Mixtecs, Zapotecs, and Chatinos

The Peoples of America
General Editors: Alan Kolata and Dean Snow

This series is about the native peoples and civilizations of the Americas, from their origins in ancient times to the present day. Drawing on archaeological, historical, and anthropological evidence, each volume presents a fresh and absorbing account of a group's culture, society, and history.
Accessible and scholarly, and well illustrated with maps and photographs, the volumes of *The Peoples of America* will together provide a comprehensive and vivid picture of the character and variety of the societies of the American past.

Already published:

The Tiwanaku: A Portrait of an Andean Civilization
Alan Kolata

The Timucua
Jerald T. Milanich

The Aztecs
Second Edition
Michael E. Smith

The Cheyenne
John Moore

The Iroquois
Dean Snow

The Moche
Garth Bowden

The Nasca
Helaine Silverman and Donald A. Proulx

The Incas
Terence N. D'Altroy

The Sioux
Guy Gibbon

Mixtecs, Zapotecs, and Chatinos: Ancient Peoples of Southern Mexico
Arthur A. Joyce

Mixtecs, Zapotecs, and Chatinos
Ancient Peoples of Southern Mexico

Arthur A. Joyce

A John Wiley & Sons, Ltd., Publication

This edition first published 2010
© 2010 Arthur A. Joyce

Blackwell Publishing was acquired by John Wiley & Sons in February 2007. Blackwell's publishing program has been merged with Wiley's global Scientific, Technical, and Medical business to form Wiley-Blackwell.

Registered Office
John Wiley & Sons Ltd, The Atrium, Southern Gate, Chichester, West Sussex, PO19 8SQ, United Kingdom

Editorial Offices
350 Main Street, Malden, MA 02148-5020, USA
9600 Garsington Road, Oxford, OX4 2DQ, UK
The Atrium, Southern Gate, Chichester, West Sussex, PO19 8SQ, UK

For details of our global editorial offices, for customer services, and for information about how to apply for permission to reuse the copyright material in this book please see our website at www.wiley.com/wiley-blackwell.

The right of Arthur A. Joyce to be identified as the author of this work has been asserted in accordance with the Copyright, Designs and Patents Act 1988.

All rights reserved. No part of this publication may be reproduced, stored in a retrieval system, or transmitted, in any form or by any means, electronic, mechanical, photocopying, recording or otherwise, except as permitted by the UK Copyright, Designs and Patents Act 1988, without the prior permission of the publisher.

Wiley also publishes its books in a variety of electronic formats. Some content that appears in print may not be available in electronic books.

Designations used by companies to distinguish their products are often claimed as trademarks. All brand names and product names used in this book are trade names, service marks, trademarks or registered trademarks of their respective owners. The publisher is not associated with any product or vendor mentioned in this book. This publication is designed to provide accurate and authoritative information in regard to the subject matter covered. It is sold on the understanding that the publisher is not engaged in rendering professional services. If professional advice or other expert assistance is required, the services of a competent professional should be sought.

Library of Congress Cataloging-in-Publication Data
Joyce, Arthur A.
  Mixtecs, Zapotecs, and Chatinos: ancient peoples of southern Mexico/Arthur A. Joyce.
    p. cm. – (The Peoples of America)
  Includes bibliographical references and index.
  ISBN 978-0-631-20977-5 (hardcover: alk. paper) – ISBN 978-0-631-20978-2 (pbk.: alk. paper)
  1. Mixtec Indians–History. 2. Zapotec Indians–History. 3. Chatino Indians–History.
4. Oaxaca Valley (Mexico)–History. I. Title.
F1219.8.M59J69 2010
972′.701–dc22

A catalogue record for this book is available from the British Library.

Set in 10/12.5pt Sabon by Graphicraft Limited, Hong Kong

1   2010

To Christine

Contents

List of Figures	ix
Preface	xiii

1	**People, Culture, and History**	**1**
	Sources of Evidence	5
	Theorizing Oaxaca's Ancient Past	17
2	**Peoples and Landscapes on the Eve of the Spanish Conquest**	**35**
	The Physical Geography of Oaxaca	36
	Mixtec and Zapotec Peoples at the Time of the Spanish Conquest	42
3	**From Foragers to Village Life**	**64**
	First Peoples	65
	The Archaic Period and the Origins of Agriculture	66
	The Transition to Sedentism	70
	Negotiating Initial Village Life	73
4	**Negotiating Community and Complexity**	**84**
	Constructing Community and Identity in the Early Formative	85
	Community and Identity in the Early Middle Formative	104
	Structures of Authority in the Early to Middle Formative	110
5	**From Village to City: The Founding and Early Development of Monte Albán**	**118**
	The Late Middle Formative Political Crisis	120
	The Founding of Monte Albán	128
	Political Consolidation and Upheaval at Monte Albán	155

6 **Political Centralization in the Mixteca and Coast**	160
Social Transformations in the Mixtec Highlands	160
Interregional Interaction and the Rise of Mixtec Centers	173
Political Authority and Ideology	177
Urbanization in the Lower Río Verde Valley	180
Political Collapse in the Mixteca and the Oaxaca Coast	195
7 **Authority and Polity in the Classic Period**	197
Classic-Period Society in the Valley of Oaxaca	199
Classic-Period Polities of the Mixtec Highlands	226
Political Fragmentation and Centralization on the Oaxaca Coast	239
8 **Collapse and Reemergence**	248
The Collapse in the Oaxacan Highlands	249
The Classic-Period Collapse and the Early Postclassic on the Oaxaca Coast	252
Postclassic Heroic History	258
Lord 8 Deer "Jaguar Claw" and the Archaeology of Tututepec (Yucu Dzaa)	266
Late Postclassic Archaeology of the Oaxacan Highlands	270
The Spanish Conquest	280
9 **Conclusions**	283
Beyond Functionalism and Neo-Evolutionism in Oaxaca	284
Poststructural Theory and the Archaeology of the Mixtec, Zapotec, and Chatino	287
Endnotes	296
Bibliography	299
Index	336

Figures

Figure 1.1	Map of Mesoamerica showing sites and obsidian sources mentioned in the text	1
Figure 1.2	Photo of Tututepec showing the colonial church and the sacred hill of Yucu Dzaa	2
Figure 1.3	The Mexican state of Oaxaca showing geographical regions, rivers, and mountain ranges	6
Figure 1.4	PEMA excavations at Monte Albán	13
Figure 1.5	Excavations at the site of Cerro de la Cruz in the lower Río Verde Valley	14
Figure 1.6	Ceramic phases in Oaxaca	16
Figure 2.1	View of the Valley of Oaxaca	39
Figure 2.2	View of the Nochixtlán Valley with the Yanhuitlán church in the foreground and the archaeological site of Cerro Jazmín in the background	40
Figure 2.3	View of the lower Río Verde Valley	42
Figure 2.4	Modern *lama-bordo* terracing in the Nochixtlán Valley	53
Figure 2.5	INAH excavations in front of the Cueva del Diablo (Devil's Cave) near Mitla	57
Figure 3.1	Archaeological sites of the Archaic through early Middle Formative periods (8000–700 BC) in Oaxaca	68
Figure 3.2	Idealized plan of Formative-period house with associated burial, oven, midden, and bell-shaped pit features	76
Figure 3.3	Group of Tierras Largas-phase figurines from the site of Hacienda Blanca, Valley of Oaxaca	78
Figure 3.4	Early Formative public buildings from Area C at San José Mogote	80

Figure 4.1	Olmec-style artifacts from Oaxaca: (a) photo of hollow baby figurine from Etlatongo; (b) fire-serpent and were-jaguar motifs	90
Figure 4.2	Early and Middle Formative figurines from the Valley of Oaxaca: (a) Guadalupe-phase female figurine; (b) San José-phase female figurine; (c) San José-phase figurine, possibly male; (d) costumed figure with ritual attire including a zoomorphic mask and necklace, San José phase	97
Figure 4.3	Burials from the Tomaltepec cemetery: (a) Burial 20 with ceramic offerings; (b) Burial 57 with ceramic offerings	101
Figure 5.1	Archaeological sites of the later Formative (700 BC–AD 300) in the Valley of Oaxaca	120
Figure 5.2	Idealized reconstruction of Rosario-phase buildings and Monument 3 on Mound 1 at San José Mogote	121
Figure 5.3	Photo of the Main Plaza at Monte Albán, looking south. The North Platform is in the foreground and the South Platform in the background	132
Figure 5.4	The Main Plaza at Monte Albán: (a) Danibaan and Pe phases (500–100 BC); (b) Nisa phase (100 BC–AD 200)	133
Figure 5.5	Carved-stone monuments from Building L-sub: (a) *in situ* monuments; (b) elder from the upper rank; (c) young adult from the first rank in the lower row of Building L-sub; (d) rain-god impersonator; (e) decapitation; (f) monuments D-139 and D-140 with hieroglyphic inscriptions	135
Figure 5.6	Late/Terminal Formative monumental art from the Valley of Oaxaca: (a) *viborón* frieze from the North Platform at Monte Albán; (b) Building J "conquest slab" from Monte Albán; (c) Dainzú ballplayers (d) Monte Albán Monument J-41	138
Figure 5.7	Late/Terminal Formative-period ceramics from the Valley of Oaxaca: (a) *cocijo* urn; (b) *comal*; (c) G-12 combed-base bowl	140
Figure 6.1	Archaeological sites of the Late/Terminal Formative in the Mixtec highlands and the lower Río Verde Valley	161
Figure 6.2	Plan of the civic-ceremonial center of Monte Negro	166
Figure 6.3	Late Formative burials from Monte Negro: (a) Burial VIII-4B; (b) Burial IX-5; (c) Tomb 1; (d) Tomb 40	168

Figure 6.4	Plan of Huamelulpan: (a) site plan; (b) plan of the Grupo de la Iglesia	169
Figure 6.5	Ceramic urn from Huamelulpan with rain-god imagery	171
Figure 6.6	High-status house from Huamelulpan	172
Figure 6.7	Yucuita Monument 1	175
Figure 6.8	Plan of upper-terrace excavations at Cerro de la Cruz	182
Figure 6.9	Late Formative cemetery beneath Structure 1 at Cerro de la Cruz	184
Figure 6.10	Plan of Yugüe	188
Figure 6.11	Plan of the Mound 1 acropolis at Río Viejo	190
Figure 6.12	Terminal Formative bone flute from the Yugüe cemetery	193
Figure 7.1	Classic-period archaeological sites of Oaxaca	198
Figure 7.2	The Main Plaza of Monte Albán: (a) Pitao phase (AD 350–500); (b) Xoo phase (AD 500–800)	202
Figure 7.3	High-status residential complex showing the location of the tomb (Tomb 104)	208
Figure 7.4	Tomb 104: (a) plan of tomb; (b) painted murals showing ancestors	210
Figure 7.5	The iconographic program of Lord 13 Night	214
Figure 7.6	Xoo-phase genealogical registers from the Valley of Oaxaca: (a) Slab 6-6059, unknown provenance; Museo Nacional de Antropología e Historia; (b) Monte Albán Stela MA-VGE-2	216
Figure 7.7	Photo of System M, a temple-patio-altar complex on the Main Plaza of Monte Albán	219
Figure 7.8	Plan of the site center at Cerro de las Minas	230
Figure 7.9	Ñuiñe urn from Cerro de las Minas Tomb 5	232
Figure 7.10	Plan of commoner residences at Cerro de las Minas	233
Figure 7.11	Classic-period carved stones from the Mixtec highlands: (a) carved slab from Yucuñudahui Tomb 1; (b) Cerro de la Caja Monument 7; (c) Cerro de la Caja Monument 2; (d) Tequixtepec Monument 17; (e) stone sculpture of a human head	235
Figure 7.12	Plan of Río Viejo	242
Figure 7.13	Yuta Tiyoo-phase carved-stone monuments from Río Viejo: (a) Monument 8; (b) Monument 11; (c) Monument 14; (d) Monument 6; (e) Monument 15	244

Figures

Figure 8.1	Postclassic-period archaeological sites in Oaxaca	250
Figure 8.2	Early Postclassic carved-stone monuments from Río Viejo: (a) Monument 3; (b) Jamiltepec Monument 1 (originally located at Río Viejo)	253
Figure 8.3	Plan of Operation RV00 A at Río Viejo	255
Figure 8.4	Scenes from the Mixtec codices: (a) the meeting of Lord 8 Deer and Lady 9 Grass at Chalcatongo; *Codex Nuttall*, codex page 44; (b) Lord 8 Deer and followers arrive at Tututepec showing the placement of sacred objects in the temple; *Codex Colombino-Becker*, codex pages 5 and 6; (c) the nose-piercing rite of Lord 8 Deer; *Codex Nuttall*, codex page 52; (d) the murder of Lord 12 Movement; *Codex Nuttall*, codex page 81	262
Figure 8.5	Tututepec Monument 6	268
Figure 8.6	Residence A at Tututepec	269
Figure 8.7	Photo of the Palace of the Six Patios at Yagul	272
Figure 8.8	Plans of Late Postclassic high-status residences in the Valley of Oaxaca: (a) Palace of the Six Patios at Yagul; (b) Group of the Columns at Mitla	273
Figure 8.9	Photo of stone mosaics at Mitla	275

Preface

The coastal and highland valleys as well as the rugged mountains of the southern Mexican state of Oaxaca are today one of the most linguistically and ethnically diverse areas of the Americas. Archaeological research has shown that this present cultural diversity extends far back into the prehispanic era. In this book I synthesize archaeological, ethnohistoric, ethnographic, iconographic, and epigraphic evidence to trace the prehispanic history of three of Oaxaca's ethnolinguistic groups: the Mixtecs, Zapotecs, and Chatinos. These groups occupy much of what is now the western half of Oaxaca, and their prehispanic past is better known than that of other Oaxacan peoples. Archaeological research on the Mixtecs and Zapotecs began in the late nineteenth century and has continued as a major research focus in Mesoamerican archaeology up to the present day. Intensive research on the Chatinos of the southwestern coastal region of Oaxaca began in the mid-1980s and has been the focus of my field research beginning in 1986. This research shows that prehispanic Mixtecs, Zapotecs, and Chatinos lived in socially complex societies with writing, cities, powerful rulers, elaborate architectural and artistic traditions, and sophisticated agricultural technologies. Their archaeology addresses many key research problems such as the origins of agriculture, the development of social complexity, ancient urbanism, and societal collapse, among many others.

My approach to Oaxaca is based on a consideration of contemporary social theory and reflects the current trend in archaeology toward theoretical perspectives drawn from poststructural, feminist, and subaltern theories. Because my approach to Oaxacan archaeology differs from most of the current research in the region, I have described my theoretical perspective in some detail. This makes *Mixtecs, Zapotecs, and Chatinos* more heavily theorized than other books on ancient Oaxaca, but I have tried to discuss theory in an accessible manner that will make the book of interest to advanced undergraduates as well as graduate students and professionals. While theory can be daunting for students, it is essential because our understandings of the past are dependent on our theoretical frameworks. Making theory explicit is therefore crucial. I have also tried to discuss the many differences of opinion and debates in Oaxacan archaeology in an inclusive and fair-minded fashion, even when I disagree with my colleagues. I feel strongly that debate can produce productive tensions that drive research, but I also think that debate in Oaxaca has not always been of this productive kind. I hope that this book opens up dialog and constructive engagements on Oaxaca's ancient past.

Like most archaeological interpretations, my arguments are based on fragmentary evidence and analogy, as well as on theoretical positions that will undoubtedly evolve with time. Certainly my own perspectives have changed over the years (e.g., A. Joyce 1991a; Joyce & Winter 1996), and the nature of archaeology as a science is such that we deceive only ourselves if we believe that a particular past is largely understood. In his discussion of the advantages of processual archaeology relative to earlier cultural historical approaches, Kent Flannery (1967:122) argued that "The process theorists assume that 'truth' is just the best current hypothesis, and that *whatever* they believe now will ultimately be proved wrong, either within their lifetime or afterward. Their 'theories' are not like children to them, they suffer less trauma when the theories prove 'wrong.'" I heartily agree with Flannery's insights here and it is sage advice for archaeologists of any theoretical persuasion. Respectful differences of opinion yield productive tensions that drive research and hopefully our understanding of past people.

Many people and institutions have supported me as I carried out the research discussed in this book and as I wrote the book itself. There have been numerous people who have aided me through years and while I cannot hope to mention everyone here, there are some that deserve special recognition.

I am grateful to Wiley-Blackwell and the two editors at the press who have worked with me on the book, Rosalie Robertson and Peter Coveney, as well as their assistants, Julia Kirk and Deirdre Ilkson. I thank Nik Prowse and Leah Morin who worked on editing and proofreading, as well as Guy Hepp who worked on the index. I wish to thank Alan Kolata who first invited me to contribute a volume to the *Peoples of America* series. While writing the book, I was supported by an ACLS/SSRC/NEH International and Area Studies Fellowship, a Faculty Fellowship from the Council on Research and Creative Works at the University of Colorado at Boulder, and a Summer Fellowship at Dumbarton Oaks. I would especially like to thank my colleagues who read the entire manuscript and provided thoughtful and constructive comments: Jeff Blomster, Michelle Butler, Guy Hepp, Mary Pye, Cynthia Robin, and Marcus Winter as well as one anonymous reviewer. The following kindly read sections of the book manuscript and I thank them for their input: Doug Bamforth, Stacy Barber, Cathy

Cameron, John Clark, Frank Eddy, Byron Hamann, James Hester, John Hoffecker, Steve Lekson, Marc Levine, Mark Mitchell, Payson Sheets, Javier Urcid, and Paola Villa. I would also like to thank Eric Berkemeyer who drafted many of the figures in the volume along with Jeff Blomster, Byron Hamann, Ray Mueller, and Javier Urcid who graciously provided a number of previously unpublished illustrations and photos. I thank the following colleagues for providing figure permissions: Andrew Balkansky, Stacy Barber, John Clark, Gabriele Daublebsky, Emily Jean Dendinger, Peggy Gough, Jorge Juárez, Lina Kopicaite, Marc Levine, Simon Lord, John Monaghan, John Neikirk, Heather Orr, Hilary Parkinson, María del Perpetuo Socorro, John Pohl, Jill Rheinheimer, Iván Rivera, María de los Angeles Romero Frizzi, Francisco José Ruiz Cervantes, Javier Urcid, Al B. Wesolowsky, and Marcus Winter.

In Mexico I have been supported by many institutions and colleagues during my research in Oaxaca. I would like to thank the Instituto Nacional de Antropología e Historia; especially the presidents of the Consejo de Arqueología: Lorena Mirambell, Mari Carmen Serra Puche, Norberto González Crespo, Joaquín García-Bárcena, and Roberto García Moll. I would like to thank the directors of the Centro INAH Oaxaca, María de la Luz Topete, Ernesto González Licón, Eduardo López Calzada, and Enrique Fernández Dávila who have supported my research. I would like to thank my colleagues in the Centro INAH Oaxaca, especially Marcus Winter, Nelly Robles, Raúl Matadamas, and Roberto Zárate. I would also like to thank the Centro de Investigaciones y Estudios Superiores en Antropología Social (CIESAS) who granted me guest-investigator status in 2008 and 2009. Many other colleagues in Oaxaca have been generous with their support over the years including Laura Arnaud Bustamante, Manuel Hermann, Alicia Herrera, Robert Markens, Cira Martínez, Iván Rivera, and Michael Swanton.

I would like to thank the people of Oaxaca who have supported my research since 1986. I greatly appreciate all of the local and regional officials and land owners in the *municipios* of Santiago Jamiltepec and Villa de Tututepec de Melchor Ocampo who have given us permission and have facilitated our field research. I would like to especially thank all of the people of San José del Progreso, Río Viejo, La Boquilla, Yugüe, and Tututepec on the Oaxaca coast who have worked with us for the past 22 years. I also want to thank my friends in the lower Río Verde region especially Doña Heriberta Avelino, Don Salomón Reyes, and Don Jaime Rodríguez, as well as the Borrozo, Castillo, Cruz, García, Herrera, Iglesia, and López families. In Oaxaca City, I would especially like to thank Cicely Winter and everyone at the Casa Arnel who have welcomed us now for more than 20 years.

Funding for my archaeological and paleoenvironmental field research in Oaxaca has been provided by grants from the following organizations: National Science Foundation (grants 8716332, 9729763, and 0508078), NASA (NNX08AO31G), Foundation for the Advancement of Mesoamerican Studies (#99012), National Geographic Society (grant 3767-88), Wenner-Gren Foundation (GR. 4988), Fulbright Foundation, H. John Heinz III Charitable Trust, University of Colorado Norton Fund and Innovative Grant Program, Vanderbilt University Research Council and Mellon Fund, Explorers Club, Sigma Xi, and Rutgers University.

In the United States, I would like to thank the University of Colorado at Boulder, especially all of my colleagues and students who have supported my work over the years. In particular, I would like to thank Doug Bamforth, Cathy Cameron, Linda Cordell, Jim Dixon, Darna Dufour, John Hoffecker, Carla Jones, Steve Lekson, Dennis Mcgilvray, Russ Mcgoodwin, Payson Sheets, and Matt Sponheimer. One of the most rewarding parts of being an academic has been my interactions with graduate students. My current and former students have challenged me to think in new and creative ways and I would especially like to thank Stacy Barber, Michelle Butler, Jamie Forde, Jeff Glover, Jessica Hedgepeth, Byron Hamann, Guy Hepp, Scott Hutson, Sarah Jennings, Stacie King, Marc Levine, Mark Mitchell, Tina Stenson, Errin Weller, and Andy Workinger. Many of these students have gone on to or are about to embark on successful careers in academia and I am proud of them.

Other friends and colleagues who have contributed to my ideas over the years and whom I would like to thank include: Pepe Aguilar, Wendy Ashmore, Jeff Blomster, Donald Brockington, Bruce Byland, Sal Capaldo, John Clark, Nicole Couture, Marcia-Anne Dobres, Mike Elam, Alex Geurds, Michelle Goman, David Grove, Gerardo Gutiérrez, Annabeth Headrick, Steve Houston, Maarten Jansen, John Janusek, Laura Junker, Steve Kowalewski, Peter Kroefges, Naomi Levin, Michael Lind, Geoff and Sharisse McCafferty, Bill Middleton, John Monaghan, Ray Mueller, Heather Orr, Michel Oudijk, Tom Patterson, John Pohl, Lucia Pou, Mary Pye, Carlos Rincón, Cynthia Robin, Ron Spores, Lauren Sullivan, Mary Thieme, Nancy Troike, Javier Urcid, Laura Van Broekhoven, Marcus Winter, and Robert and Judith Zeitlin.

Finally, I want to say a special thank you to my family who has supported me through all the work and stress, including months away from home in the field. Without the love and support of my wife, Christine, and Pepe as well as that of the Pacheco family, I would not have been able to complete this book and my life would not be as rich and happy.

one
People, Culture, and History

In early 1522, a few months after conquering the Aztec capital of Tenochtitlán, Hernán Cortés dispatched an army led by Pedro de Alvarado to the Mixtec city of Tututepec on the Pacific coast of the present-day southern Mexican state of Oaxaca (figure 1.1). Since the city's founding in

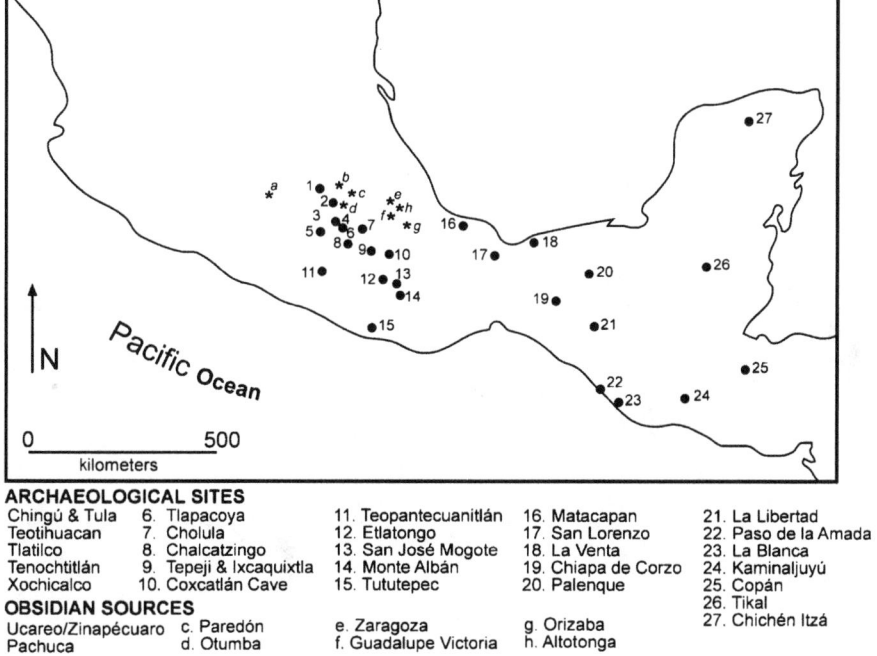

ARCHAEOLOGICAL SITES
Chingú & Tula 6. Tlapacoya 11. Teopantecuanitlán 16. Matacapan 21. La Libertad
Teotihuacan 7. Cholula 12. Etlatongo 17. San Lorenzo 22. Paso de la Amada
Tlatilco 8. Chalcatzingo 13. San José Mogote 18. La Venta 23. La Blanca
Tenochtitlán 9. Tepeji & Ixcaquixtla 14. Monte Albán 19. Chiapa de Corzo 24. Kaminaljuyú
Xochicalco 10. Coxcatlán Cave 15. Tututepec 20. Palenque 25. Copán
26. Tikal
OBSIDIAN SOURCES 27. Chichén Itzá
Ucareo/Zinapécuaro c. Paredón e. Zaragoza g. Orizaba
Pachuca d. Otumba f. Guadalupe Victoria h. Altotonga

Figure 1.1 Map of Mesoamerica showing sites and obsidian sources mentioned in the text (drawing by Eric Berkemeyer)

the late eleventh century by the legendary ruler, Lord 8 Deer "Jaguar Claw," Tututepec had been the political capital of one of the most powerful polities in Mexico (Joyce et al. 2004). By the time of the arrival of the Spanish, Tututepec dominated an empire covering 20,000 km^2 along the southern Pacific coast. The city was located in the foothills of the Sierra Madre del Sur mountain range only 15 km north of the Pacific Ocean (figure 1.2). From the city center, people looked down onto the lush agricultural fields of the coastal plain, to the estuaries and out onto the vast blue of the Pacific. The ruler or cacique of Tututepec controlled much of the wealth of this land, which early colonial-period Spanish documents tell us included minerals such as gold and copper; agricultural fields for the production of cotton and cacao; and coastal resources like pearls, salt, and fish. Cortés had heard of this rich and powerful Mixtec city from Lord Lachi, the Zapotec ruler of Tehuantepec, a traditional enemy of Tututepec, and offered an alliance with the Spanish to defeat the Mixtec Empire.

Figure 1.2 Photo of Tututepec showing the colonial church and the sacred hill of Yucu Dzaa (photograph by Arthur A. Joyce)

In February of 1522, Alvarado arrived in Tututepec with 200 Spanish soldiers and an army of thousands of Zapotecs from Tehuantepec. In describing Alvarado's arrival in the coastal city, Díaz del Castillo (1955:101–2) stated that "they were taken to reside in the most populated part of the town, where the ruler had his altars and his largest houses, and where the houses were very close together, and made of thatch . . ." [translation by the author]. Alvarado conquered Tututepec in early March and imprisoned the ruler, Lord Coaxintecuhtli, who was forced to turn over thousands of *castellanos* of gold until his death in prison. After the conquest of the south coast, Cortés ordered Alvarado to establish a town near Tututepec, which became Villa Segura de la Frontera, the second municipality in New Spain. The settlement lasted less than one year. Unhappy with the hot climate and the ravages of disease, the Spanish settlers left for Antequera in the highlands, which later became Oaxaca City.

Oppression and epidemics rapidly decimated the coastal population. A major smallpox epidemic swept through the region in 1534, followed by measles in 1544. The population of the Tututepec Empire at the time of the conquest has been estimated at more than 250,000, yet only an estimated 4,500 people were recorded at Tututepec in the census of 1544 (Dahlgren 1990:42). Spanish friars and administrators began the suppression of indigenous religion and the conversion of people to Catholicism.

The Spanish Conquest of Mesoamerica is often portrayed as a profound historical rupture disconnecting indigenous peoples from their prehispanic history and culture. The colonial history of Mesoamerica is viewed as driven by forces beyond the control of indigenous people, such as disease and the religious, social, and economic changes imposed by the Spanish colonial authorities. Yet recent studies (e.g., Gruzinski 1989; Terraciano 2001) increasingly recognize indigenous people as active players in colonial history and show that important continuities exist from the prehispanic past up to the present day. Although Native Americans were at a disadvantage, especially due to the devastation suffered because of epidemics, indigenous people creatively incorporated elements of European culture into daily practice and at times actively resisted Spanish authorities.

In the region of Tututepec, for example, Mixtecs rose up in revolt against the Spaniards in 1523 and later in 1694. While these rebellions were unsuccessful, colonial authorities had only limited success in acculturating native peoples. The prehispanic past remained in the social memory of the people of Tututepec. In 1717, the native ruler presented the *Codex Colombino*, a late prehispanic historical manuscript, as evidence in a court case to establish the boundaries of the region under Tututepec's control. In the 1990s and 2000s, the people of Tututepec worked together to build a community museum as a place to preserve and celebrate the history of the town with a focus on the prehispanic past. Despite difficulties in raising funds, and a major earthquake that destroyed parts of the town, the community worked with federal and state authorities to build and organize the museum, which was dedicated in 2004. I have come to know several of the community leaders involved in the museum project and have seen how their dedication, hard work, and desire to celebrate their rich history has resulted in the construction of the museum, which draws their past into the present and future, becoming an anchor for social memory and community identity. Rather than being solely at the mercy of distant forces, the native peoples of Oaxaca – Mixtecs, Zapotecs, Chatinos, and others – have been active participants in their histories both before and after the conquest.

This book examines the archaeology and history of the Central Valleys and the Mixtec highlands and coast of Oaxaca, which were inhabited by Mixtec, Zapotec, Chatino, and related peoples through the prehispanic period. I focus on these regions of Oaxaca because the indigenous groups that inhabited them were members of the Otomanguean language family and because these regions are the best understood archaeologically in Oaxaca. Archaeological research in these areas provides a rich picture of the impressive history and cultural achievements of ancient Oaxacan peoples. They were some of the first people in the Americas to domesticate plants and settle in permanent villages. Beginning at c.500 BC, some of Mesoamerica's earliest urban centers were founded in Oaxaca, including the spectacular mountaintop city of Monte Albán in the Oaxaca Valley and the coastal city of Río Viejo with its massive acropolis and carved-stone portraits of rulers. The history of Oaxaca's prehispanic ruling dynasties was recorded in the rich iconography of carved-stone monuments and painted murals. Oaxaca was where some of the earliest hieroglyphic writing in Mesoamerica has been discovered. The late prehispanic codices – painted screenfold manuscripts – record historical and religious narratives of the exploits of rulers and deities. Oaxaca's archaeological record also provides some of the richest evidence of the lives of common people through the prehispanic era. Archaeologists have excavated the houses of farmers and craftspeople, discovered the stone tools they used to work their fields, prepare food, and hunt; the pottery used to cook, serve, and store food; and the incense burners and figurines used to contact ancestors and deities as well as evidence for mortuary rituals preserved in burials and cemeteries.

To understand the prehispanic past, I draw on archaeological evidence along with studies of indigenous texts, early colonial Spanish documents, and iconographic analyses of prehispanic imagery. Each of these sources of data show that the prehispanic Mixtec, Zapotec, and Chatino peoples shared a history of interaction including cultural interchange, trade, warfare, alliance, intermarriage, and migration. By the time of the Spanish Conquest, for example, the degree of interaction and intermarriage created a shared noble identity that cut across ethnolinguistic differences. Common people also interacted across regions through participation in markets that brought together people from great distances as well as through warfare and migration. The history of the Mixtecs, Zapotecs, and Chatinos is therefore a shared history, although as discussed throughout the book the nature of these interactions changed through time and archaeologists have debated their significance in understanding culture change.

Sources of Evidence

Scholars are fortunate to have available a variety of complementary sources of information on prehispanic Oaxaca, including research in archaeology, ethnohistory, ethnography, and linguistics. The most important source of data for most of the prehispanic period comes from the archaeological record. Oaxaca has been a focus of archaeological research since the late nineteenth century and over the last half-century has been the locus of some of the most influential projects addressing problems such as the origins and development of agriculture, early village life, urbanism, and social complexity (figure 1.3).

Archaeological research involves the reconstruction of the past through the study of material culture recovered through systematic survey, excavation, and laboratory studies. Of course, archaeological evidence cannot tell us directly about the lives, activities, and accomplishments of past peoples. Archaeologists use analogies drawn from the present as well as indigenous and Spanish written accounts of life during the prehispanic and early colonial periods to interpret the archaeological evidence in terms of past practices, beliefs, and social institutions (see Stahl 1993; Wylie 1985).

The research of ethnographers and linguists who study the indigenous peoples of present-day Oaxaca shows that, despite the profound disruptions of the Spanish Conquest, prehispanic traditions and social memories continue to shape the lives and understandings of indigenous communities. Research on living peoples is important for gaining insights into indigenous practices and systems of meaning, involving religion, cosmology, and agriculture. Archaeologists must be cautious in uncritically using ethnographic evidence for interpreting the archaeological record, however, due to the dramatic changes that occurred in indigenous culture over the last 500 years.

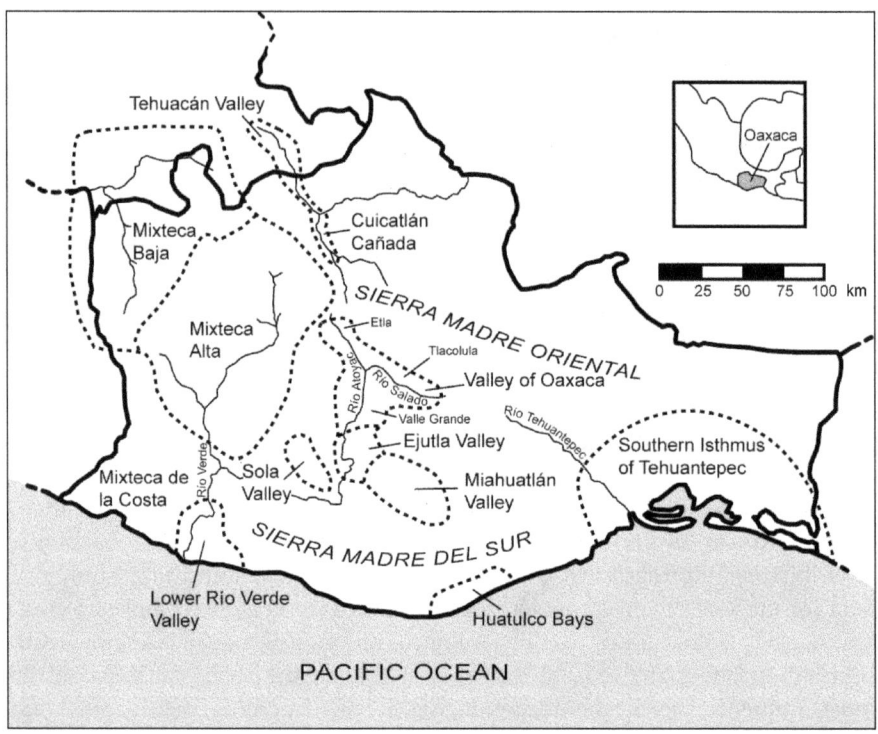

Figure 1.3 The Mexican state of Oaxaca showing geographical regions, rivers, and mountain ranges (drawing by Eric Berkemeyer)

The use of ethnographic information can be justified if there are historical sources that allow scholars to trace meanings and practices back to the time of initial encounters between Native Americans and Europeans and further back into the prehispanic period. Fortunately, Oaxaca has a rich ethnohistoric record that can strengthen analogies used in interpreting the archaeological record and, in the case of prehispanic writing systems, provide direct accounts of prehispanic life.

Ethnohistoric sources include Spanish and indigenous documents that provide information on native peoples and culture from the time of the Spanish Conquest up to the present. It is important to recognize, however, that colonial-period Spanish descriptions of indigenous society must be viewed critically with the goals and perspectives of European writers taken into account. A more significant source of observations on colonial-period culture comes from the writings of indigenous scholars recorded in both indigenous alphabetic and pictorial writing. These documents include a number of maps (*mapas*), some painted on cloth (*lienzos*), that record community boundaries as well as genealogical records of ruling families, some of which extend back centuries into the prehispanic period. The *lienzos* and *mapas* make direct historical connections between the colonial period and a series of late prehispanic screenfold books, or codices, written on deer hide in the prehispanic Mixtec pictographic writing system.

The codices are immensely important documents because they record Mixtec religious and historical texts from before the Spanish Conquest. Though only portions of eight codices in prehispanic style survived destruction, this corpus represents the largest number of preconquest documents from anywhere in Mesoamerica. The histories recorded in the codices date back to the tenth century so that, in combination with early colonial documents like the *lienzos* and contemporary ethnography, scholars have a continuous written and oral record of indigenous culture dating back more than a millennium. Still earlier written inscriptions on stone, painted murals, and a variety of portable artifacts extend indigenous texts back more than two millennia, although the prehispanic writing systems that predate the codices are only beginning to be deciphered (Urcid 2001). One bias present in all of these ethnohistoric sources – early colonial Spanish and indigenous documents as well as prehispanic writing – is that they were all authored almost exclusively by social elites, primarily male, with little mention of the lives of common people.

The combination of ethnohistory, archaeology, ethnography, and linguistics provides scholars of prehispanic Oaxaca with multiple, complementary datasets that can be used to examine the history of ancient Oaxacan peoples. In the remainder of this chapter I review the history of research dealing with each of these sources of evidence.

Ethnohistory

The earliest interest in Mixtec, Zapotec, and Chatino culture by Europeans dates to the early colonial period and includes a diverse range of documents that were part of the Spanish program of conquest and colonization (Terraciano 2001:21–31, 67–71). Information collected by Spanish religious and political authorities in the sixteenth century includes the *Relaciones Geográficas*, legal documents, and several dictionaries and grammars of native languages recorded by Dominican friars. The *Relaciones Geográficas* were compiled toward the end of the sixteenth century by order of King Phillip II of Spain and consisted of a long series of questions put to indigenous nobles, including some that pertained to people's memories of the preconquest era. Dictionaries and grammars were compiled to aid in the conversion of natives to Catholicism and have proven to be valuable sources of information on indigenous worldview and language at the time of the conquest. The most important linguistic sources of the sixteenth century included the works of Fray Francisco de Alvarado ([1593] 1962) and Fray Antonio de los Reyes ([1593] 1976) for Mixtec and Fray Juan de Córdova for Zapotec ([1570] 1989). Legal documents record a wide array of information including translations of native-language documents and trial records. One of the most important sources of evidence on contact-period Mixtec religious belief and practice comes from the records of the famous Inquisitorial investigations at the town of Yanhuitlán in the Mixteca Alta region (Hamann 2008a).

Writings on indigenous culture by Spanish scholars of the seventeenth and eighteenth centuries are not as useful as those of the early colonial period. The works of chroniclers and official historians, particularly the two-volume history of Fray Francisco de Burgoa ([1674] 1989), often do not distinguish sources of data and intersperse stories and legends of prehispanic Oaxaca with Biblical references. Other colonial-period chroniclers, including Antonio de Herrera y Tordesillas, Fray Bernardino de Sahagún, Fernando de Alva Ixtlilxochitl, and Fray Diego Dúran, mention Oaxaca, but are more important as sources of data on life in other parts of Mexico.

Although colonial-period Spanish accounts of indigenous culture and history have proven to be useful, Oaxaca also has a rich record of indigenous documents from late prehispanic times into the colonial period. The most significant documents dealing with prehispanic religion and history are the Mixtec codices. While there were probably hundreds if not thousands of codices, only a handful survived the Spanish Conquest and most are now housed in European museums. Several of the Mixtec codices were painted prior to the Spanish Conquest (e.g., the codices *Vienna*, *Zouche-Nuttall*, *Selden*, and *Colombino-Becker*). Other codices were painted in the first few decades after Spanish contact, but are rendered in prehispanic pictographic conventions with little evidence of European influences, and were probably copies of earlier ones. The extant codices are visually stunning manuscripts painted in polychrome and consist of texts that are largely religious in nature, including versions of the Mixtec creation story (Monaghan 1990), as well as indigenous historical narratives that deal with events from the tenth century up to the Spanish Conquest (Byland & Pohl 1994; Jansen & Pérez 2005, 2007; Troike 1974).

A variety of early colonial pictographic and alphabetic documents in native languages exhibit the influence of Spanish colonization and in some instances may have involved collaborations of Spanish administrators and indigenous scribes. Although these documents reflect indigenous people's encounters with the Spanish, they are still authored from a native perspective and, particularly in the case of sixteenth-century examples, demonstrate strong continuities with prehispanic writing and modes of representation, including the use of the prehispanic calendrical system (Terraciano 2001:15–65). These documents include the *lienzos* and *mapas* as well as a number of early colonial "codices." Colonial-period codices differ from those in prehispanic style in that they show a juxtaposition of native and European conventions and are executed in ink on Spanish paper. Many of the earliest colonial documents were largely pictographic with alphabetic glosses, although the transition from pictographic to alphabetic writing was well under way by the latter half of the sixteenth century (Terraciano 2001: 48–65). By this time native scribes were taking over the role of recording legal documents often in indigenous languages and, increasingly through the colonial period, in Spanish.

The modern study of Mixtec, Zapotec, and Chatino ethnohistory began in the latter part of the nineteenth and early twentieth centuries (Castellanos 1989; Gay 1881; Seler 1904, 1908; Martínez Gracida 1888). These works included general histories of Oaxaca that were often inconsistent in identifying sources of data and combined contemporary oral histories with the use of colonial-period documents, particularly Spanish-language ones. Several researchers, however, began the study of indigenous documents, including *lienzos* and codices (J. C. Clark 1912; Starr 1908).

The first major breakthroughs in the study of Oaxaca's ethnohistory was the research of the famous Mexican archaeologist Alfonso Caso, who was a pioneer in both Oaxaca's archaeology and studies of the Mixtec codices. Caso used the glosses and genealogies on several early colonial pictorial manuscripts, especially the *Mapa de Teozacualco*, as "Rosetta stones" to establish links to the prehispanic codices. His work demonstrated that the codices were from the Mixteca and showed that the histories represented in the codices continued for many centuries from the prehispanic era into the early colonial period (Caso 1949). Caso (1956, 1964, 1977, 1979) made important advances in decipherment of the codices and in understanding the prehispanic calendar along with his monumentally important archaeological research discussed below.

Beginning in the 1950s, Caso's research drew a large number of ethnohistorians and archaeologists to Oaxaca. Important ethnohistoric studies since the mid-twentieth century include work on early colonial Mixtec (Dahlgren 1990; Cook & Borah 1968; Spores 1984; Terraciano 2001) and Zapotec (Chance 1978; Whitecotton 1977, 1990; J. Zeitlin 2005) culture and society. Relatively little work has been done on Chatino ethnohistory (Greenberg 1981:47–80) perhaps due to the remoteness of contemporary

Chatino communities and a relative scarcity of colonial-period archival records. Scholars have increasingly moved away from a reliance on the official histories of the Spanish colonial authorities and toward archival sources and indigenous documents. Another important development has been the increasing number of indigenous scholars working on Oaxacan ethnohistory (e.g., de la Cruz 2002; Jansen & Pérez 2005, 2007). Indigenous scholars address early colonial and contemporary culture with an intimate knowledge of their culture and a concern for correcting biases in Western scholarship. Major advances in the study of indigenous pictographic writing have built on Caso's work and include Mary Elizabeth Smith (1973), Troike (1974), Byland and Pohl (1994), Pohl (1994), Jansen and Pérez (2007), and Monaghan (1990).

The recent advances in the study of Oaxacan ethnohistory provide a rich understanding of indigenous culture and social practices at the time of the Spanish Conquest. Ethnohistory gives us a crucial interpretive basis for understanding prehispanic culture, but it is ultimately the archaeological record that provides the bulk of the evidence on the prehispanic past.

Archaeology

The inspiring ruins of prehispanic communities like Monte Albán and Mitla have drawn scholars to Oaxaca for well over a century. During the eighteenth and nineteenth centuries scholars interested in the prehispanic past such as Guillermo Dupaix, Eduard Muhlenpfordt, Désirée Charnay, William Henry Holmes, and Eduard Seler visited the ruins of Monte Albán and Mitla, writing about the sites and speculating on their age and origins. The first archaeological work in Oaxaca was carried out in the late nineteenth and early twentieth centuries by Leopoldo Batres at Mitla and Monte Albán and by Marshall Saville at Mitla, Monte Albán, Xoxocotlán, and Cuilapan.

The first large-scale, scientific archaeology began in the 1930s with the research of Alfonso Caso at the ancient Zapotec city of Monte Albán. During this period, the Mexican government began sponsoring archaeological projects to explore the prehispanic past and develop sites for tourism. In the 1920s, Caso began research on carved-stone monuments and in late 1931 began major excavations at Monte Albán. With the discovery in early 1932 of Tomb 7, one of the richest burials ever found in the Americas, Monte Albán burst onto the world stage. Caso continued fieldwork at Monte Albán with his colleagues Ignacio Bernal and Jorge Acosta until 1958 (Caso 1942, 1969; Caso & Bernal 1952; Caso et al. 1967). The Monte Albán project focused on excavating and reconstructing the civic-ceremonial center in and around the Main Plaza, approximately 170 tombs were discovered, and stratigraphic excavations allowed for the development of a ceramic sequence for the Oaxaca Valley. Beginning in the late 1930s, Caso and his colleagues (e.g., Acosta & Romero 1992; Bernal 1948–9; Caso 1938) expanded their investigations into the Mixteca Alta north of the Valley of Oaxaca with excavations at prehispanic centers such as Yucuñudahui, Coixtlahuaca, Huamelulpan, and Monte Negro. Caso and Rubín de la Borbolla (1936) excavated the late prehispanic ceremonial center of Mitla in the eastern Oaxaca Valley. Caso and his collaborators established that the region's archaeological remains were the creations of the ancestors of Oaxaca's living indigenous peoples. Their research outlined the culture history of the Oaxaca Valley and the Mixteca Alta from the founding of Monte Albán around 500 BC to the time of the Spanish Conquest and demonstrated that highland Oaxaca gave rise to some of the most impressive cities in prehispanic Mesoamerica.

By the 1950s and 1960s, Oaxaca began to attract an international group of archaeologists. Excavations were carried out in the ceremonial and elite precincts of sites like Dainzú, Mitla, Yagul, and Zaachila in the Oaxaca Valley (e.g., Bernal & Oliveros 1988; Bernal & Gamio 1974; Paddock 1966a). Bernal (1965) began a surface survey of sites in the Oaxaca Valley, while initial reconnaissance, survey, and testing projects were begun in the Mixteca Alta (Spores 1969, 1972), Mixteca Baja (Paddock 1968), Miahuatlán Valley (Brockington 1973), and along the Pacific coast of Oaxaca (Brockington et al. 1974; Wallrath 1967). Most of the studies mentioned above also began the development of regional ceramic sequences.

An important trend of the 1960s and 1970s was the application of the methods and theories of processual archaeology to the study of ancient Oaxaca. The focus of research shifted from elite centers and culture history to a regional perspective that stressed cultural evolution and human adaptation. Two major projects in the Valley of Oaxaca exemplified the theoretical shift: the Oaxaca Human Ecology Project, directed by Kent Flannery, and the Valley of Oaxaca Settlement Pattern Project, directed by Richard Blanton and Stephen Kowalewski. The Oaxaca Human Ecology Project focused on understanding Archaic- and Formative-period ecology and cultural change, including changes in household and community form, sociocultural complexity, and subsistence patterns, extending the archaeological record of Oaxaca back to the Early Holocene (Flannery 1976a, 1986). Flannery and his collaborators developed a number of influential models dealing with the origins of agriculture, early village life, and the emergence of social complexity. The Settlement Pattern Project included surface collections and mapping of visible architectural features over an impressive

2,150 km², or 95 percent of the Valley of Oaxaca (Blanton 1978; Kowalewski et al. 1989), and provided interpretations of changing settlement patterns, economic systems, and political organization.

Since the 1970s, systematic regional survey coverage has been extended to the Mixteca Alta (Balkansky et al. 2000; Byland & Pohl 1994; Kowalewski et al. 2009; Plunket 1983), Mixteca Baja (Rivera 1999), lower Río Verde Valley (Joyce et al. 2001), southern Isthmus of Tehuantepec (J. Zeitlin 1978), Ejutla Valley (Feinman & Nicholas 1990), Cuicatlán Cañada (Redmond 1983), Miahuatlán Valley (Markman 1981), Sola Valley (Balkansky 2002), and into the mountains between the Oaxaca and Nochixtlán Valleys (Drennan 1989; Finsten 1996). These studies make Oaxaca perhaps the most intensively surveyed area in the world.

Other major projects since the 1970s focused on the cultural evolution of Monte Albán both from the perspective of the site itself and from a regional and interregional perspective. Marcus Winter (1974) of the Oaxaca Regional Center of the Mexican Instituto Nacional de Antropología e Historia (INAH) examined changes in household form and organization through excavation of residences. Since the 1980s periodic excavation and salvage projects by INAH archaeologists have continued at Monte Albán (González Licón 2003; Martínez López 1998). In the eastern arm of the Oaxaca Valley, the Institute of Oaxacan Studies surveyed and excavated several high-status residences at Lambityeco to explore social developments during the collapse of Monte Albán at the end of the Classic period (Lind 2008; Lind & Urcid 1983; Paddock 1983). Spencer and Redmond (2001, 2004) examined the impact of Monte Albán on sites in the area of San Martín Tilcajete, finding evidence for conquest by Monte Albán at the end of the Formative period.

Interaction with Monte Albán, including the possibility of conquest, has been a major research question outside the Valley of Oaxaca. Research throughout the Oaxacan interior (e.g., Balkansky 2002; Feinman & Nicholas 1990; Spencer 1982) and along the Pacific coast (A. Joyce 1991a; Workinger 2002; R. Zeitlin 1990) has led to a major debate with some scholars arguing that Monte Albán dominated an empire extending over 20,000 km² (Marcus & Flannery 1996), while others maintain that evidence supports a more limited area of political domination (A. Joyce 2003; Workinger & Joyce n.d.; Zeitlin & Joyce 1999).

Beginning in the 1970s, the INAH sponsored a series of large-scale projects directed by Marcus Winter that focused on major Formative- and Classic-period urban centers in highland Oaxaca, including Yucuita and Huamelulpan in the Mixteca Alta and Cerro de las Minas in the Mixteca Baja. Like the earlier Monte Albán project, these investigations focused on understanding sociopolitical developments, refining ceramic chronologies, and developing sites for tourism (Gaxiola 1984; Robles 1988; Winter 1989a). Other recent projects in the Mixteca Alta include Blomster's (2004) research on Formative-period Etlatongo, Pérez's (2006) excavations of Late Postclassic houses near Teposcolula, Balkansky's research on the Formative center of Tayata (Balkansky et al. 2008), and excavations by Spores and Robles (Spores 2005; Spores & Robles 2007) at the contact-period site of Yucundaa.

By far the largest and most important of the INAH projects was the Proyecto Especial Monte Albán 1992–4 (PEMA). In 1992, Mexican President Carlos Salinas de Gortari created the Fondo Nacional Arqueológico (National Archaeological Fund) for the support of 12 projects designed to explore and protect major archaeological sites in Mexico, including Monte Albán (figure 1.4). The PEMA, under the direction of Marcus Winter, excavated dozens of residences and public buildings in and around the Main Plaza, recorded 21 tombs, conducted deep stratigraphic excavations, and produced a detailed map of the site (Martínez López et al. 2000; Winter 1994a, 1995). The results of the PEMA have led to a reappraisal of Monte Albán's history, particularly the early architecture of the Main Plaza and the site's collapse at c.AD 800 (e.g., Winter 2001, 2003).

Another major contribution of the PEMA was the work of the project's epigrapher, Javier Urcid, who recorded and analyzed several new carved-stone

Figure 1.4 PEMA excavations at Monte Albán (photograph by Arthur A. Joyce)

monuments (Urcid 1994a). Since the 1980s, Urcid has worked on recording, comparing, and analyzing hieroglyphic inscriptions and iconography throughout Oaxaca. Building on the research of Caso (1965), Whittaker (1980), and Marcus (1992), Urcid (2001, 2005) uses comparative and contextual analyses to infer meanings from inscriptions and images. He has identified at least six separate though related writing systems for prehispanic Oaxaca. Other scholars making significant contributions to the study of writing and imagery include Orr (1997), Rivera (2000), and L. Rodríguez (1999).

The last two decades also witnessed an expansion of research in the Pacific coastal region of Oaxaca. Archaeological and paleoenvironmental research directed by Arthur Joyce and his collaborators (Barber 2005; A. Joyce 1991b, 2005; Joyce et al. 1998; King 2003; Levine 2007; Workinger 2002) has focused on the lower Río Verde Valley on the western coast. The lower Río Verde was probably occupied by Chatinos prior to the Late Postclassic, but they were largely displaced by Mixtecs at c.AD 1100. Research includes excavations at 18 sites, including the political centers of Río Viejo and Tututepec, and a full-coverage regional survey (figure 1.5).

Figure 1.5 Excavations at the site of Cerro de la Cruz in the lower Río Verde Valley (photograph by Arthur A. Joyce)

Paleoenvironmental studies examine the effects of highland land use on the human ecology of lowland peoples (Goman et al. 2005; Joyce & Mueller 1997). The research in the lower Verde is innovative in that it introduced poststructural theory to Oaxacan archaeology, including a concern with the social negotiation of political power, social identity, and how constructed landscapes embody power relations (e.g., Barber 2005; Barber & Joyce 2007; Forde 2006; A. Joyce 2006; Joyce et al. 2001; King 2003; Levine 2007; also see A. Joyce 2000, 2004 for poststructural studies of Monte Albán). Archaeological work in other parts of coastal Oaxaca includes INAH survey and excavation projects near Huatulco (Fernández & Gómez 1988) and Tehuantepec (Winter 2004a). The Zeitlins (J. Zeitlin 1978, 2005; R. Zeitlin 1990, 1993) have surveyed and excavated several sites in the southern Isthmus of Tehuantepec – a region that Zapotecs migrated into during the Late Postclassic period.

Building on the foundation provided by the work of Alfonso Caso, Oaxaca is now one of the most comprehensively studied regions of Mesoamerica, particularly the Valley of Oaxaca, the lower Río Verde Valley, and the Mixteca Alta (Figure 1.6).[1] In addition to the evidence provided by ethnohistory and archaeology, ethnographic and linguistic studies also provide important data on indigenous communities, beliefs, and practices that contribute to the interpretation of the archaeological record.

Ethnographic and linguistic sources

Although scholars of the late nineteenth and early twentieth centuries collected myths and made observations on indigenous communities, the first intensive, systematic ethnographic work on the Mixtec and Zapotec was associated with the community-studies approach begun by Tax (1937) and refined by Redfield (1941) based on research among the Maya. The first long-term community-based ethnography in Oaxaca was Elsie Clews Parsons' (1936) comprehensive study of acculturation at Mitla. Her work is especially important for archaeologists because she sought to identify continuities and breaks with the prehispanic past by tracing community practices and traditions back through the ethnohistorical record. Another important early community study was de la Fuente's (1949) ethnography of the Zapotec village of Yalálag.

By the 1960s and 1970s, ethnographic studies of indigenous communities in Mesoamerica were increasingly influenced by Eric Wolf's concept of the "closed corporate community." In Oaxaca, ethnographic work increased as researchers considered and critiqued Wolf's ideas, focusing on issues of religion, economy, gender, and local government in Mixtec

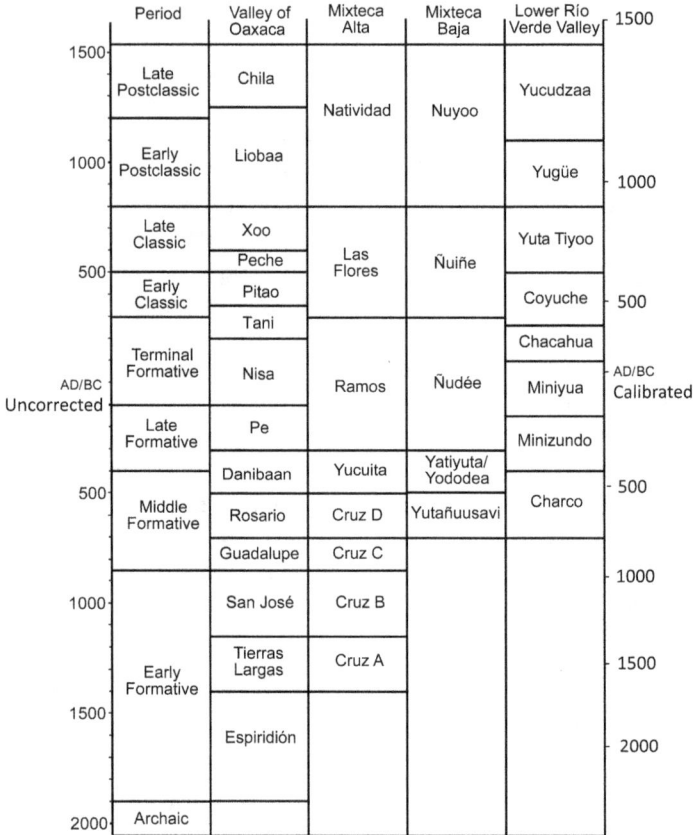

Figure 1.6 Ceramic phases in Oaxaca

(Butterworth 1975), Zapotec (e.g., Chiñas 1973; Kearney 1972; Nader 1969), and Chatino (Bartolomé & Barabas 1996; De Cicco 1969; Greenberg 1981) communities. Studies of the economics of indigenous peoples included research on market systems (Cook & Diskin 1974), agriculture (Lees 1973), and on the production of crafts, especially pottery (Hendry 1992; Thieme 2001).

Several recent ethnographic studies have explicitly linked contemporary beliefs and practices to the colonial and prehispanic past (e.g., de la Cruz 2002). The most influential ethnographic work for archaeologists has been John Monaghan's (1995) research at Santiago Nuyoo in the Mixteca Alta. Monaghan's historical ethnographic approach combines ethnohistory with research on contemporary indigenous conceptions and practices related to community and the sacred. He traces continuities and transformations in idioms like sacrifice, feasting, and community authority from the ethnographic present back to the early colonial period and even into late prehispanic times (Monaghan 1990). Research in historical linguistics has also been used by archaeologists to develop models on the divergence of ethnolinguistic groups (Josserand et al. 1984).

Oaxaca's ethnographic and linguistic record provides a means for understanding indigenous cultural principles and practices. In subsequent chapters, this view of indigenous belief and practice will provide a basis for developing relational analogies (Stahl 1993; Wylie 1985) that in conjunction with archaeological data can be used to make inferences about prehispanic society and culture. In the final section of this chapter, I discuss the theoretical approach I use to understanding the history of the prehispanic Mixtecs, Zapotecs, and Chatinos.

Theorizing Oaxaca's Ancient Past

Archaeology, ethnohistory, ethnography, and linguistics provide Oaxacan archaeologists with a variety of complementary sources of evidence to examine prehispanic history. Yet, as Wylie (1985, 1992) and others (e.g., Hodder 1999; Hodder & Hutson 2003:239–42) have pointed out, evidence is theory-laden so that an archaeologist's theoretical perspective as well as one's social and cultural settings inform interpretations of the past. Theory consists of the conceptual tools through which we define and categorize archaeological evidence, translate that evidence into understandings about past social and material worlds, and evaluate the utility of those understandings. It is therefore crucial to be explicit about theory. In this section, I discuss my theoretical perspective in relation to some of the other approaches used in contemporary Oaxacan archaeology. The complexities of archaeological interpretation mean that researchers often develop alternative interpretations of evidence depending on the analogies they use and on the theoretical approaches that inform their work. If carried out openly and respectfully, these debates can help to drive research and theoretical developments that lead to better understandings of the past. Not surprisingly, in Oaxaca, archaeologists disagree on many aspects of the archaeological record ranging from the timing and nature of early complex societies to the significance and intensity of warfare, and many of these debates are discussed in this book.

I examine the prehispanic past of the Mixtec, Zapotec, Chatino, and related peoples of Oaxaca from a perspective that considers history as the interplay between the lives of people and broader patterns of social relations, material conditions, cultural meanings, and traditions. The approach I take to understanding the past is an outgrowth of developments in social theory over the past 30 years, particularly as informed by poststructural and feminist thinkers (e.g., Bourdieu 1977; Butler 1993; Foucault 1977; Giddens 1979; Latour 2005; Sewell 1992). Archaeologists influenced by these theories have moved away from the grand metanarratives of cultural evolution and systems theory and toward a more contingent, fractured, and contested view of society and history (e.g., Hodder & Hutson 2003; Janusek 2004; Joyce et al. 2001; Pauketat 2001, 2007).

Though it would seem logical to view history in a general sense as created by the actions of people, ironically, until recently, archaeologists have largely excluded the lives of people from historical understandings. Most archaeological theory of the first half of the twentieth century was both understated and focused on issues involving chronology and the spatial definition of past archaeological "cultures" viewed as a collection of normative ideas (Spaulding 1985). Norms were seen as reflected in the distribution of different suites of artifacts across space, such that the lives and actions of people were often minimized in archaeological explanations of the past.

With the emergence of processual archaeology in the 1960s, archaeologists rejected the normative approach and developed a theoretical perspective that united ecological functionalism with cultural evolutionary theory (Willey & Sabloff 1993:214–97). Processual archaeologists sought to remodel archaeology as a science based on positivist philosophy with the goal of developing general, even universal, theories of the past (Binford 1962; Watson et al. 1971). The lives, actions, and identities of people in this framework again were minimized, as were intrasocietal tensions and conflicts. People as well as social institutions were seen as little more than functional components that contributed to the maintenance of an equilibrium state for the overall social or ecological system (Binford 1968; Butzer 1982; Flannery 1968). Only elites had power to effect social change in their role as decision-makers who monitor the system and initiate changes when needed. Material conditions (e.g., population-resource balances, energy storage for dampening resource fluctuations, and so on) were viewed as distinct from, privileged over, and largely determinant of, cultural meanings. Cultures changed as a result of systemic responses to external factors like warfare or environmental stress, or internal ones, such as the system becoming too integrated and centrally controlled, thereby destroying the natural buffering effects of hierarchy (Flannery 1972). When inherent thresholds were reached in the functioning of a cultural or ecological system, the system could evolve or devolve (Flannery 1972; Spencer 1982). Cultural evolution (or devolution) progressed (or regressed) through a series of set "levels" or "stages" of cultural complexity, the most popular formulation being Elman Service's (1962) scheme of bands, tribes, chiefdoms, and states. While archaeologists acknowledged a degree of historical variation, it was assumed that all cultures at any one level of cultural evolution shared fundamental structural and functional features. Analogies with ethnographically known cultures from the same evolutionary stage could therefore be used to fill in the explanatory gaps left by the archaeological record.

Over the past 20 years archaeologists have moved away from ecological systems theory, struggling to incorporate models of intrasocietal difference and conflict into archaeological theory and broadening or rejecting cultural evolutionist categories (e.g., Dobres & Robb 2000; Hodder & Hutson 2003; Janusek 2004; Johnson 1999; Pauketat 2001, 2007; Yoffee 2005). For example, concepts like heterarchy that focus attention on social distinctions that are unranked or that have the potential to be ranked in multiple ways have broadened views of social complexity beyond a focus on hierarchy (Ehrenreich et al. 1995). Archaeologists have worked to incorporate cognition, ideas, and meaning into theories of social change in ways that move theory beyond the earlier focus on ecology, economy, and a narrow materialism (e.g., Hodder 1982; Hodder & Hutson 2003; Renfrew & Zubrow 1994; Robb 1999). Approaches to cultural evolution have recognized a greater diversity of societal types and pathways to complexity (e.g., Blanton et al. 1996; Earle 1997). The utility of developing general theories of society and history as exemplified by systems theory and cultural evolutionism has been increasingly questioned. Archaeologists are recognizing that historical processes involve an interplay of social and ecological relations at a variety of temporal and spatial scales (Pauketat 2001). Archaeologists have also moved away from positivism and embraced a diversity of scientific methodologies (e.g., Hodder 1999; Watson et al. 1984; Wylie 2000).

Despite these trends, archaeological theory today involves a range of positions with regard to social theory, epistemology, and philosophies of science (e.g., Dobres & Robb 2000; Hegmon 2003; Hodder 2001; Hodder & Hutson 2003; Johnson 1999; A. Joyce 2008a; Leonard 2001; Pauketat 2001; Schiffer 2000; Spencer 1990; VanPool & VanPool 1999) that create productive tensions, which drive research and theoretical development. Many of the recent trends and debates in archaeological theory have been inspired by considerations of poststructural theories of practice (Bourdieu 1977; de Certeau 1984; Giddens 1979; Latour 2005; Ortner 1984, 1996; Sewell 1992) and power (Foucault 1977; Giddens 1979; Gramsci 1971), feminist theory (Butler 1990, 1993; Geller and Stockett 2006; Moore 1994), subaltern studies of the role of non-elites in political processes (J. C. Scott 1990), materiality or the study of the interconnectedness of materials and ideas (D. Miller 2005; Tilley et al. 2006), and the methodologies of hermeneutics or the science of interpretation (Collingwood 1946; Gadamer 1975; Hodder 1999; Shanks & Tilley 1992). These theoretical programs view social differences and the affiliations, tensions, and conflicts that arise from differently positioned actors as fundamental for understanding historical processes. They represent a more humanistic perspective than many previous approaches to the past in that the complex, varied lives of people take on greater significance in historical understandings. The theoretical perspective that I use to examine the prehispanic history of Oaxaca draws on these theoretical developments in the social sciences, which I discuss in more detail in the remainder of this section.

Poststructural social theory endeavors to bring people and cultural meanings into understandings of society and history (Bourdieu 1977; Giddens 1979; Latour 2005; Ortner 1984, 1996; Sewell 1992). Rather than focusing on the functioning and evolution of social groups, poststructural theories view the recursive relationship between people and the broader social and historical setting as fundamental. The argument that there is a single superior methodology in science such as logical positivism is also rejected because of the complexity and diversity of phenomena that must be examined by archaeologists. Given the importance of interpreting cultural meanings, hermeneutic methodologies have increasingly been embraced (Hodder 1999; Shanks & Tilley 1992:105–9). Hermeneutics is the science of interpretation, which is a more appropriate methodology for examining the multiple and often contested meanings of materials and practices in the past. Scientific methodologies more closely aligned with positivism are still useful in addressing material processes where explanations are more tightly constrained by observation (e.g., the presence of stone-tool cut marks on bones), but once meanings need to be inferred (e.g., the meanings associated with the cutting of bone), hermeneutic methodologies are more appropriate. Archaeologists have increasingly recognized that observation is theory-laden and reject views that data are objective and can be separated from theory (Wylie 1992). Thus, rather than a single rigid methodology to evaluate our ideas about the past, many archaeologists now embrace a variety of methodologies whose application is dependent on the nature of the phenomena under study (e.g., physical versus cultural processes; past versus present; historically contingent versus universal processes).

Practice, structure, agency, and subjectivity

In understanding the dynamics of social life, the practice theory of Pierre Bourdieu (1977) and the structuration theory of Anthony Giddens (1979,

1984) have been particularly influential in archaeology. These theories view the dynamics of social life as emanating from the recursive relationship between the practices of people and the broader social relations, structural schema, and material conditions that constitute society and culture. Practices refer to what people do and what they do is socially embedded, such that practice cannot be considered apart from the structural setting of cultural ideas, rules, and material relations. This is what Giddens (1979:5) refers to as the duality of structure. Structure is both the medium and the outcome of the reproduction of practices. What people do creates patterns of social relations and these patterns in turn imply cultural rules about how the social and material world is defined and understood. For example, as modern Zapotecs contact their ancestors through cave ceremonies, they contribute to broader cultural schemas concerning people's relationships with ancestors and the divine. These schemas include both the nature of ancestors and the divine, along with understandings about the power and drama of the material setting involving things like sacred caves, incense, and ritual performance. These understandings in turn are learned by people and become part of their social persona.

The focus on social embeddedness differentiates practice from the way that processual archaeologists conceptualized behavior. In processual approaches, behavior was seen as the actions of individuals or groups responding in rational and usually adaptive ways to external social and/or ecological conditions. Practice theory considers how human subjects and the broader social, cultural, and material settings are mutually constitutive. Cultural principles along with material and non-material resources construct who people are as cultural subjects – their beliefs, knowledge, dispositions, identities, and personhood – that is, their subjectivities, while people's actions in turn reproduce or change structure.

Structure therefore consists of cultural principles and resources (Sewell 1992). Cultural principles are the rules of social life – generalizable procedures that guide our actions in daily life. For ancient Mixtecs, Zapotecs, and Chatinos these principles included rules of etiquette, farming procedures, ritual proscriptions, and the complex symbolism associated with rulership, deities, ancestors, and the landscape, for example. These principles are generalizable in that they can be applied to a variety of contexts beyond the specific conditions in which they were first learned or are typically applied. Cultural principles may be formal prescriptions such as written laws, but more often are informal and not always discursively or even consciously understood. These principles are virtual in the sense that they are implied in regularized practices, in the patterns of social activity within groups that constitute social systems. Principles like etiquette, grammar, and bodily comportment, for example, are learned primarily through observation rather than formal instruction.

Resources are both human and non-human. Human resources include materials (e.g., physical strength, an army) and ideas (e.g., the special knowledge of a ritual specialist). Non-human resources include naturally occurring and manufactured materials such as a sacred cave, a maize plant, or a king's scepter.

It is important to recognize that cultural principles and resources are mutually intertwined, which is what we refer to as materiality (D. Miller 2005; Tilley et al. 2006). For example, ritual knowledge is both a resource that ritual specialists draw on in ceremonial performances, and a set of cultural principles that define things like the relationship between people and the divine, and the proper way to petition deities and ancestors. Material resources are the products of cultural schemes in that the activation of material things as resources and the determination of their value and social power are dependent on the cultural principles that inform their use (Sewell 1992:12). Thus, the value of ornamental shell or jade in ancient Oaxaca was a combination of their material properties and the culturally constructed meanings that were given to these properties. A cave is considered sacred because of a combination of material features like how it projects beneath the surface of the earth and its darkness, along with the meanings that have been given to these properties as passageways to the divine world of deities and ancestors. Resources in turn affect cultural schemas in the sense that, to be sustained over time, principles are reinforced and validated by the accumulation of resources resulting from their enactment. Poststructural theory therefore rejects the dualism between materialism and idealism; instead, material resources and cultural principles are seen as mutually constituting, which is what we refer to as materiality. Poststructuralism contrasts with the theories of processual archaeology, which view material conditions as distinct from and causally privileged relative to the ideational realm.

Structure, or mutually reinforcing rule-resource sets that are durable to some extent in time and space, are internalized in people, constituting them as human subjects with particular knowledge and dispositions. Bourdieu (1977) termed these interiorized dispositions "habitus," which he saw as systems of durable, transposable principles. Habitus includes interests, worldviews, recipes for action, and schemes for evaluating and perceiving the world. These interiorized principles and resources are mobilized in practice as they guide and empower human activity, which in turn reproduces social systems and structure. People living under similar conditions share a similar habitus so that members of particular status groups, genders, ethnic groups, or communities share similar dispositions. At the time of the Spanish Conquest, for example, nobles in Oaxaca shared a habitus that crosscut gender, community, and ethnic affiliations. Bourdieu has been criticized, however, for viewing habitus as largely unconscious, leaving little room for creative action that might transform society (Ortner 1996:11; Sewell 1992).

Giddens' (1979, 1984) theory of structuration provides more room for intention and creative human action with the potential to be socially transformative. He locates internalized structures not just in the unconscious, but in what he terms practical and discursive forms of consciousness. Practical consciousness, which overlaps with Bourdieu's concept of habitus, consists of the common-sense knowledge drawn on in the habitual activities of everyday life that reproduce many aspects of the social world. For example, ancient Oaxacan peoples would have drawn on these tacit stocks of knowledge in carrying out many daily farming and food-preparation activities – activities that were certainly conscious, but were not discursive in that they were not overtly analyzed or discussed as part of a broader understanding of society.

Yet, as people live, they reflect on their actions and build understandings of the conditions of their worlds that are discursive. It is this discursive penetration of the conditions of existence that allows people to creatively interact with their social world. The boundary between practical and discursive consciousness is fluid, and experience with the world can open up realms of social life to discursive penetration just as things that were once questioned can become taken for granted. In a stark example from the early colonial-period idolatry trials at Yanhuitlán, the sacrifice of slaves by Mixtec nobles led slaves to question the sacred qualities of human sacrifice (Terraciano 2001:272). Both practical and discursive knowledge is always situated knowledge that is limited and incomplete; it is a product of the particular social position and experiences of a subject. Empowered with knowledge and the resources that it mobilizes, people can transform their worlds.

As discussed by Sahlins (1981), however, the entirety of structure is never present or knowable in the conjuncture of the particular conditions of everyday actions and interactions. For example, in the cave ceremony discussed above, things such as the ritual powers of the priest, the presence of deities and ancestors, and the sense of being inside the sacred earth would be foregrounded, while other aspects of structure, like knowledge of how to make pottery or the layout of one's house, would not. Sahlins terms the conditions, principles, and resources that are activated in any setting of interaction the "structure of the conjuncture." Because of the particular structures of the conjuncture, the outcome of action is often unintended due to the incompleteness of knowledge, unacknowledged conditions, and the unpredictable outcomes of social action. For example, early colonial Spanish attempts to convert Mixtecs to Christianity resulted in only partial, incomplete, and ambiguous conversions (Terraciano 2001:361). Mixtecs understood Christian concepts and practices in their own terms so, for example, Mary, the mother of Jesus Christ, came to resemble a female creator deity.

Poststructural theory therefore differs from archaeological theory of the 1960s and 1970s in that it involves the development of a theory of the subject (Hodder & Hutson 2003:90–124; Meskell & Joyce 2003; Moore 1994; Shanks & Tilly 1992; Stockett & Geller 2006). An important concept used to explore subjectivity is identity, which describes people's affiliations with various complex, nested, overlapping, and partially contradictory collectivities (Janusek 2004; Meskell 2001). Identity is defined in relation to collectivities based on shared memory, place, ancestry, gender, age, occupation, religion, or other cultural practices. Since a collectivity "occupies a unique place within an encompassing sociopolitical order, affiliation with it embodies a distinct network of power relations" (Janusek 2004:17). People are able both practically and strategically to foreground or, conversely, to conceal different elements of identity depending on social circumstances. For example, in ancient Oaxaca, rulers used language, dress, and ritual practices to at times foreground a distinct "international" identity that connected them to likeminded nobles throughout Mesoamerica, whereas in other contexts they acted as the "father or mother" of the community, foregrounding affiliations with their subjects. At times the intersection of these local and "international" identities embodied unresolved conflicts and social tensions (Barber 2005; A. Joyce 2006). People therefore embody an intersection of identities that never represent a unified, consistent, fixed, and integrated whole.

Identity and other elements of subjectivity are never fixed within an atomized individual but are continuously produced through dwelling in and experiencing the world. As shown by Judith Butler (1990, 1993), even sex and other material aspects of the body are culturally constructed, although those constructions are constrained by the materiality of the body. In other words, rather than sex as a male–female duality that is natural, fixed, and pre-discursive, Butler (1990:7) argues that this dualistic view of sex is a product of western gender constructs. In contrast, amongst the Late Postclassic Aztec, Rosemary Joyce (2000) has shown that adult male and female heterosexual genders were crafted from the undifferentiated gender potential of infancy through the labor of adults. Another adult gender category consisted of the sexually abstinent ritual specialists of the temple, both young men and women. This example also shows how identity categories never stand alone; here gender, age, and the disciplining of labor intersect in the development of Aztec personhood. Subjectivity therefore is embodied in bodily practices, comportment, expressions, and ornamentation (R. Joyce 2000, 2004a; Meskell & Joyce 2003). As Rosemary Joyce (2004a:84) defines it, embodiment is the "shaping of the physical person as the site of the experience of subjectivity, a shaping that is simultaneously the product of material and discursive actions."

Butler (1993) argues that embodied identities are enacted via practices that cite preexisting cultural principles. These performances are the fluid media through which identities are "reflexively shaped within specific social settings" (R. Joyce 2000:7). Yet such performances of identity are never entirely closed, leaving room for agency and both the transformation and the reproduction of those principles. Within bodily practices, Connerton (1989) contrasts incorporating practices, which are similar to Butler's citational performances, with inscribed practices, depending on the media through which they are enacted and transcribed (see R. Joyce 2000, 2004a). Incorporating practices are enacted on and through the materiality of the body such as gestures, expressions, and comportment. Inscribed practices transcribe meanings and memory into more permanent material media such as carved-stone monuments, figurines, and the architectural layout and symbolism of ceremonial centers in ancient Mesoamerica (Ashmore & Sabloff 2002; A. Joyce 2004; R. Joyce 2000). Connerton suggests that inscribed practices can involve attempts to foreclose alternative meanings, while incorporating practices tend to be more open and potentially generative of new meanings. Connerton (1989) also stresses commemorative ceremonies in the production of social identities and communal memory. Commemorative ceremonies re-enact prototypical persons and events, which can be understood as either historical or mythical and which represent enactments of a master narrative that becomes a focus of communal identity. For example, sacrificial rituals in Oaxaca reenacted the cosmic creation and defined the relationship between people and the divine world of deities and ancestors (Monaghan 1990).

Who people are as cultural subjects (subjectivity) and what they do (practice) is therefore both enabled and constrained, but not entirely determined by the structural setting. I use the concept of agency to consider the relationship between peoples' subjectivities and practices, and the broader social, cultural, and material setting. Of all the concepts that have been adopted by archaeologists from social theory, agency has been the most widely defined and debated (Dobres & Robb 2000). Perhaps as a reaction to the holism of systems theory, archaeologists have tended to equate agency with western notions of individualism and economic rationality (Johnson

1989). Archaeologists from a variety of theoretical persuasions have used agency to mean the strategic actions of rational actors, as in agent-based models or optimal foraging theory (Kohler & Gumerman 2000). Agency has also been used for the aggrandizing actions of ruling elites (Clark & Blake 1994; Flannery 1999) and conversely for resistance to rulers and dominant ideologies (Shackel 2000). Finally, agency has often been equated with power, as in the ability to effect change in society. Another debate surrounding the use of agency in archaeology is whether agency exists at the level of individuals (Flannery 1999) or groups (Gillespie 2001).

I believe that much of the debate over agency in archaeology misses the point at the heart of practice theory – the recursivity of social life and the inseparability (duality) of the subject and society, including both their ideational and material dimensions. As Sherry Ortner (1996:10–11) describes broader debates over agency among social theorists:

> The debates tend to be posed in such a way that one appears to have to choose between total constructionism and total voluntarism, between the Foucauldian discursively constructed (and subjected) subject, or the free agent of Western fantasy. It is the argument of a practice theory framework, however, that this choice is both unnecessary and wrong, which brings us back, finally, to the point of departure: the construction of agency within practice theory, and its potential for resolving this problem.

I view agency as involving people's actions – a continuous flow of conduct in the world – and how their actions are enabled and constrained by the structural setting (see Giddens 1979:55–6). Agency therefore looks back and forth between the subject and structure, focusing on the ways in which cultural principles and resources constrain and enable people's conduct in the world both externally and as internalized dispositions that constitute the subjectivity of the actor. Latour (2005) extends this relational view of agency to include networks of people, ideas, objects, animals, and divine beings, amongst others. For example, in the cave ceremony described above agency involves the network of ritual specialists, audience, ancestors, deities, the sacred cave, ritual knowledge and belief, and ritual paraphernalia such as incense burners that are activated in the ceremony. Again quoting Ortner (1996:12):

> The challenge is to picture indissoluble formations of structurally embedded agency and intention-filled structures, to recognize the ways in which the subject is part of larger social and cultural webs, and in which social and cultural "systems" are predicated upon human desires and projects . . . [S]ocial

life is precisely social, consisting of webs of relationship and interaction between multiple, shifting interrelated subject positions, none of which can be extracted as autonomous "agents"; and yet at the same time there is "agency" . . .

Ortner (1996) views agency as the skill, intention, knowledge, and intelligence through which actors play the "serious games" of social life. The games of life are multiple, and their rules and goals, as well as relevant categories of actors and the significance assigned to certain acts and outcomes, are culturally organized and constructed as what Holland and her colleagues (1998:522) have called "figured worlds." The game transcends structure with structure framing and producing the rules of the game, but with people who can reflect on their circumstances and "imagine or fantasize escapes and alternatives" (Ortner 1996:14). Agency therefore cannot be universalized as economic rationality or the desire for power and prestige, but must be contextualized in history, culture, and ultimately the specific setting of social activity.

Structural properties are neither rigid nor inflexible such that Ortner's "serious games" involve constant negotiation and struggle over cultural principles and resources. Practices are always negotiations among the variably positioned actors who embody different subjectivities characterized by varying identities, interests, emotions, knowledge, outlooks, and dispositions. As discussed by Pauketat (2001:80), "practices are always 'negotiations' to the extent that power, the ability to constrain an outcome, pervades fields of action and representation . . . Any form of this practical, negotiative process of becoming is a historical process, and its explanation can only be made with reference to the genealogy of practices or the tradition of negotiations." Likewise, Hodder (1987:6) argues that "societies might best be seen as non-static negotiations between a variety of changing and uncertain perspectives." Culture and society therefore are never integrated wholes as in systems perspectives, but always contain polyvalent and potentially contestable symbols, meanings, and actions.

Power, knowledge, and negotiation

Fundamental to the outcome of social negotiations is power. Although early poststructuralist thought (esp. Bourdieu 1977) continued the tendency of social theorists to focus on power as domination, recent considerations of feminist and subaltern scholarship have focused greater attention on the ways in which structure and power are negotiated, contested, and at times resisted (Joyce et al. 2001; Ortner 1996; J. C. Scott 1985, 1990). Power is now recognized as encompassing relationships that are broader than domination and social control. This view is reflected in the distinction between *power to* and *power over* (Miller & Tilley 1984). *Power over* refers to domination, while *power to* refers to the complex ways in which cultural knowledge constructs people as cultural subjects. *Power to* encompasses power as domination, but it also includes the positive, productive, and creative aspects of cultural knowledge that create social identities and that people draw on in practice.

Foucault (1970, 1972, 1980, 1986) explores the relationship between knowledge and power, particularly the ways in which cultural knowledge, what he calls discourse, constructs human subjects. Foucault urges us not to view discourse as entirely descending from the application of the strategic power of a dominant group, as has been assumed by earlier views. For Foucault, power and knowledge are inseparable. All societies are permeated and constituted by relations of power, which cannot be established or implemented without the production and circulation of knowledge. Discourses validate certain kinds of knowledge, social relations, and subjects as legitimate or true, while excluding others. Historical periods are marked by dominant discourses that construct particular historically contingent subject positions and power relations. Thus, in ancient Oaxaca, notions of sacrifice defined the relations between people, deities, and ancestors, and distinctions based on gender, status, and occupation were in part defined by one's relations with the divine as expressed and enacted through sacrificial rituals (A. Joyce 2000, 2008b). As Foucault (1980:98) states, "it is already one of the prime effects of power that certain bodies, certain gestures, certain discourses, certain desires, come to be identified as individuals." The person is therefore an effect of power and at the same time is the element of its articulation.

Power in this sense is intrinsic to society and is manifest in cultural institutions, discourses, and social relations (Janusek 2004:13). No one is outside the reach of power but, as discussed by Giddens (1979), Ortner (1984, 1996), and others (Janusek 2004; Joyce et al. 2001; J. C. Scott 1976) to varying degrees, consciously or not, people can transform their social worlds. In this sense, power can be defined as the transformative capacity of an agent to achieve an outcome in the world which can either reproduce or change the social and structural setting (Giddens 1979:88–94). The transformative capacity of agents is determined by the compromise struck between their creativity, skill, and discursive penetration of the world along with structural principles and the properties of resources that create asymmetries in access to both material and non-material resources. All people, therefore, have some power in the sense that their practices serve to produce or reproduce social relations, cultural principles, and resource distributions. Power therefore involves what Giddens (1979:149) terms the dialectics of control, meaning that all participants in any interaction manifest some degree of power.

Foucault's prescriptions for the study of power are important in broadening our views of social relations beyond domination, but he goes too far in underplaying the ideas, institutions, and practices that actively produce and legitimate the social position of dominant groups as well as the ways in which subordinates can penetrate and resist domination. Scholars influenced by Marxist thought have explored aspects of structure and material practices that reproduce domination as the interface between hegemony and ideology (Comaroff & Comaroff 1992:27–30; Gramsci 1971:328; Janusek 2004:12–16). Gramsci (1971) defined hegemony as the unquestioned, naturalized, and universal taken-for-granted elements of a cultural field that reproduce domination. Yet domination is never total, and as knowledgeable actors, people always have some degree of discursive penetration of their social conditions. Where people penetrate structures of domination, hegemony is threatened and there is an opening for the contestation and negotiation of domination.

When aspects of a dominant discourse are opened to discursive penetration, ideologies develop to legitimate the social order that reproduces domination. Ideologies are cultural principles that create, maintain, and justify the interests of groups (Giddens 1979:184–90). As discussed by Giddens (1979:193–5), ideology operates to conceal sectional interests in three ways: (1) Ideology can represent sectional interests as universal. For example, the ancient Mesoamerican belief that nobles are the people's conduit to the gods means that it is in everyone's interest to support the nobility. (2) Ideology can deny or transmute structural contradictions. The Mesoamerican idea of reciprocal obligations between nobles and commoners denied unequal material transactions between them. (3) Ideology can naturalize or reify the present, meaning that current conditions are an unchangeable aspect of the cosmos. For example, Mesoamericans believed that the first ancestors of the nobility originated from sacred births, which fundamentally differentiated nobles from common people. Like the boundary between practical and discursive consciousness, the boundary between hegemony and ideology is fluid and can vary as people confront social conditions and become more or less aware of domination as domination. While people embody domination in bodily practices such as being deferential to those in authority, dominant ideologies are often inscribed in more permanent media as a way to foreclose alternative ideologies that contest domination (Connerton 1989). As argued by Rosemary Joyce (2000), practices of inscription therefore draw attention to sites of social tension and contestation and may involve practices that are highly charged. Throughout this book, I will describe ways in which architecture, space, imagery, and ritual were used to communicate ideologies in response to social tensions and differences that potentially threatened domination.

Recognizing that power is socially negotiated means that dominant ideologies are historically constituted through the ongoing interaction of people of different social positions such as elites and commoners, women and men, urban and rural dwellers, and people of the core and periphery. Dominant ideologies are not simple reflections of elite interests imposed on subordinates. The outcome of the negotiation of power may bolster the social position of elites, but it usually does so in ways that reflect some degree of compromise resulting from the interactions of varied social actors. For example, during the early colonial period, Spanish authorities tried to use indigenous idioms to teach Catholic doctrine so as to make it more accessible and palatable, which in turn contributed to the maintenance of many traditional beliefs and practices by Native Americans (Spores 1984:142–64; Terraciano 2001:252–317; J. Zeitlin 2005:89–118). Attempts to convert indigenous peoples to Christianity were characterized by a long and complex history of negotiation and struggle. Subordinates always have some degree of penetration of domination, which can be actualized by engaging with elites in the construction of dominant discourses, by seeking independence from institutions and practices of domination, or by resisting domination (Joyce et al. 2001; Joyce & Weller 2007). Basing their research on historical case studies, Abercrombie and his colleagues (1980) argue that subordinates at times penetrate dominant ideologies to a great extent. In these instances, the dominant ideology may serve more as a means to create social cohesion among elites than a way to justify inequality to subordinates.

Social systems are fragmented and contested to varying degrees such that there is never complete closure in any system of domination and subordinates may develop alternative ideologies that contest the dominant one. This theoretical position contrasts with processual traditions that tend to view societies as functional wholes with elites making decisions for the good of the group. James Scott (1985, 1990) shows how resistance is expressed in a variety of forms both discursively and non-discursively. Although resistance may occur in the form of active rebellion, more frequently it is expressed in subtle ways that do not directly confront authority. These subtle, although important, forms of resistance are what J. C. Scott (1990) terms the "hidden transcript" and are usually disguised or conducted outside the view of elites or their functionaries. Examples of the "hidden transcript" include distancing behavior such as humor and irony directed at dominant individuals, institutions, or ideas, which is oppositional in form if not in content (Goldstein 2003). Other examples of hidden transcripts include private rituals that challenge or bypass authority and foot dragging or withholding payments to rulers and ruling institutions in the form of labor or resources (Giddens 1979:145–50; J. C. Scott 1990). Subordinates are often limited to expressing resistance in subtle hidden forms because of the possibility of reprisals. It may also be difficult to invest in and organize more overt and challenging forms of protest because people are caught up in the daily struggle to make a living. Resistance can be undermined by geographical and cultural divisions that hinder the ability of non-elites to recognize their mutual subordination or to act in concert. Even under highly repressive and coercive forms of domination, people can at least express resistance passively. The frequency of peasant rebellions in recent history, however, indicates that people will at times express resistance overtly and at great risk in the face of coercion by dominant groups. A number of early colonial-period rebellions against the Spanish occurred in Oaxaca, for example.

Dominant ideologies provide openings for negotiation, contestation, and resistance because they usually include some form of social contract that delineates obligations of ruling authorities to their subjects. Authority can be more overtly contested if subordinates appear to affirm the dominant ideology by claiming that the social contract is not being properly enacted. For example, in ancient Oaxaca, commoners could have protested exploitation or oppression at the hands of authorities by claiming that nobles were not meeting their ritually prescribed responsibilities to their people. As a public affirmation of the dominant ideology, J. C. Scott (1990) views this as another example of the hidden transcript.

The expression of resistance in subtle and/or disguised forms often creates the historical impression that commoners have been duped by a dominant discourse, which may explain the prevalence of theories of false consciousness. The appearance of an uncontested domination is also a product of what J. C. Scott (1990) calls the "public transcript," where the dominant discourse is overwhelmingly represented in overt expressions of power in writing, architecture, art, and ritual performance. It is in the interest of elites to represent power as uncontested, while public performances of subordinates "will out of prudence, fear, and the desire to curry favor, be shaped to appeal to the expectations of the powerful" (J. C. Scott 1990:2). Rituals objectify and embody particular power relations and may create a degree of social cohesion and a shared corporate identity, but they also tolerate a considerable degree of resistance and negotiated appropriation (Bell 1992; Kertzer 1988). Expressions of resistance via the principles of a dominant ideology may also appear like affirmations of that ideology, further reinforcing hegemonic appearances. During periods of rebellion and political upheaval, however, hidden transcripts can become public and resistance is enthusiastically and openly expressed. Rebellions and periods marked by the collapse of established political orders can allow subordinates to express the anger that is stifled by coercive and oppressive systems. Such expressions of a hidden transcript of resistance are evident in several regions of Mesoamerica during and immediately following the collapse of ruling institutions at c.AD 600–900 (Joyce & Weller 2007).

History

Another implication of archaeology's embrace of poststructural theory has been an increasing convergence of archaeological and historical perspectives (e.g., Hodder 1987; Knapp 1992). Given the influence of systems theory and cultural evolutionism, archaeological theory has tended to view the past as the unfolding of general laws of social process and evolution (e.g., Flannery 1972). This approach views history as predetermined, often involving a sequence of episodic transitions from one stable system to another, which minimizes historical transformation and contingency.

In contrast poststructural theory, with its focus on the recursivity of social life, views social systems and structures as always in a state of becoming. Social conditions are never static, so there can never be a synchronic mode of analysis. Even the reproduction of cultural principles is the dynamic outcome of human activity. The negotiation of social conditions in practice is always a historical process (Pauketat 2001:80). Historical memories and tradition therefore are embedded in bodily practices and inscribed in material culture, architecture, and landscape (Connerton 1989; Pauketat 2001; A. Smith 2003). While society is always in a state of becoming, structures often persist well beyond the life of any one person (Giddens 1979; Hamann 2002; Hodder & Hutson 2003:127–45). Given the long time spans typically dealt with in archaeology, researchers have increasingly explored theories that address structural continuity and change on a variety of time scales.

The French Annales School of history examines the idea of longer-term historical processes that may underlay particular events and has been explicitly considered by a number of archaeologists (Hodder 1987; Knapp 1992). The most influential theorist from the Annales School is Fernand Braudel (1973, 1980) who argues that history occurs on three different, though interacting, time scales. Events involve the historical consequences of short-term practices of social actors. The medium scale consists of processes such as cycles of economic prosperity and decline. The long term or *longue durée* involves enduring structures, which Braudel largely assigned to the consequences of the physical environment, although other researchers extend the *longue durée* to include structures of meaning or *mentalités* (Hamann 2002; Sahlins 1996). Long-term structures of meaning can be viewed as those cultural principles that are more deeply sedimented in time due to factors such as their inscription in material media like monumental architecture and landscape (Joyce 2009a; Hamann 2002).

Sewell (1992:22), for example, differentiates between deep and superficial structures. Deep structures involve the underlying, taken-for-granted principles that generate surface structures and practices. Though deep structures are often durable over long periods, their surface manifestations are more contested and dynamic. Deep structures historically generate a variety of superficial schemas, practices, and power relations. Examples of deep structures of the *longue durée* include the capitalist commodification of things (Sewell 1992:25–6), the "search for satisfaction" in Judeo-Christian cosmology (Sahlins 1996), and the interconnected ideas in indigenous Mesoamerica of cyclical world-transforming cataclysms followed by the rise of new social orders resulting from sacrificial debts to the divine (Hamann 2002). As I discuss later in this book, while sacrificial original debt can be seen as an element of deep structure in Mesoamerica, its surface manifestations such as specific forms of sacrificial rites and the political significance of sacrifice have changed dramatically (Hamann 2002; A. Joyce 2000, 2008b).

Perspectives on the *longue durée* acknowledge that major historical transformations can occur even with continuity in structures of the long term. In contrast, Foucault's (1965, 1973, 1977, 1985) influential studies of the genealogy of knowledge have emphasized historical discontinuities or ruptures in discursive formations. Discursive formations are characterized by rules, mechanisms, procedures, and modalities analogous to deep structures that are implied in the construction of subjects. Foucault's (1972, 1973, 1977) discursive formations are never total and there are always gaps, contradictions, and subjugated forms of knowledge that create the potential for change. Foucault views historical transformations as discontinuous ruptures rather than as the result of gradual change. Historical ruptures result in the emergence of new discursive formations such as the appearance of new forms of political organization and religious ideology in Mesoamerica after the collapse of Classic-period ruling institutions at c.AD 600–900 (Blomster 2008a; Ringle et al. 1998). Ruptures, however, are never total and elements of a previous discourse can be recuperated and reconstituted under new cultural regimes (Foucault 1980; Stoler 1995). An important aspect of recuperation is that bodies of knowledge that are recuperated under new discursive formations are done so in ways which conceal their operation as a form of domination.

De Certeau (1984), however, critiques Foucault's primary focus on discursive formations. He likens Foucault's perspective to an observer looking down from a skyscraper onto the city. This observer acts as a voyeur, looking at the actions of the masses from a distance that simplifies and makes the city seem ordered and controlled. Instead, de Certeau urges us to consider the city from the perspective of the varied walkers who move through the "dark spaces" on the streets below. By this he is emphasizing that a dominant discourse is not a cohesive totality; that there are possibilities that are actualized by the "walkers" in the practices of everyday life that elude domination and constitute openings in discursive formations. As de Certeau states (1984:48): "A society is thus composed of certain foregrounded practices organizing its normative institutions *and* of innumerable other practices that remain 'minor,' always there but not organizing discourses . . . a *'polytheism' of scattered practices* survives, dominated but not erased by the triumphal success of one of their number" (italics in the original). De Certeau (1984) thus urges us to look not just at the discursive formation of the age, but at the everyday practices that may constitute openings in discourse and that can provide a reserve constituting the beginnings of major structural transformations.

Foucault's exploration of how discourse constructs subjectivities along with de Certeau's consideration of the ways in which everyday practice can create openings in discursive formations illustrates poststructuralism's movement between the micro-scale of the lives of people and the macro-scale of society and history. In this book, I apply the theoretical perspective developed in this chapter to examine the prehispanic Mixtec, Zapotec, and Chatino peoples. In the next chapter, I use ethnographic, linguistic, ethnohistorical, and environmental data to provide an understanding of indigenous culture and environments at the time of the Spanish Conquest that can be used to build analogies with which to address the archaeological record. These analogies, along with the theoretical approach outlined in this chapter, provide the interpretive tools that I will use to examine Oaxaca's archaeological record.

two

Peoples and Landscapes on the Eve of the Spanish Conquest

This book focuses on the regions occupied by the prehispanic Mixtecs, Zapotecs, and Chatinos, which with a few exceptions largely conform to the modern distribution of speakers of those languages. Today as in the prehispanic past, Mixtecs reside in the highland regions of the Mixteca Alta and Mixteca Baja, and the lower elevations of the Mixteca de la Costa. The demographic center of Zapotec-speaking peoples is the highland Valley of Oaxaca, although Zapotecs migrated to the southern Isthmus of Tehuantepec just prior to the arrival of the Spanish. Chatino speakers today live along the Pacific slope and coast of the Sierra Madre range in south central Oaxaca. I argue that, prior to the intrusion of Mixtec peoples during the Postclassic period, Chatinos also occupied the lower Río Verde Valley and hence they are included in the discussion here, although early colonial ethnohistoric data for them is limited. Today the regions occupied by Mixtecs, Zapotecs, and Chatinos are found in the Mexican state of Oaxaca as well as in small portions of the adjoining states of Guerrero and Puebla (figure 1.3).

In this chapter, I provide a geographical and cultural background to the study of ancient Mixtecs, Zapotecs, Chatinos, and related peoples. I examine the physical geography of the regions inhabited by these peoples in the prehispanic era and use ethnographic, linguistic and ethnohistoric evidence to provide an outline of indigenous culture at the time of the Spanish Conquest.

The rich historical and ethnographic records of Oaxaca allow for an understanding of cultural principles and practices at the time of the Spanish Conquest, which I will then draw on as sources of analogy for interpreting the archaeological record. Archaeologists depend on analogies based on ethnographic, historical, and actualistic observations to make inferences from the archaeological record regarding meaning and practice in the past. The observation that there are long-term continuities in cultural beliefs, practices, and institutions means that it is possible to use appropriate ethnographic and historic observations as analogies to reconstruct the past. Yet, as numerous scholars have pointed out, analogies must be used critically and with caution (e.g., Stahl 1993; Wylie 1985). For example, archaeologists cannot assume that cultural ideas and practices observed ethnographically can be applied to the archaeological record of the distant past, particularly when major historical ruptures have occurred such as the European conquest and colonization of the Americas. Rather than relying simplistically on such a direct historical approach, archaeologists have increasingly concerned themselves with both justifying the analogies that they choose (e.g., tracing back historical connections between the analogy and the archaeological case) and evaluating how well the material implications of the analogy fit with or diverge from the archaeological record (Stahl 1993:246–53; Wylie 1985:97–107).

Fortunately, Oaxaca has a rich ethnohistorical record, especially for the Mixtec and Zapotec, which allows us to gain an impressive understanding of culture at the time of the arrival of the Spanish. Although early colonial culture experienced major disruptions due to European contact, archaeologists and ethnohistorians have documented many continuities from the prehispanic past to the colonial period and up to the present day (Byland & Pohl 1994; de la Cruz 2002; Jansen & Pérez 2007:294–96; Monaghan 1990). Even when our analogies diverge from the archaeological record, the differences between the analogy and the archaeological case can provide important evidence with which to interpret the past. That is, analogy informs, but does not determine interpretation. For example, archaeological and iconographic evidence indicates that, just as in the colonial period, and even today in some Mixtec communities, sacrifice in prehispanic times was a means by which people petitioned deities for fertility and prosperity (Monaghan 1990). Yet the nature and context of sacrificial rites differs greatly between the present and the past, which gives archaeologists a basis for interpreting how sacrificial rituals and their political significance have changed through time (e.g., see A. Joyce 2000, 2008b). Ethnohistoric and ethnographic analogies have been used with success to examine the archaeological record of Oaxaca (e.g., A. Joyce 2000; Marcus and Flannery 1994).

The Physical Geography of Oaxaca

Oaxaca is characterized by incredible ecological diversity ranging from the hot, humid tropical lowlands of the Pacific coast and isthmian regions to the cool, semi-arid valleys of the Mixteca Alta. Most of Oaxaca consists of the rugged mountain ranges of the Sierra Madre Oriental and the Sierra Madre del Sur with spectacular peaks reaching 3,200 m. The mountains are interrupted in places by valleys formed through a combination of tectonic and fluvial processes. These highland valleys, as well as several lowland valleys and stretches of coastal plain, represent the only areas that have broad expanses of flat, agriculturally productive land and were the regions that became centers of prehispanic population.

Geology, climate, and vegetation

Oaxaca lies entirely within the tropics, between 16° and 18° north latitude. The Cocos and North American plates, which meet off the Pacific coast of central and southern Mexico, cause considerable tectonic activity (Rodrigo 1983). Most of the destructive earthquakes that have hit Mexico City have their epicenters along the coast of Oaxaca and Guerrero. Oaxaca periodically experiences major earthquakes such as the 1980 quake that destroyed parts of downtown Huajuapan in the Mixtec Baja and the 1999 temblor that leveled buildings in Tututepec's town square. A history of deposition, uplift, volcanic activity, and erosion have produced a diversity of rock formations and parent materials that affect soil fertility and susceptibility to erosion.

Climatic patterns in Oaxaca generally vary with elevation. Mean annual temperatures in the hot Pacific coastal lowlands reach 28° C, while the temperate highland valleys have averages from 15° C to 20° C. Although temperature differs greatly depending on elevation, it is relatively constant in any one place throughout the year. Rainfall is highly variable with mountainous areas along the Pacific slope receiving up to 2,000 mm or more annually, while the semi-arid highland valleys have annual precipitation as low as 400 mm. Rainfall is seasonal with most precipitation falling during the rainy season between May and November. There may be periods of weeks or months without any rain during the dry season from December to April. By the end of the dry season, the desiccated landscape and its vegetation is a dusty brown only to suddenly transform into lush greens once the rains return in the spring. In addition to the seasonal cycle of rainfall, precipitation can be variable and unpredictable both over the course of a single rainy season and from year to year.

Paleoclimatic research in other parts of Mesoamerica shows that significant changes in climate have occurred during the period of human occupation over the last 13,000 years (Hodell et al. 2007). Paleoecological evidence from Oaxaca is consistent with broader patterns in Mesoamerica, demonstrating the dramatic climatic and ecological changes that occurred with the end of the Pleistocene and the onset of the Holocene about 10,000 years ago (Flannery 1986). Mesoamerican data indicate a series of more subtle changes in climate during the Holocene, some of which may have had significant effects on indigenous economy and society (e.g., Hodell et al. 2007). Paleoclimatic data from Oaxaca, however, are at present insufficient to draw conclusions concerning the effects of Holocene climatic change on indigenous populations.[2]

The most dramatic ecological effects at least during the latter part of the Holocene in Oaxaca, as well as in most of Mesoamerica, were the result of agricultural practices (Dunning et al. 2002; Joyce & Mueller 1997). Human impact on the environment intensified about 3,500 years ago when the transition to sedentary agricultural villages transformed most of Mesoamerica into an anthropogenic landscape of agricultural fields, terraces, and settlements. Paleoecological research in Oaxaca has yielded little direct evidence bearing on patterns of natural vegetation prior to human disturbance. Based on analogies with modern flora, vegetation in the highland valleys probably ranged from mesic woodlands in the floodplains to more xeric thorn-cactus and mesquite forest in the piedmont (C. E. Smith 1978). In the coastal lowlands vegetation was dominated by semi-deciduous tropical forests with mangrove forests along estuaries and palm communities in drier coastal settings. Natural vegetation in the mountains is probably the least disturbed by humans and grades from pine forests in the highest areas to pine-oak and oak at lower elevations. Geomorphological studies in highland Oaxaca (Joyce & Mueller 1997), however, indicate that the use of modern flora as analogs to reconstruct pre-disturbance vegetation patterns may be problematic due to climate change and a long history of anthropogenic impacts.

Physiographic regions

The regions that became important centers of Mixtec, Zapotec, and Chatino population and where the archaeological record is reasonably well understood include the Central Valleys of Oaxaca, especially the Oaxaca Valley, along with the Mixteca Alta and Mixteca Baja in the highlands and the lower Río Verde Valley and southern Isthmus of Tehuantepec on the Pacific coast.

Surrounded by spectacular mountain peaks, the semi-arid Valley of Oaxaca is the largest area of flat, agriculturally productive land in Oaxaca with a high water table and productive soils (figure 2.1). The valley floor covers approximately 700 km^2 at an elevation of 1,500 m to 1,700 m above sea level and today continues to be a focus of agriculture by indigenous

Figure 2.1   View of the Valley of Oaxaca (photograph by Arthur A. Joyce)

Zapotec communities. Bedrock varies from Precambrian gneiss, Lower Tertiary conglomerates, and Cretaceous limestone, sandstone, and shale in the western part of the valley to Middle Tertiary andesite and volcanic ash and acid tuff (ignimbrite) in the eastern and southern parts of the valley. Although the valley floor is largely Quaternary alluvium, there are pockets of extrusive acid tufts. Standing on the summit of the ancient hilltop city of Monte Albán in the center of the valley (today a major tourist attraction), one can see that the Oaxaca Valley is Y-shaped with the arms forming three subregions: the northern arm is the Etla Valley; extending east is the Tlacolula Valley; and to the south is the Valle Grande, also known as the Zaachila arm. The Etla and Valle Grande subregions are drained by the Río Atoyac, while the Tlacolula arm is drained by the Río Salado, which meets the Atoyac just south of the present-day state capital of Oaxaca City. The Atoyac drains into the Río Verde approximately 100 km southwest of Oaxaca City and flows through a deep canyon to the coast where it discharges into the Pacific Ocean.

To the south of the Valley of Oaxaca proper are three smaller valleys, the Ejutla, Miahuatlán, and Sola valleys. The four valleys are separated by low ridges that are easily traversed and together they make up a larger Central Valleys region. The smaller valleys are somewhat drier and less productive agriculturally. Except for a small part of the eastern Miahuatlán Valley, all are part of the Río Verde drainage.

The Mixteca Alta is a high mountainous region northwest of the Valley of Oaxaca that is punctuated by several small intermontane valleys with floor elevations ranging from about 2,000 m to 2,500 m above sea level. With approximately 250 km^2 of relatively flat land, the Nochixtlán Valley is the largest valley of the Mixteca Alta (figure 2.2). Streams in the Nochixtlán Valley drain south into the Río Verde. Bedrock is dominated by the red to purple calcareous shales of the Yanhuitlán beds, which form fertile soils, although they are highly prone to erosion. When traveling through the Nochixtlán Valley, one cannot help but be struck by the stark reddish brown landscape that is the result of thousands of years of natural and anthropogenic erosion, which removed much of the topsoil and cut into the underlying beds (Joyce & Mueller 1997; Kirkby 1972;

Figure 2.2 View of the Nochixtlán Valley with the Yanhuitlán church in the foreground and the archaeological site of Cerro Jazmín in the background (photograph by Arthur A. Joyce)

Spores 1969). The two other major valleys of the Mixteca Alta are the Teposcolula and the Tamazulapan valleys west of Nochixtlán, which drain west into the Río Balsas system. Other smaller valley systems in the Mixteca Alta include the Tlaxiaco, Huamelulpan, and Coixtlahuaca valleys.

Directly west of the Mixteca Alta is a lower mountainous region, the Mixteca Baja, which consists of a series of small valleys with floor elevations ranging from 1,500 m to 1,700 m. Streams in the region flow west into the Río Balsas system. The Mixteca Baja is generally hotter and more arid than the Mixteca Alta. The geology of the region is diverse with bedrock variously including igneous, metamorphic, and sedimentary rock. The largest and agriculturally most productive area of the Baja is the Huajuapan Valley.

Along much of the Oaxaca coast the Sierra Madre del Sur descends abruptly to the sea in a steep escarpment, often forming a high, rugged coastline. In many places it is possible to look down on the expanse of beach and surf from mountaintops only a few kilometers from the ocean. There are only a few narrow strips of coastal plain and several small river valleys. Despite the abundant rainfall and warm temperatures, the lack of fertile soils limits agricultural fertility. Two regions are exceptions to this general pattern. Both the lower Río Verde Valley and the southern Isthmus of Tehuantepec have large rivers with broad floodplains that allow for productive agriculture. Access to estuaries and the ocean also provides resources such as fish, shellfish, waterfowl, and salt that are generally unavailable in interior regions. Today small communities along the coast exploit abundant populations of fish and shellfish using nets and small launches; as we will see, these were important resources in the prehispanic period as well.

The southern Isthmus of Tehuantepec marks the eastern end of the Sierra Madre ranges and the mountains descend to an expansive coastal plain 25 to 30 km wide. Several huge estuaries have formed along the coastline. Rivers in the southern Isthmus generally originate in the Pacific slope, although the Río Tehuantepec begins high in the Sierra Madre del Sur southeast of the Valley of Oaxaca. The floodplains of the rivers provide rich soils for agriculture, although soils in much of the coastal plain beyond the drainages are less productive.

The lower Río Verde Valley is located 225 km west of the southern Isthmus. The Río Verde originates deep in the interior highlands and drains an area of 17,680 km^2, giving it the largest drainage basin in the southern Pacific zone of Mesoamerica (Tamayo 1964). The Río Verde emerges from a narrow valley in the Sierra Madre onto a broad coastal floodplain approximately 20 km northeast of the river mouth (figure 2.3).

Figure 2.3 View of the lower Río Verde Valley (photograph by Arthur A. Joyce)

Bedrock in the lower Río Verde Valley consists largely of Jurassic gneiss and Mesozoic granites and granodiorite. The region's high water table means that, even during the dry season, plants never reach the desiccated state found in other regions, retaining a hint of green. In addition to the river and ocean, the region includes large estuaries, ponds, coastal plain, piedmont, and mountain zones. Paleoenvironmental research indicates, however, that modern ecological conditions emerged only in the last 3,000 years and that before that the floodplain was much smaller and the estuaries had yet to form (Goman et al. 2005; Joyce & Mueller 1997).

Mixtec and Zapotec Peoples at the Time of the Spanish Conquest

When the Spanish conquistador, Pedro de Alvarado, traveled to the Mixteca de la Costa in 1522 the number of Mixtec, Zapotec, and Chatino speakers probably numbered over a million. The major population centers were the regions discussed above – the highland valleys, the lower Río Verde valley, and the southern Isthmus of Tehuantepec. Ethnohistoric records provide a rich picture of indigenous culture at the time of the Spanish Conquest. There are few data on early colonial-period Chatino communities, so the discussion below will focus on Mixtec and Zapotec ethnohistory.

Language

In Oaxaca, the patchy distribution of fertile lands separated by high mountains acted as an isolating factor, which contributed to the emergence of considerable linguistic and cultural diversity. Today at least 16 distinctive language groups are identified in Oaxaca and when one walks through the larger indigenous markets in the state, such as the one in Oaxaca City, it is possible to hear several native languages spoken, along with Spanish. Of the indigenous Oaxacan languages, 11 belong to the Otomanguean family (Amuzgo, Chatino, Zapotec, Chinantec, Chocho, Ixcatec, Mazatec, Popoloco, Mixtec, Cuicatec, and Trique). Two languages, Mixe and Zoque, constitute the Mixe–Zoquean family, while three (Chontal, Nahuatl, and Huave) are single representatives of their families. The two most frequently spoken languages are Zapotec and Mixtec (Rodrigo 1983:125–6). Chatino is closely related to the Zapotec language. Yet this number of recognized indigenous languages masks even greater linguistic diversity. Zapotec probably includes dozens of mutually unintelligible languages (Nader 1969:331) and Chatino may have as many as three variants (Urcid 2001:20). Mixtec has perhaps more than a dozen distinct languages, although since Mixtec tends to vary continuously from community to community, it is difficult to determine a precise number (Josserand et al. 1984).

Some of the present-day linguistic diversity, however, is the result of population loss and cultural disruption following the arrival of Europeans. It is difficult to determine the precise number of indigenous languages at the time of the Spanish Conquest. In the late sixteenth century, Fray Antonio de los Reyes ([1593] 1976) distinguished six distinct variants of Mixtec. Orthographic variation in early colonial-period Mixtec documents is consistent with Reyes' scheme (Terraciano 2001:71–4). There has been less study of sixteenth-century linguistic variation in Zapotec and Chatino, although glottochronological estimates suggest that the four major variants of Zapotec may have been differentiated by this time (Marcus 1983a:7).

It should be pointed out that the terms "Mixtec" and "Zapotec" are both derived from Nahuatl, the Aztec language, and represent words used by the Aztecs to describe the peoples of Oaxaca. The indigenous word for the spoken language in the Mixteca Alta is *dzaha dzaui*. In terms of early colonial evidence for a consciously recognized social identity at a scale approximating an ethnic group, Terraciano (2001:318–28) finds that people from the Mixteca Alta identified themselves as Ñudzahui, which means "people of the place of Dzahui." In Mixtec, Dzahui means "rain" or "a divine and esteemed thing" and is the name of the rain deity. Ñudzahui, however, is not found in early colonial indigenous documents from the Mixteca Baja, suggesting that a different regional identity may have been in place. Likewise, while we do not know how people of the Mixteca de la Costa referred to themselves, colonial-period documents from the Mixteca Alta refer to the coast as Ñundehui, or "place of the sky or horizon." Zapotecs refer to themselves using variants of the term *binnizá*, which has often been interpreted as "people of the clouds," although recent linguistic studies question this reading (de la Cruz 2007:15–20). The Zapotec language is *dizaa* in the Oaxaca Valley dialect. The Chatino refer to themselves as Ne'Cha'cñâ or "people of the useful words" (Bartolomé & Barabas 1996:121).

Community and polity

Mixtecs, Zapotecs, and Chatinos lived in a variety of communities ranging from small hamlets occupied by a single family to cities with populations in the tens of thousands like Teposcolula (Yucundaa in Mixtec), Tututepec, and Tehuantepec (Joyce et al. 2004; Spores & Robles 2007; J. Zeitlin 2005). At the time of the conquest, Oaxaca was broken up politically into dozens of independent polities each ruled by a great house centered on a hereditary ruler who could trace his or her genealogy back to a founding couple. For example, the Mixtec codices depict that Lord 10 Dog "War" and Lady 8 Grass "Cloud of Ñuu Dzaui" was the founding couple of Jaltepec (Añute in Mixtec) in the southern Nochixtlán Valley from whom later rulers of the community claimed descent. Mixtecs referred to all settlements – from hamlets to entire regions – as *ñuu* and people were usually identified by their affiliation with a particular community (e.g., *tay ñuu Yucundaa* or person from the *ñuu* of Teposcolula; Terraciano 2001:103–7). A *ñuu* could be subdivided into a number of barrios or *siqui*. For example, early colonial-period Yucundaa in the Teposcolula Valley had at least 8 *siqui* (Terraciano 2001:112) and many modern Mixtec, Zapotec, and Chatino communities continue the barrio organization. While the *siqui* of a community could be contiguous, they could also be spatially separated, suggesting that a *ñuu* could encompass several spatially distinct sites defined archaeologically. Hereditary rulers generally led larger, more prominent communities. Zapotecs used the term *queche* for nucleated settlements governed by a hereditary ruler and consisting of

Peoples and Landscapes on the Eve of the Spanish Conquest 45

barrios, or *quiñaqueche*, and surrounding subject communities (Oudijk 2002:77). An early colonial-period map that accompanied the *Relación Geográfica* indicates that Tehuantepec had as many as 31 distinct barrios, which represents a decline from the 49 barrios recorded in a census conducted several decades before (J. Zeitlin 2005:41). Zapotec *queche* and Mixtec *ñuu* that were governed by ruling houses and controlled a number of smaller subject communities constituted polities (for more extensive discussions of Mixtec, Zapotec, and Chatino names and their variability see Bartolomé & Barabas 1996; de la Cruz 2007; Greenberg 1981; Oudijk 2002; Terraciano 2001; J. Zeitlin 2005).

When ruling nobles intermarried, their communities were united until the death of both spouses. Most alliances were established for strategic purposes to enhance the political prestige and military power of both royal houses (Pohl 2003). Prehispanic and early colonial documents record numerous such alliances, including several between Zapotec and Mixtec ruling houses. Alliances could result in the creation of communities with linguistically distinct barrios. For example, a series of marital alliances between Mixtec nobles and members of the ruling house of Zaachila resulted in immigration and the establishment of Mixtec barrios at Cuilapan, Zaachila, and Xoxocotlán in the Valley of Oaxaca. Alliances tended to be unstable, particularly in cases when ruling couples failed to produce an heir, leading to conflicts over succession. For example, early in the fifteenth century a succession struggle within the Zaachila ruling house allowed Cuilapan to usurp Zaachila as the dominant polity in the Oaxaca Valley (Oudijk 2002:76). The complex and shifting pattern of marriage and alliance formation among nobles contributed to the spread of a distinctive style of elite culture called the Mixteca–Puebla style that included painted codices, polychrome vessels, and styles of dress and ornamentation.

The late prehispanic political landscape was dynamic and factionalized with the fortunes of polities waxing and waning depending on success in warfare and the establishment of alliances with other ruling houses. The Mixtec codices and early colonial documents record numerous wars (Jansen & Peréz 2007; Mary Elizabeth Smith 1973). Dozens of fortresses were built, often on hilltops above communities. The most famous of these fortresses is Guiengola, whose impressive walls still stand on a mountain overlooking the Tehuantepec River, 40 km north of the Pacific Ocean (Peterson & Mac Dougall 1974). Burgoa (1674 [1989]:342–3) recounts that in the late fifteenth century a joint Zapotec–Mixtec army successfully held off an Aztec siege of a fortress believed to have been Guiengola. Defeated polities were forced to pay tribute to victorious ones and at times peace was brokered via a marital alliance between the former enemies. In some cases, a polity was conquered and its lands usurped by the victor. Warfare also provided a means to take captives as slaves and sacrificial victims. In addition to warfare among Mixtec and Zapotec polities, at the time of the Spanish Conquest, many communities in the Oaxacan highlands had been defeated and forced to pay tribute to the Aztec Empire.

Sociopolitical relations and identity

At the time of the Spanish Conquest, Mixtec and Zapotec society was made up of two hereditary categories that can be considered distinct status groups: nobles and commoners (Oudijk 2002; Spores 1984; Terraciano 2001:133–51; J. Zeitlin 2005:39–67). Noble or commoner status was a function of membership in a corporate group intermediate in scale between a family and community. There is some disagreement as to the nature of these corporate groups with some researchers suggesting that they were lineages (Oudijk 2008:101; J. Zeitlin 2005:58), others arguing that they were based on ancestral lines and were not formal lineages (Spores 1984:70), and still others viewing them as ramages or conical clans (Urcid 2005:44; Whitecotton 1977:153–7). The nature of corporate groups also may have varied among and perhaps within communities (e.g., J. Zeitlin 2005:42–52). Corporate groups usually reckoned descent back through either the paternal or maternal line to an apical ancestor. Genealogical relations were important for the social construction of status since proximity to the apical ancestor as well as the prestige of that ancestor produced the basis for inequality among corporate groups and therefore determined whether a person was a member of the nobility or was a commoner. Rights to property, privileges, and special offices were held via membership in the corporate group. Some commoners also belonged to corporate groups consisting of royal houses with commoners tied to the nobility through patronage relationships, rather than kinship (Chance 2000; Gillespie 2000; J. Zeitlin 2005:49–50).

The nobility consisted of hereditary rulers and a lesser nobility who governed barrios and were involved in the administration of local resources, trade, tribute, and religious ceremonies. Commoners made up the vast majority of people, most of whom were farmers, although many also participated in craft production and paid tribute in goods and labor to their communities. There was significant variation in wealth and status, which complicates the archaeological identification of status groups and has led to considerable debate over prehispanic social organization in Oaxaca and throughout Mesoamerica (Chase & Chase 1992).

Members of the ruling nobility (Mixtec *yya*; Zapotec *coqui*) were descended from parents of equally high status (Oudijk 2002; Terraciano

2001:134–7). Mixtecs and Zapotecs both differentiated between kings (Mixtec *yya toniñe*; Zapotec *coquitao*) and queens (Mixtec *yya dzehe toniñe*; Zapotec *coquitao xonaxi*) and, in the case of the Mixtecs, it was not unusual for queens to be the ruler of a polity. The hereditary nobility occupied the highest positions in the political and religious hierarchy. Rulers could trace their ancestry back to a deified founder of the community using genealogies recorded in codices and oral histories. The link to the founder was embodied in a sacred bundle of paper, cloth, or vegetable matter that held ritual objects often kept in the main temple and viewed as the "heart of the community."

Rulers were at the head of a ruling house (Mixtec *aniñe*; Zapotec *quihuitao*), consisting of buildings, lands, relatives, servants, and dependent laborers (Terraciano 2001:133–65; J. Zeitlin 2005:50). The ruling nobility lived in palaces consisting of numerous rooms built around a central patio or patios (Barber & Joyce 2006; Lind 1979). Palaces were built of stone or adobe with plaster floors and walls often elaborately painted and included living and sleeping quarters, kitchens, and storerooms. Noble status was therefore materially inscribed in these architecturally elaborate structures.

When individuals from two ruling families married, they united their respective communities into a single larger polity until their deaths (Smith & Parmenter 1991:20; Terraciano 2001:158–97). The accession ceremony involved a ritual whereby the new ruling couple "took possession" of the palace, symbolically constructing the polity and validating their position as hereditary rulers (Terraciano 2001:160). These rituals were performed before a select audience and involved a series of repetitive postures and gestures that commemorated and embodied sacred events and ceremonies recorded in codices and oral histories. The reed-mat throne represented both the royal marriage that created a polity (Mixtec *yuhuitayu*) and the seat of its authority.

In Mixtec society there was near gender equality in the noble class (Smith & Parmenter 1991:20; Terraciano 2001:171–9, 353–4). Rulers were chosen as heirs not based on gender or birth order, but on the advantages to be gained from the alliances resulting from a particular heir. Male heirs may have been preferred during times of conflict because of their experience as military leaders. Evidence from Zapotec society suggests, however, that rulership most often passed to the eldest male offspring of the ruling couple (Whitecotton 1977:155). Upon the death of one spouse, the other continued as the ruler of the united polity, although that alliance dissolved when the second spouse died. Each member of the ruling couple selected the succeeding ruler for their respective communities. Their heirs might continue the alliance or create a new one via marriage with a royal noble from another community. Polygyny allowed for the formation of multiple political alliances.

Rulers governed their communities, administered justice, and directed warfare and defense (Spores 1984:74–80; Terraciano 2001; J. Zeitlin 2005:39–88). The ruling house controlled large tracts of land that were worked by dependent laborers, and collected tribute from commoners and lesser nobles within their polities. Nobles and especially rulers were intermediaries between the people and the sacred realm, performing important religious ceremonies on behalf of the community. Rulers also sponsored communal feasts, usually in the palace, that tied the community together. The reciprocal obligations that rulers owed to subjects could become a focus for the negotiation and contestation of authority. Early colonial documents suggest that if rulers did not meet their communal obligations they could lose the support of, and face opposition from, lesser nobles and commoners (Terraciano 2001:148–9).

Lesser nobles (Mixtec *toho*; Zapotec *joana*) were often the hereditary ruling families of communities or barrios within a larger polity (Spores 1984; Terraciano 2001; J. Zeitlin 2005:58–9). Although the houses of lesser nobles were not as elaborate as rulers' palaces, they were generally larger and fancier than the houses of commoners. Lesser nobles paid tribute to the ruling house in goods, including such exotics as gold, jade, and cotton textiles. Perhaps more importantly, lesser nobles paid tribute in services through various administrative roles, including the collection of tribute for the ruling house, organizing of communal labor projects, organizing local militias, mediating disputes among commoners, and performing various political and religious services for their communities. It was possible for non-ruling nobles to usurp the authority of ruling houses and establish new dynasties through intermarriage, warfare, and political intrigue.

Noble identity was embodied in a variety of practices and dispositions that set them apart from commoners (Spores 1984:64–80; Terraciano 2001:134–7; J. Zeitlin 2005:57–67). The nobility embodied political and ritual authority as well as a distinctive style and elegance. Nobles were attired in fine garments of cotton, feathered headdresses, and animal skins and were adorned with jewelry fashioned from precious stones and metals like gold, silver, jade, pearls, and alabaster. They wore ornamental plugs in their ears and lips. Unlike commoners, nobles routinely feasted on turkey and deer and drank cacao and pulque. The nobility used a form of reverential and highly metaphorical speech and could read the pictographic symbols of the codices that recorded the histories, genealogies, and creation stories of their peoples. They had preferential access to a wide array of prestige goods such as gold, silver, copper, ornamental shell, turquoise, quetzal feathers, and elaborate polychrome pottery often obtained through long-distance exchange.

Both nobles and commoners were identified by calendrical names based on the date of their birth or birth naming ceremony in the 260-day ritual calendar (Terraciano 2001:150–1). Nobles were also identified by a personal name so, for example, Lord 8 Deer "Jaguar Claw" was born on the day 8 Deer and was given the personal name of "Jaguar Claw." Ethnohistoric data suggest that gender developed with age for nobles and perhaps for commoners as well. In the codices, there are few actual depictions of infants or children and even birth scenes depict people as born in fully adult form. People may not have been considered fully human until they reached gendered adulthood. This pattern resembles the one described for the Aztec by Rosemary Joyce (2000:149–56) where gender is the result of the labor of adult relatives who through ritual and training ensure that the child gradually embodies a male, female, or neutral gender. Like the Aztecs, a neutral gender category probably existed, consisting of men and women who were sent as children to train as priests and who remained celibate as long as they were in the priesthood (Spores 1984:92). Another age-related identity, at least for the Mixtec nobility, seems to have been embodied by elders (*yya nisano* or *toho nisano*; Terraciano 2001:135–6).

The vast majority of Mixtecs (*ñandahi*) and Zapotecs (*peniqueche*) at the time of the Spanish Conquest were commoners. Commoners consisted of a diverse array of men, women, and children including free commoners, dependent laborers, and slaves.

Free commoners wore modest clothing, usually made of maguey fiber, and lived in houses made from thatch and wattle and daub, sometimes with stone or adobe foundations (Spores 1984:64–84; Terraciano 2001:137–40; J. Zeitlin 2005:42–57). The patio was the focal point of daily activities where the family socialized, women wove textiles and prepared food, men returned after a day in the fields, and children played. Free commoners worked small tracts of land owned by the family or corporate lands assigned to them by their barrio or community (Terraciano 2001:203–19). Communal lands included plots used to pay royal tribute and generate community funds as well as sacred sites and communal woodlands. Some commoners also specialized at least part time in the production of crafts like pottery, lithics, textiles, and baskets; some acted as local merchants. Ethnohistoric evidence suggests at least for the Mixtec that there was considerable flexibility and overlap in the activities in which men and women engaged, although men were primarily responsible for work in agricultural fields and women focused on the daily preparation of food and on spinning and weaving of cloths (Terraciano 2001:139–40).

Tribute included labor, agricultural products, textiles, and other resources paid by commoners directly to the ruling house. The community was also required to pay tribute, which was mobilized through the working of communal lands. Cloth was particularly valued as a form of tribute in Mesoamerica, which increased the demand for and value of female labor (McCafferty & McCafferty 1998) and often put women at the forefront of resistance to requests for increased tribute (Terraciano 2001:241).

Dependent commoners farmed the lands of nobles and were servants (Terraciano 2001:140–5; J. Zeitlin 2005:33, 55). Dependents paid a portion of their harvest as tribute to the noble house and were generally poorer than free commoners. Slaves were considered the property of the nobles who captured them in battle. They labored for the noble house, could be transferred to other noble houses as tribute, and were the primary victims of human sacrifice.

Mixtec and Zapotec identities in the early sixteenth century therefore consisted of a complex set of status, gender, occupational, ethnic, kinship, corporate-group, age, barrio, and community affiliations that intersected and changed through people's lives creating a diverse set of subject positions. Social relations within and between these groupings were generally conceptualized as reciprocal, such as the complementarity of gender roles within families or the reciprocal obligations between rulers and subjects. Yet the power relations that were bound up in social practice and structure created potential conflicts of interest and inequalities, particularly among nobles and between nobles and commoners. These conflicts of interest and inequalities created the potential for societal tensions that at times resulted in the contestation of social conditions and even outright conflict. For example, internal divisions within royal houses were often revealed during succession struggles such as the conflict that broke out between factions of the Zaachila dynasty in the mid-fifteenth century, leading to the emergence of Cuilapan as the most prominent community in the Oaxaca Valley (Oudijk 2002:76; also see Terraciano 2001:175–7; J. Zeitlin 2005:76–8). Lesser nobles could be caught between their responsibilities to their barrio or community, their personal and familial interests, and their obligations to the ruling house (Terraciano 2001:195–7). Though nobles were enriched by the tribute and services of their subject communities, their social position required reciprocal obligations, which created the potential for conflict if nobles were seen as not fulfilling their ritual, political, and economic responsibilities. Tribute and service demands created a constant potential for social conflict, particularly during times of agricultural decline and when nobles requested increased payments (Terraciano 2001:145–50). Early colonial records indicate that potential conflict also existed between corporate groups and noble houses over the control of land and labor (Terraciano 2001:207).

Subsistence economy

The large populations that inhabited regions like the lower Río Verde Valley and the Valley of Oaxaca were supported by intensive systems of production developed over thousands of years (Flannery 1983a; Spores 1969; Winter 1988). The economies of indigenous communities throughout Mesoamerica were largely agrarian, although a variety of wild resources were also exploited. The Mesoamerican staples of maize, beans, and squash were the dominant crops grown throughout Oaxaca in the sixteenth century. Of these, maize yielded the highest caloric yield while beans and squash provided important sources of protein. Modern varieties of maize can be grown almost anywhere with intact soils (Rodríguez et al. 1989) and when traveling today through mountainous areas of Oaxaca it is not unusual to see people laboring to grow crops on steep slopes aided only by *machetes* and diggings sticks. Earlier varieties of maize may not have been as resilient as modern ones, which would have limited agricultural productivity relative to today.

Other crops traditionally grown by Mixtecs, Zapotecs, and Chatinos included chile, avocado, and bottle gourd (Flannery 1983a; Spores 1984: 80–1; Winter 1988). Crops that reached their greatest productivity in hot lowland climates included cacao, cotton, and perhaps manioc along the coast. Maguey was an important cultigen grown primarily in the highlands because it was used as a source of thread for textiles. Maguey was also used to produce the alcoholic drink pulque, which has a high nutritional value and is ritually important.

The most basic and widespread form of farming in the early sixteenth century was slash-and-burn agriculture that relies on rainfall to water crops (Flannery 1983a; Winter 1988:95–6). Today, as at the time of the Spanish Conquest, the wet and dry seasons in large part determined the slash-and-burn agricultural cycle. Fields are cut and burned toward the end of the dry season, which adds nutrients to the soils. Farmers are skilled at controlled burning of fields, ensuring that fires do not spread, and in March and April the air fills with smoke and ash. In May and June, seeds are sown. Crops then grow and are harvested through the rainy season. Fields are usually cultivated for one or two consecutive years before productivity falls, requiring farmers to cease planting and leave the field fallow for sufficient time for nutrient levels to return. Today fallow periods last from 2 to 5 years in fertile floodplains and as long as 6 to 10 years or more in the mountains (Rodríguez et al. 1989:224).

The areas with the best agricultural yields were the floors of the highland valleys and the floodplains of coastal rivers (Rodrigo 1983:192). Despite high potential productivity, climatic conditions and pests often make yields variable and unpredictable (Flannery 1983a:324). In all regions the timing, duration, and intensity of the rainy season can vary, which also affects the agricultural cycle and can create risk and uncertainty. In higher valleys killing frosts can damage crops. Agricultural uncertainty may be lower in the coastal lowlands, although insect infestations and destructive flooding triggered by tropical storms can create havoc for farmers.

The availability of water was a problem in the semi-arid regions of the Oaxacan interior (Flannery 1983a). Where farmers relied solely on rainfall to water crops, dry years could result in low yields. There are a few areas in the valley bottoms, particularly in the Oaxaca Valley, where the roots of plants can reach water, allowing for two to three crops to be grown annually. Elsewhere, small-scale irrigation systems were used to carry water to dry soils on the valley floors and along seasonal drainages in the piedmont zone. Irrigation techniques included the digging of wells to irrigate fields and the use of small dams and canals to divert floodwaters from drainages. Archaeological evidence suggests that in a few regions networks of small canals were used to irrigate broader areas in the piedmont (O'Brien et al. 1982).

In some parts of the highlands, especially in the Mixteca Alta, severe erosion has been a problem faced by farmers for thousands of years (Joyce & Mueller 1997). The construction of hillside terracing systems using stone retaining walls was the most common soil-conservation technique and continues to be used throughout the highlands (Flannery 1983a; Spores 1969:561–4; Winter 1988). The *lama-bordo* gully terrace system was another technology used to deal with erosion, particularly in the Nochixtlán valley (figure 2.4).

The *lama-bordo* involved the construction of a series of stone and rubble dykes, generally between 1 m and 4 m in height and up to 200 m long, in gullies descending hillslopes (Flannery 1983a:330–1; Pérez 2006; Spores 1969:561–4). The fertile red clays from the Yanhuitlán beds that eroded into these gullies from the slopes above were then trapped by the retaining walls creating flat surfaces supporting productive agriculture. Today when traveling through Nochixtlán one is struck by the extent of prehispanic terraces that cover the hills around the valley floors. Some of the terraces, including *lama-bordos*, are still used by the modern Mixtec inhabitants of the region. These soil-conservation techniques are examples of what Erickson (1999) calls landesque capital or agricultural features that require a significant initial labor investment, but that yield resources over many

Figure 2.4 Modern *lama-bordo* terracing in the Nochixtlán Valley (photograph courtesy of Raymond Mueller)

subsequent generations. Pérez (2006) argues, however, that most *lama-bordo* terraces could have been constructed by small groups of farmers.

Agriculture was the main source of food, although a wide variety of other resources were exploited (Spores 1984:67, 81–3). Wild resources included edible plants like the prickly pear fruit from the nopal cactus, avocados, coyol palm nut, and the fruit of the zapote as well as numerous medicinal and ceremonial plants like native tobacco. The alcoholic beverage pulque was made from the sap of the maguey plant. The only animals that were domesticated in the sixteenth century were dogs and turkeys, but people hunted deer, rabbits, peccary, birds, and iguanas as sources of animal protein. Coastal regions were rich in marine and estuarine resources including fish, shellfish, and migratory waterfowl. Salt was an important resource extracted from coastal areas, but also found in salt springs in a few locations in the highlands. Other economically important resources included lithics like basalt and chert used for the manufacture of stone tools, clay for pottery, palm fiber for mats and baskets, cochineal dye from a highland insect, and *púrpura* dye from a marine snail.

Commerce

Most communities in Oaxaca established contacts with distant places to gain access to resources in complementary ecological zones (A. Joyce 1993a; Terraciano 2001:231–51). In general, the coastal lowlands produced a wider range of resources than were available in the highlands. Through trade, highland people sought coastal and lowland products such as cotton, cacao, fish, shellfish, salt, tropical fruits, ornamental shell, and quetzal feathers. Given the scarcity of these resources in the highlands most were considered social valuables and access to some items was restricted to nobles by sumptuary rules such that they should be considered prestige goods. In return, highland peoples sent products like cochineal dye, pulque, and agricultural surpluses to the lowlands. Precious metals such as gold, silver, and copper as well as some precious stones like alabaster were found in restricted locations in the mountains as well as in deposits in some coastal rivers. Other resources were found only in regions well beyond Oaxaca, such as obsidian from the Basin of Mexico and the Gulf coast, and jade from Central America.

Merchants included long-distance traders who dealt mostly in social valuables, and local merchants, who traded both utilitarian and exotic goods (Terraciano 2001:231–51; J. Zeitlin 2005:78–80). Merchants traveled to places as distant as central Mexico, Guatemala, and the Soconusco coast. Mixtecs and Zapotecs traded with members of the famous Aztec merchant class or *pochteca*, who also served as diplomats and spies on behalf of the Mexica rulers. Communities such as Nochixtlán and Yanhuitlán may have had an unusual number of merchants that contributed to their prosperity.

There was a degree of economic specialization among Mixtec and Zapotec households and communities (Lind 2000:573; Oudijk 2002:83). Although full-time economic specialization was probably rare, archaeological and ethnohistoric evidence suggests that there were part-time specialists in the production of ceramics, ground- and chipped-stone tools, baskets, reed mats called *petates*, dyes, and salt. In modern Mixtec, Zapotec, and Chatino communities it is still possible to see many of these items being produced, such as pottery, textiles, and baskets. Social valuables made from exotic materials and requiring special skills to manufacture – such as shell and greenstone ornaments, copper bells, polychrome pottery, painted codices, elegant cotton textiles, and feather capes – were made by specialists attached to the elite or by nobles themselves. Copper axes and cacao were used as a form of currency, although primarily by the nobility.

Goods were exchanged in markets (*quiya* in Zapotec; *yahui* in Mixtec) found in communities all over Oaxaca as well as in special boundary locations between polities (Pohl et al. 1997; Terraciano 2001:248–51; J. Zeitlin 2005:79). Many communities had local markets that were held every five days where men and women exchanged necessities. Regional markets were established in political centers like Tlaxiaco and Teposcolula in the Mixteca Alta and Tehuantepec in the southern Isthmus. Regional markets attracted a wider variety of goods including local utilitarian products, but also prestige goods and even slaves. In addition to the market system, periodic ritual feasts also distributed resources among households.

The local and regional markets of the sixteenth century were not unlike the indigenous weekly markets held today in towns like Tlacolula in the Valley of Oaxaca and Tlaxiaco in the Mixteca Alta. At Tlaxiaco, for example, on market day the town square and nearby streets are filled with plastic-covered stalls and packed with people who traveled from all over western Oaxaca as well as the nearby states of Guerrero and Puebla to barter for goods. Low clouds blow through town, nearly touching the tops of buildings, and the early morning highland air is crisp and cold. Several indigenous languages can be heard in the crowd, including several dialects of Mixtec as well as Trique and Zapotec. Local farmers and craftspeople sell goods such as agricultural produce, turkeys, goats, pottery, baskets, and textiles. Many people come to the market because they can find goods from distant regions that are not available in local markets: dried fish and salt from coastal towns, pottery and weavings from the Oaxaca Valley, tiles from the state of Puebla to the north, and manufactured items such as tools and toys from northern Mexico and the United States.

In late prehispanic times a few regional markets, especially in boundary areas between powerful polities, were renowned for the availability of exotic goods often brought in by long-distance merchants, particularly the *pochteca* (Pohl et al. 1997). These interregional markets included Putla on the boundary between two powerful empires: the Aztecs and the coastal Mixtec Empire of Tututepec. There is some question as to whether these interregional markets operated on a regular schedule, like local and regional ones, or whether they were organized infrequently in association with religious celebrations and perhaps diplomatic exchanges. More ephemeral border markets also existed, usually on flat unoccupied mountaintops.

The economic relations of Mixtec, Zapotec, and Chatino peoples at the time of the Spanish Conquest therefore depended on resources like the quality and availability of land and water, as well as on access to commodities through trade often carried out in local and regional markets. In the following section, I will consider how political economy was embedded in sacred principles involving the nature of existence and people's relationship with the divine. Religious beliefs and practices were also ideological in that they served to create and legitimate inequalities in wealth, status, and power, particularly the distinction between nobles and commoners.

Religion and ideology

At the time of the Spanish Conquest Mixtec, Zapotec, and Chatino religion was based on the belief in a vital force that animated all "living" things. These religious concepts continue to be part of the beliefs of modern indigenous people throughout Oaxaca (de la Cruz 2007:55; Greenberg 1981; Marcus 1983b; Monaghan 1994, 1995; Terraciano 2001). For Mixtecs this force was called *ini* or *yii*, while Zapotecs called it *pèe* and the Chatinos call it *cryasa*. These terms can be translated as "wind," "heat," and "heart." Animate objects include not just people, plants, and animals but also time and the sacred calendar, rivers, rain, light, mountains, wind, earthquakes, and clouds, as well as a range of divine beings. In fact, the Mixtecs of the town of Nuyoo studied by Monaghan (1995:98) believe that all things except burned rocks are animate. Earth, mountains, and rivers are therefore not considered parts of a physical environment separate from humans, but have agency and are connected with people and deities via the sacred life force. The sacred force is also concentrated to varying degrees so that deities have more "heat" than humans and nobles have more than commoners. Within humans, the sacred force was concentrated in the heart and blood, which amongst Mixtecs today is considered the *ánima*.

Mixtecs and Zapotecs believed in a wide variety of deities, including ones associated with the cosmic creation, the sacred calendar, maize, and merchants (de la Cruz 2007; Monaghan 1995; Spores 1984:142–64; Terraciano 2001:252–74; J. Zeitlin 2005:68–76). Deities were manifest in the form of sacred bundles containing images made from stone, jade, turquoise, and other precious materials. Sacred bundles are frequently depicted in the codices where they are shown tied with a large knot and sometimes with a head or face protruding from the top. After the Spanish Conquest, indigenous nobles went to great pains to protect and conceal sacred bundles (Terraciano 2001:280–1). During the Inquisitorial trial of Yanhuitlán in the mid-fifteenth century, testimony was given against three Mixtec nobles for having maintained a religious cult focused on 20 sacred bundles that they protected within a secret vault (Byland & Pohl 1994:131–2). Romero (1994:237) describes the 1565 discovery by Spanish authorities of a cave near Mitla containing over 300 sacred bundles as well as other religious objects and the remains of human sacrifices (figure 2.5).

For Mixtecs living today in Nuyoo, the sacred force is most concentrated in Jesus who is equated with the sun and is called "the man of *yii*"

Figure 2.5 INAH excavations in front of the Cueva del Diablo (Devil's Cave) near Mitla (photograph by Arthur A. Joyce)

(Monaghan 1995:127), but there are numerous deities (*ñu'un*) associated with rain, earth, and wind. For example, Monaghan (1995:99–166) explains how each deity represents a different embodiment or "face" of the earth (*nu ñu'un*) and can be associated with a diverse array of landscape features and objects such as different bends in a river or pre-Columbian figurines found in farm fields.

In late prehispanic times one of the principal deities was a local example of the pan-Mesoamerican rain god termed Dzahui in Mixtec. For the Mixtecs of Nuyoo, the rain god (*ñu'un savi*) has many "faces" including that of "rain people" who appear as lightning bolts, and multicolored "rain serpents" that fly through the sky bringing rain (Monaghan 1995:104–9). The *ñu'un savi* live in sacred caves that are treated as shrines and referred to as "rain houses." For Zapotecs, the rain deity is Cocijo and is most closely associated with lightning. In modern Chatino the rain god is known as *ho'o ti'yu* (Greenberg 1981:83). Ethnohistoric data suggest that, like modern Mixtec deities, Cocijo had a variety of manifestations or "faces" associated with clouds, rain, hail, and wind, as well as with divisions of the ritual calendar and the four world directions and its center (J. Zeitlin 2005:69). The rain/lightning deity in Oaxaca was depicted with serpent-like features such as a bifid tongue and was associated with fertility, potency, and sacred time.

Time in ancient Mesoamerica was sacred and a manifestation of the vital force of *ini, pèe*, or *cryasa*. Mixtecs, Zapotecs, and Chatinos, like other Mesoamerican peoples, traced time through the use of solar and ritual calendars (de la Cruz 2007:331–484; Urcid 2001; J. Zeitlin 2005:68–70). The year in the solar calendar consisted of 18 "months" of 20 days along with a short 5-day month (6 days every 4 years). The 260-day ritual calendar was made up of 20 different day names, which are combined with the numbers 1 to 13. The cycle of 13 days is particularly significant because it is related to the directional divisions of the cosmos. The number 13 signifies the quadripartite division of each cosmic plane – sky, earth's surface, and underworld – along with the vertical axis that connects them. In the Zapotec calendar the ritual year was further divided into four 65-day units named *cocijo*, each consisting of five divisions of 13 days. The ritual calendar was important in divination and reflected the cyclical view of time and history in prehispanic Mesoamerica. Particular dates, for example, had magical and divinatory properties. An important cycle of time was the period of 52 solar years that it took the two calendrical systems to return to the same starting date.

Another important category of deities consisted of noble ancestors and particularly the dynastic founders of a community (Marcus 1983b; Terraciano 2001:260–5). Marcus (1983b) argues convincingly that the long lists of local deities recorded by the Spanish early in the colonial period with names taken from the 260-day ritual calendar were actually deified royal ancestors. Many of these deities consisted of male–female pairs, indicating a royal couple. It was believed that ancestors, particularly deceased rulers, could intervene with the gods on behalf of their descendants. For the Zapotec, the ancestors were associated with the clouds and referred to as *binnigula'sa'* or the "old people of the clouds." Although most deities with names from the 260-day ritual calendar were probably deceased ancestors, the Mixtec codices depict several local variants of deities found throughout Mesoamerica who were also depicted with calendrical names: Lord 9 Wind for Quetzalcoatl, Lord 7 Rain for Xipe Totec, and Lady 9 Grass for Cihuacoatl (Terraciano 2001:264).

In ancient Oaxaca, the cosmos was divided into the sky or heavens, the surface of the earth, and the earth's interior or underworld (de la Cruz 2007:88–91). The origins of the cosmos, time, deities, people, and sacred principles were the focus of indigenous creation stories. The Mixtec codices, particularly the *Codex Vienna*, present a version of the creation story that parallels an account recorded by Fray Gregorio García in the early seventeenth century and contemporary creation stories recorded by Monaghan (1990). Versions of the origin story are also found in the Quiche Maya Popol Vuh, and in Mexica writing and oral literature (Hamann 2002). Iconographic representations of portions of the creation story have been found on sculpture as well as painted pottery and murals that date back to the Formative and Classic periods (Guernsey-Kappelman 2001:93; Schele & Freidel 1990:245).

The Mixtec creation story begins in sacred time, a time of darkness (Furst 1978; Hamann 2002:358–63; Jansen & Pérez 2007:65–151; Monaghan 1990). The main actors in the beginning of the creation stories are deities and divine forces, and much of the actions depicted are associated with the town of Apoala in the Mixteca Alta. The Mixtec name for Apoala, *yuta tnoho*, is translated as the "river where the lords came up," that is, the birthplace of the Mixtec kings and queens. Early in the *Codex Vienna* the primordial creator deities, Lady 1 Deer and Lord 1 Deer, are shown making a sacrifice of powdered tobacco and incense, bringing forth sacred elements of nature, and giving birth to a number of important deities, including the patron deities of Apoala. The tobacco offering is associated with other rituals of generation, including the sacred birth from a huge flint of the deity Lord 9 Wind. Lord 9 Wind is shown in the codices establishing many of the sacred objects and practices that would come to define the identity of the nobility and the wider community. He is shown in various guises, often adorned with jade, gold, and shell ornaments, and is depicted as a powerful shaman, a sacrificer, a warrior, a sacrificial victim, and a painter of the sacred codices. After ascending to the heavens to consult with the primordial deities, Lord 9 Wind descends to the earth bringing with him several objects, including a quincunx staff, which would be important in royal rituals. In subsequent scenes, he is shown carrying the waters of heaven and bringing life and order to the Mixtec world.

Lord 9 Wind then causes the first lords to be born from a sacred tree at Apoala (Jansen & Pérez 2007:78–91). The third generation descended from the sacred tree birth includes two nobles, Lord 5 Wind and Lady 9 Alligator, who are shown seated together on a reed mat, the symbol of the Mixtec polity or *yuhuitayu* (Jansen & Pérez 2007:96). Each figure is shown with the round eyes and fanged teeth of Dzahui, the rain god. The place sign below the mat bears the symbols for Apoala, a blue river (*yuta*) and a bunch of feathers (*tnoho*). This scene therefore shows the couple establishing a polity at Apoala. The histories recorded in the codices would show that the later ruling dynasties claimed ancestry from this first royal couple at Apoala.

In the following pages of the *Codex Vienna* the first Mixtec nobles perform rituals associated with maize, pulque, and hallucinogenic mushrooms that lead to the dawn of the sun of the current age (Jansen & Pérez 2007:81–91). A key scene in this sequence shows the nobles forming a covenant with the powerful deities of earth and sky that allows people to practice agriculture (Hamann 2002:358–63; Monaghan 1990). The covenant is necessary because the turning of the soil and the harvesting and consumption of maize, the daughter of the earth and rain, causes the deities great pain. In return for being allowed to practice agriculture, the deities require that humans sacrifice their bodies in death, going into the earth where they are assimilated by the gods. The Nuyooteco Mixtecs studied by Monaghan (1990:562–3) describe this covenant by saying, "we eat the earth and the earth eats us." While the *Codex Vienna* depicts the establishment of the covenant in apparently peaceful terms, the *Nuttall* and *Bodley* codices depict the covenant as the outcome of a "War of Heaven" where gods and nobles fought against rock-skinned stone men and rain-descending cloud men (Hamann 2002:358–63). Following the establishment of the covenant, the current world begins with the first sunrise of the new era and the founding of the major ruling houses of the Mixteca Alta.

Mixtec and Zapotec creation stories therefore describe the fundamental relationship between people and the divine as a sacred covenant that established relations of debt and merit between humans and the gods, with sacrifice as a fundamental condition of human existence (Monaghan 1990, 1994). At the time of the Spanish Conquest there were a variety of religious practitioners who were responsible for carrying out sacrifices and other rituals designed to contact the deities and petition them for fertility and prosperity. Early colonial accounts suggest that there was a hierarchy consisting of high priests (Mixtec *nahanine*; Zapotec *huiatao*) and ordinary priests (Mixtec *tay saque*; Zapotec *copa pitao*), as well as terms for sacrificers, diviners, and students of the priesthood (Terraciano 2001:267–70; J. Zeitlin 2005:71–2).

Priests were responsible for sheltering, honoring, and "feeding" or making sacrificial offerings to the deities that invoked the sacred covenant (Marcus 1983b:349–50; Spores 1984:84–95; Terraciano 2001:267–71; J. Zeitlin 2005:71–6). It is not clear if women as well as men could enter the priesthood, although the codices show women performing a variety of ritual acts and early colonial documents record several powerful female diviners (Terraciano 2001:269–70). Often feasts and sacrificial rituals involved music, dancing, and the ingestion of tobacco, alcohol, and hallucinogenic mushrooms in order to communicate with deities and ancestors. Feasts could include processions to ritually important places such as sacred caves, mountains, and temples. Priests performed a number of devotional practices to honor the gods through fasting, sexual abstinence, guarding the sacred bundles, and cleaning of temples. Other ceremonies led by ritual practitioners included marriages, mortuary rituals, and the painting of codices. Ritual specialists used the sacred calendar to plan ceremonies and forecast future events. It was believed that at least some ritual specialists and rulers were able to transform into their animal-spirit companions or *naguals* and fly through the air making contact with gods and ancestors. These figures are often shown holding flint knives or human hearts and wearing a turtle carapace; they are known as Xicani priests in Zapotec and Yahui priests in Mixtec. In Nuyoo today, ritual specialists known as "rain people" perform offerings, prayers, and sacrifices in sacred caves to petition the gods for rain (Monaghan 1995:107–8).

Religious ceremonies were often carried out in temples, palaces, and ballcourts (Jansen & Pérez 2007; Marcus 1983b:349–50; Spores 1984:84–95; Terraciano 2001:252–74; J. Zeitlin 2005:67–78). Ballcourts were viewed as portals to the divine and were the sites of ceremonies related to sacred origins, sacrifice, political boundary marking, and the establishment of alliances. Since the entire landscape was imbued with *ini/pèe/cryasa*, many places were considered sacred and were locations of ritual activities. For example, sacred mountaintops were associated with rain and the cosmic creation, while springs and caves were portals to the underworld where sacrifices and offerings were made to gods and ancestors. Bundles that could include the remains of nobles were stored in sacred caves. A cave near the town of Chalcatongo contained a mummy-bundle shrine to the Mixtec goddess and oracle, Lady 9 Grass. The codices depict a number of important Mixtec rulers such as Lord 8 Deer "Jaguar Claw" consulting with Lady 9 Grass in her mummy-bundle cave shrine (Joyce et al. 2004).

Buildings like houses, palaces, and temples were ritually animated with the vital force through dedicatory ceremonies (Jansen & Pérez 2007:51–63; Marcus 1983b; Terraciano 2001:271–4). Many buildings were also equated with natural places. Temples built on pyramids were seen as sacred mountains of creation. Ballcourts, tombs, and sunken patios were equated with caves. Whole communities like Apoala and Achiutla in the Mixteca Alta, and Mitla in the Valley of Oaxaca, were religious centers. Mitla, for example, was a burial place for the Zapotec nobility as well as the town where the great priest resided. The great priest was most likely the powerful oracle, probably a god impersonator, discussed in ethnohistorical documents that curated and communicated with ancestral bundles kept in large cruciform tombs. Even ancient ruins were recognized as places of creation where ancestors resided (Hamann 2002, 2008b).

Sacrificial rituals included human sacrifice, the autosacrificial letting of blood, and animal sacrifice (A. Joyce 2000, 2008b; Monaghan 1994; Terraciano 2001:260–74). These forms of sacrifice drew on the vital force or "heat" of the body concentrated in blood and in the heart. Human sacrifice was the most powerful form of sacrifice and was most often performed on captives taken in warfare. An obsidian or chert knife was used to open the abdomen and remove the heart, which was sometimes burned as an offering. People were also sacrificed through decapitation and severed heads were at times displayed on skull racks. Ethnohistoric and archaeological evidence suggests that human sacrifice was a rare event and usually performed in association with important ceremonies, such as the accession of a new ruler, or during times of political crisis, sickness, or draught. Autosacrifice involved piercing parts of the body such as the ears, tongue, or genitals with an obsidian blade, thorn, or stingray spine. Sometimes the blood was dripped onto paper and the paper was then burned as a votive offering. Frequent participation in autosacrifice meant that priests often were scarred on the ears and tongue. A variety of animals were offered in sacrifice including doves, quails, turkeys, dogs, and jaguars. A type of tree resin called copal was also equated with blood and was burned as a sacrificial offering.

Nobles occupied a special place in relation to religious belief and practice, especially the sacred covenant and the acts of sacrifice that it required (A. Joyce 2000:73–5). In the codices the ancestors who made the first sacrifice to the earth and sky were noble priests (Hamann 2002; Monaghan 1990). The most powerful ritual specialists were nobles who were required to undertake some formal training in the priesthood. Human and autosacrifice performed by and on the bodies of the nobility were the most potent form of sacrifice.

Nobles therefore acted as intermediaries between people and the divine forces and beings that controlled the cosmos. Sacrifice was a kind of social contract between commoners and nobles (A. Joyce 2000; Monaghan 1994:23). In addition to the various types of blood sacrifice, many offerings in the form of goods and labor given by commoners to the nobility were conceived of not as tribute, but as sacrifice (Monaghan 1994:10–11). The term for ordinary priests in Mixtec, *tay saque*, may have been related to the term for tribute collector (Terraciano 2001:268). In return for sacrificial offerings, priests, rulers, and other nobles enacted the most potent forms of sacrifice that invoked the covenant, opened up contact with the divine, and provided for human and natural fertility. Noble ancestors constituted another level in this chain of interaction between humans and deities in that the rituals performed by elites contacted the sacred via noble ancestors. Noble ancestors were especially important because they were seen as bound to their corporate groups, maintaining an interest in the day-to-day affairs of their descendents (J. Zeitlin 2005:75).

The covenant was a key aspect of prehispanic ideologies since it established and reinforced both the hierarchical relationship between people and deities and that between commoners and nobles. The covenant concealed the domination of nobles as domination (Giddens 1979:193–5) since the interests of the nobility were universalized by linking their ritual practices to the maintenance of fertility and prosperity of all people. Noble status was reified by tracing the close relationship between elites and the divine to the cosmic creation and the sacred births of noble ancestors. The sacred covenant therefore established reciprocal ritual, political, and material obligations between nobles and commoners that nevertheless legitimated the privileged position of the nobility. Sacrifice was also a concept through which enemies were defined since sacrificial victims were most often war captives.

People were not entirely dependent on nobles for contact with the divine, however, since commoners could perform rituals, including certain forms of sacrifice, independent of the nobility (Winter et al. 2007). Commoners practiced autosacrifice and animal sacrifice, kept household shrines, buried their dead, burned incense, and made dedicatory and termination offerings for their homes. There are even indications that at times some commoners questioned and perhaps resisted the political and religious authority of the nobility (Joyce & Weller 2007). Despite their abilities to contact deities, people may have seen the world as a place over which individual commoners had relatively little control apart from their relations with ritual specialists, including rulers (J. Zeitlin 2005:75–6).

Religious belief and practice therefore described the sacred origins of the Mixtec and Zapotec peoples and their ongoing relationship to the divine. Religion was also ideological in that it constructed and legitimated the privileged position of the nobility as intermediaries between commoners and the sacred forces and beings that controlled the cosmos. In the next chapter, I turn from indigenous accounts of cosmic origins to archaeological accounts of the origins of the earliest native peoples of Oaxaca.

three
From Foragers to Village Life

The first people to reach Oaxaca were part of the initial migration of humans into the Americas sometime between 30000 and 10000 BC at the end of the last Ice Age or Pleistocene Epoch. The first several thousand years of the subsequent postglacial period or Holocene was marked by the initial domestication of plants in Mesoamerica, which provided the basis for the agrarian economies that supported later village and urban societies. Despite the immensely important cultural developments of the Late Pleistocene and Early to Middle Holocene, the archaeological record from this period is sparse, making it difficult to infer social relations, practices, and cultural principles for this time. The evidence does not suggest the presence of distinct regional identities so that it is impossible to differentiate between the peoples who would later become Mixtecs, Zapotecs, and Chatinos. With the beginnings of sedentary village life during the Early Formative period (1900–850 BC) the archaeological record of Mesoamerica is sufficient to provide more comprehensive understandings of society and culture.

In this chapter, I discuss the long but poorly understood period from the initial peopling of the Americas to the beginnings of village life during the Early Formative. I focus on the Early Formative both because the Mixtec and Zapotec regions have been the focus of some of the most important studies of early village life in Mesoamerica (e.g., Blomster 2004; Flannery 1976a) and because it is during this time that it becomes possible to identify many cultural traditions that can be traced through the later history of prehispanic Oaxaca. These include village life, agrarian economies based on maize, the exchange of social valuables, and rituals involving shamanism and autosacrifice that allowed people to communicate with the divine. Glottochronological and archaeological evidence suggests that by the Early Formative it is likely that the Mixtecan and Zapotecan language groups had diverged and there is evidence for cultural differences between regions later inhabited by speakers of Mixtec and Zapotec (Winter et al. 1984: 76–8). Chatino probably did not diverge from Zapotec until later in the Formative, however (Winter et al. 1984:87).

First Peoples

Human entry into the Americas has been a focus of archaeological research and debate since the beginnings of the discipline in the mid-nineteenth century (Meltzer 1983). Most archaeologists agree that people first entered the Americas at the end of the Pleistocene. Due to colder climatic conditions, continental glaciers over a mile in height covered much of what is now Canada and extended into the northern United States. The glaciers lowered sea level by as much as 150 m, exposing broad stretches of continental shelf and creating an unglaciated land bridge known as Beringia that connected Siberia and Alaska. Most researchers argue that the cold, marshy, and windswept reaches of Beringia was the point of entry of people into the New World. Archaeologists debate whether people entered by land through an ice-free corridor or used some form of sea craft to move more rapidly along the coast, although evidence is increasingly supporting the latter position (Dixon 1999, 2001; Erlandson 2007; Erlandson et al. 2007).

An even more controversial aspect of the peopling of the Americas has been determining when people arrived. Since the discovery in 1926 of an undisputed association of artifacts with extinct Pleistocene fauna at the Folsom site in New Mexico, archaeologists have agreed with a Terminal Pleistocene presence of humans in the Americas. These ice-age foragers belong to the Paleoindian period (c.10000–8000 BC) and their archaeological sites have been found from Canada to Tierra del Fuego. Paleoindians were originally thought to have been mobile foragers who specialized in the hunting of Pleistocene megafauna, but recent research has shown that they had regionally variable patterns of subsistence, settlement, and social organization (Bamforth 2007). In Mesoamerica, archaeologists have investigated a number of Paleoindian sites, especially in the Basin of Mexico (R. Zeitlin 2007:167–71).

The earliest evidence for a human presence in Oaxaca dates to the Paleoindian period. The only definite artifacts dating to this period are a surface find of a distinctive fluted chert projectile point found by the Valley of Oaxaca Settlement Pattern Project in the Tlacolula arm of the valley and two recent discoveries of fluted points near Mitla (Winter et al. 2008). Similar fluted points have been found in Paleoindian sites throughout North America and into western Mesoamerica. A major discovery is the recent excavation of the remains of a mastadon in association with chert artifacts at the site of El Pocito, about 7 km east of Mitla (Winter et al. 2008). Although the bones of the extinct Pleistocene mammal and the artifacts were spatially associated, it is possible that the artifacts were redeposited. Flannery (1983b) reports a possible Paleoindian site at Cueva Blanca near Mitla.

People therefore were clearly present in Mesoamerica by the Paleoindian period. A few sites scattered throughout the Americas, however, have raised the possibility of earlier pre-Paleoindian occupations. Evidence from sites like Meadowcroft Rockshelter in Pennsylvania, Pedra Furada in Brazil, and Tlapacoya in the Basin of Mexico suggest a human presence in the Americas dating back perhaps to 30000 BC. Yet the results from most pre-Paleoindian sites have been seriously questioned or refuted due to problems with dating, stratigraphy, or the questionable presence of artifacts. Monte Verde in Chile, however, yielded an impressive assemblage of artifacts, structures, and the remains of mastodons with multiple radiocarbon dates that extend human settlement back to perhaps 2,000 years before the Paleoindian period (Dillehay 1997). New analyses from Meadowcroft Rockshelter (Goldberg & Arpin 1999) as well as recent discoveries of other possible pre-Paleoindian sites promise to push human entry into the Americas back further in time (Dunbar & Hemmings 2004; Meltzer 2004). These data leave open the possibility that future research will extend human history in Oaxaca back tens of thousands of years. Archaeological understandings of the first Americans are far from resolved.

The Archaic Period and the Origins of Agriculture

By 8000 BC global temperatures were warming rapidly, the continental glaciers of North America were receding, and sea level was rising, flooding the continental shelf. In Oaxaca the cooler and drier conditions of the Late Pleistocene were giving way to the warmer climates of the Holocene. Paleoclimatic data from other parts of Mesoamerica indicate the establishment of warmer and moister climates by the Early Holocene from 8000 to 6000 BC (Buckler IV et al. 1998; Markgraf 1993). Between 6000 and 3000 BC temperatures, particularly during the summer, were probably higher than today. By 3000 BC paleoenvironmental evidence suggests a drying trend with conditions somewhat more xeric than today.

The small foraging populations of Mesoamerica responded to the environmental changes of the Early Holocene by exploiting a wide variety of wild plants and animals like white-tailed deer, peccary, and cottontail rabbit along with a variety of birds, reptiles, and rodents (Flannery 1986; Flannery & Spores 1983). In coastal areas like the Chantuto region of the southern Pacific coast of Mexico, investigated by Voorhies (2004), fish were the predominant source of animal protein. By perhaps as early as 8000 BC people began to domesticate squash (*Curcurbita pepo*) with a variety of other plants domesticated by the Middle Holocene including maize (*Zea mays*), beans (*Phaseolus* sp.), chile pepper (*Capsicum annuum*), and tomato (*Physalis* sp.). Recent DNA evidence indicates that bottle gourd (*Lagenaria siceraria*), once thought to be an early New World cultigen, was actually first domesticated in Asia and probably brought to the Americas, along with the domesticated dog, during the initial peopling of the continent (Erickson et al. 2005).

The long, gradual transition from Early Holocene hunter-gatherers to Middle Holocene forager-farmers belongs to the Mesoamerican Archaic period (8000–1900 BC). Archaic sites are rare in most regions, suggesting that population densities were low (Flannery 1986; Flannery & Spores 1983; Kowalewski et al. 2009:285–7; Winter et al. 2008; R. Zeitlin 2007). The few sites that have been studied suggest that people lived in small groups with permanent year-round occupations not developing until the very end of the Archaic or the beginning of the succeeding Formative period. Technological changes suggest an increase in ground-stone technologies such as manos and metates that were used to process plant foods, including early domesticates. Domesticates appear to have been a relatively small component of diets until the end of the Archaic.

Models of Archaic-period cultural change, especially surrounding the origins of agriculture, have been dominated by the results of two important archaeological projects conducted in the 1960s and 1970s in the central and southern Mexican highlands: the Tehuacán Valley Project directed by Richard MacNeish (1971; MacNeish et al. 1972) and the Oaxaca Human Ecology Project directed by Kent Flannery (1986). These projects were designed to investigate the origins of agriculture and both have dominated views of Archaic-period settlement, subsistence, and social organization in Mesoamerica. Since Flannery's research focused on the Tlacolula arm of the Oaxaca Valley and MacNeish worked in the Tehuacán Valley, located only 50 km north of the Mixteca Alta, both projects are important for understanding Archaic-period developments in Oaxaca (figure 3.1).

Winter and his colleagues (2008) recently excavated two additional Archaic-period sites several kilometers east of Flannery's research area. Winter and colleagues (2008) suggest that the presence of high-quality chert for tool-making may account for the relatively large number of early sites in this part of the Oaxaca Valley. The only other excavated Archaic site in

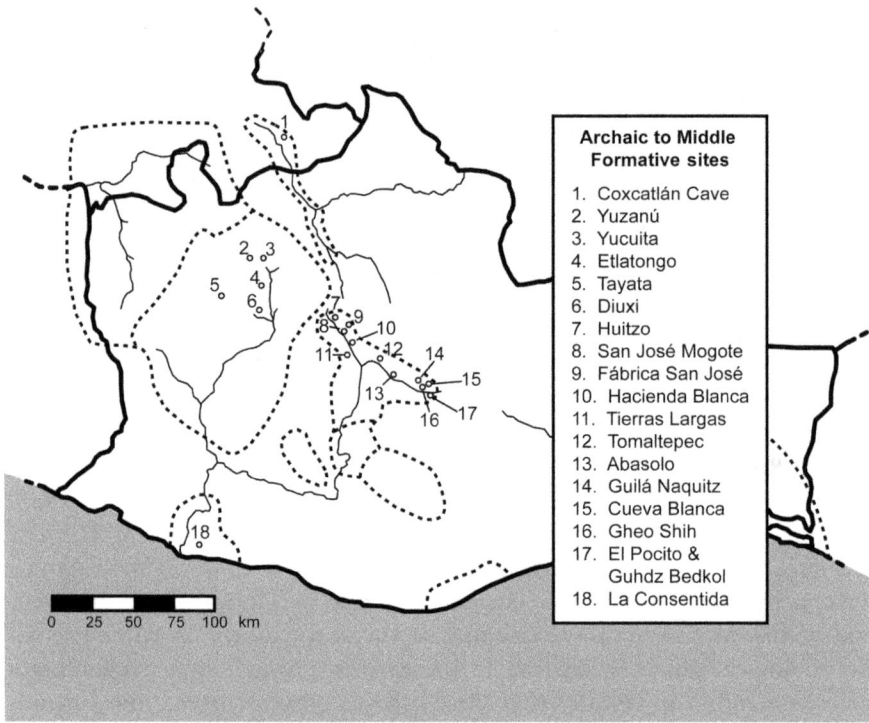

Figure 3.1 Archaeological sites of the Archaic through early Middle Formative periods (8000–700 BC) in Oaxaca (drawing by Eric Berkemeyer)

Oaxaca is Yuzanú in the Nochixtlán Valley where Lorenzo (1958) exposed a concentration of stone tools and a hearth or maguey-roasting pit. Archaic-period artifacts were also found by Winter and his colleagues (2008) in debris piles from modern brick-making at the site of Barrio Tepalcate in the southern Isthmus of Tehuantepec.

The Tehuacán and Oaxaca Valley projects focused on the investigation of dry caves and rockshelters where the remains of plant foods, especially early domesticates, were preserved. The cave sites like Coxcatlán Cave in the Tehuacán Valley and Guilá Naquitz in the Valley of Oaxaca yielded chipped- and ground-stone tools, lithic debitage, cordage, basketry, nets, wooden artifacts, floral and faunal remains, pollen, and features like small storage pits and hearths (Flannery 1983b, 1986; MacNeish et al. 1972). Many of the deposits were interpreted as living floors occupied by small groups for periods of a few days to months. Several open-air sites were also investigated. The most important of these was Gheo Shih, a 1.5 ha site near Guilá Naquitz that dates to c.6650–5050 BC (Marcus & Flannery 2004). Excavations recovered evidence for the making of drilled stone pendants and an open area of 20 m by 7 m delineated by two parallel rows of boulders interpreted as a ritual space, probably a dance ground. In the Tehuacán Valley a high proportion of excavated burials had evidence for burning, disarticulation and scraping or cut marks on bone perhaps resulting from reverential treatment of the dead or human sacrifice (MacNeish et al. 1972).

Based on the results of the Tehuacán and Oaxaca projects, the researchers developed a number of influential models of Archaic-period subsistence and settlement. MacNeish (1971) argued that nomadic nuclear-family microbands of the Early Archaic gradually shifted to a pattern of seasonal fission–fusion cycles with wet-season "macrobands" of a few dozen people that split into dry-season microbands. By the Late Archaic somewhat larger populations lived in semi-permanent hamlets. Evidence for contact with other regions includes the importation of marine shell beads and obsidian for the manufacture of stone tools. Flannery (1986) developed an ecological-systems model for agricultural origins, arguing that maize, beans, and squash were domesticated as a result of systemic adjustments by incipient agriculturalists to the effects of annual rainfall variation on plant yields. A major systemic threshold was reached once the productivity of maize was sufficient to cause people to clear mesquite forests for agriculture, which made it advantageous for people to focus on floodplain agriculture and set the stage for the development of sedentism in the Early Formative.

The arguments of MacNeish and Flannery have provided the framework for Archaic-period research over the past 30 years. Recent research and reanalysis of the Tehuacán and Oaxaca data, however, raise questions with much of the evidence on which these models were based. For example, the original dating of early domesticates was based on radiocarbon determinations of materials, usually charcoal, associated with the botanical remains. Dating of the actual domesticates using the more precise AMS technique shows that many of the original dates for maize and beans were too early, sometimes by as much as 1,500 years. Domesticated squash from Guilá Naquitz, however, proved to date to c.7000 BC, making it the earliest known cultigen in Mexico (Long et al. 1989; B. Smith 1998:150–63). Guilá Naquitz also yielded the earliest macro remains of maize, which date to 4200 BC (Benz 2001). The inconsistency among AMS dates from plant macrofossils and the standard radiometric dates from associated features is probably due to the cave deposits being more disturbed than originally thought. Hardy (1993, 1996) raises serious questions with stratigraphy, lithic typology, and cultural sequences from both Tehuacán and Oaxaca.[3] The domestic status of some of the proposed cultigens has been questioned based on ecological and morphological grounds (Buckler IV et al. 1998). Biochemical biogeographical analyses indicate that the Tehuacán and Oaxaca valleys were not the regions of origin of domesticated maize, beans, squash, and chile. Recent research along the Pacific and Gulf coasts indicates that the domestication of maize in those regions was at least as early as in the highlands (Jones & Voorhies 2004:342–3), although finds involve pollen rather than plant macrofossils. Questions also have been raised with the dating and interpretation of the rock alignments at Gheo Shih (Lawler 2005). Winter and his colleagues (2008) discovered similar rock alignments at the site of Guhdz Bedkol near Mitla. The discovery of two possible postholes and an ash deposit between two of the alignments suggests that they are the remains of structures, rather than a dance ground. Finally, the models of Flannery and MacNeish do not adequately consider social distinctions within groups and how they may have been significant in Archaic-period social change. For example, Watson and Kennedy (1991) show how women and gender relations likely played key roles in the origins of agriculture in eastern North America, given that women were most likely more intensively involved with plant collecting and early cultivation than men.

The focus on dry caves and rockshelters has almost certainly resulted in a biased sample of the full range of Archaic-period sites and occupied habitats. Without sophisticated geomorphological and paleoenvironmental modeling, it is impossible to assess the relationship of sites exposed on modern land surfaces to the original distribution of Archaic-period sites and landscape features. Geomorphological research in the Oaxaca and Nochixtlán valleys has shown that the valley bottoms were aggrading for much of the Holocene, which would have deeply buried Archaic sites (Joyce & Mueller 1997). Although similar biases exist for later periods, larger populations and substantial architecture increase site visibility even in geomorphically dynamic settings. Hopefully, the recent excavations by Winter and his colleagues (2008) will draw renewed attention to the Oaxacan Archaic and address some of the outstanding research problems in this long, important, but little understood period of Mesoamerican prehistory.

The Transition to Sedentism

Beginning sometime between 1900 and 1400 BC we find the first clear evidence for sedentary villages in Oaxaca. The transition to sedentism and the beginnings of pottery production mark the onset of the Mesoamerican Formative period. Permanent villages and ceramics make Early Formative (1900–850 BC) sites more visible than their Archaic predecessors. The transition to village life was also undoubtedly accompanied by population growth accounting for an increase in the number of archaeological sites. Archaeologists have debated the nature of political authority and social complexity during the Oaxacan Early Formative period (Blanton et al. 1999:34–42; Marcus & Flannery 1996:93–110). Although the evidence suggests some emerging distinctions in prestige, wealth, and power, it is not until the Middle Formative (850–400 BC) that indications of social complexity are clearly present. The remainder of this chapter discusses initial Early Formative-period developments among the Mixtec, Zapotec, and Chatino in the Central Valleys, Mixtec highlands, and lower Río Verde Valley. Important Formative-period sites have been found in other parts of Oaxaca such as Laguna Zope in the southern Isthmus of Tehuantepec (R. Zeitlin 1978). The southern Isthmus, however, was not occupied by Zapotecs until the Postclassic period and so is not featured in this discussion.

Origins of sedentism

In Oaxaca, the transition to Formative villages is seen first with the intriguing Espiridión Complex represented by excavations in the Etla arm of the Valley of Oaxaca at the sites of San José Mogote, Tierras Largas, and Hacienda Blanca (Flannery & Marcus 1994:45–54; Winter 1994b:130). Espiridión deposits include the remains of a house floor at San José Mogote and a bell-shaped pit at Tierras Largas. Ceramics consist of a few hundred undecorated buff-to-brown pottery sherds from hemispherical bowls and globular jars with necks. Several researchers argue that early Mesoamerican pottery forms were probably imitations of gourds used as water containers produced with new ceramic technologies adopted from lower Central America where pottery-making originated several hundred years before the earliest Mesoamerican ceramics (Clark & Blake 1994). Radiocarbon dates are not available for the Espiridión Complex although, based on comparisons with ceramics in the Tehuacán Valley, Flannery and Marcus (1994:375) argue for a date of approximately 1900 to 1400 BC.

The only other site that may approach the Espiridión Complex in age is the site of La Consentida located in a tick- and mosquito-infested woodland about 2 km north of the coastal estuaries in the lower Río Verde Valley (A. Joyce 1991a:408–10). The site covers 2.6 ha and is dominated by a mound measuring approximately 80 m by 60 m and rising 5 m above the surrounding plain. A single test excavation exposed an occupational surface as well as obsidian flakes and eroded ceramics. A charcoal sample from the site yielded an age of 3,480 +/− 60 BP, or 1530 BC (1886–1739 BC calibrated; Beta-131037). The occupation on a low artificial mound resembles other early villages along the Pacific coast of southern Mesoamerica, but further research is needed to establish both the age and the nature of the community.

Social implications of sedentism

The problems with Archaic archaeology discussed above as well as the absence of sites with a continuous sequence from the Late Archaic to the Early Formative limit understandings of village origins. Although sedentism has been suggested for the Late Archaic (Stark 1981:353–359), the earliest clear evidence for permanent villages dates to about 1900 BC and is situated along the Pacific coast of southern Mexico and Guatemala. Clark and Blake (1994) suggest that the rich coastal ecosystem created a stable and productive resource base that allowed for sedentism founded largely on an economy of hunting, gathering, and fishing. Maize was a minor component of Early Formative diets on the Pacific coast in contrast to the Mexican highlands. Marcus and Flannery (1996:71–2) argue that, in Oaxaca, sedentism occurred once the productivity of maize was sufficient for people to begin clearing mesquite trees in the alluvial plains of highland valleys. Although the creation of resource concentrations sufficient to allow for sedentism may have been an important factor in village origins, changes in social relations and in relations between people and the landscape were also needed to make sedentism possible (see Jones 2002:145–67). That is, people do not necessarily congregate in villages once the distribution and availability of resources on the landscape allow for sedentism. Village life requires new relations among people and with the landscape that may only have been developed long after environmental conditions made sedentism economically feasible.

The shift to sedentism had enormous implications for people's lives. Living year round in one place allowed for investments in fixed technologies and tools whose transportation costs would have been prohibitive for mobile populations. Ceramics, permanent structures, and an increasing reliance on storage facilities all appear with early sedentary communities. People could accumulate resource surpluses allowing for increasing competition for wealth and status, eventually leading to the emergence of status distinctions. Sedentary communities are more closely tied to fixed resources on the landscape, which allowed for an increasing reliance on agriculture. Land use and rights over the land and its resources would have become more stable, perhaps leading to patterns of familial and community land rights similar to those at the time of the Spanish Conquest.

Beyond the technological and economic implications, sedentism altered people's symbolic connections to the landscape. Sedentism changes the way in which people dwell on the land, creating domestic places where social identity and memory are inscribed in houses, monuments, paths, and farm fields that are differentiated from the outside world (Robin 2002). Of course, community was not the only place that embodied salient aspects of identity, memory, and power since landscape features like caves and mountaintops were imbued with sacred properties (Brady & Ashmore 1999; Jansen & Pérez 2007). Sedentism allowed for more intensive manipulations of space through the construction of permanent architecture. Architecture could be used to create spaces that were less visible and where access could be restricted, along with open visible spaces that in some instances were specifically demarcated as places for public gatherings (Love 1999). The physical arrangement and symbolism of buildings, plazas, courtyards, roads, and other architectural features channeled people's movements and experiences and therefore strengthened and focused memories (Hillier & Hanson 1984). Space could be manipulated through the erection of physical or symbolic barriers, especially around public ceremonial precincts, that restricted the times and places of interaction allowing for control over both the content and presentation of social discourse and the creation of meaning and memory.

Negotiating Initial Village Life

Beginning at about 1400 BC sedentary agricultural villages became established in the Valley of Oaxaca and the Mixteca Alta (Flannery 1976a; Kowalewski et al. 2009). Elsewhere in Oaxaca, few sites have been securely dated to the Early Formative. Whether this represents sampling bias or is an accurate reflection of population distributions is difficult to assess. A similarly uneven distribution of population, however, applies more generally throughout Mesoamerica for this period.

Much of the research on Early Formative villages in Oaxaca focuses on the emergence of status distinctions and how the integration of increasingly larger and more complex polities was achieved by evolving social structures (Blanton et al. 1999:34–42; Marcus & Flannery 1996:76–110). Debate involves the nature of leadership, with Marcus and Flannery (1996) preferring a cultural evolutionary model focused on the emergence of ascribed status and a restricted chiefly authority, while Blanton and his colleagues (1999) prefer a view based on a more broadly shared corporate governance. In contrast, I emphasize evidence for people's practices and how the changing structures of the Early Formative were negotiated out of earlier social conditions. Rather than focusing on the integration of society, a poststructural perspective considers the novel social circumstances created by early village life and how these conditions created social problems as well as new possibilities. The coalescence of early villages brought together previously mobile groups into permanent associations. Based on archaeological evidence from the initial Early Formative, the groups that came together in villages consisted of several small, perhaps nuclear families. Early village life undoubtedly created new opportunities involving access to land, labor, and potential mates as well as the ability to accumulate resources. Social tensions also would have resulted as people negotiated larger and more permanent associations. The new social practices, identities, and structural conditions of the Early Formative were a product of these negotiations.

Initial villages are best known from survey and excavations from the period 1400–1150 BC, which pertains to the Tierras Largas phase in the Valley of Oaxaca and the Cruz A phase in the Mixteca Alta. The most extensive excavations for this period come from San José Mogote, which sits on a piedmont spur overlooking the Río Atoyac and some of the best agricultural land in the Valley of Oaxaca. Today the site center is being encroached on by the modern village of the same name but, from the mid-1960s to the early 1980s, the site was the focus of a large-scale research project by Kent Flannery and his associates designed to investigate some of the key ideas of the New Archaeology (Flannery 1976a; Flannery & Marcus 1994). Major excavations have also been carried out at Tierras Largas, Hacienda Blanca, and Tomaltepec in the Valley of Oaxaca and Yucuita and Etlatongo in the Nochixtlán Valley of the Mixteca Alta (Blomster 2004; Marcus & Flannery 1996). In other parts of the Mixteca Alta the Early Formative is known almost entirely from surface surveys, which have not differentiated the Cruz A and Cruz B phases (Balkansky et al. 2000).

The organization of Early Formative communities has been one of the major research topics in the Valley of Oaxaca where studies pioneered household archaeology (Flannery 1976a; Winter 1972, 1986; Whalen 1981). Excavation and survey data show that early villages were generally small, covering 1 to 3 ha with estimated populations of a few dozen people. In both the Nochixtlán and the Oaxaca Valley, however, one community exceeded the others in size (Kowalewski et al. 1989; Spores 1983). In the Valley of Oaxaca, San José Mogote reached 7 ha (Marcus & Flannery

1996:78) and in the northern Nochixtlán Valley, Yucuita covered perhaps 20 ha (Winter 1982:10). Although population estimates based on archaeological data are speculative (O'Brien & Lewarch 1992), Tierras Largas-phase population at San José Mogote is estimated at 129 people (Kowalewski et al. 1989:61), while Winter (1984:188) estimates a population of 200 for Cruz A-phase Yucuita. Early Formative communities were usually located on low piedmont spurs adjacent to humid agriculturally productive land on the valley floors (Nicholas 1989:489–92). Population in Oaxaca and Nochixtlán was not evenly distributed, with concentrations of sites and population located around San José Mogote and Yucuita, respectively. It is not clear why these two areas grew more rapidly than others, although both are located adjacent to large areas of high water-table land. In the case of the Etla arm of the Oaxaca Valley, the primacy of the foundational Espiridión villages may have given the area a head start.

Family and domestic life

Archaeological excavations indicate that the focus of social life was the small family group. Early Formative sites are dominated by a set of associated domestic features and artifacts interpreted as the remains of nuclear-family households perhaps averaging 5 people (Winter 1972, 1986). Typical communities included 5 to 10 households, although San José Mogote and Yucuita both consisted of multiple barrios, each containing discrete concentrations of several households separated by sparsely occupied areas. San José Mogote consisted of nine spatially discrete residential areas or barrios (Marcus & Flannery 1996:87) and Yucuita consisted of at least three (Winter 1984:188). The barrios in the largest sites therefore appear to consist of groups of related families and were similar in composition to the more typical communities of this period. Yucuita and San José Mogote may represent the origins of the intra-community barrios that were so prevalent at Spanish contact.

Residences covered an average of about 300 m^2 and often include the remains of house structures, bell-shaped pits, human burials, and ovens (figure 3.2). Most Early Formative households consisted of a single wattle-and-daub structure typically measuring 18 to 24 m^2 and built over an earthen floor, suggesting the residence of a small family group (Winter 1986). The floors are often the only preserved feature of the house and are visible as a compressed somewhat organic clayey layer at times overlain by fine sand. Wall posts may be visible as post molds and if the house burned, chunks of daub, accidentally fired, are preserved. Wattle-and-daub houses usually

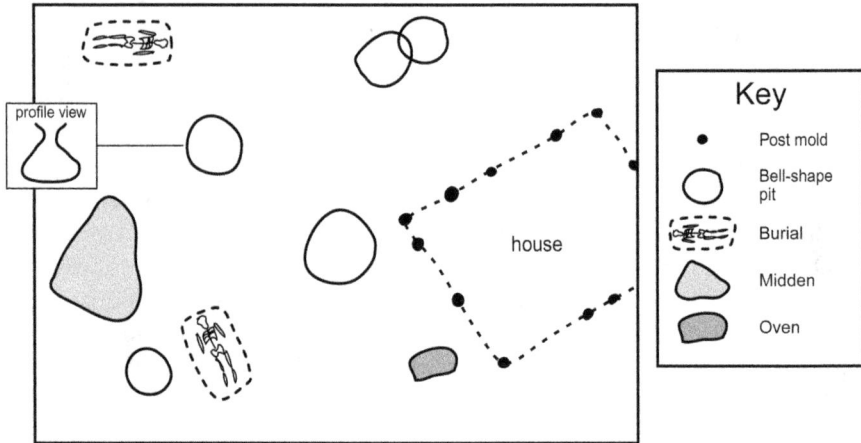

Figure 3.2 Idealized plan of Formative-period house with associated burial, oven, midden, and bell-shaped pit features (drawing by Eric Berkemeyer)

last no more than about 25 years before they have to be rebuilt, which probably accounts for the frequent superposition of sequences of house floors found in Early Formative sites.

Most practices inferred for the initial village period from 1400 to 1150 BC involved the economic, ritual, and political relations of household members (Flannery 1976b; Flannery & Marcus 1994; Flannery & Winter 1976; Whalen 1981; Winter 1976, 1986:332–40). Although people slept in houses, most daily activities occurred outside. As some family members traveled to fields to tend to crops or hunted in surrounding lands, others stayed near the house preparing meals, making tools of stone and wood, socializing with neighbors, and caring for young children. Based on analogies with late prehispanic culture, women were more involved in food preparation and cooking, and men more focused on food acquisition, although probably with considerable overlap and sharing of tasks.

Daily activities focused on acquiring and preparing food, including domesticates grown in fields near villages and wild foods hunted or collected in the valley floor, hills, and mountains beyond the community. Crops were grown on humid bottomlands relying on rainfall during the wet season. Small-scale irrigation techniques, including the digging of wells and ditches, allowed people to farm into the dry season and to extend productive agriculture into areas with a lower water table, especially in the piedmont

(Flannery 1983a). In addition to growing maize, beans, squash, chile peppers, and avocados, people continued to exploit wild plants and animals. Charred remains recovered from sites include agave and prickly pear fruit as well as the bones of deer, peccary, rabbit, opossum, mud turtle, gopher, various birds, and domesticated dog.

The patio area outside houses was the focus of routine domestic practices such as food processing, cooking, sewing, and manufacturing baskets, stone tools, and pottery (Flannery & Winter 1976; Whalen 1981; Winter 1976). Evidence for these activities include the presence of lithic debitage from tool-making, bone needles used in sewing or basket-making, stone knives and scrapers used in butchering animals and processing hides, and ground-stone tools used in the processing of plant foods, especially maize. Activities that are less visible in the archaeological record, but which undoubtedly occurred, include socializing with neighbors and the rearing and play of children. Much of the evidence for domestic practices comes from middens where refuse was discarded. Middens were sometimes associated with individual households and at other times were used by groups of households or perhaps entire communities. Cooking was done on ceramic braziers and probably ovens that have been excavated in the activity areas around many houses.

Food, tools, and valuables were stored in bell-shaped pits (Winter 1976). These pits, narrow at their opening and widening below, were sometimes large enough for a person to stand within, ranging from about 1 to 4 m^3, and were sometimes capped with stone slabs. Winter (1976:27) estimates that a typical bell-shaped pit held enough maize to feed an average family for a year, which highlights the advantages of sedentism for storage and the ability to accumulate surpluses. Bell-shaped pits often went through a "life cycle" where they were initially used for storage, and then converted to refuse dumps as they collapsed or if the house was abandoned. In some cases, bell-shaped pits were used as graves.

When people died they were interred in shallow graves or bell-shaped pits during mortuary rituals. Burials consisted of single individuals usually interred within 10 m of the house. The close spatial association between the burial of ancestors and the house inscribed and fixed the claims of the family to the land (Hendon 2000). Otherwise burial patterns were highly variable without standardization of burial position or orientation, suggesting that burial customs did not yet mark community affiliations. Burials lacked offerings, although Marcus and Flannery (1996:85) suggest that three flexed interments of adult men may have been bundle burials reflecting higher achieved status. The mortuary evidence is consistent with data on household wealth, indicating minimal wealth and status distinctions.

78 From Foragers to Village Life

Engaging the world beyond the household

The presence of burials adjacent to houses shows that residences were also an important ritual locus. In addition to human burials, evidence of household ritual practices includes a turtle-shell drum fragment recovered at Tierras Largas (Winter 1976) and perhaps imported materials such as macaws for feathers and shell for ornaments (Marcus & Flannery 1996:84). In later periods bodily ornamentation was an important marker of identity including gender, age, and status. The most common evidence for domestic rituals, however, are the ubiquitous small solid ceramic figurines in human form found in domestic contexts in the Valley of Oaxaca (figure 3.3). Figurines appear less common in the Nochixtlán Valley with most examples from redeposited contexts (Blomster 2004:81; Winter 1984:188). The Oaxacan figurines are stylistically similar to Early Formative figurines found throughout Mesoamerica (Marcus 1998; Winter 2005a). They depict nude individuals often with elaborate hairdos and sometimes body ornaments, especially earplugs, or sandals. Since genitals are not represented, gender attribution has usually relied on the presence of breasts, indicating

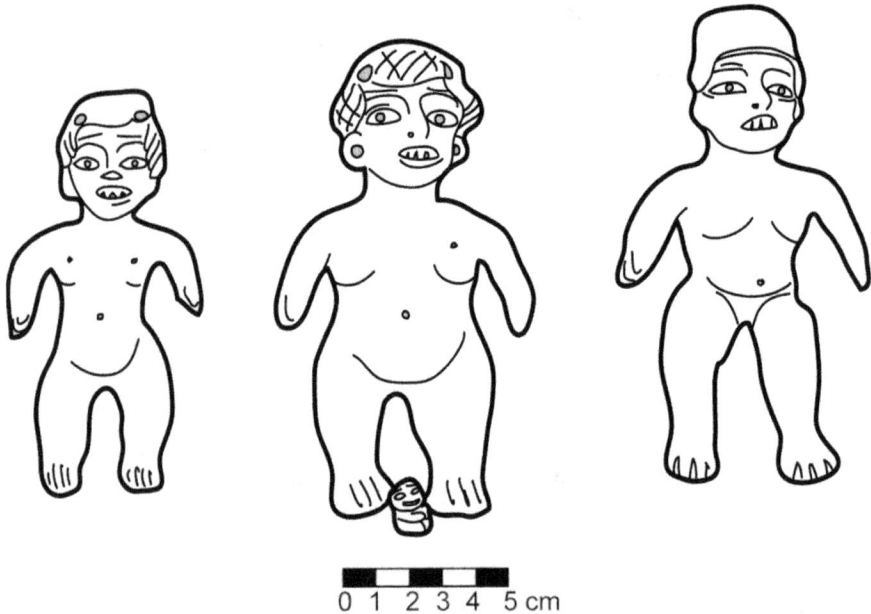

Figure 3.3 Group of Tierras Largas-phase figurines from the site of Hacienda Blanca, Valley of Oaxaca (after Winter 1994c, plate 30; drawing by Eric Berkemeyer)

women. Male or sexually neutral figurines are also present as are a small number of zoomorphic ones. Figurines gendered female appear to be young adults, many are depicted as pregnant, and at least one holds a baby (Marcus 1998:79–91). Many have perforations through the hair, probably for suspending the figurines as ornaments.

Given the abundance of figurines throughout Mesoamerica much has been written about their possible significance. Marcus (1998) views them as representations of female ancestors used in household rituals performed by women that included divination and the propitiation of ancestors represented by the figurines. She argues that this form of ancestor worship was an important means by which Early Formative society was integrated since multiple families would have been linked by their descent from a common ancestor. Cyphers (1993) agrees with Marcus that the figurines were used in household rituals carried out by women, but she interprets these rituals as involving life-crisis ceremonies involving the transition to puberty, pregnancy, and child rearing.

Rosemary Joyce (2000:28–53) has carried out a broad comparative study of Early Formative figurines. Her analysis focuses on how the figurines "were a medium for the objectification of stereotyped social identities" embodied in bodily practices involving gender, age, and, later in the Formative, status. Following Joyce, the foregrounding of young nude female bodies sometimes shown pregnant on the Tierras Largas-phase figurines can be seen as a reflection of societal tensions and the negotiation of identity surrounding the sexuality of young women. The figurines would represent attempts to foreclose certain practices and shape the identity of young women whose "sexuality may have been both a resource and a problem for house elders" (R. Joyce 2000:53; also see Lesure 1997). Joyce (2003:259) views zoomorphic figurines as representations of another aspect of the experience of embodiment – that of a person's animal-spirit companion or *nagual*. The most common animals represented on the figurines were dogs and birds, which in later periods were frequently sacrificed as parts of mortuary ceremonies, suggesting that these animals may have held unusual power. Elements of the various interpretations of Formative figurines are not mutually exclusive, although Rosemary Joyce's approach (2000, 2003) has the advantage of more fully engaging the imagery and interpreting it within the broader social setting of the Formative.

Evidence for ritual practices that engaged people beyond the household have been found at San José Mogote. In the westernmost barrio at San José Mogote (Area C), Flannery (1976b:334–5; Marcus and Flannery 1996:87–8) excavated remains of eight rectangular one-room buildings (figure 3.4), measuring no more than 4 m by 6 m, that date to the Tierras Largas phase and continue into the early San José phase (1150–850 BC).

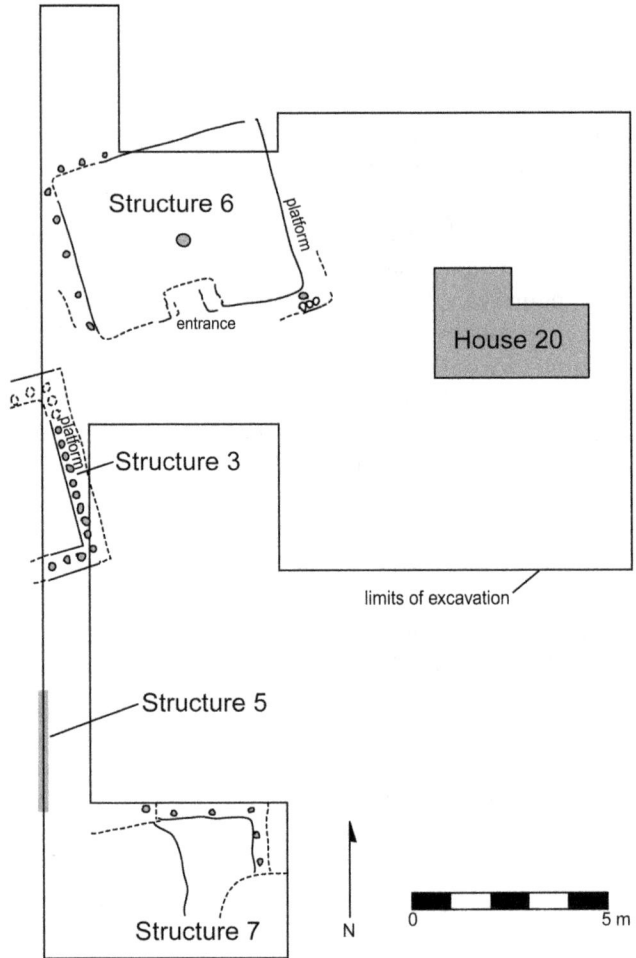

Figure 3.4 Early Formative public buildings from Area C at San José Mogote (after J. E. Clark 2004, figure 2.2; redrawn courtesy of Wiley-Blackwell Publishing; drawing by Eric Berkemeyer)

These structures differ from typical residences in that they were built using heavy pine posts with a plaster floor surrounded by a narrow platform. The walls of the buildings were covered with lime plaster with evidence of replastering episodes. Unlike typical residences, floors were swept clean and no figurines were recovered. Based on analogies with ethnohistorically recorded Zapotec practices, Marcus and Flannery (1996:87) suggest that small circular depressions in the floors, in some cases filled with powdered lime, were used in rituals where the lime was mixed with ceremonial plants like native tobacco. These buildings were all oriented roughly 8° west of true north, an orientation that differed from most houses, but which was shared by later public buildings in highland Oaxaca. The best preserved of the structures (Structure 6) also included three fragments of possible ceramic dance masks, a small metate covered with powdered lime, and a quartz pestle with traces of red hematite used in Mesoamerica to coat ritually important objects. These data create a strong case for the buildings having been used for ritual purposes, although Winter (1986:336) raises the possibility that they were residences of more prestigious families.

Based on analogies with small-scale societies in the American Southwest and New Guinea, Marcus and Flannery (1996:87–8) argue that these buildings were "Men's Houses" where prominent men from throughout the community met to plan raids or hunts and to carry out "men's rituals," thereby acting as an integrative mechanism. John Clark (2004:48–52) points out, however, that the buildings would have accommodated no more than two dozen people, activities within them would not have been visible to the broader community, and the buildings were restricted to only a single barrio rather than placed in a more central, "public" location. In addition, the relevance of analogies drawn from peoples so distant in time and space can be questioned. I agree with J. E. Clark (2004:52) that these buildings are better interpreted as ritual buildings associated only with a select part of the village. Given their location in one of the site's residential barrios, they seem to have been associated with only one group of families rather than the community as a whole. Perhaps ritual buildings were present in other barrios and in other communities or, alternatively, the Area C barrio may have been the locus of a ritual specialist. The evidence does not suggest, however, that these special buildings enhanced the wealth or status of people living in the barrio.

People also engaged in the world outside their communities through trade and exchange. Evidence from the Oaxaca Valley shows that people imported obsidian, shell for ornaments, and fancy pottery from distant regions (Pires-Ferreira 1975; Winter 1984:183–8). Obsidian used as cutting and scraping tools consisted of small flakes found mostly in middens. The closest sources of this volcanic glass are found hundreds of kilometers away in the Basin of Mexico and in the mountains overlooking the Gulf coast. All households had some access to obsidian, although chemical-sourcing studies show that the sources accessed by different households varied greatly, with some acquiring material primarily from the Otumba source in the Basin of Mexico and others relying more on exchange networks linked to Guadalupe Victoria in Veracruz. Winter (1972:177) argues that the distribution of obsidian reflects a pattern whereby each household acquired its obsidian independent of others, probably via reciprocal exchange with nearby villages. Small quantities of finely made imported ceramics, possibly from the Gulf coast, as well as probable local imitations of those vessels have been recovered at both San José Mogote and Tierras Largas. Imported shell included Pacific coast species and freshwater snail probably from the Atlantic drainage. Marine shell ornaments were more abundant at San José Mogote than at smaller sites, suggesting that some families there may have invested more heavily in long-distance exchange and the use of exotic materials for bodily ornamentation.

Evidence for more diffuse forms of interaction are suggested by ceramic styles that both the Valley of Oaxaca and the Nochixtlán Valley share with much of western Mesoamerica from the Basin of Mexico to the southern Isthmus of Tehuantepec. Winter (1984:183–4) calls this the Red-on-Buff Horizon, which is characterized by bowls, bottles, and jars with thin walls and buff, brown, or black surfaces sometimes decorated with red paint. What accounts for these shared ceramic styles is not clear, although researchers have suggested broadly shared cultural and linguistic traditions as well as trade (Flannery & Marcus 1994:66; Winter 1984).

A village, but not a community?

The evidence from 1400 to 1150 BC in the Oaxacan highlands suggests that most early sedentary communities consisted of less than a dozen small family groups each constituting an individual household. If Flannery (1986) and MacNeish (1971) are correct in viewing later Archaic-period settlement as including seasonal congregations of multi-family macrobands then early villages involved the development of a permanent and continuous association of these groups. The organization of San José Mogote and Yucuita with their multiple barrios resembles a conglomeration of loosely affiliated multi-family groups.

The social identities of Early Formative subjects were defined primarily by their affiliations with family, age-grades, and gender, while wealth and status distinctions were minimal. There are few indications of social practices or concepts that brought people together as members of a community or barrio. The ritual buildings at San José Mogote are the strongest indicator of practices that engaged multiple households, although it is not clear whether they served only the Area C barrio or the entire community. As argued by J. E. Clark (2004), the evidence does not yet indicate the kinds of inscriptive practices, especially the creation of ceremonial centers, that anchored social memory and embodied notions of community identity in later Mesoamerican societies. If correct, communities at this time may be better viewed as co-resident groups rather than communities united by a sense of belonging characterized by perceptions of shared interests, history, and identity.

There is little direct evidence for the sorts of corporate practices and intersubjective understandings out of which broader community identities would have been forged, although it can be surmised that families did engage in cooperative enterprises. Many practices hypothesized for earlier macrobands would have continued, such as seasonal subsistence pursuits that required the labor of multiple families (e.g., clearing of fields and crop harvests), barrio rituals, and mating, along with everyday socializing. The creation of multi-household and perhaps community-wide middens also suggests shared spatial sensibilities and practices.

Yet living in larger, permanent settlements would have created social tensions, resulting from disputes with neighbors and competition over resources, including land, mates, and social valuables. Although domestic spatial organization was open, making activities on patios visible to passersby, resources including social valuables could have been hidden in bell-shaped pits so as to reduce tensions and jealousy surrounding competition for surpluses (Hendon 2000:45). The imagery of figurines perhaps suggests tension and negotiation surrounding the sexuality and mating choices of young women. It is possible that the continuous availability of potential mates from one's own or nearby communities compromised the ability of elders to influence mating choices in contrast to earlier times when courting opportunities were limited to periods when multiple families came together. The negotiation of these new social relationships, particularly the permanent and ongoing association with neighboring families, produced the structural conditions of initial village life and set the stage for developments later in the Early Formative.

four
Negotiating Community and Complexity

By the late Early Formative and the early Middle Formative (1150–700 BC) evidence from the Valley of Oaxaca and Mixtec Alta (figure 3.1) indicates increasing population, social inequality, trade, and the emergence of a salient identity centered on community as embodied in various rituals and inscribed in public buildings and communal cemeteries. Archaeologists have debated the nature of social organization during this period and how long-distance contacts, particularly with the Gulf-coast Olmec, influenced Mixtec and Zapotec culture. In other parts of the Oaxacan highlands and in the lower Río Verde Valley, people lived in small egalitarian communities until the Middle/Late Formative (Feinman & Nicholas 1990:222–5; A. Joyce 2005:17–18; Winter 2005b:88) and in some regions settlement has not been recorded until the end of the Formative (Balkansky 2002:35; Markman 1981:63).

Much of the population growth reflects major increases in the largest sites, including San José Mogote in the Valley of Oaxaca, Diuxi in the Tilantongo area, Tayata in the Huamelulpan Valley, and Etlatongo in the Nochixtlán Valley (Balkansky et al. 1998a:45–9; Balkansky et al. 2000, 2004; Blomster 2004; Kowalewski et al. 1989:61, 2009:287–90; Spores 1972). In the Valley of Oaxaca, San José Mogote expanded to about 70 ha with estimated population increasing from 129 during the Tierras Largas phase to 1,384 by the San José phase (1150–850 BC; Kowalewski et al. 1989:61). Most people lived in the Etla arm near San José Mogote and the estimated population of the Oaxaca Valley increased from 327 to 1,800 by the Guadalupe phase (850–700 BC; Nicholas 1989, table 14.13). Settlement studies in the Mixteca Alta reveal a pattern of settlement clusters with estimated populations ranging from 250 to 1,500 people (Kowalewski et al. 2009:287–9). In the Nochixtlán Valley, Yucuita declined in size, while Etlatongo grew into a large village covering 26 ha (Blomster

2004:31). It is not clear why Yucuita lost population, although the lack of unifying symbols and practices may have made ongoing social relations tenuous such that social tensions were more likely to be dealt with by fissioning than in later times when a stronger sense of community had developed. By the late Early Formative, people in San José Mogote and Etlatongo were successful in forging broader corporate symbols and practices that created social cohesion and a greater sense of community identity.

Constructing Community and Identity in the Early Formative

I argue that the late Early Formative was a time of increasing variation and probably competition among households in craft production, access to long-distance exchange, and perhaps control over ritual knowledge and authority, all of which resulted in increasing social distinctions, including inequalities in wealth and status among individuals and households. At the same time, variation in craft production and interregional contacts created greater dependencies among households, barrios, and communities. Larger corporate groups engaged in social, economic, and ritual practices that increasingly produced salient identities at the scale of the barrio, community, and perhaps groups of nearby communities. I assert that communal ritual practices carried out in public ceremonial spaces, including buildings and cemeteries, was a way in which rising inequality was negotiated within the context of a more traditional egalitarian ethos.

Crafting social distinctions

Houses from this period have been excavated primarily from San José Mogote, Tierras Largas, and Tomaltepec in the Valley of Oaxaca (Flannery & Marcus 1983a; Whalen 1981:27–63; Winter 1972) as well as Etlatongo in the Nochixtlán Valley (Blomster 2004:65–145) and Tayata in the Huamelulpan Valley (Duncan et al. 2008). Most San José-phase residences in the Valley of Oaxaca continued the earlier pattern of small, single-room wattle-and-daub structures. Some residences, however, featured somewhat more elaborate architecture such as walls with whitewash, larger posts, drains, and stone foundations. San José Mogote House 16–17 included a residential building (House 17) and a roofed work area (House 16) where occupants manufactured chert bifaces. Higher-status residences at Etlatongo may have been differentiated by their construction on low platforms and the presence of larger-capacity storage pits, but the extent of residential excavations at present is insufficient to assess the variation in houses (Blomster 2004).

In the Valley of Oaxaca, households competed to produce resource surpluses through the production of a wide variety of crafts, and both the volume and the variety of crafting increased relative to earlier periods. Broad horizontal exposures of Early Formative residences, such as those carried out by Marcus Winter (1972) at Tierras Largas, provide data on a wide range of social practices. Residential excavations show that all households participated to varying degrees in crafting, including the manufacture of stone and bone tools, pottery, baskets, and shell and mica ornaments along with woodworking, sewing, and the spinning of cloth (Flannery & Winter 1976; Parry 1987; Pires-Ferreira 1975). There is no evidence, however, that the scale of craft production exceeded the household. Households developed alternative economic practices, especially involving craft production, which resulted in differential success in accumulating surpluses that further differentiated social identities. For example, House 1 at Tierras Largas had evidence for cloth production, sewing, and stone-tool production (Winter 1972, 1976:31), while House 13 at San José Mogote had evidence for sewing, modest production of shell ornaments, and perhaps some limited working of mica ornaments and magnetite mirrors (Flannery & Marcus 1983a:55). In contrast, House 16–17 at San José Mogote had evidence for a wide variety of crafts including the production of chert bifaces, baskets, shell ornaments, and mold-made pottery (Flannery & Marcus 1994:333). Gendered activities are difficult to infer at this time except by analogy with later Mesoamerican patterns, the strongest being an association of spinning and weaving with female identity. At Tayata in the Huamelulpan Valley there is evidence for household production of ceramics and shell ornaments as well as evidence for the manufacture of obsidian tools and ornaments of mica and greenstone (Balkansky et al. 2008:37; Duncan et al. 2008:5315). Excavations at Etlatongo in the Nochixtlán Valley indicate that people were involved in stone-tool production and perhaps the manufacture of shell and mica ornaments (Blomster 2004).

Beyond the household, certain barrios, communities, and perhaps broader social networks developed economic practices that tied them to particular sources of exotic raw materials. For example, evidence of shell working in the Valley of Oaxaca comes almost entirely from San José Mogote and Tierras Largas in the Etla arm (Flannery & Winter 1976:39). People used imported shell to make beads, pendants, and perhaps holders for magnetite mirrors. Though most households made shell ornaments, there was great variation in the types of shell used. At San José Mogote some households worked shell from the Atlantic drainage, while others focused on shell from the Pacific. Some households also imported finished shell ornaments from sources that differed from those that they used in ornament production (Pires-Ferreira 1976:316). These data suggest that households acquired ornamental shell by negotiating their own exchange relations with particular trade partners, without the involvement of communal or regional authorities.

The demand for shell ornaments was great with almost all excavated households throughout the Valley of Oaxaca exhibiting evidence for their consumption. People may have also traded ornaments to nearby regions (Blomster 2004:94). High demand would have encouraged expansion of this craft. Why shell-ornament production did not spread to communities beyond Etla is not clear, although it is possible that production sites in other areas have been missed. Given the large population of the Etla arm and perhaps more competition for prestige, demand there may have been greater. Etla crafters may also have sought to monopolize relations with trading partners, making it difficult for others to enter the market.

Iron-ore mirrors, mostly made of local magnetite, were another craft item whose production was spatially restricted. Mirrors were made by polishing lumps of iron ore with an abrasive material like sand or hematite powder to create a surface with a degree of reflectivity. People used mirrors as adornments, often worn high on the forehead or as pendants. Mirrors were prestigious objects associated with status and ritual practice, although their precise symbolism is not well understood for Formative Mesoamerica.

In the Valley of Oaxaca, the only location with evidence for mirror production is the Area A barrio at San José Mogote (Flannery & Marcus 1994:301–5), indicating that barrios were distinguished both spatially and through economic activities. In Area A, four superimposed houses have evidence for mirror production, which shows generational continuity in this craft. In a 1-ha sector of Area A, 500 pieces of iron ore were recovered, including whole and broken mirrors, unfinished mirrors, and worked and unworked lumps of iron ore (Pires-Ferreira 1975:58–9). Iron-ore mirrors are much more restricted in their distribution than other exotic goods and may have been more closely tied to high status. The only iron-ore mirror found in Oaxaca in a well-dated context outside San José Mogote is from the small site of Tomaltepec, where a mirror was interred with an adult woman buried together with an adult male in the community cemetery. Offerings associated with this burial suggest relatively high status. Few mirrors appear to have been distributed to Zapotecs outside the Area A barrio, although evidence shows that mirrors from San José Mogote were traded to important sites in distant regions including Etlatongo and the Olmec center of San Lorenzo (Pires-Ferreira 1975:49–63). Pires-Ferreira (1975:61) dates the Oaxacan mirrors discovered at San Lorenzo to the period from

1000 to 750 BC or from the latter part of the San José phase to the early part of the succeeding Guadalupe phase. In addition to their role as makers of mirrors, the identities of people in the Area A barrio at San José Mogote were also distinguished by their establishment of exchange relations, tied directly or indirectly to important communities in distant regions of Mesoamerica.

Importing prestige

Another way in which individuals, households, and communities were becoming differentiated was by establishing exchange relations with prominent people in distant places. Throughout indigenous America, people equated geographical space to cosmological distance such that materials and ideas from far-off places were seen as imbued with sacred power (Helms 1991). By the latter part of the Early Formative, evidence throughout much of Mesoamerica indicates the development of social relations linking distant places through which goods and ideas were exchanged (Hirth 1984). Many of the materials and ideas that people exchanged involved religious beliefs and practices along with bodily ornamentation (Grove & Gillespie 1992a).

The most common recognized material imported to Oaxaca was obsidian, which could be used in ritual bloodletting, but more typically was used as an effective cutting tool for everyday utilitarian tasks. The late Early Formative marks the earliest appearance of prismatic blades in Oaxaca, which is concurrent with beginnings of long-distance trade in blades throughout Mesoamerica. In the Valley of Oaxaca and at Etlatongo in the Nochixtlán Valley all households had access to obsidian and there appears to be little variation among households in the quantity of obsidian (Blomster 2004:180; Winter & Pires-Ferreira 1976). Imported obsidian has also been reported at Tayata (Duncan et al. 2008). Instrumental neutron activation analyses (INAA) show that most of the San José-phase obsidian in the Valley of Oaxaca came from the Guadalupe Victoria source on the Gulf coast, Otumba in the Basin of Mexico, and Zinepécuaro in West Mexico. Sources varied considerably among houses at Tierras Largas suggesting that families may have independently established trade relations that linked them to different sources of obsidian. In contrast, at San José Mogote there is consistency in the distribution of sources accessed by different households, which could mean that obsidian was pooled by an important person or family who controlled exchange (Winter & Pires-Ferreira 1976:309). Mixtecs from Etlatongo participated in different obsidian exchange networks from those of Oaxaca Valley Zapotecs, since at Etlatongo obsidian from the central-Mexican source of Paredón was the most common, along with material from Otumba, also in central Mexico, and Orizaba on the Gulf coast (Blomster 2004:94, 109).

There was significant variation in the success of households in establishing trading partners through which exotic goods like jade, marine and freshwater shell, imported ceramics, and fish spines were obtained (Flannery & Marcus 1994:333). The distribution of exotic goods obtained via long-distance exchange mirrored variation in crafting with residences like House 16–17 at San José Mogote having access to a greater amount and variety of imported materials. The evidence suggests that some households were able to transfer more labor into craft production, which allowed them to expand their networks of local and long-distance exchange partners, generating sources of wealth that probably enhanced their ability to establish advantageous social ties through marriage and alliance.

Imports included bloodletting implements and ornaments such as beads, pendants, and ear spools made of jade and shell. Ornaments made from exotic materials became more important in the late Early Formative throughout Mesoamerica. Rosemary Joyce (1999:19) argues that ornaments were a means by which people "beautified" their bodies, enhancing their appearance and the positive evaluation of others, which contributed to personal influence in these face-to-face societies. The intimate association of costume ornamentation with the visible body, subject to social assessment, made ornamentation a medium for the creation of individuality. Obsidian blades, stingray spines, and fish spines used in autosacrificial bloodletting were also common imports recovered in domestic settings (Flannery 1976b:341–4). Autosacrifice allowed people to petition gods and ancestors for fertility and prosperity.

Imported ceramics include vessels and figurines. In the Valley of Oaxaca, imported pottery from San José-phase sites, while rare, appears to be most frequently from the Gulf coast (Blomster et al. 2005). Suspected imports based on visual similarities, but unconfirmed by ceramic characterization studies, include pottery possibly imported from the Tehuacán Valley, the Basin of Mexico, Chiapas, and perhaps Morelos (Flannery & Marcus 1994:286). A few Olmec-style figurines from the Valley of Oaxaca may include imports from the Gulf coast, although most are probably locally produced (Blomster 2002).

Blomster (2004) has recovered evidence for interaction with the Olmec at Etlatongo located on a hill and surrounding floodplain at the confluence of three major rivers in the Nochixtlán Valley. Early Formative settlement was concentrated in lower-lying areas around the Río Yanhuitlán where his excavations recovered a wider variety of Olmec-style pottery than

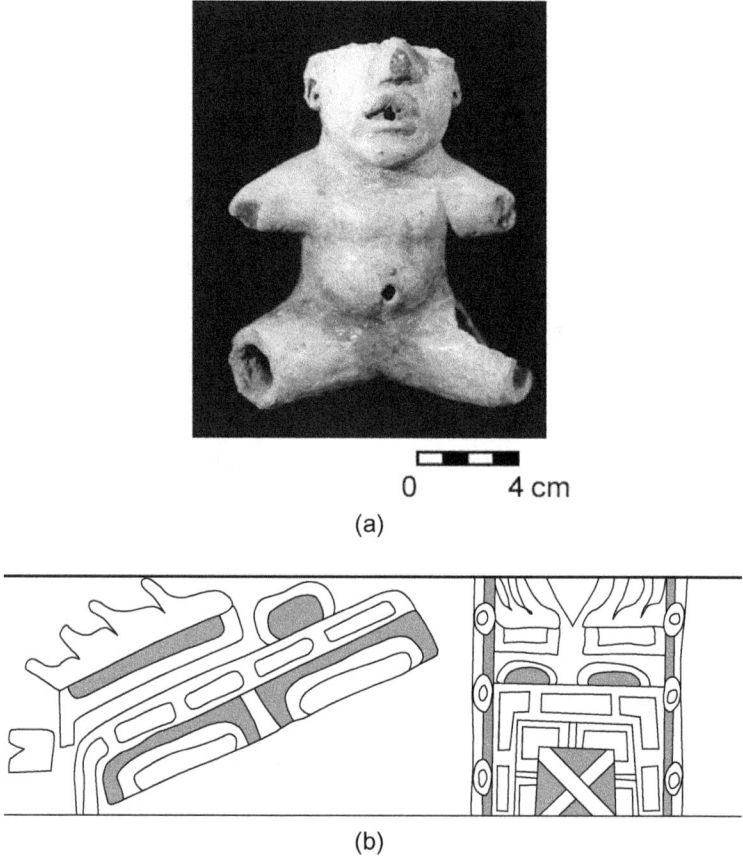

Figure 4.1 Olmec-style artifacts from Oaxaca: (a) photo of hollow baby figurine from Etlatongo (photograph courtesy of Jeffrey Blomster); (b) fire-serpent and were-jaguar motifs (after Joralemon 1971, figure 120; redrawn courtesy of Dumbarton Oaks Research Library and Collection, Trustees for Harvard University, Washington, DC)

found in the Valley of Oaxaca (Blomster 2004). Perhaps the most important discovery at Etlatongo occurred while Blomster was removing the fill from a bell-shaped pit (Blomster 2004:88–92). Near the top of the lowermost stratum that had filled the pit, he recovered an elaborate hollow baby figurine, probably imported from the Gulf coast; in style, it is identical to the few hollow babies from sites in the Gulf coast, central Mexico, and Soconusco (figure 4.1a).

Mixtecs, Zapotecs, and the Olmec

Long-distance contacts led to the creation of broader social affiliations through which religious concepts and perhaps aesthetic values related to bodily adornment and prestige may have been appropriated. Data from chemical-sourcing studies and iconography point to the Gulf-coast Olmec as an important source of ideas as well as materials for Mixtec and Zapotec peoples. Understanding patterns in the exchange of ideas and symbols is more difficult than tracking the movements of material goods. Often archaeologists assume that exotic objects exchanged over wide distances had the same meaning and function wherever they were found. For example, the hollow baby figurines of the Early Formative have been interpreted as prestigious symbols of chiefly authority and icons of a regional religious cult linked to increasing inequality (Blomster 1998). This perspective, however, ignores the observation that objects can develop complex biographies as they are made, exchanged, used in different cultural settings, taken out of and put back into circulation, and discarded (Appadurai 1986; Kopytoff 1986). What this means is that people appropriate foreign ideas and symbols, working them into their own traditions of belief and practice in ways that change to varying degrees their original meaning, context of deployment, and material expression. For ancient Mesoamerica, the spread of influential ideas and symbols has, not surprisingly, engendered heated debates, and this is especially true as it relates to the Gulf-coast Olmec (e.g., Blomster et al. 2005; Flannery & Marcus 2000; Sharer & Grove 1989).

For many years debate surrounding the interregional impact of the Olmec coalesced around two competing models (Grove 1997; Lesure 2004). The "mother-culture" model, first developed in the 1940s, views the Olmec as Mesoamerica's first civilization, which dominated Formative-period culture and interregional relations, thereby establishing many of the religious and political principles that would come to define the Mesoamerican tradition. In the late 1960s, researchers working mostly outside the Gulf coast recognized that many symbols and artifacts previously viewed as "Olmec" actually originated in other regions, leading to the development of the "sister-culture" model. These scholars argue that societies in regions like the Valley of Oaxaca, the Morelos Valley, and the Basin of Mexico were comparable in complexity to the Gulf-coast Olmec and that mutual interaction among the people of these areas led to the spread of materials and ideas. More recently, scholars have moved toward a more sophisticated middle ground between the "mother-culture" and "sister-culture" positions (Blomster et al. 2005; Lesure 2004). This new perspective recognizes that Olmec centers like San Lorenzo were far larger and more complex than contemporary polities in other regions, implying that the Olmec probably had greater influence on ideas and symbols that were circulating interregionally. On the other hand, researchers argue that foreign ideas were used, manipulated, and reproduced in locally distinct ways (Blomster et al. 2005:1071). Although there is variation in the degree to which scholars stress the role of the Olmec, they argue that for each region the specific social circumstances that patterned interregional relations must be considered.

In Oaxaca, the style and symbolism of decorated ceramic vessels and figurines reflect widespread patterns of exchange and interaction. Ceramics in the Valley of Oaxaca and the Mixteca Alta share some general trends seen in many regions at this time such as the use of white slips and an increase in cylindrical vessel forms (Blomster 2004:115–32; Flannery & Marcus 1994:135–286). Debate, however, has focused on ceramic vessels, usually cylindrical or conical bowls, with carved symbols (figure 4.1b). These vessels, especially the carved symbols, closely resemble ceramics found in many parts of western Mesoamerica, particularly in the Gulf coast, in the Basin of Mexico, and in Chiapas. The images on Oaxacan pottery are stylized versions interpreted as representations of two sacred figures – a saurian being known as the "fire-serpent" and a cleft-headed jaguarian creature called the "were-jaguar." Traditionally these images have been seen as originating in the Gulf coast and so have been referred to as "Olmec-style," although proponents of the "sister-culture" model strongly disagree.

Debate has surrounded the origins and interpretation of fire-serpent and were-jaguar symbolism. Flannery and Marcus (1994:387–8), following Grove (1989), see the fire-serpent and were-jaguar as local manifestations of pan-Mesoamerican supernatural forces of "sky" and "earth," respectively, that may have been widely shared even before they were first represented on ceramic vessels at c.1200 BC. Marcus and Flannery (1996:95–6) show that in the Oaxaca Valley the distributions of the two designs are almost mutually exclusive with the fire-serpent image found at Abasolo and Tomaltepec and the were-jaguar at Tierras Largas. At San José Mogote different barrios had either one design or the other. Given their distribution and the association of these vessels only with male burials, Marcus and Flannery (1996:95–6) argue that the two motifs represent the celestial ancestors of ranked patrilineal descent groups. Blanton and his colleagues (1999:39–42) disagree with Marcus and Flannery based on the lack of evidence for unilineal descent in indigenous Mesoamerica. Instead, Blanton and colleagues suggest that the motifs represent a moiety system that involved corporate governance without social ranking. Blomster (2004:122) questions that the motifs even represent a duality – whether forces, lineages, or moieties – since the images have been shown to be different views of the same creature. The possibility that the two designs simply reflect chronological variation would negate both models (Winter 1994b:135).

J. E. Clark (2004) argues that the fire-serpent and were-jaguar motifs are manifestations of related deities he calls Z-gods, or zoomorphic gods, that originated first among the Olmec and represented the elements of sky, earth, water, and the underworld. He suggests that these and other early deities were closely associated with the emergence of powerful hereditary rulers among the Olmec and that gods were fundamental in the legitimation of royal power and authority. A reanalysis of the age of ceramics exhibiting Olmec-style motifs by Di Castro and Cyphers (2006) shows that the earliest examples are indeed found at San Lorenzo in the Gulf coast.

Recent evidence suggests that people appropriated Olmec imagery from actual Olmec ceramics imported into regions like the Valley of Oaxaca and the Nochixtlán Valley. Although Mixtecs and Zapotecs made local vessels with Olmec-style imagery, an extensive INAA study shows that in the sample the overwhelming majority of "Olmec-style" vessels traded during the late Early Formative consisted of ceramics imported from the Gulf coast to regions including the Valley of Oaxaca, the Nochixtlán Valley, the Isthmus of Tehuantepec, the Basin of Mexico, Central Chiapas, and the Soconusco coast (Blomster et al. 2005). In fact, the researchers found no evidence that these vessels were exported from regions other than the Gulf coast.

Similarly, hollow white-slipped figurines depicting nude sexless divine babies or dwarfs were probably imported from the Gulf coast and then emulated in local styles (Blomster 2002). In the Valley of Oaxaca hollow baby figurines are rare and most excavated examples consist of limbs or limb fragments (Marcus 1998), making it impossible to interpret their total imagery. Blomster (2004) recovered a nearly complete Olmec-style hollow baby, probably imported from the Gulf coast, from a bell-shaped pit at Etlatongo, along with several examples that were likely local imitations. Most researchers view the hollow baby figurines as divine beings. Rosemary Joyce (2000:196–7) suggests that similar dwarf images found on monumental Olmec art are associated with underworld disorder that must be ritually kept at bay by powerful rulers. Like J. E. Clark's (2004) argument concerning ceramic motifs, Joyce views these images as implicated in Olmec ideology and the legitimation of political authority.

Although Olmec-style imagery on ceramics and hollow baby figurines were associated with hereditary rulership and its legitimation in the Gulf coast, it is doubtful that these artifacts were deployed in the same way in Oaxaca. The evidence from the Valley of Oaxaca and the Mixteca Alta indicates only modest differences in wealth, power, and status. Archaeologists have debated whether hereditary inequality was present in Oaxaca at this time and I agree with Blanton and his colleagues (1999:36–42) that the evidence is weak (see below). Both Olmec-style ceramic vessels and hollow baby figurines are found primarily in domestic contexts like house floors, middens, bell-shaped pits, and burials suggesting associations with the sharing of meals, including ritual feasting, as well as mortuary ceremonialism and modest status distinctions (Blomster 2004; Lesure 2004; Marcus 1998).

Ceramics with Olmec-style designs, both imitations and imports, were fancy serving vessels used on special food-sharing occasions probably including ritual feasting associated with mortuary ceremonies (Lesure 2004: 83). Meals, feasts, and ceremonies associated with them are communal events where social relations are negotiated on a face-to-face level. Exotic designs on serving vessels created an appearance of difference in the local setting and associated users of these pots to each other both locally and on a broader pan-Mesoamerican scale. I argue that these vessels were actively engaged in the creation of social difference through commensalism (i.e., the act of eating together), rather than being a passive reflection of preexisting social distinctions. People who acquired and deployed Olmec-style vessels, whether imports or imitations, in the context of shared meals invited assessment and risked rejection in an attempt to enhance prestige and wealth (R. Joyce 2000:27). The significance and value of Olmec-style pottery was not acquired wholesale from the Olmec, but was produced locally through the negotiation of wealth and status in the settings in which these exotics were deployed as well as through the social relations by which they were acquired (see Appadurai 1986). Likewise, burial vessels found in graves are not a direct indicator of the personal status of the deceased, but instead reference the social networks in which the person participated during life and which were threatened by the person's death. Regardless of whether feasting occurred as part of mortuary ritual, the use of serving vessels invokes the commensal settings and social relations in which they were used, and are a way in which survivors display regard for the deceased and try to ensure the continuation of social relations through that person (R. Joyce 1999:17–21). Grave goods may indirectly reflect the status of the deceased because high status often correlates with the extent of a person's social affiliations and the regard in which that person is held.

In Oaxaca the lack of evidence for large-scale feasting and the small number of vessels found in even the most elaborate burials suggest that the commensal practices referenced by serving vessels involved relatively small networks. Given the distribution of Olmec-style designs, commensalism and mortuary ceremony probably involved the negotiation of corporate relations at the scale of small communities, or barrios in the case of San José Mogote. The mutually exclusive distribution of Olmec-style designs suggests that they represent corporate groups such as lineages, ramages, moieties, barrios, or communities (cf. Blanton et al. 1999; Marcus & Flannery 1996). Since vessels with Olmec designs are restricted to male burials, it is likely that these vessels were associated with male identity and perhaps were used to assert the prestige and affiliation of men as members of certain households or corporate groups.

Since the ceramic designs reference distant peoples and places, it is also likely that the display of Olmec-style vessels during special meals and rituals involved the negotiation of prestige and status as well. Exchange placed Mixtecs and Zapotecs in at least indirect contact with the Olmec. People who made and used Olmec-style vessels and figurines associated themselves with a distant, powerful, prestigious, and probably sacred place. People displayed these symbols and the broader social relations that they referenced during communal ceremonies, which reflected attempts to enhance personal and familial prestige. Whether the Olmec-style designs reflect more intensive forms of interaction such as the spread of a religious cult (Blomster 1998) is difficult to assess, although the modest hierarchies and relatively small communities of Oaxaca differ from the Olmec, where religion legitimated hereditary rulership and united communities that dwarfed the largest sites in Oaxaca.

Hollow baby figurines are not as common as Olmec-style vessels and the ways in which they were deployed are not as clear. Like the Olmec-style vessels, hollow baby figurines referenced affiliation with the Gulf coast and were likely another way in which prestige was asserted. Most of the figurines, at least the more common local imitations of Olmec-style ones, were discovered in domestic contexts where they could have been displayed to visitors during normal meals and feasts, or they may have been used in more restricted domestic rituals. Although these figurines may have maintained an association with underworld disorder as argued by Rosemary Joyce (2000:196–7) for the Olmec, evidence suggests that, among the Mixtec and Zapotec, rituals did not involve hereditary elites.

Ritual and status

During the late Early Formative, people continued many earlier rituals such as the use of figurines, feasting, and autosacrifice, although there is evidence for the emergence of new ceremonial practices conducted in public buildings and communal cemeteries. These rituals engaged larger groups and contributed to the production of a sense of shared communal history and identity.

Evidence for rituals involving figurines as well as typical bloodletting implements like obsidian blades have been found in nearly all excavated households and do not appear to be linked to status distinctions. Other ritual paraphernalia, however, seems to correlate with household status as measured by elaborate architecture and greater evidence for craft production and exotic trade items (Flannery 1976b; Marcus 1998). Exotic bloodletters, such as stingray spines, are found only in higher-status houses. Shell, mica, and jade ornaments as well as magnetite mirrors generally increase in frequency with measures of status, but the ritual significance of these objects is unclear. Flannery (1976b:336) reports a possible shrine from House C3 in Area A at San José Mogote. High proportions of serving vessels and more deer bone were found in houses with other indicators of high status (Duncan et al. 2008; Flannery & Marcus 1994:329–39; Whalen 1981:59), suggesting that meals and perhaps ritual feasts sponsored by higher-status families were somewhat larger and more sumptuous. Unusual types of ritual paraphernalia such as ceramic masks and conch-shell trumpets have been found in both residential areas and public buildings, but there are too few to associate them with known social distinctions such as status. Masks and conch-shell trumpets could have been used by priests or shamans, otherwise the evidence does not support the presence of ritual specialists.

The most frequent evidence of household ritual in both the Valley of Oaxaca and the Mixteca Alta continues to be solid anthropomorphic figurines (Blomster 2004:77–96; Duncan et al. 2008; Marcus 1998). The majority of figurines continue earlier themes of nude women sometimes shown pregnant, or occasionally holding children (figure 4.2a and 4.2b).

Hairdos are highly variable, although less elaborate than on earlier figurines. Bodily adornments including beads, necklaces, pendants, earspools, and noseplugs are more common, perhaps reflecting a greater focus on beautification. Interpretation of the ritual uses of these figurines continues to range from divination and ancestor worship to dance rituals and life-crisis ceremonies. Figurines may continue to reflect societal tensions and the negotiation of identity surrounding the sexuality of young women. Given the importance of marriage for establishing strategic relations with other households, especially from other communities and regions, tensions surrounding sexuality, mating, and childbirth are not surprising. Archaeologists generally agree that female figurines were used by women primarily in household ceremonies and were an important way in which female identity and subjectivity was materialized (for an exception, see Winter 2005a).

There is an increase in figurines that depict male or sexually neutral figures, based on the absence of breasts, genitalia, and sometimes hair (Marcus 1998:93–108; Winter 2005a:41–4; figure 4.2c). One of the more common

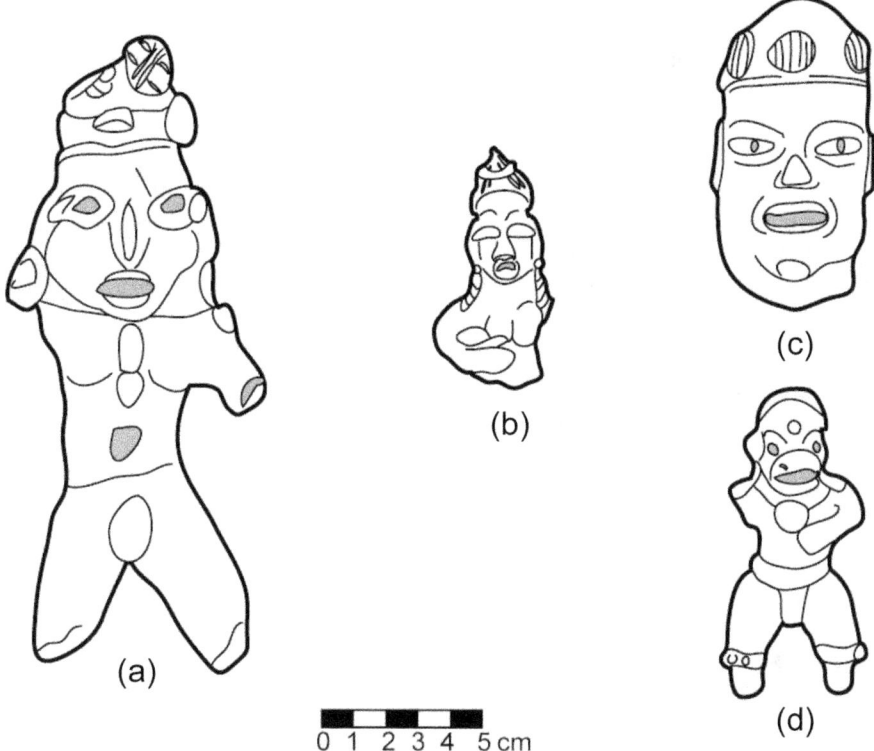

Figure 4.2 Early and Middle Formative figurines from the Valley of Oaxaca (drawings by Eric Berkemeyer): (a) Guadalupe-phase female figurine (after Winter 2005a, figure 9a); (b) San José-phase female figurine (after Winter 2005a, figure 6f); (c) San José-phase figurine, possibly male (after Winter 2005a, figure 7a); (d) costumed figure with ritual attire including a zoomorphic mask and necklace, San José phase (after Winter 1989a:26)

figurine types depicts individuals with shaved heads and at times wearing caps or close-fitting helmets. Some examples exhibit what might be intentional cranial modification; several San José-phase burials also exhibit cranial deformation. Other figurine types depict people clothed for ritual, including what may be ballgame paraphernalia. Some examples show people wearing zoomorphic masks or helmets (figure 4.2d), which Marcus (1998) interprets as dance outfits, although they may represent people taking on the guise or "face" of their animal-spirit companion, a practice that is indicated by later prehispanic imagery (Urcid 2005) and that was common at the time of the Spanish Conquest.

Most San José-phase figurines have been found in secondary contexts, although a few are from caches and burials. The majority of figurines found in caches and burials represent naked personages without genitals or breasts and often with earspools and pendants. Marcus (1998) interprets these as male, although they are best described as sexually neutral. The most elaborate cache consists of four solid figurines found buried beneath the floor of House 16 at San José Mogote, a possible open annex attached to House 17. One of the figurines was seated, while the others were extended with their arms folded across their chests. Marcus (1998:177–81) interprets the scene as showing a seated person in a position of authority on top of three supine retainers shown in positions of subordination. Two similar seated figurines were found with a burial of an adult woman at the Tomaltepec cemetery (Burial 35). Both House 16–17 and Burial 35 had indications of higher status (Marcus & Flannery 1996:104; Whalen 1981).

Elaborately dressed figurines, at least some of which were male, along with ungendered figurines from caches and burials suggest new themes by the San José phase (Marcus 1998:93–108; Winter 2005a:43). It is possible that these new figurine types reflect societal tensions and the negotiation of social identity surrounding emerging status distinctions in Mixtec and Zapotec societies, which had previously been characterized by more egalitarian social relations. Since many of these figurines foreground ritual action, they may have served to legitimate inequality by stressing special ritual qualities rather than involvement in crafting and trade. Evidence for ritual practices, however, is weakly associated with household wealth and status, although it is possible that prominent people were controlling ritual in ways that are archaeologically invisible.

Ritual and community

Evidence for ritual practices that engaged people beyond the household increases during the late Early Formative, and includes the construction at San José Mogote of what was probably the first centrally located, community-wide ceremonial precinct in Oaxaca. At San José Mogote, Zapotecs continued to use rectangular one-room temples in the Area C barrio into the early part of the San José phase. By the middle of the San José phase the construction of public buildings shifted to the Area A barrio near the households specializing in magnetite mirror production. It is in Area A that the first ceremonial precinct in Oaxaca was constructed.

The earliest public building built in Area A was Structure 16, a one-room structure on a puddled adobe platform with traces of a lime-plastered cell sunken beneath the floor, possibly for storage (Flannery & Marcus

1994:362–3). The full dimensions of Structure 16 could not be ascertained, although it appeared comparable to the earlier public buildings in Area C. The building was oriented roughly 21° east of north, which differed from most Early/Middle Formative public buildings in Mesoamerica.

A similar building was excavated at the small (1.2 ha) site of Tomaltepec located in the piedmont of the Tlacolula arm of the valley about 20 km southeast of San José Mogote (Whalen 1981). At Tomaltepec, Michael Whalen (1981) sought to investigate household and community organization away from the main center of population and economic activity in the Etla arm. The most elaborate early San José-phase building exposed by Whalen was Structure 11, which was oriented 16°–17° east of true north. The building included a well-preserved adobe-plastered cell similar to the one in Structure 16 with a volume of about 9 m^3, which is about six times the capacity of the average bell-shaped pit. A dense refuse deposit excavated within the cell included unusually high concentrations of deer and rabbit bone, and stone and bone butchery tools. Lithics included over 50 percent of the total Early Formative obsidian recovered at the site as well as a variety of ground-stone tools. The archaeologists recovered large quantities of charcoal, mostly pine, and the remains of maize, teosinte seeds, and avocado pits. Pottery included a much higher proportion of serving vessels than in typical houses. Researchers have struggled with whether to interpret these structures as public buildings or high-status houses (Flannery & Marcus 1994:362; Whalen 1981). I agree with Flannery and Marcus (1994:362) that the evidence leans toward public buildings. The large storage features and high volume of domestic refuse probably resulted from ritual feasting, rather than normal domestic activities. Given the small size of Tomaltepec, it is likely that feasts associated with Structure 11 would have involved the entire community, while those associated with Structure 16 at San José Mogote may have been limited to the Area A barrio.

Late in the San José phase Structure 16 and the nearby residences in Area A at San José Mogote were covered by a much larger public architectural complex (Flannery & Marcus 1994:367–71). The complex consisted of two east-facing monumental terraces that elevated ceremonial activities and perhaps supported public buildings that have not survived. For the most part construction of the terraces involved the use of established architectural practices such as stone walls, puddled adobe, and earthen fill; the terraces, however, included the first use of adobe brick known in Oaxaca. The lower, eastern terrace was designated Structure 2 and its 1-m-high retaining wall was faced with boulders and included two narrow stairways that allowed access to the terrace surface to the west. The stairways forced people into a single file procession as they entered the lower terrace, perhaps allowing access to be controlled. A retaining wall runs east from the southeastern corner of the terrace and demarcates an open plaza or perhaps a sunken patio to the east. Two small carved-stone monuments, the earliest reported in Oaxaca, appear to have fallen out of the east–west running retaining wall. Marcus and Flannery (1996:109–10) identify one as a feline and the other a raptorial bird. The second terrace, Structure 1, was built on the surface of Structure 2 approximately 10 m west of the latter's retaining wall and reached a height of 1.5 m. Plazas and carved-stone monuments displayed in accessible settings (i.e., not in tombs) are characteristic of later public buildings in Oaxaca, rather than residences.

Construction of the architectural complex represented by Structures 1 and 2 represents the first monumental building known in the Oaxaca Valley. The complex was more visible than earlier public buildings and probably could have accommodated hundreds of people during ritual performances. Given the scale of the complex, it may have required labor from beyond the Area A barrio in order to build. Both the construction of the architectural complex and the rituals carried out there suggest practices that engaged the entire community of San José Mogote and perhaps surrounding ones (Marcus & Flannery 1996:110). These practices can be seen as a "scaling up" of both established architectural techniques and rituals that probably included dance, divination, and bloodletting. Through these shared communal practices, people inscribed notions of collective identity, history, and memory in the ceremonial complex, thereby reorganizing space and creating the first ceremonial center in the region.

The construction of a separate ceremonial precinct marked by the size and durability of monumental buildings, and reinforced by the carved stones depicting divine beings, resulted in a zonation of space within the community and region such that sacred locales for the enactment of communal ceremonies were segregated (see R. Joyce 2004b; Love 1999). The lack of evidence for significant status differences, especially hereditary ones, indicates that the construction of the ceremonial complex was not directed by powerful leaders, but instead was a communal project designed to build an expanded ceremonial space to communicate with the sacred realm and as a space where various community activities were carried out, perhaps including feasts, dances, and games. The larger collectivities mobilized by the construction and use of the ceremonial complex, however, could have provided opportunities for influential people to expand social networks and influence as suggested by Aldenderfer (2004) for Late Preceramic monumental architecture in parts of the Andean highlands. I argue therefore that the construction of Structures 1 and 2 at San José Mogote was not the result of powerful rulers, but may have created conditions conducive

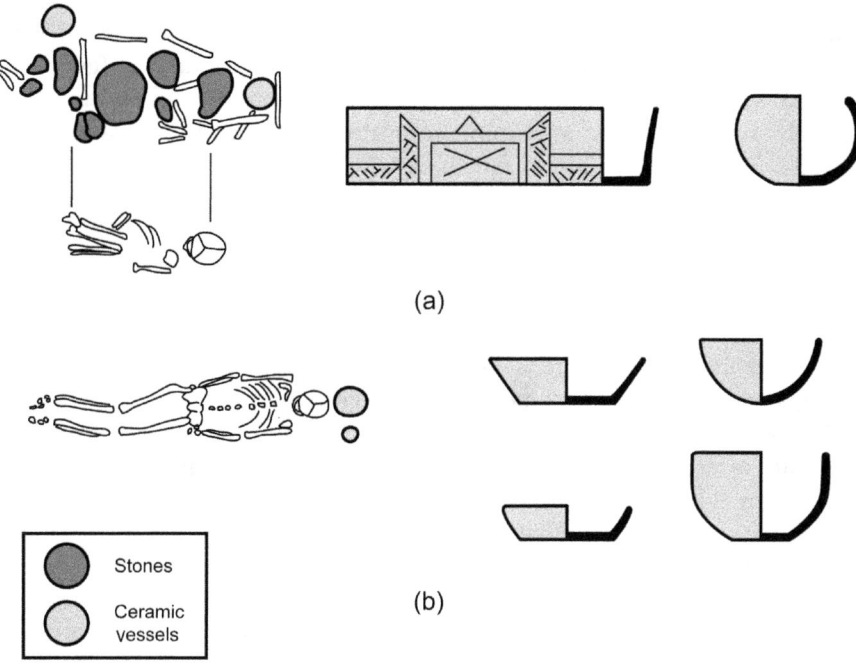

Figure 4.3 Burials from the Tomaltepec cemetery: (a) Burial 20 with ceramic offerings; (b) Burial 57 with ceramic offerings (after Whalen 1981, figures 31, 33, 35, and 39; drawings by Eric Berkemeyer)

to power building. The zonation of space also set the stage for the later appropriation of ceremonial precincts by nobles at the end of the Middle Formative. Although the intention of the original builders may not have been to create a focal point of community identity, the resulting institution – a ceremonial complex that connected the community to the divine – became a tradition that would continue through the remainder of the prehispanic period and up to the present as embodied in the churches found today in communities throughout Oaxaca.

Ritual practices that engaged people on the scale of small communities like Tomaltepec or barrios at San José Mogote are also suggested by the discovery of communal cemeteries. The largest and best documented of these Early Formative cemeteries comes from Whalen's (1981) excavations at Tomaltepec in the Tlacolula arm of the valley. At Tomaltepec, Whalen (1981) excavated a cemetery in the northern part of the site where most of the adult members of the community were interred, including a nearly equal number of men and women. Almost 70 burials containing the remains of 80 individuals were recovered (figure 4.3). Positioning and orientation of burials was very uniform with most individuals laid prone with their head to the east, although 10 burials, probably all male, were interred in a flexed position. Burials were in simple pits, although a few were covered with stone slabs. Some burials included an adult man and woman, possibly marital pairs, a pattern seen more frequently in subsequent periods. It is also possible to recognize several clusters of about a dozen burials, which could represent households or larger corporate groups (cf. R. Joyce 1999:23).

Offerings were present with 54 percent of the buried individuals and included ceramic vessels and figurines; jade, shell, and magnetite ornaments; a greenstone celt, bone awls, obsidian, and ground stone (Whalen 1981). A number of burials were also accompanied by secondary interments, perhaps ancestors, usually limited to a detached skull. Offerings were generally modest with most consisting of one to three ceramic vessels. The most elaborate offering was found with Burial 11-1, a flexed interment of a 30- to 40-year-old man accompanied by three ceramic vessels, including one with Olmec-style designs, a necklace of 15 greenstone beads, a single greenstone bead placed in the person's mouth, and a greenstone celt. The greenstone artifacts interred with Burial 11-1 represent nearly all the greenstone found in the cemetery. Another elaborate interment was Burial 42, a probable woman in her 20s, accompanied by seven ceramic vessels, a fragment of a solid figurine, and half of a broken stone pendant. Flexed burials of males over 30 years of age at death had significantly more Olmec-style vessels and were more likely to be covered with stone slabs and accompanied by secondary burials. Senior flexed male interments tended to have more elaborate offerings than typical burials, although several flexed junior males were unaccompanied by offerings. As discussed above, only males were interred with Olmec-style vessels, perhaps reflecting their affiliation with interregional social networks. Only females were interred with figurines (Winter 2005a, table 2), which underscores the female gendering of figurine production and use.

Burials at San José Mogote are found in a small cemetery in the Area C barrio as well as individual interments near residences (Marcus & Flannery 1996:97–106). Mortuary patterns at San José Mogote differ somewhat from those of Tomaltepec with adults of both sexes and children interred in the barrio cemetery. Like at Tomaltepec, most burials were prone with some examples of slab-lined graves and male–female pairs; flexed burials have not been found. All burials in the Area C cemetery were accompanied by relatively modest offerings, including ceramic vessels and greenstone and shell ornaments. Mourners placed a greenstone bead in the mouth of nearly every adult burial at San José Mogote, but not in those of children.

Children at San José Mogote, Tomaltepec, and other sites like Abasolo were therefore interred with offerings, including vessels with Olmec-style designs, although they were differentiated from adults either by burial location or by the absence of certain offerings. The burials at San José Mogote were adorned more frequently with ornaments than those at Tomaltepec and other sites in the valley. There were also several individuals with cranial modification, although Saul and Saul (2001:181) have found no significant correlation between cranial modification and social status in Mesoamerica (also see Geller 2004). In San José-phase Oaxaca, cranial modification does not seem to correlate with other status indicators.

The burial evidence from the Oaxaca Valley suggests that mortuary ritual constituted a nested set of social affiliations, contributing to the construction of identities linked to individuality, status, age-grade, household, and community. Burial in cemeteries returned people to the corporate body at death in a way that emphasized shared history and identity, contributing to the construction of identities at the scale of the barrio and small community. Affiliations with smaller groups, probably family and/or co-resident groups, are suggested by the burial clusters at the Tomaltepec cemetery. Small-group affiliations are also suggested by the scale of mortuary ceremony and commensal practices referenced in the relatively low number of vessels left as offerings. Bodily ornaments interred with some men and women, particularly at San José Mogote, suggest that people expressed individuality and attempted to enhance personal influence through beautification. Status appears to have been most strongly associated with age as indicated by differential mortuary treatment. For example, at Tomaltepec children were excluded from the community cemetery, while at San José Mogote, they did not have greenstone beads placed in their mouths like adults.

Overall, the data indicate that by the late Early Formative settlements were more than co-resident groups lacking a strong sense of *communitas*, as I have suggested for earlier periods. People at San José Mogote and other settlements viewed themselves as part of a distinct community with its own history, traditions, and relations to the divine as embodied in the site's ceremonial center. The construction of a community identity would have acted against the rising social distinctions of household, status, and perhaps barrio, which created tensions that could have driven communities apart. It is difficult to untangle the relationship between this shared sense of *communitas* and the success of people in the Etla arm, especially at San José Mogote, in craft production and the establishment of long-distance contacts, as well as the rapid growth of these sites. Nevertheless, by the end of the Early Formative San José Mogote was seen as a special place because of its size and success in crafting and long-distance exchange, but also as a ceremonial center.

It is likely that similar developments were occurring at sites like Etlatongo, Tayata, and Diuxi in the Mixteca Alta (Balkansky et al. 2000; Blomster 2004). At Tayata, archaeologists have found evidence for a higher-status residence characterized by the production of ceramics and shell ornaments, high quantities of dog and fish bones, evidence for ritual feasting, and special mortuary rituals involving the *in situ* burning of the corpse shortly after death, followed by burial (Balkansky et al. 2008; Duncan et al. 2008). Taken together, these data suggest relatively high status comparable to evidence from other sites in Oaxaca. Until more data are reported from Tayata, however, it will be difficult to access the degree of inequality and whether there were indications of hereditary status distinctions. Balkansky and his colleagues (2008:37) report a ceremonial plaza at Tayata measuring more than 90 m on a side, which, if dated to the Early Formative, would represent an impressive performance space for public ceremonies.

Community and Identity in the Early Middle Formative

There is significant continuity in social conditions from the late Early Formative through the early part of the Middle Formative until about 700 BC. The Middle Formative is best known from the Valley of Oaxaca where horizontal excavations have exposed occupations from the Guadalupe phase (850–700 BC) sites of San José Mogote, Fábrica San José, Tierras Largas, Huitzo, Hacienda Blanca, and Tomaltepec (Drennan 1976; Flannery & Marcus 1983a; Whalen 1981; Winter 1972). Survey and excavation data show that social distinctions continued to be reproduced through practices like crafting, long-distance exchange, ritual, bodily ornamentation, and the expansion of social ties via marriage and the creation of debts and obligations through feasting and gift giving. Public buildings where ritual practices inscribed a sense of community identity increased in scale and are found at more communities. Inequalities in wealth and status, as indicated by residential data and mortuary practices, increase slightly, although it is still unclear if hereditary status distinctions had developed. Elsewhere in Oaxaca, there are fewer data to assess Middle Formative social systems and structural conditions, although the available evidence suggests similarities to the Valley of Oaxaca in the scale of communities and in the degree of social inequality (Balkansky et al. 2000, 2004, 2008; A. Joyce 2005:18; Kowalewski et al. 2009).

Evidence for craft production continues for everyday utilitarian items like stone and bone tools, ceramics, cloth, baskets, and woodworking (Drennan 1976:75–110; Flannery & Marcus 1983a; Whalen 1981:34–63; Winter 1972:147–68). The specialized production of shell and mica ornaments continued; a small number of ornaments were also made from materials like travertine, as well as from dog and deer teeth. Differences in craft production did not distinguish households to the degree that they did in the Early Formative since most crafting activities were widely practiced. Possible evidence for part-time craft specialization comes only from Fábrica San José, a 1.2-ha site in the piedmont located adjacent to a small drainage and near mineral springs that provide a good source of edible salt along with large travertine deposits. Robert Drennan, who excavated the site in the early 1970s, was interested in relations between this small community and San José Mogote located only 5 km to the west. At Fábrica San José, Drennan (1976) excavated several Guadalupe-phase houses, including one with evidence for higher-than-normal quantities of decorated serving vessels, mica, shell, obsidian, and deer bone, suggesting relatively high status. Located nearby was a midden with evidence for the specialized production of shell ornaments and possibly the manufacture of ornaments from animal bone and stone. One of the shell artifacts was a finely crafted ornament in the form of the blood motif usually associated with sacrifice in later Mesoamerican imagery (Drennan 1976:107–8, figure 78d). The midden also yielded a fragment of a possible turtle-shell drum. Fábrica San José also yielded evidence for community specialization in salt production, which was a minor activity carried out in nearly every household.

The decline in shell-ornament production is consistent with evidence suggesting a decrease in the importation of Pacific- and Atlantic-coast shell (Pires-Ferreira 1975:80). Other data suggest further changes in interregional relations. In particular, evidence for interaction with the Gulf-coast Olmec decreases significantly by c.850 BC. Olmec-style ceramic vessels and figurines no longer were imported or imitated in Oaxaca. There are general similarities in ceramic styles between the Valley of Oaxaca and the Mixteca Alta, but broader ties, such as the Olmec motifs of the Early Formative, are much less evident (Winter 1994b:138–9). A decline in trade with the Olmec Heartland is also indicated by the end of iron-ore-mirror production in the Valley of Oaxaca. In Pires-Ferreira's (1975) sourcing study, obsidian from the Gulf-coast sources of Guadalupe Victoria and Altotonga decreases from 37 percent in the Early Formative to 22 percent by the Middle Formative, while central-Mexican obsidian increases with the most common source being Otumba (25 percent). The overall amount of obsidian imported into the valley decreases by the Middle Formative (Parry 1987:134).

Bloodletting implements including fish and stingray spines continue to be imported and, while rare, tend to be associated with higher-status residences or public buildings (Flannery 1976b).

People continued to import greenstone ornaments into the Valley of Oaxaca, which may have taken on a more important role in the creation and display of status both when worn as ornaments and when interred as burial offerings. Throughout Mesoamerica trade in greenstone increased during the Middle Formative with ornaments deployed as luxury goods used to display personal and household prestige and establish alliances through gifting (Grove & Gillespie 1992a, 1992b). Certain types of greenstone ornaments, particularly bead belts and earspools may have been widely recognized badges of nobility in regions where hereditary status distinctions had developed, such as the Gulf coast, Morelos, the Chiapas Central depression, the Soconusco coast and as far south as Honduras (R. Joyce 1999:39). In these regions greenstone was symbolically linked to wealth, prestige, status, maize, agricultural fertility, and sacred power (Grove & Gillespie 1992a:29–30; Taube 2000). In the Valley of Oaxaca, however, it is difficult to quantify changes in the amount of imported greenstone, although ornaments appear to be at least as common in burial offerings as during the San José phase. The majority of greenstone ornaments were small round or tubular beads that were available to people regardless of status. The elaborate ornaments that embodied noble status in other parts of Mesoamerica have not yet been recovered in Oaxaca.

Until the Rosario phase (700–500 BC) variation in crafting and imported goods as well as other indicators of inequality continue to indicate relatively modest status distinctions. During the early Middle Formative, higher-status households are distinguished by some combination of evidence for shell-ornament production, greater access to imports, higher proportions of decorated serving vessels, burials with more elaborate offerings, and special ritual objects. Yet again, the differences among Middle Formative houses are fluid and relatively modest. For example, in Drennan's (1976) analysis of Middle Formative households from Fábrica San José, the higher-status ones are distinguished most often by above-average proportions of decorated serving bowls. Other indicators of prestige vary widely so that one high-status house (LG-1) had 27 pieces of imported shell and 9 pieces of mica, while other houses with high proportions of decorated serving vessels had little or no shell. Household LG-6 did not have a high percentage of decorated serving vessels, but was associated with the specialized production of ornaments. Many of the households with higher proportions of decorated serving vessels had associated burials with few or no offerings. Again, Household LG-1 was an exception with four burials all accompanied by offerings, including three burials of children each accompanied by offerings of greenstone beads. The fourth interment, Burial 39, was the most elaborate recovered in the region prior to 600 BC. Burial 39 was a woman approximately 60 years of age at death interred in a prone position and accompanied by three ceramic vessels, including a cylindrical drinking vessel, which she grasped in both hands. Red pigment was visible on the cylinder and on the woman's mandible. Her mouth was filled with 47 round greenstone beads, 6 tubular greenstone beads, 1 round bead of brown stone, and 1 greenstone pendant. The large quantity of exotic ornaments suggests high status, although it is also possible that these objects marked a special role, such as ritual specialist.

Despite the elaborate offering in Burial 39 and evidence for shell and mica ornaments, House LG-1 was architecturally similar to the other houses excavated at Fábrica San José. Architectural elaboration is often a better indicator of wealth and status differences since it reflects the long-term ability of households to mobilize resources (Michael Smith 1987). Both households with indications of higher status (LG-1 and LG-6), however, were built over the earliest houses at the site, which date to the early Guadalupe phase. These data suggest that the founding families may have had an advantage in status competition due to factors such as the ability to claim the best land or their broader social affiliations within the community.

Burials from other Middle Formative sites in the Valley of Oaxaca exhibit a range of offerings similar to what was found at Fábrica San José (Marcus & Flannery 1996; Whalen 1981; Winter 1972). Most burials lack offerings or were interred with only a few ceramic vessels or greenstone beads. Marcus and Flannery (1996:113–15) argue that the higher-status female burials at Fábrica San José, as represented by Burial 39 as well as an elaborate Rosario-phase interment, were the result of women from prestigious families at San José Mogote marrying into families and moving to the former site. While this is a plausible scenario, it is also possible that women born at Fábrica San José were able to achieve prestige on their own.

The practice of placing greenstone ornaments in the mouths of deceased people continues during the Middle Formative. The meaning of this practice is not well understood, although it may relate to reciprocal relations between people and the gods as later delineated by the sacred covenant. As discussed in chapter 2, this covenant gave people the ability to grow crops and, in return, people agreed to offer sacrifices to the gods, with the most basic form of sacrifice being to go into the earth at death. It is possible that the placement of greenstone in the mouths of dead people was a way in which the sacrificial offering of the body was enhanced.

Greenstone may have equated the human body with maize, which was returned to the earth in death, completing a transaction whereby sustenance in the form of maize had been taken from the earth in life (Taube 2000). This practice also would have removed greenstone ornaments that had been displayed on costuming in life and hidden them within the body of the deceased, perhaps as a way of de-emphasizing personal wealth and prestige at death.

Mortuary patterns during the Middle Formative indicate a shift away from community or barrio cemeteries. Most burials are associated with households and sometimes include multiple interments consisting of an adult male and female and occasionally children (Marcus & Flannery 1996:117). Distinctions between adults and children in mortuary ceremony lessened. In small communities like Fábrica San José and Tierras Largas there is evidence for the persistence of small cemeteries, although these cemeteries did not serve the entire community (Drennan 1976:126–9; Winter 1972). The number of ceramic vessels accompanying burials continues to suggest relatively small-scale funerary rituals and modest status distinctions as inscribed on bodies via ornamentation and perhaps cranial modification.

The reason for the shift from communal cemeteries to interments associated with households and the family is not clear, although the change suggests a greater focus on the household and its ancestors. Marcus and Flannery (1996:117) argue for a shift toward bilateral descent with a focus on family membership. The decrease in specialized economic activities at the barrio or community level suggests that identities linked to mid-range corporate groups (i.e., above the level of the household, but below that of entire communities) were no longer produced by shared productive activities. The salient social affiliations of the Middle Formative seem to have been focused more on the household, which was reproduced through practices involving economic, ritual, and kinship relations; and the community or polity, which was constructed largely via practices involving religion and politics. Households may have been increasingly differentiated within mid-range corporate groups like the lineages and ramages documented ethnohistorically, as families competed for resource surpluses and prestige. Perhaps the change in mortuary practices reflects social tensions surrounding inequality that was displayed in mortuary ceremonies and in the luxury goods interred with the deceased.

Household rituals show considerable continuity from the Early Formative and include autosacrifice, feasting, and the use of solid ceramic figurines. Probable bloodletting implements are found in residences of all status levels, although the few bloodletters made from imported fish spines were associated with either higher-status houses or public buildings (Flannery

1976b). Greater proportions of decorated serving vessels were associated with higher-status houses. These data suggest that people from high-status families participated in more frequent and perhaps larger meals where fancy serving vessels were displayed, including ritual feasts, which established social ties and created debts and obligations with other households in their community and beyond (also see Marcus & Flannery 1996:115–16). Sites in Etla have more decorated serving vessels than sites in other parts of the valley, suggesting that feasting and the display of prestigious ceramics contributed to the prominence of San José Mogote and the subregion in general.

Middle Formative figurines continue earlier themes with the majority depicting young women usually shown with more elaborate ornamentation than during earlier periods and frequently with elaborate hairdos, head wraps, and sandals; some wear small pubic aprons (Marcus 1998). Some figurines have perforations on the top of their heads for suspending them as ornaments. Figurines depicting pregnant women and women with children, however, appear less common than in earlier times. Marcus (1998) argues that the greater ornamentation on Middle Formative female figurines reflects rising status distinctions. The high degree of ornamentation, however, diverges from the rare occurrence of shell, mica, or jade ornaments recovered in residential excavations, particularly in lower-status ones. Ornaments, especially earspools, are also rare in burials and jade ornaments, which were the most common type in burials, were usually not worn, but instead were placed in the mouth of the deceased. These data suggest a divergence between embodied practices and practices of representation. If the use of these female figurines in household rituals was a medium for the objectification of stereotyped social identities, then the figurines seem to emphasize an enhancement of personal attractiveness to a degree that few women would have been able to achieve. Like the placement of jade ornaments in the mouths of deceased people, this disjunction between embodied practice and representation may reflect tensions surrounding rising inequality. Few women may have been able to meet the stereotyped identities represented on figurines.

Public buildings continued to be built during the Guadalupe phase, although none exceeded the scale of San José Mogote Structures 1 and 2 that were abandoned by the end of the San José phase (Flannery & Marcus 1994:371). During the Guadalupe phase people at both San José Mogote and Huitzo built public buildings made from bun-shaped adobes and earthen fill faced with stone and oriented 8° west of true north. Structure 8 at San José Mogote was a low platform that supported a puddled adobe floor of a large wattle-and-daub building that appears to have been built over the Area C barrio cemetery (see Flannery & Marcus 1994, figure 9.3). It is not clear whether Structure 8 represented a shift in the site's ceremonial center away from Area A, where Structures 1 and 2 had been built during the San José phase, or if Structure 8 was a ritual building for the Area C barrio only. It is possible that different factions were competing for the ritual participation of community members, although a community-wide ceremonial center might also lie buried within Mound 1, a huge platform that supported Rosario-phase public buildings.

Flannery (1976b:335) excavated another Guadalupe-phase public building at the site of Huitzo, located in northern Etla near the confluence of a small stream with the Río Atoyac. Structure 4 at Huitzo was a platform measuring more than 15 m wide and 2 m high that supported a series of buildings that may have been one-room temples. During the Rosario phase, what may have been an even larger public building was constructed in this area although, like the earlier buildings, it was badly damaged by recent adobe-making. Given the scale of the public buildings at Huitzo, it is likely that they were built and used by the entire community and perhaps other nearby ones (Flannery 1976b:335), indicating that by c.850 BC the community had its own ceremonial core. The people of Huitzo may have competed with San José Mogote for prestige and followers (Marcus & Flannery 1996:113). At Tomaltepec, the community's public building was rebuilt on a much larger scale and continued in use until 300 BC when it was replaced by an even larger public structure (Whalen 1981:88–90).

Structures of Authority in the Early to Middle Formative

The period from approximately 1150 to 700 BC was a time of relative stability in structural conditions where social distinctions related to age, gender, household/family, status, barrio, and community were generally reproduced over the course of hundreds of years without major historical disjunctures. This relative stability does not imply stasis since there *were* changes in demography, identity, external relations, and the kinds of objects that symbolized prestige. Furthermore, practice theory shows us that even apparent "stability" is a product of ongoing social activity. The archaeological record indicates that many of the social changes of the time were a result of the effects, both intentional and unintentional, of people expanding on earlier practices involving crafting, exchange, and ritual. These practices materialized social distinctions such that people's identities were constituted by a complex, nested, and changing series of affiliations related to gender, age, labor, household/family, status, barrio, and community. The relatively modest changes in wealth and status differences as well as in the scale of public architecture and ritual seem to have involved intensification, or "scaling up," in the practices that generated these structural conditions relative to conditions before 1150 BC. Yet the relational fields that reproduced social distinctions and limited social inequality remained fairly stable.

Hereditary inequality

The most hotly debated development of the San José and Guadalupe phases in the Valley of Oaxaca has been whether hereditary status distinctions were present (Blanton et al. 1999:36–42; Marcus & Flannery 1996:93–110). Marcus and Flannery (1996:93–110) base their model on traditional evolutionist views of chiefdoms, including the development of ranked descent groups and the emergence of a centralized chiefly authority that directed community projects such as the construction and use of the ceremonial complex at San José Mogote. Blanton and his colleagues (1999:36–42) contest the chiefdom model, arguing instead for a corporate form of governance without inherited status distinctions where members of prominent households, rather than a singular chief, contributed to political decision-making.

My reading of the evidence agrees more closely with Blanton and his colleagues (1999). Social structures that constructed and legitimated later hereditary status distinctions among Oaxaca Zapotecs are not evident prior to 700 BC. These structures include the following aspects:

1 Nobles had exclusionary control of prestigious goods, symbols, and rituals that embodied hereditary status, particularly the belief in special ritual abilities, which made nobles mediators between people and the divine. These ritual abilities included the right to carry out human sacrifice.
2 Nobles had the right to mobilize goods and labor as tribute or sacrifices that enacted the sacred covenant and contributed to their ability to petition the gods on behalf of their followers.
3 Nobles were spatially segregated in elaborate residences associated with ceremonial buildings and spaces that further symbolized the close connection between people and the divine.
4 Nobles were closely associated with deities, and had the ability to impersonate certain deities, especially the rain god.
5 The ancestors of the nobility were revered and may have been seen as becoming deities at death. Rituals petitioning the divine via noble ancestors included tomb-reentry ceremonies where the bones of the

ancestors could be consulted or used as ritual paraphernalia. Imagery showed noble ancestors as powerful beings that had ongoing relationships with the living.

When considering the evidence from Oaxaca prior to the Rosario phase, few of these cultural principles, material relations, and associated practices are indicated. There is no question that inequalities in wealth, status, prestige, and power are evident by the San José phase, but the evidence from both domestic and mortuary practices suggests only relatively minor and continuous differences. Evidence from residences show a modest degree of inequality based on variation in crafting activities, long-distance exchange, special meals, and the use of bodily adornments. At present, there is no evidence for high-status residences spatially associated with ceremonial precincts. Differences in the architectural elaboration of houses, such as the use of whitewashed walls and stone foundations, represent only minor investments of labor above that of most residences. A similar modest variation in wealth and prestige is also suggested by mortuary evidence. The clearest indicator of status is age with mortuary practices that differentiated adults from children and with the most elaborate offerings usually associated with older men and women. I believe that people were occasionally able to pass wealth, status, and influence onto their children and to circumvent leveling mechanisms, but hereditary status distinctions were not institutionalized.

Exotic goods, symbols, and ritual practices that Marcus and Flannery (1996, chapter 8) suggest were restricted to a hereditary elite include cranial deformation, Olmec-style vessels, greenstone, and iron-ore mirrors. Cranial deformation in Mesoamerica was not generally correlated with social status (Geller 2004:385–90; Saul & Saul 2001:181) and, in Early/Middle Formative burials in Oaxaca, it does not appear to correlate with the wealth of burial offerings or other status indicators (Marcus & Flannery 1996:106). Cranial deformation was probably another kind of beautification through which people sought to increase influence by enhancing the appearance of their children, but which was not necessarily productive of hereditary status distinctions. Marcus and Flannery (1996, chapter 8) suggest that Olmec-style vessels, greenstone, and mirrors were prestige goods that, when found as offerings in child burials, demonstrate hereditary status. As discussed earlier, the presence of ceramic vessels as offerings in the burial of children is more likely to reflect the social connections and indirectly the status of the family of the deceased, rather than the status of the buried individual (see Blanton et al. 1999:38; R. Joyce 1999). Greenstone was present in burials of children as well as adults, although during the San José phase children were distinguished by the absence of greenstone beads placed in their mouths.

Based on comparisons with other regions of Formative Mesoamerica, the best candidates for prestige goods restricted to hereditary elites are iron-ore mirrors, as well as bead belts, elaborate earspools, and celts made from greenstone (Grove & Gillespie 1992b; R. Joyce 1999). Bead belts have not been recovered in Oaxacan burials, while a handful of greenstone celts and earspools as well as a single magnetite mirror have been recovered as mortuary offerings. All of the burials were older adults, mostly over 30 years old at death. People in the Area A barrio at San José Mogote specialized in the production of iron-ore mirrors for export although, other than mirrors, there are relatively few indicators of high status. The presence of a small number of unusual greenstone objects like celts and earspools are the best evidence for special status. Given the lack of other indicators of hereditary status distinctions, I argue that control of these objects was a way in which people sought to distinguish themselves and elevate status, rather than a passive reflection of pre-existing status differences.

Marcus (1998) interprets increasing ornamentation on Early and Middle Formative figurines as reflecting the rise of hereditary status distinctions, although alternative interpretations have been offered (e.g., Cyphers 1993; R. Joyce 2000). A correlation between the relative status of households and the ornamentation of associated figurines has not been shown, which would be expected if the figurines represented ancestors that were contacted via figurine-based rituals.

Marcus and Flannery (1996:106–8) also rely on regional data to argue for the rise of chiefdoms in the San José phase. Using traditional cultural evolutionary indicators for chiefdoms, they argue that a two-tiered settlement hierarchy and the presence of public buildings at San José Mogote show that the site was a chiefly center. Settlement hierarchies, however, are poor indicators of the kinds of complex social and political relations that archaeologists should be interested in when considering the emergence of social complexity (e.g., Cowgill 2004:543). As discussed above, the Oaxacan data show few direct indicators for complex social relations involving tribute extraction, political domination and control, and the presence of powerful hereditary rulers. The construction of the first monumental buildings and the creation of a ceremonial center at San José Mogote indicate the mobilization of communal labor. The scale of the buildings, however, is modest compared to contemporaneous public structures at San Lorenzo in the Gulf coast and at Paso de la Amada in the Mazatan region of coastal Chiapas where the presence of status distinctions are clearer (J. E. Clark 2004). Furthermore, the evidence for a continuum in power differentials and the lack of evidence for an overall singular ruler or ruling family (Blanton et al. 1999:34–42) suggests that the construction of the ceremonial center may have been initiated as a communal project, perhaps involving a number of influential community members.

Comparing Early/Middle Formative-period social complexity

The evidence for Early Formative hereditary status and social complexity in the Valley of Oaxaca and the Mixteca Alta is much weaker than in the Gulf coast and in the Mazatan region. By the Early Formative San Lorenzo phase (1150–900 BC) the Olmec center of San Lorenzo reached 500 ha and had an estimated population of perhaps 10,000 to 15,000 people (J. E. Clark 1997; Cyphers 1997). In the Mazatan region the primary center is Paso de la Amada, which reached 140 ha and an estimated 1,950 to 2,600 people by the Locona phase (1450–1300 BC; J. E. Clark 2004). Mortuary evidence for hereditary inequality in both the Gulf coast and the southern Pacific coast is ambiguous until the Middle Formative, but high-status houses have been excavated in both regions that are far more elaborate architecturally than any Oaxacan residence. Most residences excavated at San Lorenzo and Paso de la Amada approximate in size and architectural elaboration Early Formative houses in Oaxaca. At San Lorenzo, however, a probable royal residence known as the Red Palace had plastered and painted walls, large basalt column roof supports, a stone drain or aquaduct, and a red gravel floor estimated at 400 m^2 (Cyphers 1997:101). Structure 4, the most elaborate residence excavated at Paso de la Amada, was an apsidal structure with clay walls measuring 22 m by 12 m (J. E. Clark 2004:56–7). The high-status residences at San Lorenzo and Paso de la Amada were both associated with large public ceremonial spaces, suggesting a link between high status and public ritual.

In addition to the Red Palace, evidence for powerful leaders among the Olmec includes monumental stone portraits of rulers and public works projects that involved the mobilization of thousands of laborers (J. E. Clark 1997). Early Formative monumental sculpture includes the famous Olmec colossal heads as well as thrones and representations of nobles depicted as ballplayers and warriors. The colossal heads and thrones were also communal labor projects since they weighed up to 50 tons and were quarried from sources about 50 km away. Major architectural projects at San Lorenzo far exceeded the scale of public architecture in Early Formative Oaxaca. Monumental buildings at San Lorenzo include large earthen mounds, causeways that served as dikes and docks (one measures 600 m long by 75 m wide), and a sunken patio surrounded by low earthen platforms (Cyphers 1997:106).

The ceremonial center at Paso de la Amada with its plaza, ballcourt, and high-status residence would have been a large-scale public project (J. E. Clark 2004). The ballcourt measures 87 m by 33 m, while the plaza measures almost 200 m in diameter. The ceremonial complex at Paso de la Amada is therefore far greater in scale than the Structure 1 and 2 terrace complex at San José Mogote, which measured approximately 18 m by 20 m and reached about 3 m in height (Flannery & Marcus 1994:367). By the Middle Formative the scale of monumental architecture at sites like La Venta on the Gulf coast and La Blanca on the Pacific coast of Guatemala exceeded the scale of public architecture even at Early Formative San Lorenzo (Grove 1999; Love 1999).

Although future discoveries may alter my view, I believe the balance of evidence does not suggest hereditary status distinctions or the presence of strong centralized leadership in the Valley of Oaxaca or the Mixteca Alta until after 700 BC. Archaeological evidence for social complexity in Oaxaca is much weaker than in regions like the Gulf coast and Mazatan. In fact, at Paso de la Amada, John Clark (2004:61) argues that the construction of the ceremonial center preceded the development of hereditary inequality and centralized leadership. Instead, Clark (2004:61) views the ceremonial center as a communal project directed and promoted by lineage leaders, which is essentially the scenario I envision for Oaxaca. The chiefdom model (e.g., Marcus & Flannery 1996, chapter 8) does not fit well with the evidence from Oaxaca. The evidence is more consistent with Hayden's (1995) model of transegalitarian societies, particularly the more complex examples that exhibit rising inequality without institutionalized hereditary status distinctions. These communities have many properties traditionally assumed to indicate hereditary inequality such as modest public architecture, social valuables accompanying some child burials, variation in the wealth and power of households and corporate groups, prestige items, interregional exchange of luxury goods, and religious legitimation of the position of prominent people.

Mixtec and Zapotec social structure at 700 BC

Until the end of the Middle Formative, the structural conditions of Mixtec and Zapotec society were largely egalitarian, constraining the ability of individuals and families to acquire wealth and prestige or to institutionalize status distinctions. There were opportunities, however, for individuals, households, and corporate groups to acquire modest advantages in wealth and prestige through craft production, long-distance exchange, ritual, personal beautification, and the expansion of social ties via marriage and the creation of debts and obligations through feasting and gift giving. Differences in wealth and status were most strongly correlated with age, with the most elaborate burial offerings associated with adult men and women. Status distinctions were re-inscribed in practices like the display of Olmec-style vessels or the construction of somewhat more elaborate houses distinguished by features such as whitewashed walls and drains. Rather than tightly integrated by structures of governance, whether centralized or corporate, social relations from 1150 to 700 BC were the outcome of social negotiations that left considerable autonomy for households and families. For example, I argue that, rather than an inherent property, the value of exotic items like iron-ore mirrors and greenstone was an outcome of ongoing competition to acquire and transform goods into social valuables that allowed people to establish important marriages and other alliances and to expand social obligations (see Appadurai 1986). People in Etla may have helped build the ceremonial center at San José Mogote, but there is no evidence that they were compelled by a strong centralized authority as suggested by Marcus and Flannery (1996:110). If people from other settlements participated in communal labor projects and rituals at San José Mogote, it is more likely to have been the product of cooperative social ties among households and corporate groups rather than coercion by a powerful ruler.

In addition to egalitarian principles that limited inequality, I argue that the dominant discourse also included a strong communal identity, particularly in relation to the divine, with public rituals held in ceremonial centers and cemeteries. The community produced by these ritual practices perhaps extended beyond individual settlements such as at San José Mogote where people from surrounding settlements may have participated in public ceremonies. Shared ceramic styles, the emulation of Olmec-style ceramic designs, and similarities in public architecture suggest broader cultural affiliations shared by Valley of Oaxaca communities. Differences in mortuary ritual, ornamentation, and crafting, however, suggest variation among communities in cultural principles and resources within the Valley of Oaxaca.

My view is that by 700 BC life in Mixtec and Zapotec communities was far more heterogenous than it had been at the beginning of the Early Formative. Social identities were increasingly differentiated by affiliations linked to crafting, long-distance contacts, wealth, and status. People were also forging community identities inscribed in public buildings and communal cemeteries. The evidence suggests that practices of affiliation such as large-scale construction projects and communal rituals were corporate endeavors and not under the direction of a centralized authority. These projects resulted from negotiations among households and corporate groups with relatively modest differences in wealth, power, and status. Some prominent people and households may have had more influence in communal decision-making, but the cultural ethos was linked to family and increasingly to community. Rising inequality coupled with an egalitarian ethos and strong community affiliations would in the long run generate structural contradictions and societal tensions between household, corporate group, and community. Through the remainder of the Formative period, the negotiation of these contradictions would increasingly affect Mixtec and Zapotec history.

five

From Village to City: The Founding and Early Development of Monte Albán

Beginning at c.700 BC people in Oaxaca and in many parts of Mesoamerica participated in a dramatic social transformation that included rising inequality as well as the emergence of hereditary status distinctions and centralized political authority. By the end of the Formative, the subjectivities of Mixtec and Zapotec peoples were defined not just by affiliations marked by age, gender, household, occupation, and community, but by one's relationship to powerful, hereditary rulers who were seen as mediators between people and the divine. Practices that emerged at this time increasingly associated nobles with the sacred realm and set them apart from common people. These practices included the production and use of material symbols of elite status and identity, including ceramic effigy vessels depicting deities, hieroglyphic writing, and elaborate ornamentation restricted to nobility. People communicated with the divine through ritual practices seen in Oaxaca for the first time, including human sacrifice and ballgame ceremonies. Nobility controlled both of these rituals, which were linked to another important trend: an increase in the significance of warfare. Daily lives changed dramatically as many people left the communities of their ancestors and moved to new, densely occupied cities that were centers of religion, political power, and commerce. The centerpiece of these early cities was their ceremonial precincts defined by monumental buildings and public plazas that were built as *axis mundi* or points of communication and mediation between humans and the divine. Monumental buildings, visible over great distances, were socially meaningful places that embodied the shared identities and histories of the emerging political formations of the Late/Terminal Formative. Even the identities of people in the countryside were tied to urban centers through ritual and political beliefs and practices that engaged people both physically and symbolically in a larger community embodied in the ceremonial center and its rulers. People also experienced changes in domestic and political economy as they had more children, increasingly relied on craft specialists, and were subjected to greater tribute demands.

Rather than the adaptive unfolding of new levels of political integration, as in traditional cultural evolutionary theory (Flannery 1972; Spencer 1990), I argue that social transformations at the end of the Formative resulted from tensions and negotiations between a traditional discourse that was more local, communal, and egalitarian and a newer more hierarchical, regional, and centralized one. The outcome was the emergence of powerful hereditary rulers, centralized political institutions, and cities from the more communal, egalitarian, and rural life of the earlier Formative. Rulers had greater power over political and religious institutions, long-distance exchange, and the mobilization of labor than their Middle Formative predecessors. Political authority, however, was not exclusionary or focused on the aggrandizement and power of individual rulers and ruling dynasties. Instead political authority was focused on rulers as part of a larger corporate body and the power of rulers was constrained by competing ideas and institutions. Although the overall pattern of rulership at this time may appear to be corporate, it was not necessarily the result of a structural unity as implied in Blanton's (1998) corporate-network model, but was instead an outcome of social negotiations between traditional communal authority and identity and the newer more restricted, exclusionary, and unequal forms of power. Ongoing tensions between exclusionary and communal forms of authority created political instability and led to the collapse of many of Oaxaca's first urban centers by the very end of the Formative.

The region where these social transformations can first be seen is the Valley of Oaxaca and their outcome resulted in the emergence of Monte Albán, Oaxaca's earliest and largest prehispanic city (figure 5.1). Monte Albán was a powerful hilltop city and ceremonial center that came to dominate political relations in the Valley of Oaxaca and perhaps several nearby regions. The rise of Monte Albán as an urban center was marked by major changes in social, political, and religious relations. Cities like Monte Albán are seats of political, religious, and economic power, although they vary in the degree to which each of these factors is prominent (Cowgill 2004; A. Joyce 2009b; A. Smith 2003; Michael Smith 2008). Ancient Oaxacan cities were primarily centers of political and religious authority that produced relations of dominance and dependence among the people of the urban center and their hinterlands. In Mesoamerica, indigenous terms that accord most closely with our notion of cities refer to the seats of power of ruling dynasties that extend beyond particular settlements to the broader territory claimed by the ruler (Gutiérrez 2003; Marcus

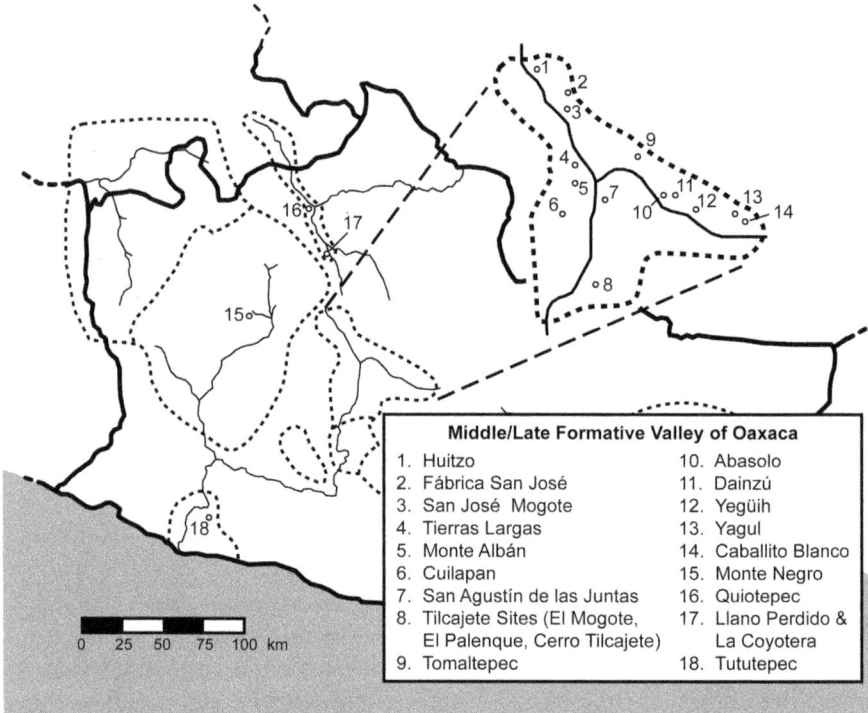

Figure 5.1 Archaeological sites of the later Formative (700 BC–AD 300) in the Valley of Oaxaca (drawing by Eric Berkemeyer)

1983c:226; Michael Smith 2000). City dwellers are differentiated from those in other communities according to practices; occupations; experiences; and the complexity of social relations, possibilities, and conflicts, especially as understood by notions of identity (Chase & Chase 2007; Cowgill 2004: 527; Janusek 2004:24; M. L. Smith 2003:24–8; Yaeger 2003). This chapter examines the origins and development of Monte Albán from 700 BC to AD 200. Chapter 6 will then consider the origins and early development of cities and centralized polities in the Mixtec highlands and in the lower Río Verde Valley.

The Late Middle Formative Political Crisis

The beginnings of this historical transformation in Oaxaca can be seen in events inferred from the Rosario-phase (700–500 BC) archaeological record of the Oaxaca Valley, especially at San José Mogote, the community that had been the largest and most influential in the region for the previous millennium (A. Joyce 2000). At this time, survey and excavation data indicate that the political landscape of the Valley of Oaxaca became increasingly competitive with warfare and changes in interregional relations threatening rulers. Despite the political crisis at San José Mogote, some of the community's leaders were able to gain greater control over sacred knowledge and authority leading to the establishment of hereditary status distinctions. The late Middle Formative therefore marks the first clear evidence for social complexity in the Valley of Oaxaca.

Political transformation and conflict at San José Mogote

Although population in the Valley of Oaxaca remained nearly constant from the San José phase (1150–850 BC) until the Rosario phase (700–500 BC), the evidence suggests that by 700 BC San José Mogote experienced a major demographic loss with the site decreasing from 70 ha to 34 ha (Kowaleski et al. 1989).[4] The Etla arm also seems to have lost some of its demographic advantage (Blanton et al. 1993:66). Despite the decline in population, excavation data show a great increase in the scale of monumental architecture, especially as represented by the site's ceremonial center at Mound 1 (figure 5.2).

Mound 1 was a natural hill architecturally modified into a huge platform whose summit towered 15 m above the rest of the community and faced a large open plaza (Marcus & Flannery 1996:126–9). Joyce Marcus and Kent Flannery (1996:126–34) and more recently Enrique Fernández (1997) carried out major excavations on Mound 1 so much of its sequence

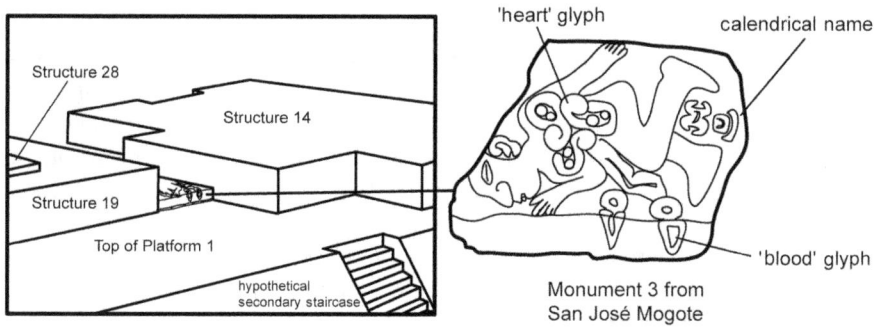

Figure 5.2 Idealized reconstruction of Rosario-phase buildings and Monument 3 on Mound 1 at San José Mogote (after Urcid 2005, figure 1.3; redrawn with permission from Javier Urcid)

of occupation is known, although its earliest building phases have not yet been exposed. During the Rosario phase the residents of San José Mogote built a series of substructures supporting public buildings on Mound 1. The best-studied substructure was Structure 19, which was built of large limestone blocks transported from a source 5 km to the west. Structure 19 was oriented 8° north of east and in its final form consisted of a platform measuring 22 m by 28 m that was approximately 2 m high. Structure 19 supported a wattle-and-daub public building (Structure 28) constructed on a lime-plastered adobe and earth-filled platform. Zapotecs buried an offering of a single large ceramic serving vessel beneath each corner of the platform, which might reference ritual feasting involved with the dedication of the building as well as the quadripartite division of the cosmos. Like earlier public buildings at San José Mogote, the floor of Structure 28 was recessed into the platform; a broken imitation of a stingray spine bloodletter made from a large obsidian blade was found on the temple's floor. Structure 14, another large substructure supporting public buildings, was constructed just north of Structure 19. Mound 1 also supported an unusual circular platform approximately 50 cm high, which Marcus and Flannery (1996:131) speculate was used for dance performances.

I argue that Mound 1 represents a further "scaling up" of public architecture and ritual performance, which engaged larger numbers of people in practices which defined the San José Mogote community and its broader polity. The evidence suggests that at the core of this corporate identity was the relationship between the community and the divine with sacrifice and perhaps feasting and dance as rituals through which people contacted the sacred.

A possible reason for the construction of Mound 1 involves status competition among communities in the Valley of Oaxaca. While San José Mogote was declining in size, political centers emerged in the other arms of the Valley (Kowalewski et al. 1989:72–7). El Mogote near the modern town of San Martín Tilcajete in the Valle Grande increased to 25 ha (Spencer & Redmond 2001:217), while settlement at Yegüih in the Tlacolula arm covered about 8 ha. Both El Mogote and Yegüih had possible Rosario-phase public buildings (Kowalewski et al. 1989:79). San José Mogote, El Mogote, and Yegüih were all surrounded by clusters of smaller communities perhaps tied to the center through ritual, political, kinship, and maybe economic relations. Evidence that the subregional centers were in conflict with one another includes a high frequency of burned daub at Rosario-phase sites, suggesting an increase in structures destroyed by fire, as well as a sparsely occupied buffer zone separating Etla from the rest of the valley (Kowalewski et al. 1989:70–5). Winter (2001:282), however, has discovered

Rosario-phase ceramics from deep deposits at two sites in the proposed buffer zone, causing him to question this interpretation. By c.300 BC evidence for conflict involving El Mogote is much clearer with the destruction and abandonment of the community's ceremonial center (Spencer & Redmond 2001:218–19). It is also possible that polities from outside the Oaxaca Valley, particularly in the nearby Nochixtlán Valley, became a threat (Blanton 1978:40).

Stronger evidence for warfare is found at San José Mogote (Flannery & Marcus 2003). At about 600 BC, the Structure 28 temple was burned to the ground, which Marcus and Flannery (1996:129) argue was the result of raiding. If correct, the most restricted and ritually important part of the site was penetrated by a raiding party who destroyed perhaps the most sacred building in the community. To the people of San José Mogote, the charred remnants of the temple would have been a stark demonstration of a profound political and religious crisis.

At about the same time as the destruction of Structure 28, a carved-stone monument depicting a sacrificial victim was placed in the corridor between Structures 14 and 19. Monument 3 has incredible political and religious significance because it represents the earliest evidence for human sacrifice, writing, and calendrics in Oaxaca (figure 5.2). Monument 3 depicts a naked man with eyes closed and with the trilobe heart glyph on his chest with blood emanating from the heart. In Mesoamerica most victims of human sacrifice were captives taken in warfare. The person on Monument 3 is identified by a glyph showing his name in the 260-day ritual calendar, suggesting high status. Elsewhere in Mesoamerica, the Middle Formative is also the first period with clear evidence for human sacrifice and hieroglyphic writing. There has been debate concerning the age of this carved stone (Cahn & Winter 1993), although recent radiocarbon dates indicate that it was set in place between 630 and 560 BC (Flannery & Marcus 2003). Overall, the evidence suggests that San José Mogote was increasingly under threat and losing both its demographic advantage and its political power relative to other communities in the Valley of Oaxaca (A. Joyce 2000).

It is likely that the changing fortunes of Oaxaca Valley polities were related to developments throughout Mesoamerica. The latter part of the Middle Formative from about 700 to 400 BC was a time of political upheaval that disrupted long-standing political relations and networks of interregional interaction. Many of the most important Middle Formative political centers declined in size and political power, including La Venta and San Lorenzo on the Gulf coast; Chalcatzingo, Teopantecuanitlán, and Tlatilco in the central-Mexican highlands (Grove 1987; Martínez Donjuán 1994; Tolstoy & Paradis 1970); and La Blanca on the Pacific coast (Love 1993:18). In the central depression of Chiapas, monumental construction at Chiapa de Corzo decreased for a time and other regional centers such as La Libertad were abandoned (Clark et al. 2000). Factors responsible for the decline of these Middle Formative centers are not clear, although conflict and the disruption of interaction networks are indicated.

At San José Mogote, people responded to this period of political crisis with radical changes in social relations probably initiated by one or more of the leading families within the community. Immediately following the destruction of Structure 28, archaeological evidence suggests major changes in the use of Mound 1 with the construction of a series of high-status residences built over the ruins of the temple (Flannery & Marcus 1983a). The best preserved of these residences consisted of parts of three adobe structures (Structures 25, 26, and 30) surrounding a patio. Structure 26 included a storage room that contained several large serving vessels perhaps for ritual feasting. Ritual objects associated with these residences included three fragments of obsidian lancet bloodletters (Parry 1987:126), and a ceramic anthropomorphic effigy brazier used to burn incense as a ritual offering (Marcus & Flannery 1996:131–3). The residences included the first formal stone-masonry tombs known from the Oaxaca Valley. Tomb 10, located beneath the patio, was a two-chambered tomb largely emptied at the very end of the Rosario phase, but which still contained a deposit of red ochre and 11 obsidian projectile points. The projectile points from Tomb 10 along with four others found in Rosario-phase contexts on Mound 1 constitute 63 percent of the projectile points recovered from Early and Middle Formative excavations in the Valley of Oaxaca, which supports arguments for increased conflict (Parry 1987:125). Two burials interred in simple graves were also discovered in Structure 26. Burial 55 was an adult buried beneath a wall at the time of the construction of the building. Flannery and Marcus (1983a:58) interpret Burial 55 as a possible sacrificial victim. Burial 60, an adult woman interred beneath the floor of Structure 26, exhibited cranial modification and was interred with three jade ornaments.

All of the Tomb 10 projectile points as well as two of the lancets from Mound 1 were manufactured from obsidian from the Pachuca source in the Basin of Mexico (Parry 1987:124–32). Pachuca is the only widely distributed source of green obsidian in Mesoamerica and so is easy to identify visually. The fact that Rosario-phase projectile points and lancets have been found almost exclusively on Mound 1 at San José Mogote suggests the establishment of exchange relations between high-status Zapotecs and people in central Mexico who were exploiting the Pachuca source.

Elsewhere at San José Mogote and at other sites in the valley, most residences continued to consist of small wattle-and-daub or adobe houses that exhibited only very modest differences in wealth and status. Social distinctions like gender and crafting as well as mortuary ritual exhibited patterns similar to those of the Guadalupe phase (Drennan 1976; Marcus & Flannery 1996:121–34; Whalen 1981). Zapotecs expanded the size of public buildings at Huitzo and Tomaltepec, suggesting an increase in the scale of communal projects. An intriguing discovery from both Huitzo and Tomaltepec were the first burials interred in the fill of public buildings in the Valley of Oaxaca (Flannery & Marcus 1983a:62; Whalen 1981:67), which may have been dedicatory interments, perhaps sacrificial victims.

Religion and politics on the eve of the founding of Monte Albán

Evidence from Mound 1 at San José Mogote indicates a major change in political discourse by the latter half of the Rosario phase, including the emergence of the first hereditary nobles in the Valley of Oaxaca. An important component of an emerging noble identity was the belief in their special ritual abilities that made them mediators between people and the sacred. The construction of high-status residences on Mound 1 transformed the structure from an area strictly for public ceremonial activities to an area combining public politico-religious buildings and elite residences in a distinct precinct. For the first time in Oaxaca a high-status residence was spatially and symbolically segregated from the rest of the community and incorporated into the ceremonial center. On a daily basis, people would have been constantly reminded of the sacred power of the ruling family as they viewed the inhabitants of Mound 1 from residential sectors of the site below. The linkage of noble status and divine authority would have been inscribed architecturally in Mound 1 by the close spatial association of the temples and the high-status residence. The residential complex consisting of Structures 25, 26, and 30 was larger and more elaborate architecturally than typical residences with at least three buildings surrounding a central patio. The association of high-status residences with the ceremonial precinct suggests that the authority of noble families and perhaps the corporate groups to which they belonged included the ability to mobilize labor for communal projects.

Although people used autosacrificial bloodletting to make offerings to the deities as early as the Early Formative, the innovation of human sacrifice represents a new and more spectacular ritual practice used to communicate with the divine. It is likely that the performance of human sacrifice was restricted to Rosario-phase nobles, given that evidence for this practice was associated only with public buildings and elite residences and that only nobles carried out the ritual in later periods (Boone 1984; Schele & Miller 1986). Nobles acted as intermediaries between people and the sacred realm with human sacrifice as a new ritual form probably linked to warfare. Elaborate obsidian bloodletters and the anthropomorphic brazier suggest the presence of luxury goods and ritual paraphernalia restricted to nobles.

The use of formal masonry tombs shows that prominent people were now buried in special locations that differentiated them from non-tomb interments. If a version of the sacred covenant was part of Middle Formative beliefs, then people interred in tombs would not have sacrificed their bodies at death in the same way as people buried in simple graves. We know from later times that ancestors buried in tombs were directly consulted by their living descendants through tomb reopening ceremonies. Tombs were reopened to add recently deceased persons to the tomb, to perform rituals in the presence of the ancestors, which sometimes included painting bones with red pigment, and to remove parts of the skeletons of ancestors for use as ritual heirlooms (Urcid 2005:34–40). Tombs suggest an increasing concern of household residents with their ancestors. Likewise, Marcus and Flannery (1996:131) argue that the anthropomorphic brazier recovered from Structure 26 may have been a precursor to later incense burners used in ceremonies designed to communicate with ancestors.

Another indication of changes in religious belief and practice during the late Rosario phase was a shift in the orientation of buildings constructed on Mound 1. After the burning of the temple, all of the structures built on Mound 1 were oriented 3 to 6° east of north, which represents a change from the 8° west of north orientation of earlier public buildings in Etla. By 500 BC, 3 to 6° east of north would become the dominant orientation of public buildings at Monte Albán (Peeler & Winter 1992). In prehispanic Mesoamerican worldviews, there was a close association between site orientations and layouts, the movement of celestial bodies/deities, and conceptions of time (Ashmore 1991; Sugiyama 1993).

Despite the emergence of hereditary nobles, it is likely that the construction of monumental buildings, the enactment of public ceremonies like human sacrifice, and the pursuit of warfare were probably still seen in communal terms. Given that hereditary inequality emerged out of a more communal and less hierarchical discourse, it is reasonable to assume that the power of nobles was dependent on their being seen as acting on the behalf of their communities. These early nobles undoubtedly had ritual and political obligations to their communities like Zapotec and Mixtec rulers at the time of the Spanish Conquest. It is likely that nobles earned the allegiance of commoners through the sponsoring of public ceremonies, including ritual feasting, as well as through success in warfare and perhaps the gifting of certain luxury goods. Nobles deployed human sacrifice as another way to maintain allegiance since it was the most potent way in which the sacred covenant could be activated to petition deities for fertility and prosperity on behalf of the community. Given the physical setting of Monument 3, the audience for these sacrifices was probably restricted, much like the setting of Middle Formative iconography dealing with human sacrifice in other parts of Mesoamerica (A. Joyce 2008b). By taking captives and offering them as sacrifices to the gods, nobles at San José Mogote demonstrated their ritual and political power as well as generosity to their communities. Human sacrifice was also a dramatic ritual performance in both its sacred and its violent qualities that would have bound people to the deities, ancestors, and other symbols of the community on whose behalf the sacrifice was realized.

Even if people saw nobles as acting on behalf of the community, the emergence of hereditary status distinctions created potential points of tension and conflict. I suspect that ritual and political decisions once made communally by prominent members of barrios or other corporate groups were increasingly influenced by hereditary rulers. Decisions surrounding warfare, important public rituals, and relations with leaders from other communities would have been complicated by these emerging status distinctions. While the causes of the demographic decline of San José Mogote are not clear, it is possible that resistance to the novel political relations of the Rosario phase led some people to "vote with their feet" and join relatives in other communities or establish new ones. Warfare and the destruction of the temple on Mound 1 would have been a crisis for the entire community that may have led people to leave San José Mogote. Greater labor demands for warfare and the construction of public buildings might also have created dissatisfaction for commoners. Further research is needed to tease apart the implications of social developments at Rosario-phase San José Mogote. Research on new communities established at this time perhaps by emigrants from San José Mogote might also identify social, political, or religious differences that reflect resistance to or distancing from the new religious and political discourse.

Though innovations in religion and politics are evident for the latter half of the Rosario phase at San José Mogote, these cultural changes did not result in the return of the community to political preeminence in the Valley of Oaxaca. Whether due to internal resistance, external conflict, or other factors, the demographic and political decline of San José Mogote continued during the Danibaan phase (500–300 BC). At about 500 BC, monumental construction activities on Mound 1 ceased and the site may have declined still further in size (Kowalewski et al. 1989:89–91). Other Rosario-phase sites in Etla such as Fábrica San José and Tierras Largas also declined in size or were completely abandoned. Many people who left the former San José Mogote polity participated in the founding of a new political and religious center at Monte Albán at c.500 BC. As discussed in the next section, from its very beginning, Monte Albán exemplified the historical transformation that began in Rosario-phase San José Mogote.

The Founding of Monte Albán

Monte Albán was founded about 500 BC in the midst of the political crisis at San José Mogote. The site is located on several unoccupied hilltops that rise over 300 m above the valley floor. Monte Albán is an ideal location for political and military control since it is located in the center of the valley where the three arms meet. The view from the ancient city stretches out for dozens of kilometers and, as in the ancient past, it is possible to look down upon surrounding communities and view people moving on the plain below. Today in the cool breeze of the hilltop center, one can view rainstorms moving across the valley and hear the explosion of fireworks from celebrations or funerals. Important landmarks like roads, churches, and town squares are clearly visible from the heights of Monte Albán. From the valley floor below, the impressive platforms and temples of the Main Plaza – the site's civic ceremonial center – are clearly visible for many kilometers, silhouetted against the blue sky of the valley. One can also make out the faint traces of the thousands of terraces that supported the houses of common people and once covered the slopes of the hills.

Similarities in architecture, iconography, and mortuary practices between San José Mogote and Monte Albán indicate that people from the former site founded the latter (Flannery & Marcus 1983b). The founding and early development of Monte Albán represents a dramatic transformation in social and political relations in the Oaxaca Valley. By 300 BC, 200 years after its founding, Monte Albán far exceeded any other site in the valley in size, population, and scale of monumental architecture. During the Late Formative Pe phase (300–100 BC) the city grew to cover 442 ha with an estimated population of 10,200 to 20,400 (Blanton 1978:44), and the population of the valley as a whole increased an estimated 27-fold (Kowalewski et al. 1989:123–6). The first several centuries following the founding of Monte Albán were characterized by warfare, changes in settlement patterns and social organization, and innovations in religion, ideology, and economy. Like other early urban centers such as Cahokia and Uruk, Monte Albán was not founded gradually, but was instead the result of a "big bang" that dramatically transformed history (Pauketat 2009).

Explaining Monte Albán

Most archaeologists focus on warfare among the Oaxaca Valley's Middle Formative communities as the principal cause for the founding of Monte Albán (e.g., Marcus & Flannery 1996:139–54; Spencer 2003; Winter 2006). Indeed the evidence for warfare during the several hundred years before and after the founding of Monte Albán suggests that defensive concerns were one reason for establishing the site. Its location on a series of hills in the center of the Oaxaca Valley made it a natural fortress. Graphic depictions of sacrificial victims, probably war captives, on carved-stone monuments as well as evidence for the military conquest of other communities in the Oaxaca Valley indicate that the people of the hilltop center periodically waged war with their neighbors. During the late Pe phase (300–100 BC) or early Nisa phase (100 BC–AD 200), the inhabitants built a defensive wall around portions of the community (Blanton 1978:52–4).

Despite the evidence for warfare, I believe that defensive concerns alone cannot explain the dramatic social transformation that occurred with the founding and early development of Monte Albán (A. Joyce 2000, 2004:198–204). Most researchers who view warfare as the key factor explaining the founding of Monte Albán argue that rulers strategically initiated the resettlement due to external military threats (e.g., Balkansky 1998b:460–1; Marcus & Flannery 1996:139–54; Winter 2006). For example, Marcus and Flannery (1996:140–3) argue that Monte Albán was founded as a result of a more general process termed synoikism whereby several villages come together to form a city in the face of an overwhelming external threat. These models, however, do not adequately consider the social and economic implications of moving to the unoccupied hilltop. The synoikism model views the founding of Monte Albán as a total societal response with elites as decision-makers and organizers, but there is little concern with the ways in which people of varying identities may have differentially participated in and been affected by the move and the resulting social transformation.

Explanations for the founding and early development of Monte Albán must consider why people other than nobility would have left their traditional homes to relocate to the barren hills of Monte Albán. The move meant people were uprooted from their communities, homes, and agricultural fields. People left the places where they had grown up, had families, and where their ancestors had lived and were buried. It is important not to minimize the personal significance that such a move potentially had for the founders of Monte Albán. Gaining an advantage in warfare may have provided an economic and political advantage to rulers, but it is difficult to construct a plausible argument for the economic advantages of moving to Monte Albán for common people. Though additional research on the nature and scale of prehispanic warfare is needed, the evidence suggests that Formative-period warfare most often involved raiding focused on ceremonial centers like Mound 1 at San José Mogote, rather than large-scale engagements that threatened entire communities (Workinger & Joyce n.d.). The establishment of Monte Albán probably had a negative effect on the economic circumstances of many people because of increased tribute demands and because living on the infertile slopes of Monte Albán required people to travel a greater distance to work their agricultural fields and obtain water. It is unlikely that at 500 BC rulers had the military might to force thousands of people to move to the hilltop center. Instead, there must have been some inducement to relocate beyond narrow economic interests or blind obedience to rulers.

The evidence suggests that the political crisis facing the people of the San José Mogote polity created several factors that motivated the move to Monte Albán. These factors include:

1 a disruption in long-distance trade and interaction that threatened the ability of San José Mogote's leading families to maintain alliances with high-status families in other parts of the valley and to maintain support from members of their own community;
2 warfare that threatened the ceremonial center of the community. I do not believe that conflict created economic hardships for most people or that casualties were very great. Instead warfare was as much a spiritual as a physical danger since the destruction of the temple on Mound 1 threatened the ability of people to contact the divine and further diminished the power and prestige of the community and its leaders;
3 the development of a religious movement that involved innovations in ritual ideas and practices through which people contacted deities and ancestors, with rulers gaining power as mediators between people and the divine. Because of the interconnectedness between religion and politics these ritual innovations also had political implications;
4 social tension and conflict surrounding the emergence of hereditary status distinctions.

Although some commoners embraced the new religious and political ideas, institutions, and practices of the time, the demographic decline of San José Mogote suggests that other people rejected these innovations and either left the community prior to the founding of Monte Albán or refused to relocate to the hilltop center. The problem therefore wasn't simply defense, but was responding to the more general social disruptions and insecurities of the period. The political crisis was important in motivating the decision to relocate to Monte Albán, but the evidence strongly indicates that Monte Albán was founded by a new religious movement that engaged a broad spectrum of people who set out to build a ceremonial center on the sacred hilltop.

Therefore, in addition to defense, Monte Albán was founded as a ceremonial center. Both leaders and common people traveled to the barren hilltop and began constructing the ceremonial center in order to communicate with the sacred realm in new and more powerful ways. One of the earliest activities at the site was to construct the Main Plaza ceremonial precinct, which was an unprecedented labor project. Even during its first few centuries, the scale of the Main Plaza and its monumental architecture far exceeded earlier ceremonial spaces in the Valley of Oaxaca, indicating that performances of politico-religious ceremonies were important in the founding and early history of the site. Understanding and dealing with political problems through ritual is consistent with the cultural logic of Mesoamerican peoples, both past and present (Freidel et al. 1993; Monaghan 1994). The construction of the Main Plaza precinct involved a program of place-making that materialized the founding community and its innovative political and religious ideas, institutions, and practices.

Place-making, monumentality, and the Main Plaza

The ceremonial core of Monte Albán was the Main Plaza, a huge public plaza measuring roughly 300 m north–south by 150 m east–west (figure 5.3). In its final form the Main Plaza was bounded on its north and south ends by high platforms supporting numerous public buildings. The North Platform was the largest single structure at the site measuring roughly 230 m by 200 m. A huge central stairway leads up to the top of the platform, which rises approximately 10 m above the plaza and supports the remains of a huge sunken patio as well as numerous temples and elite residences. The South Platform is also massive, measuring about 130 m on a side and supporting two large substructures separated by a patio with an altar in the center. Running along the northern edge of the top of the South Platform is a defensive wall built during the Postclassic period, which postdates the time when Monte Albán was a city. The eastern and western sides of the Main Plaza were defined by rows of monumental buildings, including a ballcourt in the northeastern corner of the plaza, a large palace

Figure 5.3 Photo of the Main Plaza at Monte Albán, looking south. The North Platform is in the foreground and the South Platform in the background (photograph by Arthur A. Joyce)

complex on the southeastern end, and a platform displaying a gallery of sacrificial victims in the southwestern corner. A third row of structures ran north to south through the center of the plaza and included temple platforms; the southernmost platform is an unusual pointed structure that contained carved images of places conquered by Monte Albán. The monumental buildings around the plaza were faced with stone masonry and would have been covered with white plaster making them stand out against the blue of the sky above. Below the Main Plaza are the remains of more than 2,000 terraces that supported the houses of most of the inhabitants of the site (Blanton 1978:30). Other architectural features discovered on the hill slopes of Monte Albán include roads, defensive walls, and reservoirs. Monte Albán is a spectacular archaeological site, although the structures visible to the visitor today are the result of more than 2,500 years of human activity. When the founders first arrived at Monte Albán it was an unoccupied hilltop, which they soon began to convert into a ceremonial center and home.

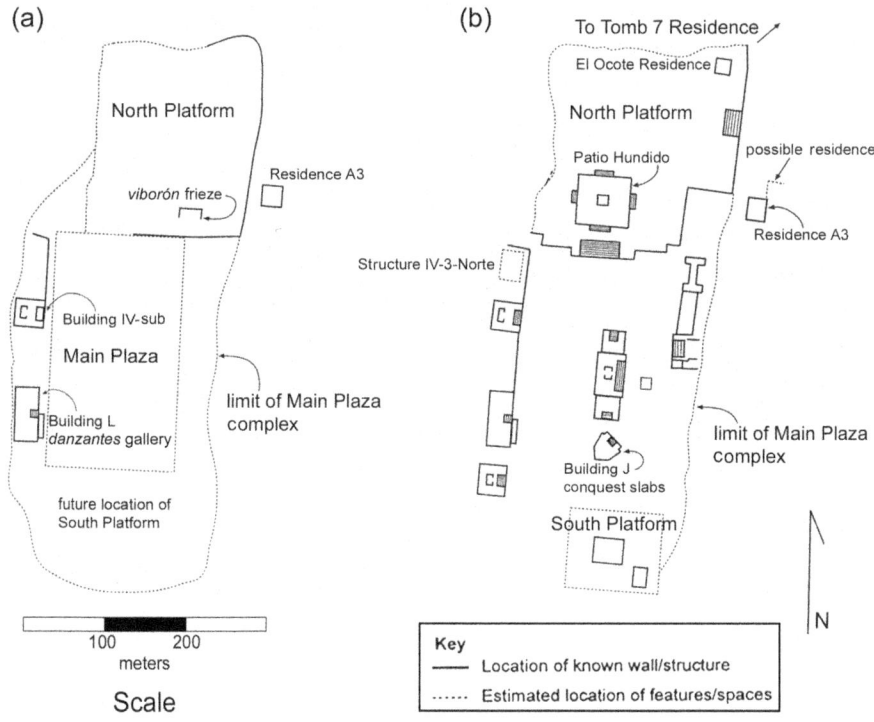

Figure 5.4 The Main Plaza at Monte Albán: (a) Danibaan and Pe phases (500–100 BC); (b) Nisa phase (100 BC–AD 200) (after Barber & Joyce 2006, figures 8.2 and 8.3; reproduced with permission of the University of Texas Press)

The initial version of the Main Plaza, dating to the Danibaan and Pe phases (500–100 BC), consisted of the plaza, along with the western row of buildings and much of the eastern half of the massive North Platform (Winter 2001:284–6; figure 5.4a). Although it is not clear if the plaza was covered with a plaster floor at this time, the evidence shows that it was created by leveling bedrock outcrops and filling in areas to create a flat surface, which would have required considerable labor (Marcus Winter, personal communication 2009). Public buildings constructed during Monte Albán's first few centuries included Building L-sub along the southwestern end of the plaza, whose walls consisted of huge monoliths, many of which displayed carved imagery (Caso 1935; Flannery & Marcus 1983c:89–90; Marcus 1976; J. F. Scott 1978a, 1978b; Urcid 2008). Building IV-sub along the northwestern end of the plaza was a massive platform that included a 6-m-high sloping wall. The Late Formative version of the North Platform consisted of a huge architectural complex that encompassed much of the eastern half of the platform's final area and included structures that reached heights of 15 m above the Main Plaza. On top of the North Platform excavations recovered the remains of a possible Danibaan-phase temple that included an offering of dozens of fancy gray-ware serving vessels (Winter 2004b:37) that may reference ritual feasting associated with building-dedication ceremonies. The southeastern corner of the North Platform's retaining wall included a semi-circular architectural projection of unknown use, but which resembled the Rosario-phase feature from Mound 1 at San José Mogote. Immediately south of this column was a low platform that was probably an area for public ceremonies, though perhaps more restricted than those on the Main Plaza. Platforms facing the Main Plaza were constructed of rubble fill and the stone used in structures was mostly quarried locally from the hills around Monte Albán (Winter 1989a:42–3).

The labor invested in constructing the Main Plaza leaves little doubt that religious belief and practice were important to the early occupants of the site. As I have argued previously (A. Joyce 2000, 2004), the symbolism and spatial arrangement of architecture and iconography suggest that the Main Plaza symbolized the Zapotec version of the cosmos where rituals could be performed, reenacting and commemorating the cosmic creation. Directional symbolism, so important to Mesoamerican conceptions of the cosmos, was present from the founding of the site. The builders of the city oriented the structures on the Main Plaza to the cardinal directions as they did temples and residences throughout the site. The sacred properties of many buildings on the plaza were activated with offerings, including human burials. Since Monte Albán's Main Plaza was built on the top of an imposing mountain, it is likely that Zapotecs considered the entire ceremonial precinct as a sacred mountain of creation and sustenance (Schele & Guernsey-Kappelman 2001). By the Pe phase (300–100 BC) the plaza resembled ceremonial centers at other Mesoamerican cities where the cosmos was rotated onto the surface of the site such that north represented the celestial realm and south the earth or underworld (A. Joyce 2000:81–4).

The southern end of the Main Plaza contains iconographic references to sacrifice, warfare, and underworld. Building L-sub was the location of a gallery of nearly 400 carved-stone monuments known as the *danzantes* (J. F. Scott 1978a), which is the single largest corpus of carved stones for Late Formative Mesoamerica and constitutes roughly 80 percent of the total monument record from Monte Albán (figure 5.5).

The only monuments found *in situ* were in Building L-sub, although most were removed from their original location leaving open the possibility that some may have initially been located in other buildings as well. The *in situ*

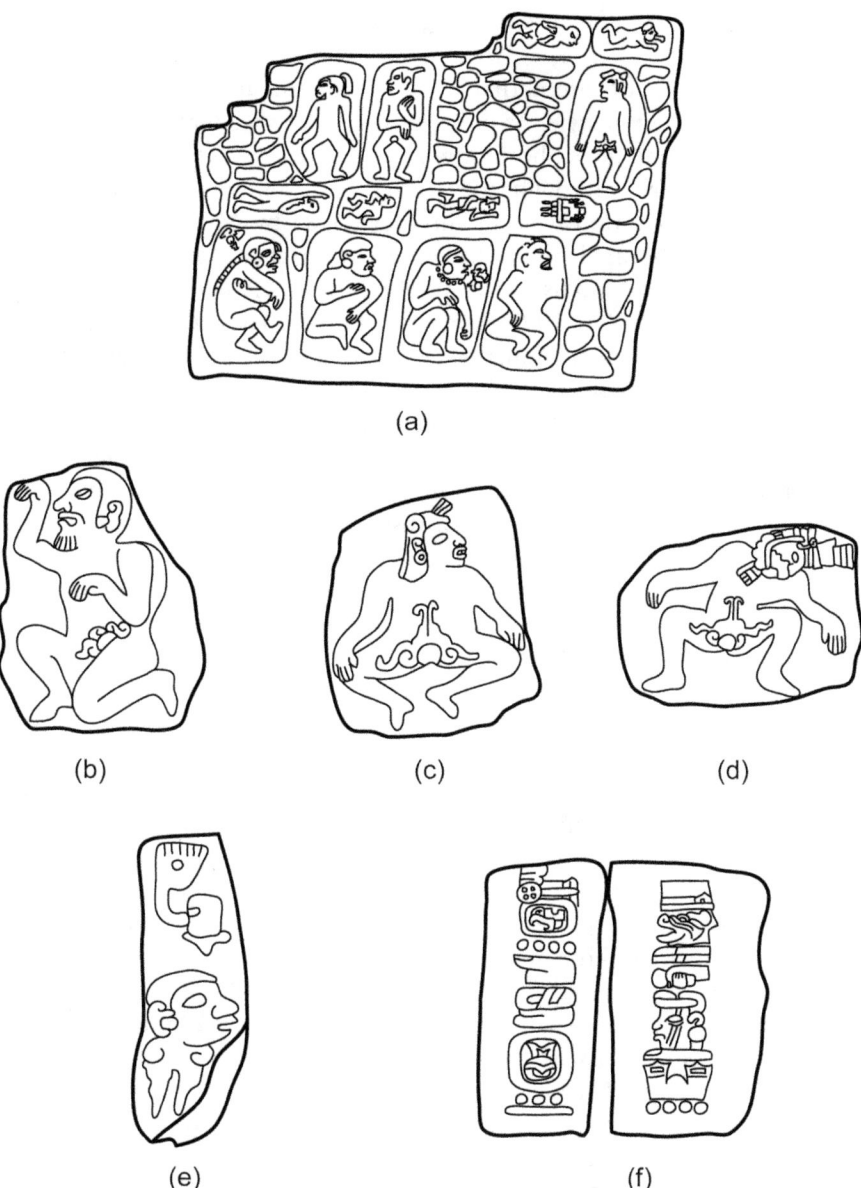

Figure 5.5 Carved-stone monuments from Building L-sub: (a) *in situ* monuments (after Winter 1989a:53); (b) elder from the upper rank (redrawn with permission from Javier Urcid); (c) young adult from the first rank in the lower row of Building L-sub (redrawn with permission from Javier Urcid); (d) rain-god impersonator (redrawn with permission from Javier Urcid); (e) decapitation (redrawn with permission from Javier Urcid); (f) monuments D-139 and D-140 with hieroglyphic inscriptions (redrawn with permission from Javier Urcid)

monuments consist of alternating rows of horizontal and vertical stones that differ somewhat in style. At present, there are two interpretations of the Building L-sub monuments, both of which relate the sculptures to sacrificial rituals and warfare, although they differ in several important regards.

The first interpretation was initially developed by Michael Coe (1962) and has been elaborated on by numerous researchers, particularly Joyce Marcus (Flannery & Marcus 1983c:89–90; Marcus 1976, 1992:391–4; also see A. Joyce 2000:81; Orr 1997; J. F. Scott 1978a). These researchers argue that the Building L-sub monuments depict victims of human sacrifice often shown in contorted poses with closed eyes and sometimes accompanied by hieroglyphic inscriptions. The personages are naked except for elaborate headdresses and sometimes adornments like necklaces and earplugs; many have prominent scrolls over their lower stomachs or genitals, which can be interpreted as genital mutilation or disembowelment. Genital mutilation suggests a combination of earlier forms of autosacrifice with death sacrifice. In four cases, a severed head is shown with blood emanating from the neck. Nudity in Mesoamerica was usually shown in the context of humiliated war captives, often destined for sacrifice. Sacrificial victims went to the underworld at death. Several carved stones included only brief hieroglyphic texts without the personages.

Recently, Urcid (2008) presented a compelling argument that the Building L-sub monuments include several related sculptural programs dating from the Danibaan phase to the Nisa phase. Using pan-Mesoamerican contextual comparisons, Urcid (2008) argues that the figures carved on vertical stones represent men in the act of bloodletting by perforating their penises, with genital scrolls interpreted as blood. He interprets the horizontal figures as ancestors contacted through the act of autosacrifice. Acts of human sacrifice are represented by the four depictions of decapitated heads.

In a more speculative vein, Urcid (2008) views the sculptural program as a pictorial narrative with both historical and mythical elements much like the later codices. Through identification of a number of different types of figures, he suggests that the stones were arranged so as to display a four-tiered ranking system based on age and acquired status with higher-status individuals displayed on the walls of the superstructures and lower-status ones on the face of the platform below. He views these personages as members of a warrior sodality with the higher-status positions including elders and people depicted as rain-god impersonators. Based on ethnohistoric and epigraphic evidence, Urcid (2008) argues that Zapotecs used autosacrifice to invoke the ancestors as oracular conduits to prognosticate the outcome of battles. Subsequent programs dated to the Pe and Nisa phases appear to replicate these general themes on a smaller scale.

A question raised by Urcid's (2008) reconstruction of a relatively large council of elders, warriors, and religious specialists is: where were the hereditary rulers of the community? He answers this question through an analysis of the hieroglyphic inscriptions on the carved stones. Though incomplete, the inscriptions on the early monuments refer to at least three rulers, their enthronements, genealogical statements, and the defeat and decapitation of an enemy. Both interpretations therefore stress sacrifice and warfare. Urcid's model has the advantage of explaining the variability and complexity of the corpus, but is admittedly hypothetical in its reconstruction of the layout of the sculptural program and its social significance.

Themes of warfare, sacrifice, the underworld, and the sacred covenant are found in another program of carved-stone monuments located in the southern end of the Main Plaza (Urcid 1994b). During the Pe phase or the early Nisa phase, approximately 50 carved-stone slabs were set in a monumental building. The original location of this program is not certain, but during the Nisa phase the inhabitants of Monte Albán reset the slabs in the walls of Building J, an unusual arrowhead-shaped building whose orientation differs from other structures on the Main Plaza. These monuments, known as the "conquest slabs," have been interpreted as places conquered by Monte Albán (Caso 1938, 1947; Marcus 1983d, 1992:394–400; figure 5.6b).

The slabs depict the terrestrial "hill" or place glyph with another glyph directly above it signifying the name of a particular place (e.g., the temple place illustrated on Monument J-38; figure 5.6b). Most of the slabs depict a human head, interpreted as the decapitated head of a ruler, extending down beneath the terrestrial hill glyph with vegetation sprouting from the top of the hill sign. The association of sacrifice, warfare, and fertility is indicated. Some of the slabs also include short hieroglyphic inscriptions, including calendrical dates, which probably record historical information related to the conquered places. Since the Zapotec hill glyph may have been derived from the depiction of caves as sectioned quatrefoils, as seen at Middle Formative Chalcatzingo (Grove 2000:283), the conquest slabs may also reference the descent of sacrificial victims into the underworld via a cave portal.

In contrast to the southern end of the Main Plaza, the North Platform included iconographic references to sky, rain, and lightning. The earliest celestial reference is found with the Late Formative stucco frieze known as the *viborón* or serpent located beneath the southeast corner of the North Platform (Orr 1997). Though incomplete, the frieze includes a sky band with scrolls representing clouds or perhaps shells, also a water-related symbol (figure 5.6a). Scrolls face one another to form serpentine figures

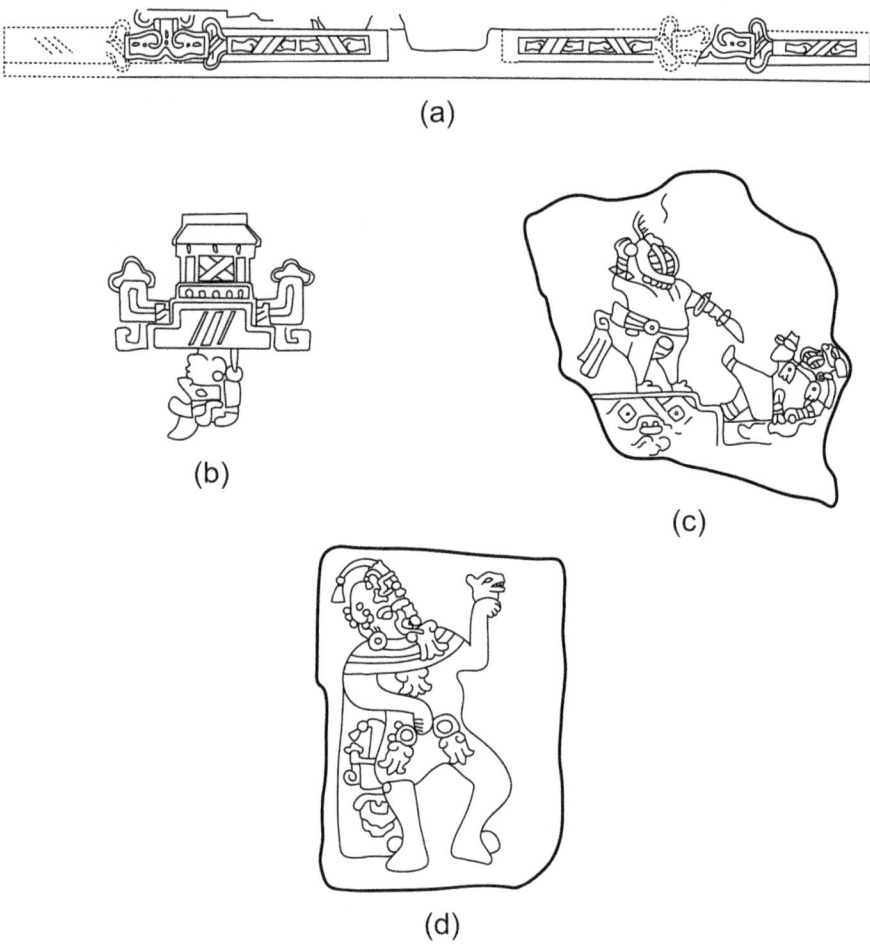

Figure 5.6 Late/Terminal Formative monumental art from the Valley of Oaxaca: (a) *viborón* frieze from the North Platform at Monte Albán (after Urcid 1994a, figure 7; reproduced with permission from the Instituto Nacional de Antropología e Historia); (b) Building J "conquest slab" from Monte Albán (after Caso 1947, figure 41; reproduced with permission from the Instituto Nacional de Antropología e Historia); (c) Dainzú ballplayers (after Orr 1997, figure 2.26); (d) Monte Albán Monument J-41 (redrawn with permission from Javier Urcid)

resembling Cocijo, the Zapotec rain/lightening deity, with rain symbols issuing from the figure's mouth. The frieze covers the sides of what may have been a sunken court. Ancient Mesoamerican peoples considered sunken or enclosed plazas and ballcourts to be interfaces with the divine (Freidel et al. 1993:350–5).

The Zapotec view of the cosmos was therefore materially inscribed on the art and architecture of the Main Plaza with references to sacrifice, warfare, and the underworld to the south and the celestial realm to the north. If I am correct in my interpretation of the Main Plaza, then rituals like human sacrifice and ancestor veneration, which invoked the cosmic creation, were performed amid a material symbol of the Zapotec cosmos. The scale, accessibility, openness, and symbolism of the Main Plaza indicate that it was constructed as an arena where thousands of people could have participated in public rituals. Until the Nisa phase, the Main Plaza was open on its eastern side, making activities on the plaza accessible to commoners living on the terraces below. Crowds could have entered the plaza from the east, moving from the everyday world of their homes below into a sacred space materializing symbolic references to the sacred past of ancestors, deities, and the cosmic creation. Ceremonies included a blending of traditional activities such as autosacrificial bloodletting, ancestor veneration, divination, and ritual feasting with new practices like human sacrifice (Blanton et al. 1999:105–7; A. Joyce 2000, 2004; Orr 1997, 2001; Urcid 2008). The images on the Building L-sub and Building J programs could be viewed as processions moved past and would have continually communicated the significance of sacrifice and warfare. Sacrificial practices, especially human sacrifice, were particularly significant in contacting deities and ancestors, reenacting the cosmic creation and the sacred covenant, and renewing the world (A. Joyce 2000; Monaghan 1990). Human sacrifice now linked the activation of the sacred covenant to warfare. Enemies would have been redefined not just as competitors, but also in sacred terms as potential sacrificial victims.

Ballgame rituals played a part in this newly configured warfare and human-sacrifice-based covenant, and it is during the Late/Terminal Formative that the earliest ballcourts are found at Monte Albán (Kowalewski et al. 1991). A program of carved-stone monuments at the site of Dainzú explicitly depicts the association of the ballgame with warfare and human sacrifice (Orr 1997, 2001). New religious cults are also indicted by the first occurrence of effigy vessels depicting deities like Cocijo, the Old God, and the wide-billed bird deity (figure 5.7a). Rain-god imagery, sacrifice, and the preponderance of effigy vessels in the form of water-related animals probably reflect the development of a Cocijo cult that linked sacrifice, fertility, and the rain god.

The symbolism and many of the rituals that defined the ceremonial center were new to the Valley of Oaxaca, although evidence suggests that the founders of Monte Albán drew on established ideas from other parts of Mesoamerica (J. E. Clark 2001; A. Joyce 2004:201–2; Winter 2006: 229–31). Although centers such as La Venta, Chalcatzingo, and Chiapa

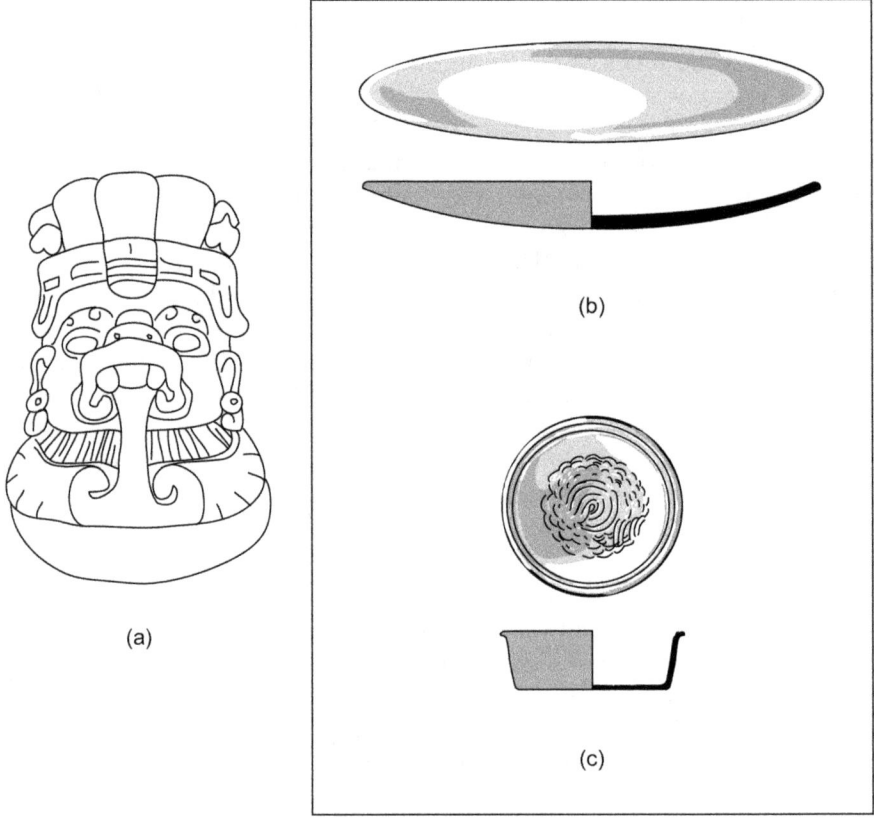

Figure 5.7 Late/Terminal Formative-period ceramics from the Valley of Oaxaca: (a) *cocijo* urn (redrawn from Joralemon 1971, figure 179; redrawn courtesy of Dumbarton Oaks Research Library and Collection, Trustees for Harvard University, Washington, DC); (b) *comal* (redrawn from Caso et al. 1967, figure 178; reproduced with permission from the Instituto Nacional de Antropología e Historia); (c) G-12 combed-base bowl (redrawn from Caso et al. 1967, figure 130b; reproduced with permission from the Instituto Nacional de Antropología e Historia)

de Corzo were in decline at this time, ideas and practices that defined relations between people and the divine were carried forward in altered form by the Zapotecs of Monte Albán. Similarities in spatial organization and symbolism suggest that Zapotecs appropriated ideas about sacred space from those earlier centers (J. E. Clark 2001). For example, Chalcatzingo like Monte Albán is aligned along a north–south axis with references to rulers/ancestors to the north and themes of sacrifice and fertility to the south (Grove 1999). Monte Albán also resembled La Venta and Chiapa de Corzo in having large plazas demarcated by a pyramid or tall platform to the north and lower linear mounds on at least one side (J. E. Clark 2001). Ballcourts and the ballgame are found in other parts of Mesoamerica long before they appear in Oaxaca. Zapotec hieroglyphic writing and rain-god imagery show similarities with Olmec examples from the Gulf coast (Covarrubias 1946; Urcid 2002). Like the Zapotecs at Monte Albán, the Olmec depicted rain-god impersonators associated with high status and sacrifice (Coe 1972). Rain and cloud symbols found at Monte Albán occur in earlier iconography at Chalcatzingo and among the Olmec (Sellen 2002: 11; Taube 1996:97).

The evidence suggests that the construction of the Main Plaza was an exercise in place-making that materialized a new corporate identity in the Valley of Oaxaca centered on Monte Albán. This identity was embodied in new deities and rituals, including warfare-dependant human sacrifice. Though most of these symbols and practices first occur in the Valley of Oaxaca at San José Mogote during the late Rosario phase, they were foregrounded in the initial construction of the new ceremonial center at Monte Albán. Since novel deities and rituals characterized later millennial movements in Mesoamerica (Gruzinski 1989; Monaghan 1994; Ringle et al. 1998), it is possible that Monte Albán was founded by adherents of a new social and religious movement in reaction to the political crisis of the late Middle Formative. The choice of an unoccupied hilltop in the middle of the valley had the effect of distancing Monte Albán from traditional centers of settlement and politico-religious power, making the site a more effective symbol for new social formations. The hereditary nobility was a component of the new collectivity centered on Monte Albán, although evidence indicates that contradictions and tensions between more traditional corporate identities and forms of authority and hereditary rulers was part of the social dynamics of the early years of Monte Albán.

Negotiating status and authority

As exemplified by Urcid's (2008) model of the Building L-sub program, Late/Terminal Formative-period Monte Albán was characterized by both communal forms of authority and hereditary rulers. Although hereditary nobles are increasingly evident in the archaeological record, representations of rulers are muted in public expressions of political and religious authority. The authority of the nobility may have been simultaneously couched in, but in dynamic tension with, traditional forms of authority that were more communal, egalitarian, and locally based. Residential and mortuary data, however, indicate increasing social differentiation in the Oaxaca Valley during the Late/Terminal Formative (Barber & Joyce 2006:223–9; Martínez López et al. 1995:236–38; Winter 1986:341–2).

Although there was a trend away from building houses of wattle and daub and toward more substantial structures with stone foundations and mud-brick walls, low-status residences continued to include features like bell-shaped storage pits, ovens, and human burials (Whalen 1981; Winter 1974). Household rituals continued to be dominated by small, modeled figurines similar to those of earlier periods (Martínez López & Winter 1994), suggesting that the domestic rituals of common people had not changed significantly with the founding of Monte Albán. By the Nisa phase, zoomorphic figurines in the form of frogs are common and perhaps related to rituals involving water and rain. At Monte Albán, commoners lived in houses on terraces built on the slopes leading up to the Main Plaza (Blanton 1978). The identity of people living on the terraces at Monte Albán may have been defined in part by the fact that they looked down upon their counterparts on the valley floor below, while looking up at the sacred precinct and elite residences that loomed above.

During the Late/Terminal Formative, high-status people at Monte Albán tended to live in areas around the North Platform (Barber & Joyce 2006:223–9; A. Joyce 2000). High-status residences were larger and more elaborate architecturally than typical houses. The northern part of the Main Plaza precinct therefore was an elite ceremonial precinct that was spatially segregated from the rest of the community and symbolically linked nobles and noble ancestors to the celestial realm. The earliest excavated high-status residence (Structure A3A) was built east of the North Platform in an area with several huge terraces with platforms supporting residences. The A3A residence consisted of several foundation walls surrounding a stuccoed patio; the eastern wall had remnants of red paint. The most elaborate Late Formative tomb (Tomb 204) yet found at Monte Albán was discovered beneath the patio and included a chamber and antechamber; the tomb was largely cleaned out in antiquity, although 15 Pe-phase vessels remained.

Mortuary practices were highly variable, but also reflected increasing social differentiation with continuities in wealth and status (Caso et al. 1967; Flannery & Marcus 1983c:90–1; Martínez López 1998; Winter 1995). Most interments were associated with residences and included simple graves, *fosas* (graves lined with stones or adobes), cists (sepulchers that are smaller and less formal than tombs), adobe tombs, and stone-masonry tombs. There is a general correlation between the wealth of burial offerings and the elaboration of the grave, but with considerable variability. Burials in simple graves, *fosas*, and cists typically were without offerings or contained a few ceramic vessels and sometimes ground-stone tools, obsidian blades, and adornments of shell, bone, or greenstone. The most elaborate burial from the early years of the site is Burial VI-12 with an offering of 29 vessels and onyx drill cores, perhaps a specialist involved in the production of onyx ornaments. An early Pe-phase burial in a stone and adobe *fosa* contained two adults and two children accompanied by 14 ceramic vessels, 40 worked shell adornments, and 5 pieces of worked bone, including 3 needles, the needles suggesting an association with textile production (Winter et al. 1995:60–72). In contrast, some tombs could have very modest offerings such as adobe Tomb 174 with only four vessels. Stone-masonry tombs with rich offerings were likely interments of nobles and in some cases rulers such as Tomb 43, which included 72 ceramic vessels, and Tomb 111 with 51 vessels. The large number of ceramic vessels in these tombs suggests that the deceased had broad social networks in life.

Although stone-masonry tombs are associated with architecturally elaborate houses, other burial types do not seem to correlate with residential architecture. Several adobe tombs excavated by Winter (1974) were from typical houses located about 1 km northwest of the Main Plaza. Tombs often contained multiple individuals, which may represent successive interments of household heads as in later periods (Urcid 2005:36–43). Children appear to have been interred in less elaborate graves than adults, although Tomb 33, associated with a residence north of the North Platform, contained a girl approximately 10 years old accompanied by at least 34 objects, mostly ceramic vessels.

If the number of vessels interred as burial offerings is related to a person's commensal networks and perhaps to the number of people participating in the mortuary ceremony, then both nobles and influential commoners had extensive social ties. Effigy vessels and urns, sometimes depicting Cocijo, and a variety of zoomorphic vessels usually representing animals associated with water including ducks, conch shells, frogs, and toads are much more common in tombs and burials with elaborate offerings. These data suggest that associations with rain and the rain god were related to status, both achieved and ascribed by birth. Recent iconographic interpretations suggest that specialized ritual abilities may have been the prerogative not just of nobles, but also of high-ranking commoners who achieved positions of ritual authority (Urcid 2008; Urcid & Winter 2003).

The political and religious authority of the nobility is therefore increasingly evident in the residential and mortuary data of the Late/Terminal Formative. An increasing association between elite residences and religious symbols and artifacts during the early years of Monte Albán indicates that nobles gained greater control of politico-religious ideas, practices, and institutions (Joyce & Winter 1996:36). Human sacrifice, in particular, was a new ritual practice controlled by elites since only nobles would have had the resources and power to sponsor raids, take captives, and organize public ceremonies. Allusions to human sacrifice by the nobility include the hieroglyphic texts associated with the sculptural program on Building L-sub (figure 5.5f) and Monument J-41 from Building J (figure 5.6d), which depicts a ruler of Monte Albán in the act of decapitation sacrifice (Urcid & Winter 2003). Human sacrifice was a more dramatic and potent means to communicate with the sacred realm than earlier practices of autosacrifice and would have been a means by which nobles demonstrated both their power and their generosity to supporters. The founding of Monte Albán, the construction of the Main Plaza, public rituals, and warfare were activities that were almost certainly organized and led by nobles.

The power of the nobility was also manifest in greater access to exotic non-local goods like imported pottery, obsidian blades, and ornaments of greenstone and shell (Winter 1984). While these valuables were not restricted to the nobility, evidence suggests that high-status families controlled trade relations through which many imported goods entered the Oaxaca Valley. In turn, nobles or craft specialists attached to the nobility manufactured local valuables like urns and onyx ornaments. Both nobles and commoners sought social valuables to enhance personal and familial prestige and to solidify alliances, including marriages. By the Pe phase, evidence suggests that high-status families throughout the Oaxacan highlands were exchanging prestigious goods and ideas, involving political and religious authority. High-status people in the Oaxaca Valley were probably in contact with elites of political centers in more distant regions such as Teotihuacan in the Basin of Mexico and Chiapa de Corzo in the Chiapas Central depression.

Despite increasing political and religious authority, public settings like the Main Plaza stressed the symbols of communal authority and an emerging corporate identity, while muting representations of the increasingly powerful rulers of the city. Although nobles lived near the ceremonial precinct and directed public rituals, until the Classic period (AD 300–800) the Main Plaza itself had few overt representations of local nobles and there were no high-status residences directly facing the plaza. Rulers were represented solely in the hieroglyphic inscriptions set in Building L-sub, which were probably understandable only to the literate nobility. The earliest known ruler's portrait, Monument J-41, dates to c.AD 100. The size, accessibility, and symbolism of the Main Plaza suggest to me that during Monte Albán's first four centuries the plaza was a focus of public ceremonies participated in by people of varied identities including different statuses, corporate groups, and communities. The plaza emphasized public buildings, public spaces, and cosmic symbolism including images depicting sacrifice, warfare, ancestors, and the shared Zapotec view of the cosmos. The Building L-sub program was probably polysemic with different components aimed at different audiences (Urcid 2008). Following Urcid (2008), sculptures in the east face of Building L-sub would have been visible to large groups of people on the plaza and stressed the ritual and military actions of lower-ranking people. Images of higher-ranking members of the military sodality, including elders and rain-god impersonators, were located on buildings on top of the platform, which were probably restricted to higher-status audiences of both prominent commoners and nobles. Beyond Monte Albán, the buildings on the Main Plaza were visible for great distances so that its power as a sacred mountain and political center was present in the everyday lived experiences of people throughout the region, although the plaza's accessibility and visibility also presented possibilities for the discursive penetration of these beliefs (Hutson 2002).

Although the Main Plaza was a public space focused on cosmic symbolism and community, ritual practices carried out there also contributed to the power of the nobility and an increasing separation of noble and commoner identities (A. Joyce 2000; Urcid 2008). Based on the iconographic and epigraphic evidence, as well as analogies with the early colonial period, public ceremonies were probably organized and led by nobles, and perhaps high-ranking members of religious and military organizations. The role of nobles as ritual specialists, especially sacrificers, dramatically communicated and reinforced their identities as mediators between commoners and the sacred. Participation in public ceremonies created powerful memories that bound people to the rulers, the symbols, and the new social order centered at Monte Albán. Warfare also could have united people behind rulers and ruling institutions (Joyce & Winter 1996:38–9). Participation in public ritual performances contributed to the production of larger-scale corporate identities internalized in people's dispositions and externalized in social practices like contributing tribute, allegiance, and labor to rulers. At the same time, the separation of status groups was reinforced by the role of nobles as ritual specialists and by the visible association of elite residences and the North Platform, which symbolized the linkage between nobles and the celestial realm. Nobles gained materially from these new social relations, but were obligated to organize and lead rituals on behalf of the community. Control over religious ideas, spaces, and practices by nobles increased their power to attract followers, mobilize resources, defeat competitors, and interact with the sacred.

Yet nobles shared politico-religious power with communal organizations, which probably included high-ranking commoners as leaders (Urcid 2008). These two potentially competing forms of authority – communal and noble – carried inherent contradictions and potential points of tension. Powerful nobles threatened the traditional authority of communal institutions, while the latter constrained the power of the nobility. The possible representation of a communal organization on the Building L-sub program depicts non-elites as rain-god impersonators and references human and probably autosacrifice. Likewise, hieroglyphic inscriptions and early images of rulers (Monument J-41) also reference rain-god impersonation, warfare, and sacrifice. These data suggest that the settings in which hereditary nobles and communal organizations negotiated and contested political authority probably included public rituals, access to special ceremonial roles like rain-god impersonator, as well as activities related to the preparation for and conduct of warfare. The potential for conflict can only be suggested, although evidence from elsewhere in the valley more clearly indicates that some individuals, families, and communities did not welcome the religious and political innovations that marked the founding and early history of Monte Albán.

Monte Albán and its hinterland: social and economic relations

The historical changes of the Danibaan phase involved political and religious institutions tied to Monte Albán, although the social transformations of the time also profoundly affected the daily lives of common people. Unfortunately, only a few low-status residences have been excavated for the Late/Terminal Formative – primarily at Monte Albán and Tomaltepec – which limits inferences regarding the domestic practices and daily lives of commoners. With the founding of Monte Albán, many people left their homes and migrated to new communities severing traditional ties to place, land, ancestors, and history. Participation in rituals, labor projects, and other practices tied to Monte Albán in turn incorporated people into a larger-scale political formation and a social identity symbolized by the ceremonial center and its associations with cosmic creation and renewal. People also probably traveled to Monte Albán and other locations to visit markets and participate as soldiers in military expeditions. People had larger families and so had to care for more children and grow more food. People adopted new technologies such as the use of *comales* or ceramic griddles, and some individuals, families, and communities specialized in craft production. Most people continued to be farmers, but were increasingly dependent on craft specialists for basic items like pottery. The social identities of people living in and around Monte Albán were no longer defined just by affiliations with their families and communities, but were increasingly tied to the political and religious institutions and rulers of Monte Albán. Monte Albán had become an urban center connected to its hinterland through political, economic, and religious relations as well as through a shared identity.

Elsewhere in the Oaxaca Valley, evidence suggests a range of political and economic relations with Monte Albán. During the Danibaan phase, there were relatively few changes in settlement and economic relations outside Etla and the area surrounding Monte Albán (Kowalewski et al. 1989, chapter 5). Differences in ceramic wares and types as well as in monumental architecture suggest that El Mogote in the Valle Grande arm and Yegüih in Tlacolula continued as centers of competing polities (Spencer & Redmond 2001:202–7).

Tomaltepec is one community with evidence for significant ties to Monte Albán. The occupation of the higher-status Rosario-phase residence at Tomaltepec continued during the Danibaan phase, although there were few clear links to the structural changes occurring at Monte Albán (Whalen 1981:75–87). During the Pe phase, however, the high-status residence was rebuilt such that it more closely resembled residences from Monte Albán (Whalen 1981:88–105). The residence included a slab-covered, adobe-walled tomb containing burials of two adults and a child along with offerings of jade and 37 ceramic vessels, including several effigy vessels. The Pe-phase residence at Tomaltepec was more elaborate than other houses, although its structural and tomb architecture was not as fancy as that of Monte Albán Residence A3.

Marcus and Flannery (1996:169–70) suggest that the inhabitants of the high-status residence at Tomaltepec were sent by the rulers of Monte Albán to administer this community. It is equally plausible, however, that they were the descendents of Tomaltepec's earlier prominent families who were now emulating and perhaps affiliating with the hilltop ceremonial center 15 km to the west. Interments with elaborate offerings including effigy vessels recovered at Abasolo and Yagul may also reflect increasing emulation of and perhaps affiliations with Monte Albán by the leading families of these communities (Chadwick 1966; Marcus & Flannery 1996:170).

Practices of affiliation that tied members of rural communities to Monte Albán included providing tribute (probably in the form of crop surpluses) as well as participation as warriors and laborers for the construction of monumental buildings. It is also possible that commoners worked the land of nobles as a form of tribute in the way they did at the time of the Spanish Conquest, although this is difficult to demonstrate archaeologically. In return, people received the benefits of participation in ceremonies on the Main Plaza. People acquired social valuables such as decorated pottery and greenstone from the increasingly powerful leaders of the urban center. Nobles may have adjudicated disputes among their subjects. Affiliation with Monte Albán's leaders, whether high-ranking commoners or nobles, would have been a way for the leading families of rural communities to gain prestige and power by acquiring special ritual knowledge, social valuables, and perhaps military protection. As the city grew, it would also have been an important center for trade, craft specialization, and marketing, all of which would have tied people to the center.

Between the Danibaan and Pe phases, three quarters of the population increase in the entire valley occurred within 20 km of Monte Albán (Kowalewski et al. 1989, chapter 6). I argue that similarities in Pe-phase high-status residences, mortuary ceremony, public buildings, and ceramics at sites in the Etla arm and east to Tomaltepec and perhaps Yagul and Abasolo resulted from the development of a shared identity as well as from political, religious, and economic relations between Monte Albán and surrounding communities. Though it is difficult to assess the precise nature of these intercommunity relations, it is possible that ties to new political authorities and religious institutions at Monte Albán were sufficient to consider these settlements part of a polity with its capital at the hilltop center. The new religious movement centered on Monte Albán's Main Plaza appears to have attracted large numbers of followers. Economic relations and warfare, however, are also implicated in the growth of the polity.

Many researchers argue that the infertile hills of Monte Albán necessitated the establishment of economic ties with surrounding communities (Kowalewski et al. 1989:123–6; Marcus & Flannery 1996:149–50). The inhabitants of Monte Albán grew some crops in terrace gardens, including areas cultivated using small-scale canal irrigation (O'Brien et al. 1982). Even with small-scale irrigation and access to fields on the valley floor, the huge population of the city probably created provisioning problems that by the Pe phase required crops to be brought in from other communities (Kowalewski et al. 1989:123–6). Population growth in the area around Monte Albán would have increased labor available to farm land around the urban center. Researchers have also suggested that an increase in settlement in the middle and upper piedmont, especially in the Etla arm, constituted a "piedmont strategy" whereby small-scale irrigation techniques were used to generate surpluses for Monte Albán (Kowalewski et al. 1989:123–6). These communities were established in previously unoccupied areas where land disputes would have been minimal. By the Nisa phase many of the piedmont sites were abandoned, perhaps due to soil erosion

(Joyce & Mueller 1997). I think it likely that generating crop surpluses for Monte Albán gave people greater access to the ritual, economic, and military benefits of affiliating with the city, but had disadvantages such as increasing labor demands for both men and women.

Economic relations with Monte Albán had a variety of unanticipated consequences. The increasing reliance on the tortilla as inferred from the first use of *comales* (figure 5.7b) may have resulted from increasing travel by members of outlying communities to Monte Albán to provide tributary labor, engage in market exchange, or participate in ritual or military activities (Winter 1984:213). In contrast to the consumption of maize in the form of gruel or roasted cobs, tortillas can be easily transported and stay fresh for up to several weeks if toasted. Making tortillas, however, requires considerably more labor than making maize gruel or roasting cobs and so would have increased work demands, especially on women (Brumfiel 1991:237–43). During the Danibaan and Pe phases the overwhelming majority of *comales* recovered by the settlement study were from the core area around Monte Albán, indicating that these changes in domestic economy occurred here first (Kowalewski et al. 1989:149).

A possible explanation for population growth is that productive intensification by people in communities surrounding Monte Albán increased demand for labor, making it advantageous to have larger families. Of course, having larger families would have required greater efforts in child rearing. Coupled with increasing food-preparation costs, it is possible that increased family size altered gender roles and perhaps created tensions along gender lines and perhaps between Monte Albán and its hinterland communities. The contradiction between increasing labor demands in the hinterland and the ritual and economic benefits of affiliation with Monte Albán created social dynamics that should be further explored.

As people spent more time and energy in farming, some communities began to specialize in certain crafts, taking advantage of the fact that most people would have had less time to carry out the full array of productive tasks that they had previously undertaken. Communities specialized in the production of pottery, chipped-stone tools, and possibly lime and salt (Winter 1984:198–9). Specialized potting communities include Tomaltepec and San Augustín de las Juntas located 6 km southeast of Monte Albán. Excavations at both of these sites recovered kilns used to fire gray-paste ceramics as well as misfired sherds (Whalen 1981:88–105; Winter 1984: 195). The kilns were simple ovoid pits dug into the ground with two chambers separated by adobe bricks (Whalen 1988:302–3). The walls of the kiln were fire reddened. Kilns were widely distributed among households, including the high-status residence at Tomaltepec. Fargher's (2007) petrographic study of Late Formative ceramics from Monte Albán indicates that people imported gray-ware pottery from a variety of small production centers in the Oaxaca Valley, perhaps including Tomaltepec and San Augustín de las Juntas.

A common Pe-phase gray-ware conical bowl with incised lines on the interior rim and a combed base, designated type G-12 in the Oaxaca Valley ceramic sequence (Caso et al. 1967; figure 5.7c), has a degree of standardization suggesting the use of larger-scale production techniques (Kowalewski et al. 1989:113). The distribution of the G-12 bowl suggests that it was exchanged throughout the valley, perhaps via markets. People may have developed markets to provide a central location to obtain products manufactured by specialists. Markets are difficult to identify in the archaeological record, however, and only indirect evidence is available to support their presence (Blanton et al. 1982:55–68). I suspect that Monte Albán was one marketing location given its large population and centrality in terms of politics, religion, and economy. It is unlikely that a market was located on the Main Plaza as suggested by Winter (1984:200), however, since markets were rarely located in ceremonial precincts of ancient Mesoamerican cities. Increasing craft specialization and markets are usually viewed as processes that led to greater integration within the Oaxaca Valley, but it is also likely that increasing economic dependence on people from other communities and the working out of exchange values may have created tensions among interacting communities as well.

Overall, I view the political, economic, and religious changes of the Danibaan phase as having dramatically changed Zapotec culture and society. While these changes had their roots in the Rosario phase, it is with the founding of Monte Albán that the profound social transformation was realized. It is tempting to view changes in ruling institutions, ideologies, religious belief and practice, urbanism, and ties to land and community as a kind of Foucauldian rupture in discourse. There is no doubt that the Danibaan phase saw profound changes in cultural principles, material relations, and practices. Yet there are also clear continuities from the Guadalupe and Rosario phases to the Danibaan phase. Ritual practices such as autosacrifice and ancestor veneration show continuities through this period, suggesting that people's relations with the divine did not change completely. Forms of communal authority present in the Danibaan phase were probably similar to those of earlier periods. Figurines suggest continuities in domestic ritual and perhaps gender relations. Clearly the founding of Monte Albán transformed many aspects of political authority and people's relations with the sacred, yet this was not a total rupture in discourse and many of the roots of this period of change can be seen in Middle

Formative social relations. In addition, not everyone in the Valley of Oaxaca embraced the social changes of the Danibaan phase and there is evidence for conflict and resistance.

Monte Albán and its hinterland: conflict and resistance

People in the Etla arm and the central part of the valley were increasingly incorporated into a large-scale political formation centered on Monte Albán, although there undoubtedly were different degrees of compliance and involvement with unifying rulers, institutions, and practices (A. Joyce 2004). In some cases, commoners and nobles in other parts of the valley attempted to remain independent from or actively resisted the emerging political structures and rulers of Monte Albán. During the Pe phase people expanded into the margins of the Oaxaca Valley and into the Ejutla, Miahuatlán, and Sola valleys, as well as into nearby mountainous regions (Balkansky 2002; Drennan 1989; Feinman & Nicholas 1990; Finsten 1996; Kowalewski et al. 1989:123; Markman 1981), perhaps in an attempt to maintain independence from Monte Albán and avoid increasing conflict within the Oaxaca Valley. For these people, Monte Albán may not have been recognized as a sacred place, but instead could have been seen as a source of conflict and unwanted social change. As Monte Albán's size and power grew, independence and resistance became increasingly risky, as shown by representations of human sacrifice, presumably of war captives, in the Building L-sub program and in the slabs incorporated into Building J.

The best evidence for conflict comes from El Mogote in the Valle Grande, which grew to 53 ha in the Danibaan phase and included a public plaza surrounded by monumental architecture (Spencer 2003; Spencer & Redmond 2001). Spencer and Redmond (2001:218) argue that El Mogote was independent of Monte Albán given differences in the orientation and layout of their ceremonial precincts as well as a lack of evidence for the exchange of ceramics. At c.300 BC El Mogote was attacked and the ceremonial precinct burned. People then relocated the site center to a more defensible position about 800 m uphill to the west at the site of El Palenque. On El Palenque another plaza complex was constructed with a high-status residence on its northern end that included a possible storage room and a room for preparing food for ritual feasting. Feasting may have occurred in a paved courtyard east of the residence covering about 51 m^2. No interments were found in the residence. Evidence for warfare continues during the Pe and early Nisa phases with possible defensive walls constructed along the more gradual slopes of El Palenque. At c.20 BC, the ceremonial center of El Palenque, including the high-status residence, was burned and the site was abandoned.

There are a variety of likely reasons why Monte Albán's rulers would have fought against their rivals in the Valley of Oaxaca. Warfare may have been designed to conquer and incorporate independent communities, eliminate competing leaders, gain control of agricultural land, and control trade in non-local goods like obsidian, shell, and greenstone. The iconographic and epigraphic evidence further indicates that warfare was linked to ritual beliefs and practices with captives taken for human sacrifice (A. Joyce 2000).

Several researchers argue that Monte Albán was engaged in large-scale "predatory" warfare designed to "fight relentlessly to subjugate their political rivals" (Flannery & Marcus 2003:11,804; also see Spencer 2003). This view of relentless conquest warfare, however, is difficult to support with the available evidence (A. Joyce 2003; Workinger & Joyce n.d.; Zeitlin & Joyce 1999). For example, the persistence for at least 300 years of El Mogote/El Palenque as an independent community in conflict with the huge urban center of Monte Albán indicates that warfare was not as large-scale, destructive, and relentless as the predatory-warfare model suggests. Furthermore, during the Pe phase, most of the population remained at the more vulnerable site of El Mogote, which covered 44 ha, while settlement at the defensible position of El Palenque covered only 28 ha and included the site's noble families and ceremonial precinct (Spencer & Redmond 2001:219). Although the evidence indicates that El Palenque was eventually conquered, it was more likely the result of sporadic warfare over the course of several centuries perhaps fought mostly by community leaders.

Proponents of the predatory-warfare model further argue that Monte Albán expanded militarily into surrounding regions during the Pe and Nisa phases, eventually conquering and administering an empire covering 20,000 km^2 (Balkansky 1998b:469; Marcus & Flannery 1996:206–7; Redmond & Spencer 2006:377). Comparative research on ancient empires indicates that imperial elites can pursue a variety of strategies for dealing with provinces (e.g., Schreiber 1987; Smith & Montiel 2001). These strategies range from territorial conquest to hegemonic forms of imperialism. Territorial empires conquer provinces and establish imperial outposts to directly administer the region. In addition to administrative elites, imperial garrisons often include a military presence to suppress potential revolts. Hegemonic control involves conquest, or at least the threat of military action, followed by the establishment of tributary relations achieved largely through the cooperation of provincial elites, as was the case for most of the Aztec Empire. The predatory-warfare model argues that the Monte Albán Empire primarily exerted a form of territorial control over most of its provinces (Marcus &

Flannery 1996:195–207; Redmond & Spencer 2006:365–77; Spencer 2003). Imperial subjugation and direct administration of these regions would have allowed Monte Albán's rulers to control trade routes from the Pacific coast to central Mexico. The predatory-warfare model is further asserted to be a frequent if not universal cause of pristine state origins, whereby the organizational necessities of militaristic expansion give rise to the administrative institutions of the state (Spencer 2003). Monte Albán's relations with surrounding regions is one of the most hotly debated issues in Oaxacan archaeology (e.g., Balkansky 1998b, 2001; Balkansky et al. 2004; A. Joyce 2003; Joyce et al. 2000; Marcus & Flannery 1996:198–207; Workinger & Joyce n.d.; R. Zeitlin 1990; Zeitlin & Joyce 1999).

The Monte Albán imperialism argument was originally developed by Marcus (1976, 1983d) based on her reading of the Building J conquest slabs from Monte Albán. As discussed above, the conquest slabs were interpreted by Caso (1938) as representations of places conquered by Monte Albán. Marcus and Flannery (1996:197) expanded on Caso's interpretation, arguing that the difference between slabs showing an effigy head and those that do not is that the former refer to places incorporated into the Zapotec empire by conquest, while the latter were subjugated by colonization. Marcus also sought to identify locations represented on the slabs by comparing the place names with names recorded in the *Codex Mendoza*, a sixteenth-century Aztec tribute list, as well as with names in Nahuatl, the Aztec language, given to towns in Oaxaca in the sixteenth century. Initially, Marcus argued that the conquest slabs recorded places within the Monte Albán Empire, including in the Valley of Oaxaca. Later she altered her approach, arguing that, like the colonial-period *lienzos*, the conquest slabs recorded polity boundaries and so map the extent of Monte Albán's Empire (Workinger 2002:30–6). Among the places she identified are Miahuatlán, Tututepec on the Pacific coast, Cuicatlán about 100 km northwest of the Oaxaca Valley, and Ocelotepec in the mountains south of Miahuatlán.

Survey and excavation in the Cuicatlán Cañada provide the strongest case for conquest (Redmond 1983; Redmond & Spencer 2006:365–75; Spencer 1982), although questions remain as to whether Monte Albán was involved (Urcid 1994b; Workinger & Joyce n.d.). Several lines of evidence suggest military conquest followed by the imperial administration of the region by Monte Albán. Surface survey shows a shift in settlement patterns from the high alluvium to defensible piedmont locations. The site of Llano Perdido was burned and suddenly abandoned at c.300 BC. Excavations at the nearby site of La Coyotera exposed the remains of a skull rack, exhibiting victims of warfare or sacrifice. Spencer and Redmond (Redmond 1983:107–20; Redmond & Spencer 2006:365–75; Spencer 1982:220–1) infer conquest by Monte Albán based on similarities in ceramics and a Valley of Oaxaca style tomb eroding from the surface at the fortified site of Quiotepec, which was argued to have been a Zapotec administrative outpost. An unoccupied buffer zone separating the Cañada and the Tehuacán Valley to the north presumably marked the frontier of the Monte Albán Empire. New forms of political organization are inferred from changes in public architecture and settlement patterns, while an expansion of irrigation agriculture could have been designed to produce surpluses in the form of tropical crops for tribute payments to Monte Albán (Spencer 1982).

Although Spencer and Redmond provide a strong case for warfare in the Cuicatlán Cañada, the identification of Monte Albán as the conqueror of the region can be questioned. Most damaging has been Urcid's (1994b) demonstration that the indigenous Cuicatec name for the region, Yivacu or "Hill of the river of houses," differs from the Aztec Cuicatlán or "Place of the song," which Marcus (1976, 1983d) relied on to identify the place shown on the Building J slab. Marcus' reliance on Aztec names recorded 1,500 years after the conquest slabs were carved is a significant problem for all of the place attributions that she has proposed. The archaeological evidence for a Zapotec presence can also be questioned, since there were close affinities in ceramic styles both before and after the hypothesized conquest, and the Zapotec-style tomb dates to the Classic period (Pareyón 1960:101–2), postdating the presumed takeover.

Despite these problems, the data from the Cuicatlán Cañada still leave open the possibility that Monte Albán conquered the region. Direct evidence for Zapotec conquest of other regions, however, is thus far rare. Evidence for warfare is present in much of the Oaxacan highlands although, as discussed below, the data are more consistent with a model involving conflict among multiple competing polities, than one involving defense solely against Zapotec imperialism (A. Joyce 1994a). Outside the Cuicatlán Cañada, Marcus and Flannery (1996:198–207) rely on indirect evidence of a Monte Albán presence to argue for imperial subjugation. In particular, they argue that the spread of gray-ware ceramic styles from the Valley of Oaxaca is one of the best lines of circumstantial evidence for a Monte Albán takeover, either through conquest or through colonization. Subjugation is demonstrated in "those regions whose previously autonomous ceramics are literally swamped or replaced by Monte Albán gray wares" (Marcus & Flannery 1996:199). Yet research in regions within the proposed Monte Albán Empire, such as the area around Tututepec (A. Joyce 2003; Workinger 2002), Monte Negro in the Mixteca Alta (Balkansky et al. 2004) and much of the Peñoles region west of the Oaxaca Valley (Finsten 1996:84), has failed to support the hypothesized imperial takeover. These regions exhibited ceramic crossties with pottery from Monte Albán, although their ceramic assemblages included many regionally distinctive forms and decorations. The Oaxaca data are consistent with comparative studies of ancient empires indicating that general similarities in ceramic styles are a poor indicator of conquest (Schreiber 1992:263; Stark 1990). In other areas of the hypothesized empire, either evidence is equivocal or research has been insufficient to assess relations with Monte Albán. Monte Albán may have periodically gone to war with people in neighboring regions and perhaps even conquered some communities outside the Oaxaca Valley, but the evidence at present does not support the hypothesis that Monte Albán controlled a substantial empire. It is also unlikely that Monte Albán could have dominated an area as large as the one proposed by Marcus and Flannery (1996) given the logistics required to conquer and control a territorial empire of this scale, especially in a region as rugged as Oaxaca (Zeitlin & Joyce 1999:388). By the Late Formative period, the scale of polities in much of the Mixteca and in the lower Río Verde would have made it difficult for Monte Albán to subjugate these regions.

Political Consolidation and Upheaval at Monte Albán

By the Nisa phase, Monte Albán's nobles were increasingly consolidating power through control over the ceremonial center (A. Joyce 2004:205–7). Early versions of the South Platform and the eastern row of buildings were constructed effectively closing off the Main Plaza (figure 5.4b). The central row of structures was also built, which restricted and channeled traffic during ceremonies. By closing off the Main Plaza nobles were able to more effectively control access to and the use of the ceremonial precinct. The North Platform was expanded and the *viborón* court was built over, but an even larger sunken court, the Patio Hundido, was constructed in the southern end of the platform. Zapotecs built a ballcourt on the northeastern corner of the plaza. Ballcourts, like sunken courts, were seen as portals to the sacred realm and were associated with warfare, sacrifice, and the negotiation of political relations (Gillespie 1991). In addition to the control of space, the ritual calendar allowed nobles to control the timing of important ceremonies and perhaps certain types of warfare.

Control of space was reflected at a smaller scale by the Zapotec two-room temple, which was a common form of public architecture beginning in the Nisa phase (Martínez López 2002). Some Nisa-phase temples were reached by a secret passageway, which allowed ritual specialists to enter them without being seen, thereby limiting access to the temple and heightening the drama of ritual performance. These temples often have sooty deposits on their floors, resulting from the burning of incense, and sometimes the remains of sacrificed quail along with obsidian knives or blades used in sacrificial rituals. Many Nisa-phase temples had elaborate offerings, often placed in stone-masonry boxes, that included ornaments and mosaics of greenstone, shell, and turquoise along with pottery, jade figurines, effigy braziers and urns, and occasionally ceremonial burials. These offerings resembled the sacred bundles of the late prehispanic era.

Perhaps the most elaborate Nisa-phase offering was Burial XIV-10, a ceremonial burial found in the cistern beneath the *adoratorio*, or sunken altar, in the Main Plaza (Martínez López et al. 1995:237). It contained two adult males, two adult females, and a sub-adult accompanied by jade necklaces and earspools as well as ornaments of marine shell and pearl, and an elaborate jade bat-god mask. The males were interred wearing stone mosaic pectorals. Near the cistern was evidence for ritual feasting including circular ovens that contained hundreds of small bowls, a large cooking jar and serving bowl, and extensive evidence of burning. Ceremonial burials like Burial XIV-10 were the result of special mortuary rites, possibly involving the interment of sacrificial victims.

Noble residences continued to be concentrated north of the Main Plaza and by this time some were built on the North Platform itself (Barber & Joyce 2006:228–9). The El Ocote residence, built on the northeastern end of the North Platform, was larger and more complex than other high-status residences of this period. In Area IV-Norte on the northwestern side of the Main Plaza Zapotecs built the first high-status residence directly facing the Main Plaza, which might suggest that it was more "public" than others, although the entrance to the structure was to the north rather than to the east onto the Main Plaza. Interred beneath this residence was Burial 1994–62, which included an adult male with dental modification accompanied by four ceramic vessels and a necklace of 158 shell beads. High-status residences were located in some areas of Monte Albán beyond the Main Plaza, probably indicating the emergence of the pattern of neighborhoods or barrios that was clearly present in the city by the Xoo phase (AD 500–800).

Immediately north of the Area IV-Norte residence was a curious architectural complex, the Conjunto Plataforma Norte Lado Poniente (Conjunto PNLP), that consisted of a patio open to the west, surrounded on its other sides by several structures, including a temple (Martínez López & Markens 2004). The lack of burials and domestic refuse indicates that the Conjunto PNLP was not residential. Artifacts recovered from the complex included 2,683 pieces of Pacific coastal shell, including finished ornaments, mosaic pieces, and needles as well as worked and unworked pieces. Archaeologists also found more than a thousand pieces of obsidian, mostly prismatic blade fragments and over a thousand pieces of chipped chert and quartz. These artifacts represent the remains of specialized production of shell ornaments and perhaps obsidian blades. The shell data are consistent with the presence of specialists – either nobles, perhaps residing in the Area IV-Norte residence, or attached specialists, who were manufacturing adornments for the nobility.

A construction phase of the Conjunto PNLP that predates evidence for shell working included a large oven measuring 3.9 m^3 that was probably used in the production of fancy cream-ware pottery, which was an important locally made prestige item (Martínez López & Markens 2004:80). These cream wares were expensive to manufacture, often with post-fire scratch incising and large hollow supports, and their distribution was markedly status linked. Excavation on and around the North Platform has exposed 29 ovens, many of them unusually large or clustered in groups of three or four that were also used to make fancy cream wares.

These data suggest that nobles had preferential access to exotic imported goods like marine shell and obsidian, and were involved in the production of social valuables like shell ornaments and cream wares. The control of prestige goods would have been one way for nobles to expand their power and influence, by using ornaments in bodily display and by exchanging valuables to establish social ties through alliance, obligation, and intermarriage. Design motifs, especially step-fret designs on cream-ware vessels were also part of a pan-Mesoamerican system of elite display, suggesting that Zapotec nobles gained influence through the exchange of ideas and materials with nobles in other parts of Mesoamerica.

By the Nisa phase, the rulers of Monte Albán through alliance, religious persuasion, and military conquest had probably extended their authority over the entire Valley of Oaxaca and perhaps into the contiguous valleys of Ejutla, Miahuatlán, and Sola. At c.20 BC the Valle Grande center of El Palenque was finally overthrown by Monte Albán (Redmond & Spencer 2006:378–9). The ruler's palace at the site was burned to the ground and there is evidence for the destruction of a temple. Following the attack on El Palenque, Zapotecs established a new ceremonial center at Cerro Tilcajete, a hilltop site located about 1 km to the north (Elson 2006; Spencer & Redmond 2001). People at Cerro Tilcajete now had access to ceramics manufactured in the area of Monte Albán, especially fancy cream-paste pottery and perhaps urns.

Evidence for emerging conventions in public architecture and elite art and ceramics, as well as the appearance of nobles at sites throughout the valley, has led many researchers to assume that by the Nisa phase the Valley of Oaxaca was unified under the leadership of the rulers of Monte Albán (e.g., Joyce & Winter 1996; Marcus & Flannery 1996). For example, two-room temples, ballcourts, and high-status residences have been identified at several sites, including San José Mogote, Cuilapan, and Cerro Tilcajete (Elson 2006). At San José Mogote, which had recovered to become a 65-ha center, people built the ceremonial precinct as a copy of Monte Albán's Main Plaza with a ballcourt, high status residence, and at least 10 two-room temples. At 46 ha, Dainzú was the largest Nisa-phase site in the Tlacolula arm of the valley (Kowalewski et al. 1989:162). Dainzú's ceremonial center was located at the base of Cerro Dainzú where a gallery of carved stones depicting victorious ballplayers dominating defeated ones was set into the face of a monumental terrace (figure 5.6c). The Dainzú gallery exhibited similar themes to those represented on Building L-sub and Building J since versions of the ballgame involved a kind of staged mock combat, leading to the eventual sacrifice of defeated ballplayers who usually were war captives (Orr 1997). Several of the ballplayers are depicted as rain-god impersonators. Petroglyphs on Cerro Dainzú depict defeated ballplayers as decapitated heads similar to the severed heads on Building L-sub. Other than Building J at Monte Albán, the only other arrowhead-shaped building discovered in the Valley comes from Caballito Blanco in the Tlacolula arm. Excavations of high-status houses and elaborate burials or tombs have also been discovered at sites like Fábrica San José and San Augustín de las Juntas. The Pe-phase settlement clustered around Monte Albán dispersed by the Nisa phase, probably due to soil erosion in the piedmont (Joyce & Mueller 1997) and perhaps due to Monte Albán defeating its competitors within the valley, thereby lessening defensive concerns (Kowalewski et al. 1989:159–61).

Nobles living in communities throughout the Central Valleys were probably affiliated socially, politically, and economically to varying degrees with the rulers of Monte Albán, and some probably paid tribute to the regional center. Though the rulers of Monte Albán may have come to politically dominate the Central Valleys, there is reason to believe that social, political, and economic relations among communities were not well integrated or tightly administered. Kowalewski and his colleagues (1989:193) argue that local rulers had political and economic ties to Monte Albán, but there was little integration among local political centers. Sherman (2005:278–81) argues that variability in public architecture and building orientations between the Valle Grande and Monte Albán reflects the persistence of local architectural traditions and perhaps a degree of resistance to the Monte Albán polity. The rulers of Monte Albán also probably had little control over the daily activities of people in the countryside other than the symbolic presence of the hilltop center visible in the distance. These conditions would have fostered rivalries among local nobles and created points of tension between the rulers of Monte Albán and the local nobility at communities throughout the valley. Increasing labor demands on men and women and the economic differentiation of the valley may have also created social tensions.

As the rulers of Monte Albán increasingly gained power by appropriating the Main Plaza and defeating their competitors in the Valley of Oaxaca, tensions between traditional communal leadership and the nobility may have intensified. Evidence from the end of the Nisa phase suggests that these tensions may have erupted in a major political upheaval at Monte Albán at c.AD 200. At this time the Building L-sub iconographic program was dismantled and the structure was demolished or buried under Building L (Urcid 2008). The building in which the conquest-slab program was originally displayed was dismantled and the monuments were later reused in Building J. Other poorly understood narrative programs were also dismantled and a temple on the north end of the North Platform was burned (Winter 1994d:15).

Indications of conflict include the construction of a defensive wall around the most vulnerable slopes at Monte Albán as well as the relocation of people behind the wall from outlying parts of the site (O'Brien et al. 1982:207). The wall also served to dam a large gully, creating a reservoir, and may have been a means of controlling movement into the city. It has usually been assumed that the wall was constructed to defend against external enemies, but it is also possible that it offered defense against internal factions who had been expelled from the city. Another indication of conflict comes from the Conjunto PNLP, which, in addition to an area of craft production, acted as a control point for entry onto the Main Plaza (Martínez López & Markens 2004). The recovery of 27 projectile points in the Conjunto PNLP suggests that coercive force was now used to monitor access to the plaza.

The destruction of the narrative programs at Monte Albán by dismantling structures, covering up carved stones, and breaking others to use them as construction fill points to a major societal upheaval. These programs emphasized corporate leadership (Building L-sub) as well as military victories and sacrificial rituals enacted on the part of the community (conquest slabs), while underplaying the authority of the nobility. The destruction of these programs, as well as the formalization of status distinctions by the Early Classic Pitao phase (AD 350–500), suggests that powerful nobles were successful in overthrowing competing corporate forms of leadership.

six

Political Centralization in the Mixteca and Coast

Archaeological research in the Mixteca and in the lower Río Verde Valley shows that, as in the Valley of Oaxaca and throughout much of Mesoamerica, the Late/Terminal Formative was a time of major social transformations. Data from these regions suggest population growth, settlement nucleation, and trends toward political centralization during the later part of the Formative from 700 BC to AD 300 (Balkansky et al. 2000, 2004; Blomster 2004; A. Joyce 2005; Kowalewski et al. 2009). Political centers and complex polities developed by c.300 BC in the Mixtec highlands and perhaps as early as 400 BC on the coast (figure 6.1).

Evidence from these regions shows variability in political organization and monumentality. Though trends toward population growth, settlement nucleation, and political centralization generally paralleled those of the Oaxaca Valley, there were significant differences in architectural layouts, social organization, domestic culture, and political history. Yet, as in the Oaxaca Valley, data from the Mixtec highlands and from coastal Oaxaca suggest that one important dynamic that drove social change was the negotiation of political hierarchy in the context of traditional social structures that were more communal and egalitarian. Because research in the lower Río Verde Valley and especially in the Mixtec highlands is not as extensive as in the Oaxaca Valley, my arguments concerning social developments of the later Formative are more speculative.

Social Transformations in the Mixtec Highlands

Research on the years immediately preceding the emergence of complex polities in the Mixteca is limited primarily to survey augmented by small-scale excavations, which suggest population growth during the late Middle Formative. Survey data in the Mixteca Alta (Balkansky et al. 2000:370–1;

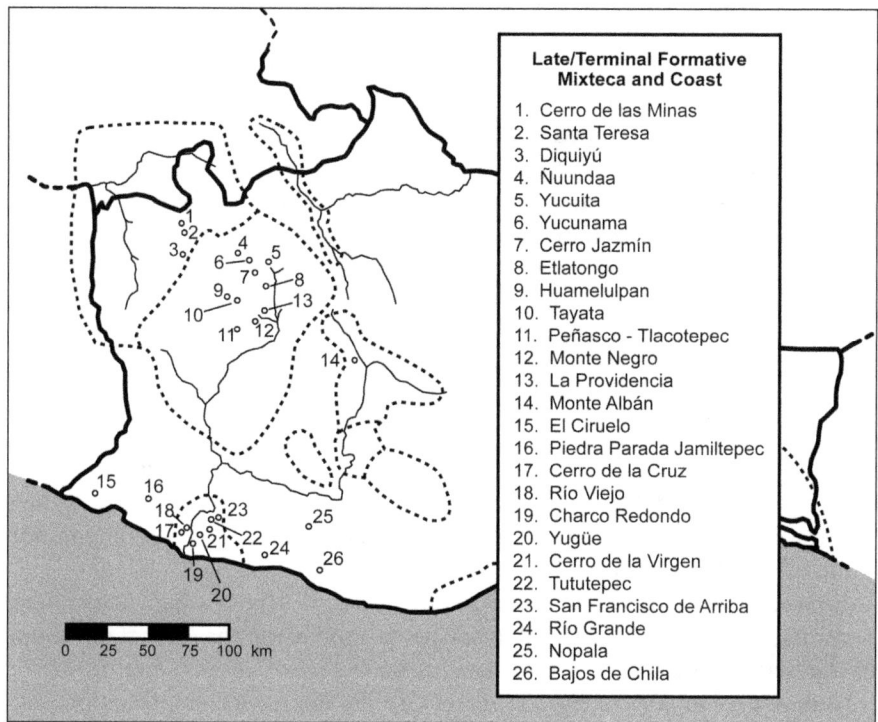

Figure 6.1 Archaeological sites of the Late/Terminal Formative in the Mixtec highlands and the lower Río Verde Valley (drawing by Eric Berkemeyer)

Kowalewski et al. 2009) show a pattern of settlement clusters around large communities like La Providencia at the southern edge of the Nochixtlán Valley (92 ha) and Tayata in the Huamelulpan Valley (77 ha). Settlement in the Mixteca Baja consisted of small communities of only a few hectares until the Late Formative period (Winter 2005b).

Models of demographic change in the Mixteca Alta will be improved once the recently defined Yucuita phase (500–300 BC) is distinguished in regional surveys (Blomster 2004:168–76). Settlement studies in several valleys of the Mixteca Alta show that during the Yucuita phase or its equivalent larger communities in the 20 to 100 ha range were probably centers of political, religious, and perhaps economic power (Balkansky 1998a; Balkansky et al. 2000, 2004; Byland 1980; Plunket 1983; Spores 1972). Demographic centers include La Providencia near Tilantongo, Tayata in the Huamelulpan Valley, Peñasco-Tlacotepec south of Huamelulpan, and

Ñuundaa in the Tamazulapan Valley, as well as Yucuita and Etlatongo in the Nochixtlán Valley.

The paucity of excavation data for the Yucuita phase makes it difficult to infer aspects of social organization. In the Mixteca Alta, the presence of large sites with mounded architecture suggests rising inequality and the concentration of politico-religious authority, perhaps similar to the Rosario phase in the Valley of Oaxaca. Excavations by Blomster (2004:148–70) at Etlatongo exposed the remains of residences and burials suggesting only modest status differences, however. Burials include stone-lined cists covered by stone slabs as well as a burial of three individuals within a bell-shaped pit. A stone-lined cylindrical chamber extended from a later floor down into the bell-shaped pit, perhaps suggesting communication with ancestors. Burial offerings were modest with the most elaborate consisting of 13 ceramic vessels, perhaps interred with a household head. Data also suggest increasing specialization in ceramic production and the first manufacture of *comales*. In the Mixteca Baja only small sites no greater than a few hectares have been identified; test excavations and survey suggest only minor status distinctions (Rivera 1999; Winter 2005b).

Between 400 and 300 BC the Mixteca Alta and Mixteca Baja underwent a demographic explosion and nucleation similar to the one that began in the Valley of Oaxaca a century or two before (Balkansky et al. 2000; Kowalewski et al. 2009:297–303; Rivera 1999; Winter 1994e). Demographic nuclei arose at Yucuita, Monte Negro, Huamelulpan, Cerro Jazmín, and Etlatongo in the Mixteca Alta as well as at Cerro de las Minas and Diquiyú in the Mixteca Baja. Populations relocated to higher elevations, especially densely occupied hilltop centers that undoubtedly included the first cities of the Mixteca with populations of several thousand (Balkansky 1998a; Balkansky et al. 2000:373–6, 2004; Kowalewski et al. 2009:299; Plunket 1983; Rivera 1999). Evidence is limited on the nature of relations between center and hinterland, however, often making it difficult to assess the degree of urbanism. Some large Cruz D- and Yucuita-phase settlements,[5] such as Tayata, Peñasco-Tlacotepec, and La Providencia were depopulated and probably became the source of the founders and early occupants of communities like Huamelulpan and Monte Negro. Sites like Yucuita and Etlatongo, however, grew from preexisting communities into demographic and political centers. In much of the Mixtec highlands total population increased with estimates more than doubling by the Ramos phase. In the Tilantongo area, however, existing communities founded the hilltop center of Monte Negro without significant population growth (Balkansky et al. 2004:44–6; Winter 1986).

Rising population in the Mixtec highlands may have been supported by the development of new agricultural technologies. Based on survey evidence,

Balkansky (1998a; Balkansky et al. 2004) argues that Mixtecs began constructing agricultural terraces, including *lama-bordo* systems, by the Late Formative, and Kowalewski and colleagues (2009:290) suggest that these cross-drainage terraces may have begun as early as the late Middle Formative. The development of these new soil-conservation technologies was a response to anthropogenic erosion that began in the Early Formative, but may have intensified with the settlement shift to higher, more erodible settings in the Late Formative (Joyce & Mueller 1997; Kowalewski et al. 2009:300).

Survey and excavation at Yucuita, Huamelulpan, Monte Negro, and Cerro de las Minas show that labor was mobilized to construct monumental buildings, suggesting the presence of rulers (Acosta & Romero 1992; Balkansky 1998a; Balkansky et al. 2004; Gaxiola 1984; Robles 1986; Winter 1982, 1986, 2007; Winter et al. 1991). Monumental architecture in the Mixteca Alta, however, differs from that in the Valley of Oaxaca and the lower Río Verde Valley in stressing platforms and terraces, rather than pyramidal mounds or massive acropoli (Kowalewski et al. 2009:303). Mortuary patterns and residences indicate, however, that differences in wealth, status, and power were not as great as in the Valley of Oaxaca. Political authority may have been vested in multiple corporate groups within each polity, rather than in the hands of exclusionary rulers. Early centers in the Mixtec highlands do not seem to have a single focal public space like the Main Plaza at Monte Albán. Instead, Mixtecs built cities with multiple public areas often surrounded by clusters of residences that constituted some form of corporate-group organization consisting of families of different status levels. The corporate groups may represent different communities that came together to found the demographic centers and could have been based on lineage ties or early versions of the barrio organization found at the time of the Spanish Conquest. Smaller communities were probably tied to rulers, institutions, and symbols at political centers through ritual, political, and economic relations. Mixtecs built monumental buildings in some smaller communities as well as in demographic centers, which might suggest the presence of political and religious institutions of a regional polity. Few hinterland sites surrounding political centers have been sufficiently studied, however, to assess the specific relations that may have constituted polities and the identities that they embodied.

Yucuita

Yucuita covers a hill and long ridge in the northern end of the Nochixtlán Valley about 8 km north of Etlatongo. From Yucuita it is possible to see the valley for dozens of kilometers to the south and the floodplain immediately below the site includes some of the richest farm land in the region. The site was excavated by Ronald Spores in the 1960s and early 1970s and by Marcus Winter from 1976 to 1980. As discussed in chapter 3, Yucuita was an important Early Formative site, although settlement declined by c.1200 BC. During the Ramos phase, Yucuita experienced a resurgence with the community growing to 100 ha and covering the slopes around the hill known as Cerro de las Flores in Spanish, or Yucuita in Mixtec (Winter 1982, 1986:346–52).

Excavations at Yucuita have focused on the slopes south of Cerro de las Flores, which was the Ramos-phase site center. In Area DFK, on a ridge projecting south from the hill, Winter (1982:20–1) excavated a monumental platform with a retaining wall 5 m high that supported probable public buildings, a drain, and an unfinished stairway. There is no evidence, however, for a sizeable plaza where ceremonies could have engaged large groups of people. Spores (1974:44) recovered evidence of ritual feasting from a test pit in this area.

Evidence for corporate groups within the community was exposed in Area M where Robles (1986:32–4; also see Winter 1986:346–52) excavated a public plaza measuring approximately 24 m by 28 m, surfaced with plaster. Two elaborate residences were built along its northern and southern sides, although the residences did not open directly onto the plaza. The residences were larger than typical Ramos-phase houses with well-made stone foundations, plaster floors, and rooms that entirely enclosed an interior patio. No burials were recovered.

In the area near the plaza, Robles (1986) excavated portions of six other houses that were more typical of the Rosario phase. The houses consisted of one or two rooms with stone and adobe foundations around a patio. Floors were usually of tamped earth, although thin plaster floors were present in some rooms. Associated features included middens, bell-shaped pits, ovens, hearths, and burials. Burials included graves, stone-lined cists, and simple adobe tombs, occasionally with stone-slab roofs. Interments in graves did not have offerings or were accompanied by a few ceramic vessels and sometimes a few shell ornaments. Tombs included anywhere from one to eight individuals, usually with somewhat more elaborate offerings. The most elaborate tomb contained eight adults accompanied by 10 vessels, including possible Oaxaca Valley imports, along with 29 bone and 3 greenstone beads. Multiple burials in tombs probably represent household heads interred at different times during the use life of the residence. A few skeletons exhibited cranial and/or dental modifications.

Evidence for a second corporate group, consisting of several low-status households and at least one higher-status one, was associated with a probable public building excavated in Area A (R. Fernández 1981). Mixtecs built Residence A-1 on a low platform covering 817 m². The residence consisted of seven rooms forming a U-shaped complex that opened onto a large patio; floors were plaster and there were several large drains. One room had a roof supported by a column and opened onto a small patio. The size of residences increased through time, suggesting an increase in the size of the family occupying the house. Archaeologists discovered a stone-cist burial beneath the southern room of the residence, while a looted and partially dismantled stone-masonry tomb was exposed beneath the patio. Evidence for several low-status houses was recovered in Area CE less than 100 m northeast of Area A. Adjacent to Residence A-1 was a probable public building that may have been a focus of the social, ritual, and political life of the group. The high-status residences in both Area M and Area A were spatially associated with public spaces, suggesting that elites had greater influence over politico-religious rituals and other activities.

Monte Negro

Monte Negro is located on a mountain overlooking the important Late Postclassic community of Tilantongo south of the Nochixtlán Valley. At 2,680 m above sea level, Monte Negro can be cold and misty during the rainy season like many of the hilltop sites in the Mixteca Alta. Monte Negro was founded early in the Ramos phase by people who migrated from surrounding communities (Acosta & Romero 1992; Balkansky et al. 2004). Like Monte Albán, Monte Negro was unoccupied prior to its founding and rapid emergence as a demographic nucleus, but was settled only during the early Ramos phase (300–100 BC) when it grew to cover 78 ha. Balkansky and his colleagues (2004) argue that the agriculture necessary to feed the people of this hilltop center was produced through the use of the *lama-bordo* terrace system that was so important in the Mixteca during later periods. Numerous *lama-bordo* terraces, some immense in scale, were built in arroyos descending the slopes of Monte Negro, which converted the infertile hills into productive agricultural land. Excavations are needed to verify when the terraces were constructed and used (see Pérez 2006) since the site lies adjacent to a major Postclassic community that could have built and farmed the terraces near the earlier site.

Monte Negro rises 500 m above the surrounding valley and its flatter summits are covered with multiple complexes consisting of concentrations of public buildings and high-status residences (Acosta & Romero 1992; Balkansky et al. 2004; Geurds & Jansen 2008). Commoner houses were built on terraces on the slopes below, although most of the excavations at the site focused on the ceremonial complexes (figure 6.2). This

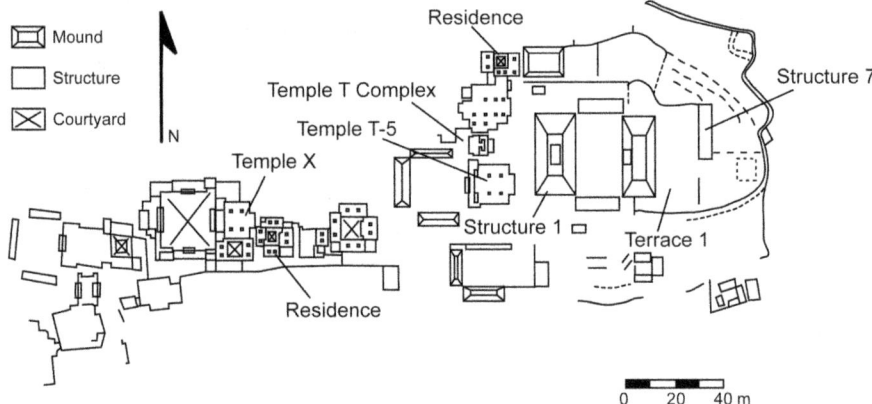

Figure 6.2 Plan of the civic-ceremonial center of Monte Negro (after Balkansky et al. 2004, figure 9; © 2004 Society for American Archaeology; reproduced by permission of *Latin American Antiquity*, volume 15, number 1; redrawn by Eric Berkemeyer)

decentralized or multiple-nuclei pattern (Balkansky et al. 2004:47) resembles Yucuita and other early political centers in the Mixtec highlands. At least four corporate complexes, perhaps the ceremonial centers of barrios, have been identified. Each complex consists of a small plaza measuring between 400 m² and 700 m², surrounded by buildings constructed on low platforms.

Excavations show that the buildings concentrated in the core of each corporate complex included both temples and high-status residences surrounding small plazas (Acosta & Romero 1992; Geurds & Jansen 2008: 401–14). Mixtecs dedicated many of the buildings with offerings of ceramic vessels interred beneath the surfaces of platforms and patios. The westernmost of the two complexes excavated by Acosta and Romero (1992) included an east-to-west running street along its length. Balkansky and his colleagues (2004) identified a possible ballcourt between the two complexes, although Geurds and Jansen (2008:409) question this interpretation.

Temples at Monte Negro had plaster floors, broad stairways, and doors with roofs supported by columns; otherwise they varied considerably in size and form, ranging from 56 m² to 160 m² (Acosta & Romero 1992; Geurds & Jansen 2008). Some temples included altars and offering basins or niches. In several instances ritual paraphernalia was found such as an anthropomorphic urn on the altar in Temple X and two obsidian knives found in

Temple T.S. Carved into the risers of some steps on Temple T.S. is the circle-and-triangle blood glyph (however, see Geurds & Jansen 2008:407–9). Monte Negro's temples differed considerably from the contemporaneous elongated, multi-room temples found at El Palenque in the Valley of Oaxaca (Redmond & Spencer 2008). They are somewhat closer in form to the columned, two-room temples found in the Valley of Oaxaca beginning in the Terminal Formative (Martínez López 2002:242–9), although those at Monte Negro have a more open floor plan.

High-status residences were somewhat larger and better made than typical ones in the Mixteca Alta (Geurds & Jansen 2008:411–14; Winter 1986:343–5), consisting of rooms with stone foundations supporting wattle-and-daub or adobe walls that surrounded an interior patio sometimes floored with stone slabs. Rooms had dirt floors and columns. Mixtecs built several residences that were connected to temples by roofed passageways, indicating a close association between high-status people and politico-religious buildings as at other early political centers in Oaxaca. The adobe tombs and burials beneath the floors of some temples as well as in residences are another indication of this association (Acosta & Romero 1992).

Like the variation in residences, burials suggest modest differences in status and the extent of social networks that participated in mortuary ceremonies. Burial types included simple graves, stone-lined cists, and adobe tombs with wooden or stone roofs (Acosta & Romero 1992). Unfortunately, Acosta and Romero (1992) do not report the inventory of offerings or context of many of the burials. Given the available data, variation in the quantity of burial offerings appears relatively low with tombs on average having more elaborate offerings (figure 6.3). Simple graves and cists usually had no offerings, although about a third had a few ceramic vessels. All the excavated tombs had offerings of up to about a dozen vessels, including zoomorphic and anthropomorphic forms. Most of the burials with preserved skulls exhibited cranial modification and one individual had pyrite inlays in his upper canines. Although these examples of bodily alteration may have signaled status distinctions, there is no correlation with burial type or the quantity of offerings. The individual with dental inlays did not exhibit cranial modification.

The most elaborate offering was the 21 ceramic vessels accompanying Burial VIII-3, an older adult female interred in a simple grave in the southern end of Temple T.S. just below a niche in the wall. Burials in temples were unusual in that 67 percent were of advanced age whereas only 14 percent of the other burials were elders. These data show a strong correlation between age and interment in temples, suggesting that elders may have acquired special status as ritual specialists probably for the corporate group. This

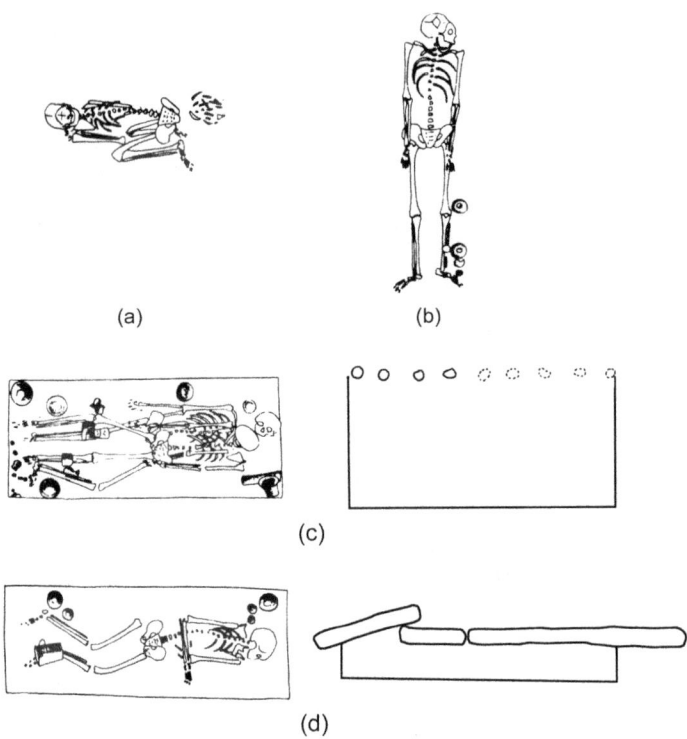

Figure 6.3 Late Formative burials from Monte Negro: (a) Burial VIII-4B; (b) Burial IX-5; (c) Tomb 1; (d) Tomb 4 (after Acosta & Romero 1992, figures 19 and 82; reproduced with permission from the Instituto Nacional de Antropología e Historia; drawing by Eric Berkemeyer)

inference is consistent with Urcid's (2008) reconstruction of sodality organization from the Building L-sub program at Monte Albán.

Huamelulpan

Huamelulpan is a major Late/Terminal Formative site located on a hill and surrounding ridges that rise to 200 m above the floor of the Huamelulpan Valley (figure 6.4). Today the site overlooks the quiet valley as well as numerous small Mixtec communities, including the one built on the site itself. Gaxiola excavated parts of the site center in 1974 and Winter expanded the excavations and reconsolidated some of the architecture in the early 1990s. The Huamelulpan Valley and surrounding hills were surveyed in the mid-1990s (Balkansky 1998a). Survey and excavation at Huamelulpan

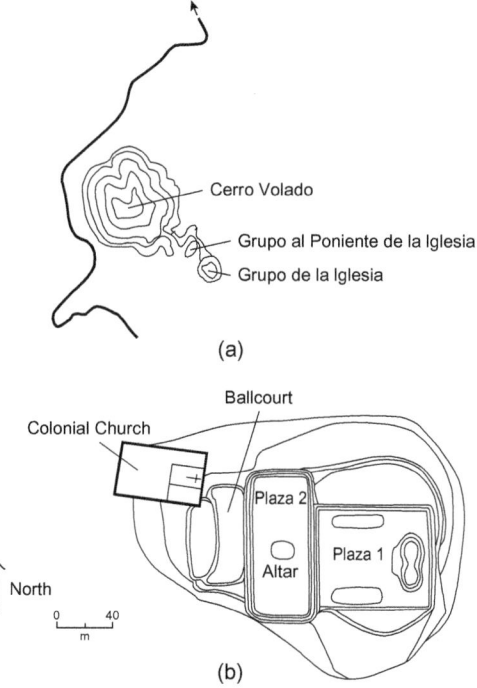

Figure 6.4 Plan of Huamelulpan: (a) site plan; (b) plan of the Grupo de la Iglesia (after Winter et al. 1991, figures I.2 and I.3; reproduced with permission from the Instituto Nacional de Antropología e Historia; drawing by Eric Berkemeyer)

show explosive growth with the site increasing from 6 ha in the Cruz D and Yucuita phases to 155 ha in Early Ramos and 212 ha by Late Ramos (Balkansky 1998a; Gaxiola 1984; Winter et al. 1991). Settlement within the Huamelulpan Valley also increased dramatically from 68 ha in the Cruz D and Yucuita phases to 892 ha by Late Ramos with people moving into higher elevations and many living on terraces. Based on survey data, agricultural practices included farming of the valley floor, small household gardens, and *lama-bordo* systems (Balkansky 1998a). Specialized production of chipped-stone tools is suggested by surface collections from some terraces.

Huamelulpan exhibits the dispersed pattern of public architecture found at other Mixtec centers. A public space on the summit of Cerro Volado, the highest part of the site, consists of a large plaza (100 m by 50 m) flanked by two monumental structures. Based on surface collections, Balkansky

(1998a:50–1) dates the plaza complex to the Ramos phase, although Winter and colleagues (1991:8–9) argue that it is primarily Classic period. Based on surface evidence, Balkansky (1998a:50) identified a possible high-status residence on the uppermost terrace on Cerro Volado, just below the plaza.

Another Ramos-phase public area surrounded by residential terraces is the Grupo de la Iglesia with two large plazas located on a hilltop in the southeastern end of the site (Winter et al. 1991). Plaza 1 measures 1,600 m^2 on the eastern end of the ridge and is demarcated on its northern, eastern, and southern sides by monumental buildings. A midden probably from ritual activities was discovered adjacent to the southern structure and contained burned human and animal bone, ceramics, and mica adornments. A monumental stairway descends 6 m from the western, open side of Plaza 1 to Plaza 2, which covers 4,000 m^2 and has an *adoratorio* or altar in its center. Directly west and beneath Plaza 2 is an I-shaped ballcourt.

A third ceremonial area is the Grupo al Poniente de la Iglesia located between Cerro Volado and the Grupo de la Iglesia (Gaxiola 1984:47–55). Construction began in the Early Ramos phase, but Mixtecs built most of the complex during Late Ramos, including at least three large platforms along with a sunken patio. Platforms had plaster floors and ranged from 2 m to 3 m in height and were as much as 49 m on a side. Builders used huge stone blocks to construct the platform corners and some were carved with hieroglyphic inscriptions. Gaxiola (1984:51–2) discovered a stone altar, the Altar de los Craneos, adjacent to the southeastern end of this complex. Three skulls were found on the altar; each had two holes drilled in the forehead for suspension. Artifacts found on the altar included shell and serpentine pendants, and a greenstone axe. Another skull was found at the base of the altar with unfinished perforations on the forehead. All of the skulls were from adults; three were male and one was female (Gaxiola 1984:51–2). The suspension of skulls in Mesoamerica is most often associated with the display of sacrificial victims, usually war captives. A ritual offering was found mostly on the plaster floor in front of the skulls, which consisted of ceramic urns, braziers, jars, and bowls probably related to ritual feasting. Some urns had images of the rain god similar to those found in the Oaxaca Valley (figure 6.5) and others exhibited bird attributes, perhaps related to the wide-billed bird deity that also appears in the Oaxaca Valley at this time.

Several meters east of the altar, Gaxiola (1984:60–2) excavated part of a possible Early Ramos-phase house consisting of two rooms around a patio; a low platform lies to the north. The architecture as well as the burial of a 3-year-old child with a single eeramic vessel does not suggest high

Political Centralization in the Mixteca and Coast 171

Figure 6.5 Ceramic urn from Huamelulpan with rain-god imagery (after Joyce & Winter 1996, figure 4a; © Wenner-Gren Foundation for Anthropological Research)

status. Since both rooms had hearths and abundant remains of deer as well as rabbit and dog, it is possible that this was not a residence, but instead was a structure used for the storage and preparation of food for ritual feasting in the ceremonial complex.

Approximately 100 m south of the Grupo al Poniente de la Iglesia the archaeologists exposed a high-status house with thick plaster floors (Gaxiola 1984:62–4; figure 6.6). Beneath the largest of the rooms in the house was a stone-masonry tomb consisting of a single chamber with three niches. The tomb was disturbed in antiquity, but still contained the remains of a female about 40 years old at death and a male about 70 years old, accompanied by eight ceramic vessels and a bone needle. In the northeastern corner of the residence were two concentrations of vessels covered with charcoal, interpreted as deposits related to ritual feasting. One feature included a hearth with abundant charcoal and burned pieces of human skull and possibly deer, along with three complete bowls, a metate,

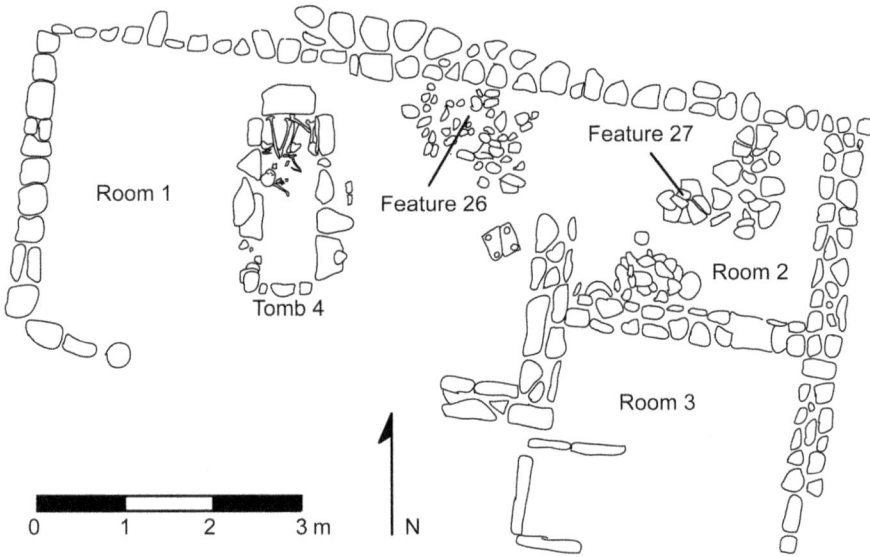

Figure 6.6 High-status house from Huamelulpan (redrawn from Gaxiola 1984, figures 49 and 50; reproduced with permission from the Instituto Nacional de Antropología e Historia)

and a gray-ware anthropomorphic urn. The second feature had two concentrations of whole ceramic vessels including 15 large gray-ware bowls, 2 braziers, and a fragment of a gray-ware anthropomorphic urn. Gaxiola (1984:64) reports that these vessel types were atypical of the overall site assemblage. The fact that most of the vessels were complete could be the result of the residence having been abandoned suddenly. Gaxiola (1984:64–5) excavated another possible Late Ramos-phase residence to the north of the Grupo al Poniente de la Iglesia.

Cerro de las Minas

Cerro de las Minas is located on a hilltop rising 100 m above the floor of the Huajuapan Valley on the edge of the modern city of Huajuapan. Looking down on the site from the road to Mexico City, Cerro de las Minas today seems like an island in the urban sprawl, but in the Late/Terminal Formative the site was the location of the Mixteca Baja's earliest political center. Cerro de las Minas was excavated by Winter (2007) from 1987 to 1993 and has been the focus of several salvage projects.

Cerro de las Minas was a small political center that emerged during the Ñudée phase (300 BC–AD 300). Ñudée-phase settlement covered much of the site's 55 ha and the majority by volume of the site's monumental architecture was constructed at this time (Winter 2007:76). The civic-ceremonial core was located on the summit of the hilltop. During the Classic period the site center consisted of three monumental platforms supporting both public buildings and high-status residences, separated by two plazas. The Late/Terminal Formative configuration of the site center is not clear, although excavations have exposed walls, floors, middens, and column bases. Adjacent to the central platform is a ballcourt that may have been constructed in the Ñudée phase.

In the southern end of the site excavations exposed portions of several Ñudée-phase residences built on terraces. Winter and Montague (1991) exposed only small sections of walls, plaster floors, middens, and a possible hearth. The archaeologists recovered eight burials in simple graves or cists partially lined with stones or adobes. Burials were primary interments with one or two individuals, and most either lacked offerings or had a few ceramic vessels. One burial was interred with a stone bead and numerous mica pieces. The most elaborate offering consisted of eight ceramic vessels and a perforated shell disc.

Santa Teresa was another important Ñudée-phase site in the Huajuapan Valley (Winter 2005b). At Santa Teresa a large public plaza measuring approximately 150 m by 150 m was built at this time and was bordered by large mounds on its eastern, southern, and western sides. Two looted stone tombs were discovered adjacent to the northeastern end of the plaza. The plaza complex resembles the corporate complexes at other Mixtec centers, although its size exceeds any other known Formative-period plaza in the Mixteca.

Interregional Interaction and the Rise of Mixtec Centers

Late/Terminal Formative political changes in the Mixtec highlands are often argued to have been the result of interactions with Monte Albán. Political centralization and settlement nucleation in the Mixteca has been seen as driven by military threats from the Zapotec capital (Balkansky 1998a; Balkansky et al. 2004; Flannery 1983c) and others have suggested that political changes in the Mixteca may have resulted from the adoption of elements of Zapotec ideology (Joyce & Winter 1996). Political centralization and settlement nucleation appears to have occurred in the Oaxaca Valley a century or two earlier than in the Mixteca, although chronological refinements may push these trends in the Mixtec highlands back to the founding of Monte Albán. Even if Monte Albán predates the Mixtec centers, this does not demonstrate that the former dominated interregional relations.

Evidence from the Mixtec highlands suggests some similarities with the Zapotec polity centered at Monte Albán in innovations in politico-religious ideas and practices. Like at Monte Albán, Mixtec centers exhibit themes of warfare, sacrifice, ballgame ceremonialism, and the sacred covenant, including depictions of prominent people dressed in the guise of the rain god. Evidence for decapitation sacrifice includes trophy skulls recovered at Yucuita, Monte Negro, Huamelulpan, and Cerro de las Minas, and several decapitated burials from Yucunama in the mountains north of the Teposcolula Valley (Winter 2005b:92). Burned human bone in ritual features at Huamelulpan and Yucuita may relate to the ritual treatment of sacrificial victims (Gaxiola 1984:63; Spores 1984:24). The blood glyph carved into the risers on Temple T.S. at Monte Negro also appears on some of the carved monuments of the Building L-sub program at Monte Albán and is probably a reference to sacrificial blood.

The relationship between sacrifice, fertility, and the sacred covenant is referenced on carved stones removed from their original context, but dated stylistically to the Ramos phase at Huamelulpan and Yucuita (Urcid n.d.). Yucuita Monument 1 depicts a person in the guise of the rain god with blood issuing from the mouth as in autosacrifice (figure 6.7). Above the personage is a representation of Glyph J, symbolizing maize, along with what may be an image of a mountain of sustenance with depictions of maize at various stages of growth from seeds to mature plants (Urcid n.d.). Similarly, Monument 3 from Huamelulpan depicts a named person in the guise of the rain god silhouetted on a hill glyph perhaps representing a mountain of sustenance. Zapotecs depicted similar themes of rain-deity impersonation, sacrifice, and fertility on Monument J-41 at Monte Albán. Another compelling representation of the sacred covenant can be seen in the evidence from the Altar de los Craneos at Huamelulpan with its trophy skulls, urns in the image of the rain god, and ceramic vessels perhaps holding offerings of food symbolizing fertility. Mixtec hieroglyphic writing and the style of anthropomorphic urns with avian and rain-god imagery stylistically resemble, although are not identical to, Zapotec writing and urns. Certain features of monumental architecture, such as I-shaped ballcourts, *adoratorios*, and large stone columns are found in both the Oaxaca Valley and the Mixteca Alta.

There are many differences in monumental architecture and public spaces among Mixtec and Zapotec political centers, however (also see Balkansky

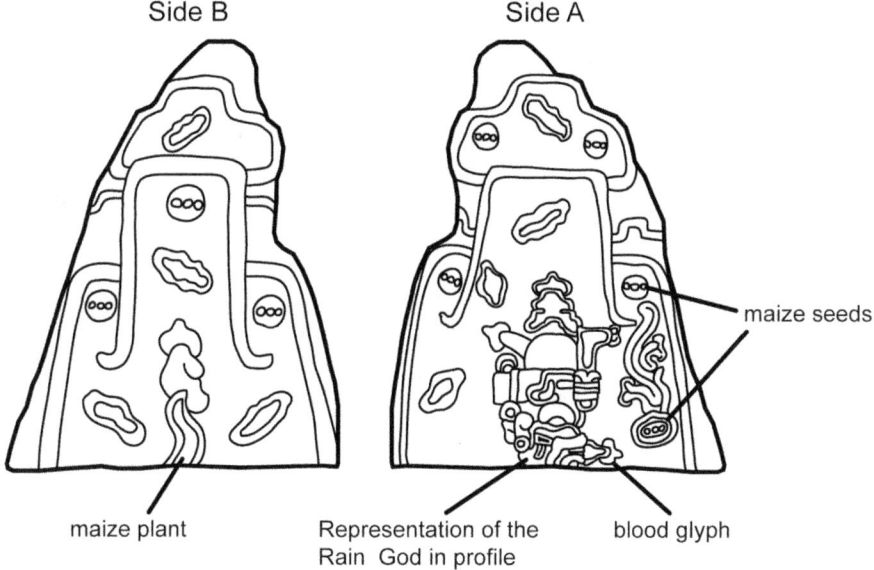

Figure 6.7 Yucuita Monument 1 (drawing courtesy of Javier Urcid)

et al. 2004:55–6). For example, the smaller-scale and multiple-nuclei pattern of Mixtec ceremonial centers differs significantly from the pattern in the Valley of Oaxaca. The architectural layout of Mixtec ceremonial centers does not appear to exhibit the cosmic symbolism found at Monte Albán.

In addition to politico-religious ideas, Mixtec elites also exchanged social valuables with nobles from the Oaxaca Valley and other regions. Non-local items like obsidian, greenstone, marine and freshwater shell, and well-made pottery were imported into communities in the Mixtec highlands (A. Joyce 1991a:537–46). These items were social valuables preferentially controlled by elites, but available to common people as well and used as symbols of prestige and means through which status could be advanced. Exotic items like shell or greenstone ornaments may have been used in beautification and as resources to establish more prestigious kinship ties through marriage.

Interaction among commoners as well as social elites in the Mixtec highlands and the Valley of Oaxaca is suggested by comparisons of ceramic styles. Late/Terminal Formative ceramics in the Mixtec highlands and Valley of Oaxaca exhibit stylistic crossties, particularly among gray wares (A. Joyce 1991a:570–9; Levine 2002). The strongest interregional ties are seen in a category of conical bowls decorated with two incised lines on the interior rim and sometimes a combed base (type G-12 in the Valley of Oaxaca ceramic typology). This ceramic type was also executed in tan wares in the Nochixtlán Valley. Ceramic compositional studies show that people made gray wares locally in all these regions (Joyce et al. 2006). It is difficult to determine patterns of ceramic diffusion, however. Gray wares are more common in the Valley of Oaxaca and it is usually assumed that gray-ware style originated there and spread to other regions (e.g., A. Joyce 1991a:571; Marcus & Flannery 1996:199–206), although locally made gray wares date back to the Early Formative in the Mixteca Alta (Spores 1972:37–45). Although there are stylistic crossties among regions, the overall assemblage in each region remains distinct. In addition, focusing solely on the Oaxaca Valley as the source area for the spread of gray-ware styles ignores other potential patterns of ceramic similarity that might be important for understanding Late/Terminal Formative interaction (A. Joyce 1993b). For example, a type of thin-walled composite silhouette bowl found in both the Mixteca Alta and the Mixteca Baja includes vessels that are almost identical to one another in technology, form, and style.

A recent compositional study of ceramic pastes shows that pottery was exchanged among people of the Mixtec highlands and the Valley of Oaxaca (Joyce et al. 2006). Oaxaca Valley gray wares, including G-12 bowls, and cream-ware vessels were exported to the Mixteca Alta and Baja, although most G-12 bowls in the Mixteca were locally produced. Brown-ware bowls were in turn exported from the Mixteca Alta to the Valley of Oaxaca. Although these ceramic types constituted some of the more elaborate ceramics of the period, they were certainly widely available, suggesting that pottery exchange between the Valley of Oaxaca and the Mixteca may have been carried out among both elites and commoners. Trade could have contributed to the spread of ceramic styles. The exchange of actual vessels as well as the diffusion of ceramic styles primarily involved serving vessels like the G-12 gray-ware bowls. The Late Formative saw an increase in the production of serving vessels that might have been used in ritual feasting (Blanton et al. 1999:105; Levine 2002) and some of these vessels, such as the G-12 bowls, may have been produced by specialists. These data suggest a possible expansion of ritual feasting where elaborate serving vessels were on display and viewed by people from other communities; vessels may also have been exchanged during feasts. The adoption of G-12-like bowls in many regions could also be attributed to emulation of a popular vessel type associated with the powerful political and ceremonial center of Monte Albán.

Flannery (1983c) suggests that similarities in monumental architecture and ceramic styles in some parts of the Mixteca Alta may be the result of conquest by Monte Albán. Warfare in the Late Formative Mixtec highlands is indicated by the presence of trophy skulls at many political centers and a shift in settlement to defensible hilltops (Balkansky et al. 2000; Joyce & Winter 1996:39–42; Rivera 1999). Monte Negro, Cerro de las Minas, and Diquiyú were built on imposing hilltops, while Yucuita and Huamelulpan were on lower hills or ridges. Possible defensive walls were built around parts of Yucuita, Huamelulpan, Cerro de las Minas, and Diquiyú and at smaller sites in several regions (Balkansky 1998a:52; Winter 1989a:37, 102). Yet, as discussed in the last chapter, there is little evidence for the conquest of any of the polities in the Mixteca Alta by Monte Albán (also see Balkansky et al. 2004:51–6; A. Joyce 1991a:593; 1994a:66–8). Instead, I argue that Mixtec polities probably periodically went to war with each other and with political centers in other nearby regions, perhaps including Monte Albán. Although polities and coalitions may have at times defeated rivals, political fortunes were dynamic and no single center probably ever gained supremacy over the Mixteca.

I interpret the evidence as suggesting a variety of forms of interaction through which ideas and practices may have spread among the people of different regions of Oaxaca. Though further research is needed, I prefer to draw on an analogy based on interpolity relations at the time of the Spanish Conquest to interpret Late/Terminal Formative interregional relations. At this time, interregional relations consisted of shifting patterns of conflict, competition, and cooperation among political centers. Nobles interacted through warfare, alliance, intermarriage, and the exchange of prestigious goods and ideas. Common people also interacted via trade, market exchange, intermarriage, and migration. Ceramic styles and other aspects of domestic culture may also have spread if slaves were taken in warfare (Junker 2008:125–9). If interpolity interaction involved dynamic relations among multiple centers, then evidence for innovations in politics, religion, ceramic styles, and militarism cannot be attributed to Monte Albán alone. Regardless of the exact nature of interpolity and interregional relations, the evidence suggests more frequent, varied, and intense contacts among the people of highland Oaxaca.

Political Authority and Ideology

Though Mixtec and Zapotec elites were clearly exchanging materials and ideas concerning religion and rulership, forms of political authority in the Valley of Oaxaca and the Mixteca differed. The available evidence from the early centers of the Mixtec highlands suggests to me that political authority was dominated by multiple corporate groups, perhaps based on kinship ties or early versions of the type of barrio organization present at the time of the Spanish Conquest. Each corporate group was centered on a public area often including a plaza and temples. The scale of public spaces, in terms of both plaza area and the volume of monumental architecture, was much less than Monte Albán's Main Plaza. In the Mixteca, groups of residences surrounded the public spaces with higher-status families more closely associated spatially with ceremonial areas. As in the Oaxaca Valley, higher-status individuals and families had preferential control over prestige goods, important ceremonies, and ritual knowledge. Elites were probably ritual specialists as well as political leaders for their corporate groups.

Based on present evidence, however, it appears to me that status and wealth distinctions in the Late/Terminal Formative Mixtec highlands are much less pronounced than in the Oaxaca Valley, and evidence for exclusionary rulership is difficult to find. Calendrical dates carved into monumental stones that formed the corners of the platforms at the Grupo al Poniente de la Iglesia at Huamelulpan could be interpreted as either a ruling genealogy or the names of leaders of corporate groups that formed a ruling council. Images of rain-deity impersonators on carved stones at Huamelulpan and Yucuita might be exclusionary rulers, although they could also be leaders of corporate groups as suggested by Urcid (2008) for the Building L-sub program at Monte Albán. These data raise the possibility that, rather than having a single overall ruler, early political centers in the Mixtec highlands may have been administered by a council of leading families drawn from the corporate groups that constituted the community and probably the broader polity (see Beekman 2008). The corporate groups may have been descended from the different communities that founded the demographic centers.

If political authority in the Mixtec highlands was based on a council of leaders, rather than a single ruler or ruling dynasty, then Late/Terminal Formative Mixtec society may have avoided structural contradictions and tensions between corporate and exclusionary forms of authority, as hypothesized for the Oaxaca Valley. Primary affiliations with corporate groups, however, would inhibit the formation of an overarching political identity linked to the polity as a whole. The subjectivities of Mixtec peoples appear to have been only weakly defined by affiliations with the political center or polity, and instead continued traditional identities linked to corporate groups perhaps tied to communities of origin as well as affiliations with family, occupation, gender, age, etc. Conversely, Late/Terminal Formative polities in the Mixteca may have contained structural contradictions between corporate organization, shared rulership, and the cohesion of the polity that caused them to be inherently unstable and subject to factional competition and conflict. The collapse of many of these early political centers after only a few centuries demonstrates their instability (see below).

If I am correct in these inferences concerning political authority, then it raises questions about urbanism in the Mixtec highlands during the Late/Terminal Formative period. Urbanism creates complex social distinctions and relations between those that live in cities and those in the countryside, while cities are usually seats of political, economic, and cultural power. There is no doubt that communities like Yucuita, Monte Negro, and Cerro de las Minas were places of political power and religious authority. The ways in which hinterland communities were tied to these demographic centers is less clear, however. In some parts of the Mixteca, particularly the area around Monte Negro, the founding of Late Formative centers significantly depopulated surrounding communities, thereby severely depleting the hinterland population (Balkansky et al. 2004:44–6). People in the hinterland may have participated in public rituals at Mixtec centers like Yucuita and Huamelulpan, although the scale of public ceremonial spaces is relatively limited. Mixtec centers may also have been the location of markets and fortifications that periodically attracted people from surrounding areas. The leading families of Mixtec centers may have exercised political authority over the countryside and mobilized tribute in the form of agricultural surpluses, labor, and military service, although again the evidence is lacking. The pattern of multiple corporate groups, each with their own leaders, may mean that people in the hinterland were affiliated with a specific corporate organization, rather than with the urban center and polity as a whole.

Relational definitions of urbanism potentially allow for smaller centers to be seen as urban. For example, in his discussion of Aztec cities, Michael E. Smith (2005, 2008:6) extends settlements with urban functions to both cities and towns. The key distinction between urban and non-urban settings is the relationship between center and hinterland, and the evidence for these kinds of relations in the Late/Terminal Formative Mixteca is currently lacking. I should be clear, however, that I find it difficult to imagine that places like Cerro de las Minas and Huamelulpan were not viewed as distinctive given their public architecture, monumental art, concentrated populations, and leading families. Future research in the Mixtec highlands should explore the relationship between center and hinterland more fully. I suspect that such research will find that relations of dominance and dependency were present between Mixtec centers and their hinterlands. The degree of urbanism in the Mixteca, however, was almost certainly less than in the Oaxaca Valley, and the nature of urban relationships was undoubtedly different.

Urbanization in the Lower Río Verde Valley

Late/Terminal Formative-period social developments in the lower Río Verde Valley on the Pacific coast of Oaxaca parallel those of the highlands with settlement nucleation and the development of centralized polities. As in the Oaxacan highlands, evidence from the lower Verde suggests tension and perhaps conflict between traditional structures of authority and newer more regional, centralized, and hierarchical ones. Political centers probably arose in adjacent river valleys along the western Oaxaca coast and Pacific slope at sites like El Ciruelo, Piedra Parada Jamiltepec, Río Grande, Bajos de Chila, and Nopala; research at these sites, however, is insufficient to assess their history of occupation (Brockington et al. 1974; Joyce 1993a).

Population increased significantly through the Formative period in the lower Río Verde Valley (Joyce 2005). The occupational area in the full-coverage survey increased from 5 ha in the Early Formative to 64 ha during the Middle Formative Charco phase (700–400 BC) and to 299 ha by the Late Formative Minizundo phase (400–150 BC). By the Middle Formative, Charco Redondo on the floodplain east of the Río Verde emerged as a demographic nucleus covering 62 ha, making the site one of the largest in Oaxaca at the time. During the Late Formative a second demographic center emerged as the population of San Francisco de Arriba exploded with the site reaching 95 ha, while Charco Redondo grew to 70 ha. Both of these communities overlapped in size with the largest sites in the Mixtec highlands, probably with populations exceeding 1,000 people. As discussed for the Mixtec highlands, the evidence at present is insufficient to determine if these communities should be considered urban centers, although again I think future research will bear this out.

One factor that has been suggested as contributing to Formative-period social developments in the lower Río Verde Valley is environmental change, particularly during the Early and Middle Formative periods. Paleoenvironmental research in the valleys of the upper drainage basin of the Río Verde indicates two periods of anthropogenic erosion during the Formative. In the valleys of Nochixtlán, Oaxaca, and Ejutla erosion and increased runoff into the drainage system was likely triggered by agricultural expansion during the Early Formative and the movement of people into higher elevations at the beginning of the Late Formative (Joyce & Mueller 1997). While people in the highlands developed terraces to control erosion, our data suggest that anthropogenic landscape change had a major impact on lowland environments as well. The eroded sediment and runoff from the highlands were carried down the drainage basin to the lower Río Verde causing major changes in floodplain and coastal environments. Paleoenvironmental research in the lower valley indicates a major shift in the form and position of the river. Data from sediment cores show an increase in flooding and sediment load that triggered a shift from meandering to more braided river conditions by the Late Formative (A. Joyce 1991a:440–511, 1991b:133–8; Joyce & Mueller 1992). More important for human populations was an expansion of the Río Verde's agriculturally productive floodplain. Preliminary data from cores in the coastal lagoons suggest that the increase in sediment carried by the river also accelerated the formation of bay-barrier features along the coast (Goman et al. 2005). By c.400 BC the formation of the bay barriers closed off the coastline, forming the estuaries. Like the floodplain, the Verde's coastal estuaries are rich in resources used by human populations such as fish, shellfish, and waterfowl. Deepika Fernández (2004:135–7) shows a trend toward increasing utilization of estuarine resources as represented by faunal remains recovered from sites in the region, which is consistent with the formation of the estuaries at the end of the Formative. It is tempting to argue that the ecological changes contributed to population growth in the region after 700 BC, although we have not yet established a clear causal link between environmental change and demographic expansion. Construction of massive residential platforms during the Late/Terminal Formative at many sites in the lower Verde's floodplain was probably a response to increasing rainy-season flooding and the need to elevate residences above floodwaters during years of severe inundations.

Identity and status in Late Formative Chatino communities

Excavations at Cerro de la Cruz provide data on a Minizundo-phase Chatino community as well as evidence for practices that constituted community identity and emerging status differences (A. Joyce 1991a, 1994b). Cerro de la Cruz is located 4 km west of the river and occupies about 1.5 ha of a low spur extending from a hill in the floodplain. The site is adjacent to an abandoned channel of the Río Verde that might have been an oxbow pond at the end of the Formative. When we first discovered Cerro de la Cruz in 1986, it had been recently bulldozed for road fill. Though I feared that little remained of the site, horizontal excavations in 1988 exposed portions of three Minizundo-phase residential terraces that included four probable low-status residences characterized by stone foundations, earthen floors, burials, and small cooking features.

Our excavations on the upper terrace (figure 6.8) exposed a granite flagstone patio surrounded by stone foundations of five structures (Structures 1–5). The evidence from the upper terrace indicates an association

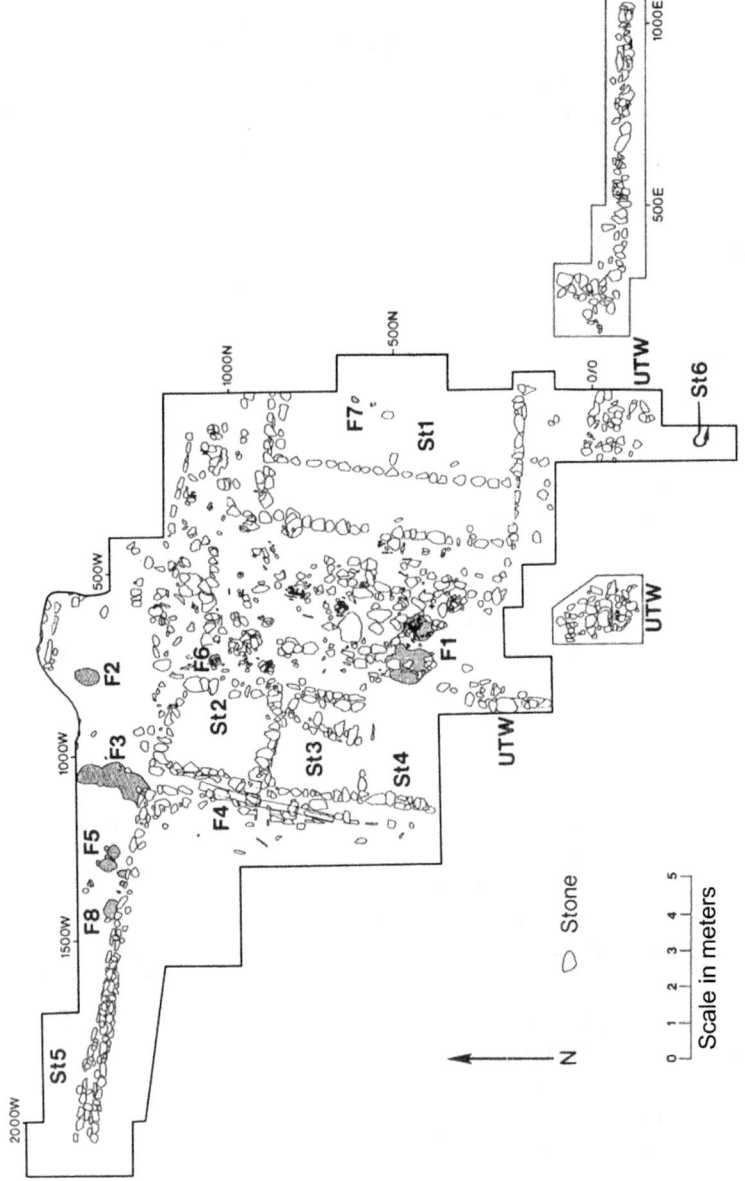

Figure 6.8 Plan of upper-terrace excavations at Cerro de la Cruz (after Joyce 1991a, figure 5.2)

between a probable residence (Structure 5), presumably of a prominent family, and public space for rituals participated in by a broader corporate group, which resemble patterns identified in the Mixtec highlands. The granite flagstone patio included two large hearths. One hearth was completely excavated and measured 3 m^2 in area, intruding up to 0.4 m into the surface of the patio. The size of the hearth exceeds typical cooking features associated with lower-Verde residences, suggesting its association with communal feasting events. Two middens that we excavated at the base of the terrace wall south of Structure 1 contained ash, charcoal, and charred maize along with a higher frequency of sherds from imported vessels (3.4 percent versus 0.4 percent) relative to typical Minizundo-phase contexts (A. Joyce 1991a). These data suggest that people used exotic imports during ritual feasts. Three of the structures surrounding the patio (Structures 2, 3, and 4) were small storage rooms with their floors deliberately sunken beneath the level of the patio. They may have been used to store goods associated with feasting. Deposits at the base of one of the rooms included charred maize and shell. Evidence for communal feasting has also been recovered in the form of large hearths or cooking pits containing charred remains of comestibles like maize, coyul palm nut, marine shell, and animal bone at the sites of Río Viejo (A. Joyce 1991a:361) and Yugüe (Barber 2005:98). Hepp (2007:100–3) suggests that whistles and ceramic figurines recovered from Late and Terminal Formative-period contexts may have been used in ceremonies associated with ritual feasting.

The most surprising discovery at Cerro de la Cruz was a Late Formative public cemetery associated with Structure 1, where non-elite adults and rarely children were interred (A. Joyce 1991a:248–61, 718–44, 1994b:152–3). A total of 48 individuals, including 41 adults, was recovered from beneath two successive floors and along the walls of Structure 1 (figure 6.9).[6] An additional nine individuals were interred along the interior of the terrace wall that supported the patio complex. None of the burials recovered from the upper terrace were accompanied by offerings. The prevalence of adult burials suggests that the achievement of adult status, which permitted interment in the cemetery, depended on age-related ceremonies, as argued by Rosemary Joyce (2000) for other parts of Mesoamerica. The burials associated with the patio complex were interred over the course of several generations, as shown by frequent instances of later burials having disturbed earlier ones. The dense placement of burials in the cemetery as well as the frequent disturbance and movement of the bones of earlier interments by later ones can be interpreted as an assertion of collective identity and a denial of the individual (see Shanks & Tilley 1982).

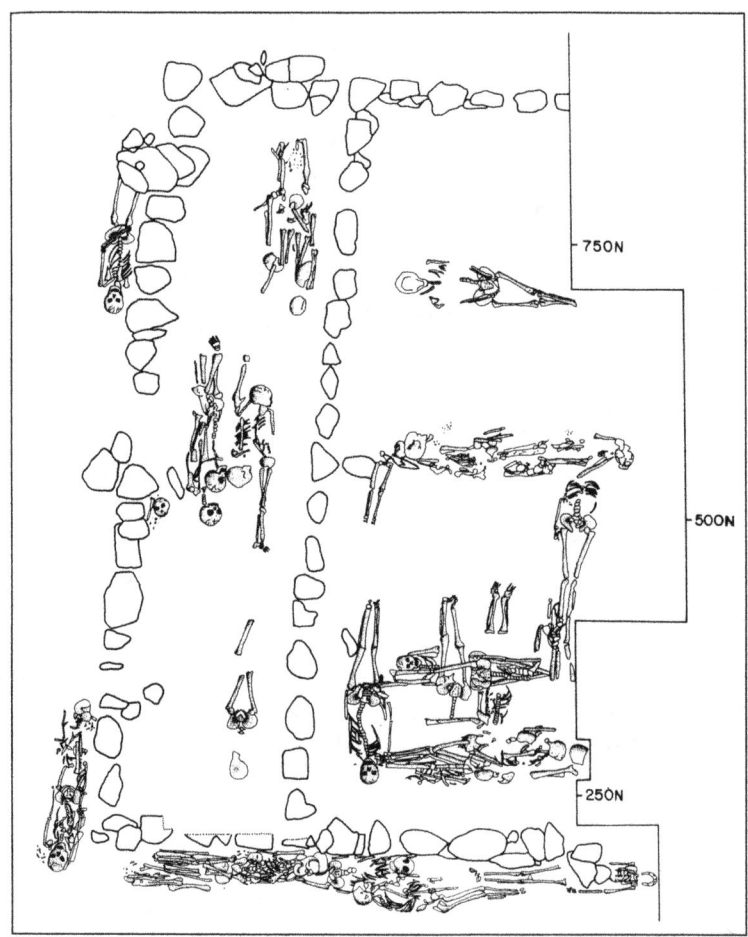

Figure 6.9 Late Formative cemetery beneath Structure 1 at Cerro de la Cruz (after Joyce 1994b, figure 9; reproduced from *Journal of Field Archaeology* with the permission of the Trustees of Boston University)

Communal identity was also constituted through collective labor and the construction of public spaces and buildings during the Minizundo phase (Barber 2005:99–100; A. Joyce 2006; Workinger 2002). Block excavations by Workinger (2002:171–222) at San Francisco de Arriba indicate that Chatinos built much of the site's massive public acropolis over the course of several building phases using rubble fill. The scale of construction suggests that political authorities at San Francisco de Arriba were able to mobilize a large labor force. On a more modest scale, a well-made stone retaining wall, probably part of a low platform, exposed in a deep trench at Río Viejo may also have been part of a public building; organic deposits at the base of the wall suggest ritual feasting (A. Joyce 1991a:365). Construction of the terraces at Cerro de la Cruz and other Minizundo-phase sites also represent communal building projects.

Evidence for ritual feasting, communal cemeteries, and collective labor used to build public structures indicates the construction of socially meaningful places tied to the identity of corporate groups consisting of multiple households and perhaps entire communities (Barber 2005:95–101). In the case of the complex around Structure 1 at Cerro de la Cruz, shared pasts were a component of communal identity with burials and sequential rebuildings referencing history and the ancestors. The repetition of feasting and burial inscribed meaning and memory onto the Structure 1 complex through which collective histories were remembered and recreated.

Mortuary data, residences, and the distribution of imported goods suggest modest status distinctions (A. Joyce 1991a; 1994b). The only Minizundo-phase burials accompanied by offerings at Cerro de la Cruz were found interred in Structure 8, a probable residence exposed on the lower terrace. A total of 15 individuals were recovered from beneath four sequential floors in Structure 8, representing at least seven different burial events. Unlike the cemetery, the Structure 8 burials included both adults and children. The most elaborate burial offering that we discovered at Cerro de la Cruz was a sash of 45 carved marine shells found with Burial B13-I9, an adult male. Another burial included a juvenile with a bowl placed over the person's head along with a necklace of 22 perforated dog canines found around the face and neck. Burials accompanied by offerings in Structure 8 were interred over several generations, suggesting that status distinctions were inherited. The nature of variation in offerings and the fact that most grave goods were locally available indicate that social inequality was relatively modest. Architecture may also have been used to enhance status since the terrace retaining wall immediately south of Structure 8 was the most elaborate exposed at the site. Another possible higher-status residence with three sequential burials was excavated at Río Viejo. Grave offerings again were modest, mostly shell ornaments, although an adult male was interred holding a conch shell, perhaps a trumpet. The mortuary evidence from Cerro de la Cruz and Río Viejo indicates relatively modest status distinctions, although it is likely that the most powerful and prestigious families in the region resided at demographic centers like San Francisco de Arriba and Charco Redondo.

The prevalence of adornments on buried individuals differs from other regions of Oaxaca and suggests that people were enhancing their status and influence through beautification. The rarity of ceramic vessels accompanying Late Formative burials in the lower Río Verde Valley also differs with patterns elsewhere in Oaxaca. Participation in mortuary rituals may have been restricted, or perhaps commensal affiliations were not referenced in these ceremonies. The interment of high-status people beneath the floors of houses rather than in communal cemeteries suggests some degree of concealment, perhaps indicating that status inequality was a source of social tension (Barber 2005:290).

Distributional studies show a correlation between the frequency of imports and independent evidence for locations associated with public ritual and/or high status such as Structure 8 at Cerro de la Cruz and the acropolis at San Francisco de Arriba (A. Joyce 1994b:160–1; Workinger 2002:313–25, 372–6). Most sherds from imported vessels were from the Valley of Oaxaca and an as-yet-unidentified region, although imports sourced to the Mixteca Alta and probably the southern Isthmus of Tehuantepec have also been identified (A. Joyce 1991a; Workinger 2002:347–54). INAA shows that the dominant source of obsidian imported into the lower Verde was Paredón in the Basin of Mexico, over 400 km to the northwest (Joyce et al. 1995; Workinger 2002:313–21). Another central-Mexican source was the high-quality green obsidian from Pachuca, which constituted 28 percent of the obsidian at San Francisco de Arriba. Pachuca obsidian was not recovered from smaller Late Formative sites like Cerro de la Cruz and Río Viejo, suggesting that the rulers of San Francisco de Arriba had special relationships with elites and/or merchants from the Basin of Mexico. Exotic imported pottery and Pachuca obsidian were social valuables used to enhance status, create obligations, seal alliances, and exchange for other goods.

Negotiating tradition and authority in the Terminal Formative

Population growth and nucleation as well as political centralization culminate during the Terminal Formative with the emergence of an urban center at Río Viejo (A. Joyce 2003, 2005, 2006). Río Viejo increased in size from 25 ha in the Minizundo phase to 225 ha by the Miniyua phase (150 BC–AD 100), and the area occupied in the entire survey zone increased from 299 ha to 446 ha over the same period. By the late Terminal Formative Chacahua phase (AD 100–250) regional settlement increased still further to 699 ha. Local centers that were probably tied to Río Viejo through political, religious, and economic ties include San Francisco de Arriba, Charco Redondo, Cerro de la Virgen, and Tututepec. These sites ranged in size from about 60 to 72 ha and all had monumental public spaces and probably powerful individuals and families. Social inequality increased at this time as shown by mortuary offerings, domestic architecture, and monumental architecture (Barber 2005; A. Joyce 2005, 2006, 2008a). The evidence suggests that rulers at Río Viejo and other political centers were struggling to expand their influence through practices including the construction of monumental buildings and large-scale public ceremonies.

Unlike the Oaxacan highlands, there is no evidence for changes in the intensity of warfare such as shifts to defensible positions or evidence for the burning or abandonment of sites (A. Joyce 2003). Conflict in the highlands, however, may have disrupted exchange routes to the coast. Pottery imported from the Valley of Oaxaca decreased during the Terminal Formative and there was a decline in the importation of obsidian that may have reached the coast via highland exchange routes (Barber 2005:106; Joyce et al. 1995; Workinger 2002). In response, people may have strengthened ties to the southern Isthmus of Tehuantepec, as indicated by an increase in ceramics imported from that region (Workinger 2002:357–8).

During the Terminal Formative, feasting, caching, and mortuary rituals continued to reproduce community identity (Barber & Joyce 2007). For example, Levine's (2002) analysis of Miniyua-phase ceramics shows a significant increase in the proportion of fancy serving vessels in non-elite ceramic inventories, perhaps indicative of an increase in ritual feasting. Decorated serving vessels primarily consist of two gray-ware ceramic categories: incised conical bowls that resemble vessels found throughout the Oaxacan highlands (the G-12-type vessel) and regionally distinctive thin-walled composite silhouette bowls and cups with incised decoration in panels on the exterior wall.

The association of feasting and communal mortuary ceremonies identified for the Late Formative at Cerro de la Cruz continued in the Terminal Formative as shown by the results of Sarah Barber's (2005) horizontal excavations at Yugüe. Yugüe stands out in the floodplain on the east side of the Río Verde because much of the site consists of a huge mixed-use platform on which the prehispanic community was built. Yugüe was a focus of Barber's (2005) dissertation project, which showed that the site was first occupied during the Minizundo phase. By the Terminal Formative, Yugüe had grown to 10 ha and was dominated by the platform that covered nearly 5 ha and was as high as 10 m above the floodplain (figure 6.10).

Chatinos built three substructures on the platform, with the largest being Substructure 1 (Barber 2005:150–206). During the Miniyua phase, people constructed a public building on Substructure 1. The building was modified at least twice, with two more construction episodes during the Chacahua phase. Feasting is indicated by a cooking feature just outside the public building that included two large jars, burned on their exterior surfaces; one still contained whole shells of estuarine mussels. Middens containing sherds, ash, bone, and estuarine shells resulted from

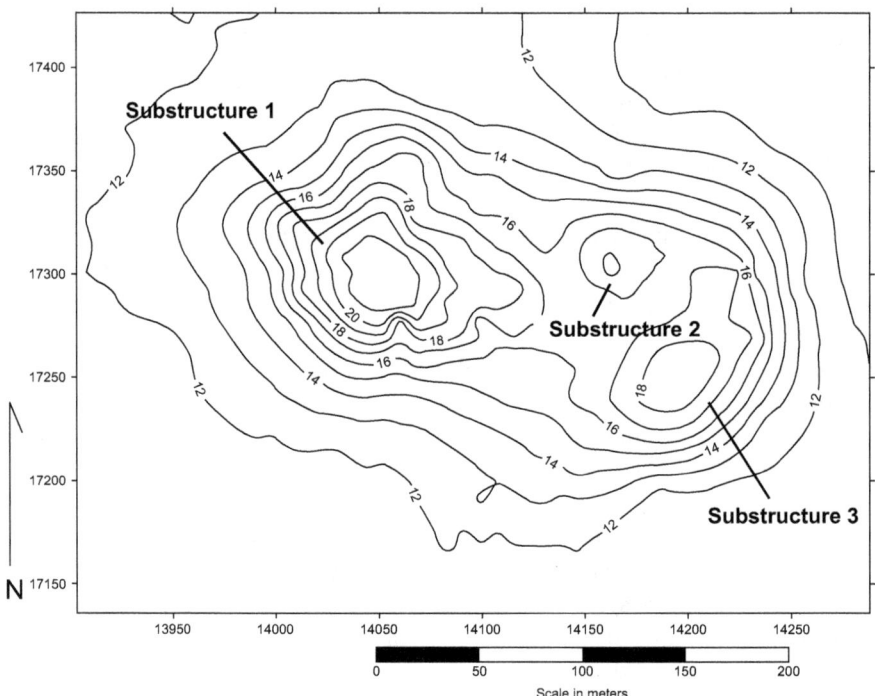

Figure 6.10   Plan of Yugüe

a number of distinct feasting events. Three Miniyua-phase burials were recovered in the fill of the building on Substructure 1; each interment had offerings of up to 4 vessels.

As Barber proceeded with her investigations of Substructure 1, she excavated an area immediately east of the church in the small village that now occupies the site. Almost immediately she began to expose dense deposits of human bone. It soon became obvious that these deposits were the remains of another Formative-period communal cemetery like the one I had excavated in 1988 at Cerro de la Cruz. Although only exposing an area of slightly less than 7 m², Barber (2005:183–92, 382–406) recovered the remains of at least 40 individuals, both male and female. Like the Cerro de la Cruz cemetery, the one from Yugüe included earlier burials disturbed by later ones and only three burials were fully articulated. Unlike Cerro de la Cruz, the later cemetery included people of varying status levels and ages. The repetitive use of the cemetery would have reproduced community identity by referencing community history and reaffirming collective affiliations.

Additional evidence for the repetitive use of community ceremonial spaces is in the form of ritual caches used to dedicate the construction of public buildings. During the Miniyua phase, Chatinos placed a cache of 20 vessels in the fill of the public building on Substructure 1 at Yugüe (Barber 2005:164–5). By the Chacahua phase at least 50 cylindrical vessels were cached sequentially in Substructure 1 perhaps as a way to "feed" the sacred structure (Barber 2005:175) much like burials in Mesoamerican cosmology were viewed as a way of feeding the gods (Monaghan 1990, 1995). At San Francisco de Arriba, people left five ritual caches in the fill of different building phases of the site's largest public structure (Workinger 2002:185–214). Most of the offerings consisted of ceramic vases and jars similar to those cached at Yugüe. The most elaborate cache, however, contained 356 greenstone beads, 27 rock-crystal beads, 109 beads of an unidentified stone, 2 greenstone bird-head pendants, 2 rock-crystal pendants, fragments of iron ore, 9 locally produced miniature gray-ware jars, and disarticulated animal bone. The rituals involved in the caching of these objects, like the cemeteries, was another way in which community identity was reproduced.

Major communal works projects during the Terminal Formative involved the construction of monumental buildings at Río Viejo and at least nine other sites including Charco Redondo, San Francisco de Arriba, Cerro de la Virgen, and Yugüe (Barber 2005:117–18; A. Joyce 1991a:393, 2005:20–23; Workinger 2002:147–230). The scale of monumental construction was considerable, even at some smaller sites, with most consisting of large mixed-use platforms that supported both residences and public buildings. For example, the mixed-use platform at Yugüe measured approximately 300 m by 150 m and reached 10 m at its highest point. At Río Viejo Mound 9-Structure 4 measured as much as 200 m by 125 m by 3 m. Chatinos probably built these huge platforms in part to raise living surfaces off the floodplain and protect residences from seasonal flooding. Paleoenvironmental data indicate that the intensity of floods increased during the latter part of the Formative due to highland erosion and perhaps increased El Niño frequencies (Goman et al. 2005:257; Joyce & Mueller 1997:90). Like in the highlands, the reliance on the tortilla as inferred by the earliest *comales*, may have allowed people to more easily transport food while working on communal labor projects away from their home communities.

The largest monumental building was the Mound 1 acropolis at Río Viejo, which was the civic-ceremonial center of the site (figure 6.11). With an estimated volume of 395,000 m^3, Mound 1 was one of the largest structures in prehispanic Oaxaca. The platform supports two large substructures each reaching 15 m above the current floodplain, along with

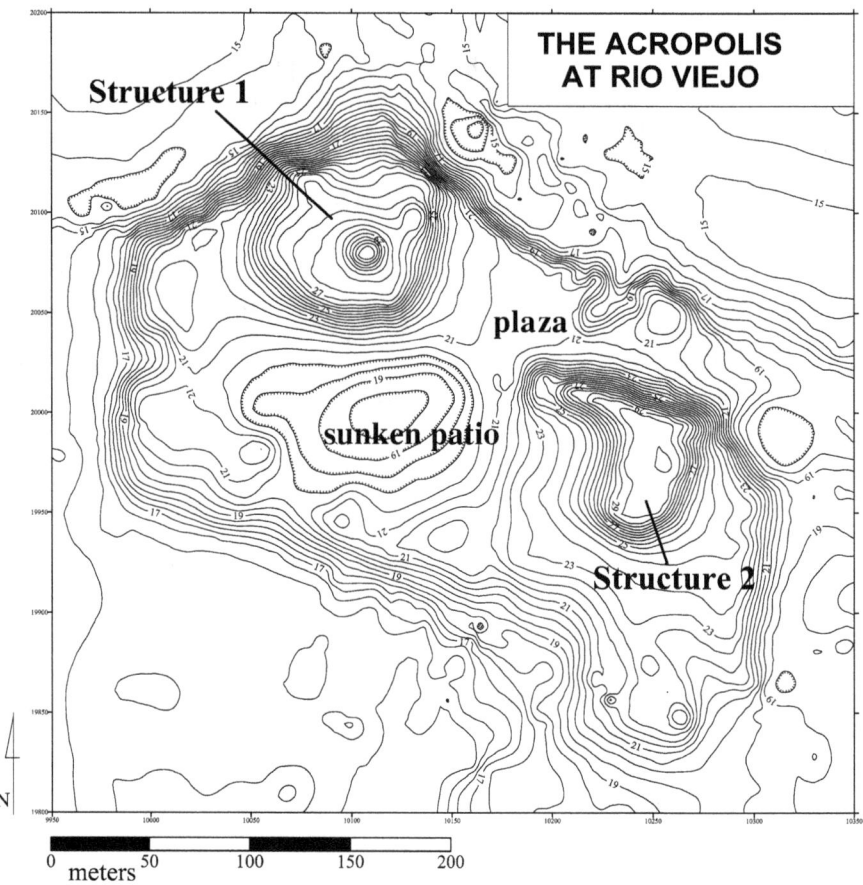

Figure 6.11 Plan of the Mound 1 acropolis at Río Viejo (after Joyce 2005, figure 6)

five smaller buildings, a plaza, and a sunken patio. Excavations have thus far been limited to the eastern substructure (Structure 2), which exposed an area of 242 m² and penetrated in places to a depth of 3.2 m (A. Joyce 2006). The evidence indicates that Structure 2 was built almost entirely during the late Terminal Formative. At that time, our excavations show that Structure 2 consisted of a large stepped platform rising approximately 14 m above the floodplain. Platform fill consisted of a mix of large, unfired adobe blocks secured with a calcareous mortar as well as undifferentiated fill. At least four distinct construction units were identified, suggesting that work parties from different communities may have participated in the construction of the acropolis. On the summit of the platform, excavations revealed remnants of a poorly preserved adobe building. The recovery of pieces of faced stucco, which apparently covered portions of the building, as well as painted adobes indicates that it was an architecturally elaborate structure, while the lack of domestic refuse indicates that it was a public building.

Participation of commoners in the construction of the acropolis as well as the rituals carried out there would have acted as practices of affiliation that constituted new social groups and contributed to the creation of a corporate identity centered on the symbols, institutions, and rulers at Río Viejo. Based on the assumption that the data from Structure 2 can be generalized to the acropolis as a whole, Levine and his colleagues (2004) estimate that it would have taken 1,000 laborers working two months per year a total of 29 years to build the acropolis; 5,000 workers would have taken six years. Monumental public buildings and spaces therefore materialized the collectivities involved in their construction and these collectivities were in turn recreated by the subsequent use and modification of these spaces. Barber and Joyce (2007; also see Barber 2005; Joyce 2006, 2008a) argue that the acropolis was sponsored by rulers attempting to expand their influence beyond the community of Río Viejo to a broader region. Monumental buildings like the acropolis embedded regional political authority in particular places, which were visible for great distances, making them a prominent focus for collectivities tied to that authority (Barber & Joyce 2007). Ritual feasting, probably at times associated with monument construction, was another communal activity that engaged large groups of people in ways that contributed to the social production of a larger-scale corporate identity.

It is not clear if people from the entire region were engaged physically and symbolically in practices of affiliation centered on Río Viejo and its politico-religious institutions and authorities. Ceremonial centers on a smaller scale are found at Yugüe and San Francisco de Arriba as well as with the public plaza at Cerro de la Virgen. While it is tempting to assume that the hierarchy of public buildings and settlements represents an administrative hierarchy through which Río Viejo governed the region (e.g., A. Joyce 2003), the evidence at present does not support such relationships. Despite the prevalence of monumental architecture, there was considerable variability in construction techniques and materials as well as in architectural form and use, arguing against the presence of architectural, political, and ritual principles imposed by a single centralized, regional authority. Rather than being unified under a singular regional polity, it is likely that political relations among communities were more dynamic and negotiated (Barber 2005; Barber & Joyce 2007; A. Joyce 2008a). I suspect that, while Río Viejo was the most powerful political center, leaders of other communities were able to strategically strengthen ties with or create distance from rulers and ruling institutions at Río Viejo. This kind of polity would be more open, dynamic, and negotiated than the modern nation state or the evolutionist visions of bounded, tightly integrated states of the ancient world.

The caches and cemetery, along with evidence from residences and public buildings, further indicate that social inequality increased during the Terminal Formative (Barber 2005:284–321; Barber & Joyce 2007; A. Joyce 2005:19–23, 2006:86–8, 2008a:223–8). Most people interred in the Yugüe cemetery did not have offerings or were accompanied by a few ceramic vessels or beads made of greenstone or shell. One interment, however, was discovered with two remarkable objects indicating high status and perhaps a special ritual role for the person. This burial was a male, aged 15 to 17, interred wearing a plaster-backed iron-ore pectoral, probably a mirror, and holding an intricately incised bone flute made from a deer femur (figure 6.12).

This interment was one of the few in the cemetery that was left undisturbed by later burials. The instrument is the most elaborate flute yet recovered for Terminal Formative Mesoamerica. Its vivid incised imagery depicts a skeletal male speaking or exhaling, probably an image of the death god (Barber 2005:186–91). Luxury goods like iron ore and greenstone, recovered in caches and as burial offerings, were obtained through networks of interregional exchange among Mesoamerican nobles. These exchange networks linked nobles in the lower Río Verde Valley to elites in other parts of Mesoamerica, contributing to the formation of a distinctive noble identity. Two other unusual burials were recovered in the cemetery at Yugüe (Barber 2005:186). One was a juvenile wearing a long bracelet of greenstone and shell beads as well as a greenstone pendant carved as a highly stylized human face. The other was an adult woman who had round pyrite inserts placed in her teeth, similar to a burial from Monte Negro. The relationship of dental inlays to status is unclear for the Oaxacan Terminal Formative, although it is possible that they marked the person as holding a special role, perhaps involving ritual knowledge, given the symbolism of mirrors in ancient Mesoamerica (Taube 1992).

Evidence for social inequality also comes from the excavation of a high-status residence at the site of Cerro de la Virgen (Barber 2005:234–70). Cerro de la Virgen is located on a hill that rises 200 m above the coastal plain approximately 14 km north of the Pacific Ocean. The site was one of the largest communities in the region during the Chacahua phase with settlement covering 60 ha. Most of the occupants of Cerro de la Virgen

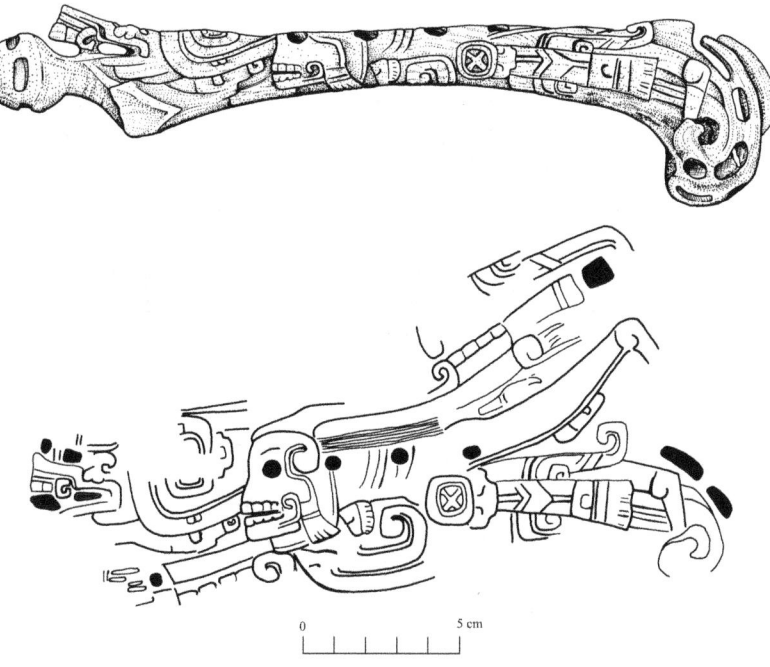

Figure 6.12 Terminal Formative bone flute from the Yugüe cemetery (drawing courtesy of Sarah Barber)

lived on residential terraces, many of which are still visible beneath the vegetation on the site's surface. A spectacular view of the coastal plain, estuaries, and ocean can be seen from the high-status residence excavated by Barber, which was built on a large terrace near the summit of the hill. The residence consisted of several rooms with stone benches surrounding a patio. The overall area of the house was 476 m² including the patio, which measured 13 m by 13 m, making this residence far larger and more elaborate than typical Late/Terminal Formative residences in Oaxaca (Elson 2006:56; Robles 1988; Winter 1974). The house overlooked and was spatially associated with a monumental public plaza to the northwest that measured approximately 2,800 m² and was surrounded by a ballcourt and several possible residences.

Despite increasing inequality and the development of political affiliations and identities at the regional scale, distinctions between nobles and commoners were not emphasized in public action (Barber & Joyce 2007:235–6; A. Joyce 2008a:227–8). The consumption of socially valued goods in burials and caches along with the construction of monumental buildings contributed to status inequality and regional authority, but were practices that transformed hierarchy into expressions of traditional communal principles. Luxury goods obtained through long distance exchange linked nobles in the lower Verde to elites in other parts of Mesoamerica and contributed to the materialization of a noble identity. The use of socially valued goods in community rituals, particularly caches in public buildings, however, transformed these objects from prestige items that embodied high status into offerings that materialized corporate identities. By obtaining the exotic items through which collective pasts were celebrated, nobles would have become pivotal community members. Likewise, monumental buildings were constructed with voluntary labor that foregrounded corporate action and identity, rather than exclusionary political authority. Public social practices therefore continued to materialize social relations as corporate, while restraining the expressions of exclusionary and individualized authority. Social identity tied to regional political authority resembled a scaled-up version of earlier materializations of community that revolved around public spaces and ceremonies such as those inferred for Cerro de la Cruz. By casting status inequality and regional authority as expressions of communal history and identity, these practices communicated an ideology that denied emerging hierarchy.

Yet there is reason to believe that the ritual transformation of inequality into an ideology of communalism was not completely closed, providing openings for discursive penetration. For example, both nobles and commoners were increasingly drawn away from traditional sites of social interaction tied to their local communities as people participated in the construction of monumental buildings and public rituals. Nobles were increasingly involved in wider interregional networks of exchange and interaction, which distanced them from commoners. Social tensions between emerging institutions of rulership that were more unequal and regional in scope, and traditional structural principles that were relatively egalitarian and community-based, can be seen in the mortuary data from the cemeteries at Yugüe and Cerro de la Cruz. As discussed above, most of the skeletons in the cemeteries were interred in dense concentrations where individual bodies were often rearranged and piled together as a result of successive burial events, thereby losing their individuality and becoming incorporated into the social group at death. Some burials, especially high-status ones, however, were left as intact skeletons, suggesting a more restricted form of authority focused perhaps on individuals or particular kin groups and linked to emerging supra-community political institutions as symbolized, for example, by Río Viejo's acropolis. Mortuary rituals may have been an important setting in which divergent forms of political authority were negotiated and contested.

Political Collapse in the Mixteca and the Oaxaca Coast

The evidence from the Mixteca and the lower Río Verde Valley shows that the rulers of Late/Terminal Formative centers had greater power over political and religious institutions, long-distance exchange, and the mobilization of labor than their Middle Formative predecessors. As in the Oaxaca Valley, however, the collapse of political institutions at the end of the Formative suggests that Mixtec and Chatino polities may have been more tenuous and contested than traditional evolutionist models have assumed.

In the Mixteca Alta, most of the Late/Terminal Formative political centers collapsed after only a few hundred years and several areas such as the Teposcolula Valley and western Nochixtlán may have been largely abandoned (Kowalewski et al. 2009:303–4). The first political center to collapse was Monte Negro, which was abandoned by 100 BC (Balkansky et al. 2004); Cerro Jazmín collapsed at about the same time (Balkansky et al. 2000:375; Kowaleski et al. 2009:35). By AD 200 Yucuita, Huamelulpan, and Cerro de las Minas also declined considerably in size and political power. Parts of Yucuita were burned and construction ceased on monumental buildings (Winter 1982:15). The populace at Cerro de las Minas may have entirely abandoned the site between AD 200 and 350 (Winter 1991:158). Settlement at Huamelulpan decreased from 212 ha in the late Ramos phase to 45 ha by the Classic-period Las Flores phase (Balkansky 1998a:49, 57; Winter et al. 1991).

In the lower Río Verde Valley, Río Viejo collapsed, perhaps violently, at c.AD 250 (Joyce et al. 2001; A. Joyce 2008a:234–40). The elaborate public building on the acropolis was abandoned. Burned adobes and floor areas demonstrate that the structure was destroyed by fire, although whether or not the burning was intentional is not known. The summit of the Structure 2 platform remained unoccupied for 250 years, resulting in the erosion and disintegration of most of the adobe superstructure. Río Viejo decreased in size from 200 ha in the Chacahua phase to 75 ha by the Early Classic Coyuche phase. Several other large Terminal Formative floodplain sites with mounded architecture, including Yugüe, declined significantly in size or were abandoned.

The evidence from the Mixteca and the lower Río Verde Valley demonstrates that early urban polities were not stable or long-lasting, although causes of the collapse are not clear. In the Mixtec highlands, conflict among centers may have weakened them politically. External threats might also have contributed to the collapse. Winter (2005b:95) suggests that Monte Albán and Teotihuacan competed for dominance of the Mixtec highlands, while I suggest that Teotihuacan might have played a role in the collapse of the Río Viejo polity (A. Joyce 2003:64–8). Yet in Mesoamerica, military defeat often did not result in major long-term political reorganizations. For example, in the case of the Aztec Empire, the rulers of conquered polities were often left in power and there was continuity in political, demographic, and economic centers. Researchers have failed to demonstrate that external conquests occurred or to explain how conquest would have affected political organization (Workinger 2002:394–402).

Another factor in the collapse of Río Viejo could have been tension between traditional communal forms of authority that were more local and egalitarian and the more exclusionary, hierarchical, and regional forms of rulership that were emerging at the end of the Formative (Barber & Joyce 2007; A. Joyce 2008a:223–30). Conflict with neighboring polities and/or with distant powers could have exacerbated these tensions. In instances where massive monumental structures were built, such as Río Viejo's acropolis, labor demands may have increased internal tensions. After the destruction and abandonment of the acropolis, this important political and religious building, which had taken considerable communal labor to construct, and which presumably was an important symbol of the Terminal Formative polity, was left to slowly disintegrate for 250 years even though flat elevated surfaces were ideal locations on which to live in the hot climate of the Oaxaca coast. It is possible that Structure 2 was not rebuilt or reoccupied during the Early Classic because it symbolized a failed political system.

Although further research is needed to determine the causes of the collapse of Mixtec and Chatino political centers, subsequent developments suggest a period of political decentralization and a return to more local forms of authority. During the Classic period, discussed in the next chapter, a more formal and status-oriented social structure emerged, reflecting the ascendancy of exclusionary forms of authority.

seven

Authority and Polity in the Classic Period

The political upheaval of the Terminal Formative was followed in the Classic period (AD 300–800) by the development of more formalized distinctions among status groups. The dominant discourse that embodied the power relations of the Classic period exhibited continuities with that of the Late/Terminal Formative – the relationship between religion and political power; between sacrifice and fertility; between ancestors, rulers, and the gods; and the quadripartite division of the cosmos. Political authority differed from the Formative period, however, with powerful, exclusionary rulers celebrated in portraits on carved stones and painted murals. Classic-period society was not characterized by the kinds of structural contradictions between communal and exclusionary forms of authority that created conflict and instability in early urban polities. Yet Classic-period society may have had its own contradictions and tensions – along status lines and between polity rulers and increasingly independent nobility.

Although the available evidence suggests that the daily lives of common people continued much as they had before with farming, food preparation, child rearing, craft production, and marketing as major occupations, in this chapter I argue that people may have been increasingly disengaged from ruling ideas and institutions. Common people no longer had access to the kinds of corporate organizations that shared power with rulers. The Classic period had fewer of the kinds of communal projects, especially the construction and use of monumental public spaces, which created affiliations between people and the symbols, institutions, and rulers of regional polities. Although people participated in decision-making and could achieve status within their local communities and/or barrios, they were largely excluded from leadership at the supra-community level. The subjectivities of commoners were increasingly subjugated when it came to regional leadership, warfare, and large-scale public rituals carried out at ceremonial centers.

The subjectivity of the nobility was now distinct from that of common people. Mixtec, Zapotec, and Chatino nobles participated in a shared identity with nobles throughout Mesoamerica, establishing important ties to distant polities, especially the powerful city of Teotihuacan in the Basin of Mexico. Nobles were distinguished from commoners by dress, access to exotic goods, control of esoteric knowledge (e.g., special rituals, literacy), participation in restricted rituals, and by residing in architecturally elaborate houses. Perhaps nowhere is the special social position of nobility as clearly portrayed as in imagery on carved-stone monuments and tomb murals. Nobles are shown in elaborate attire, sometimes dressed as jaguars, richly ornamented and often shown in the act of dominating captives, performing human sacrifice, marrying, or communicating with ancestors. Part of this noble identity included jockeying for power in the competitive political landscape of the Classic period, which resulted in competition and conflict among political centers and their ruling dynasties.

As discussed in this chapter, the social conditions of the Classic period emerged from the chaos at the end of the Formative (figure 7.1). In the

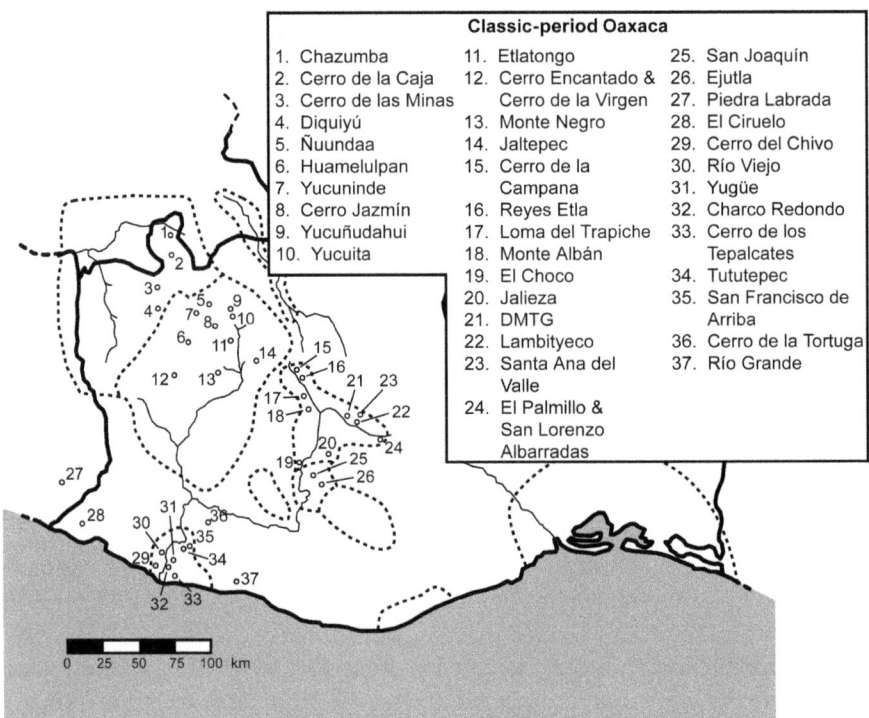

Figure 7.1 Classic-period archaeological sites of Oaxaca (drawing by Eric Berkemeyer)

Valley of Oaxaca, political upheaval was followed by the ascendancy of the nobility. In other regions, the collapse of Terminal Formative political centers was followed by a period of fragmentation before powerful ruling dynasties established control, and urban centers once again coalesced. Cerro de las Minas and Cerro Jazmín reemerged as political and demographic nuclei by AD 350 to 400, a century or two after the Terminal Formative collapse. Yucuita and Huamelulpan continued as important communities, but never returned to their status as major political centers, while Monte Negro was not reoccupied. Many of the people who left Yucuita at the end of the Formative probably relocated to the hilltop site of Yucuñudahui, which developed into the dominant Classic-period political center of the Nochixtlán Valley. In the lower Río Verde Valley the political landscape remained fragmented until the Late Classic, when a regional polity once again emerged with its capital at Río Viejo.

Classic-Period Society in the Valley of Oaxaca

Oaxacan archaeologists have often viewed the Classic period as a "Golden Age" where the institutions of the Monte Albán polity reach their greatest power and complexity with the Central Valleys united as a single polity (Joyce & Winter 1996; Kowalewski et al. 1989; Marcus & Flannery 1996). Recent research, however, has questioned the degree of unity and integration within the Valley of Oaxaca. Winter (1998) argues that Monte Albán was conquered and controlled by Teotihuacan during the Early Classic Pitao phase (AD 350–500). Researchers also point to evidence suggesting that the Valley of Oaxaca was increasingly fragmented politically during the Classic (Elson 2007; A. Joyce 2004:211; Winter 2004b:53–4). In this section, I consider evidence for political, economic, and religious practices and representations that may have integrated people in the Central Valleys along with evidence for political unity or fragmentation.

Difficulties in distinguishing temporally diagnostic ceramic phases have complicated understandings of Late Classic archaeology in the Central Valleys. Recent seriation studies have found that pottery once thought to belong to separate Late Classic and Early Postclassic phases should be lumped into a single Late Classic phase termed the Xoo phase (Markens 2004; Martínez López et al. 2000).[7] A separate Early Postclassic Liobaa phase has been differentiated from ceramics previously assigned to the Late Postclassic; the latter is now termed the Chila phase. The revised ceramic sequence resolves a number of questions that resulted from the earlier chronology. In particular, relying on the earlier ceramic sequence, the survey project suggested that Late Classic settlement was confined largely to Etla with Early Postclassic settlement almost a mirror image concentrated in the remainder of the valley (Lind 1991–2). The revised chronology now has the entire valley settled during the Late Classic, although models of Early Postclassic settlement will have to await reanalysis of the survey data.

Estimated population in the Oaxaca Valley increased significantly from 41,319 people at the end of the Formative to 115,226 by the Early Classic Pitao phase (Nicholas 1989, table 14.13). Population estimates increase in the adjacent valleys of Ejutla (Feinman & Nicholas 1990:234–6) and Sola (Balkansky 2002:51–3), but may have declined in the Miahuatlán Valley (Markman 1981:67). Population also rose in mountainous regions north and west of the valley (Drennan 1989; Finsten 1996:80–1). By the Late Classic, population estimates increase to about 150,000 people in the Valley of Oaxaca (Nicholas 1989, table 14.13).[8] Some population growth may have been the result of immigration by people from Ejutla, where estimated population decreased from 14,656 to 3,029. Zapotecs moved into higher elevations during the Classic period, especially hilltop sites with extensive residential terraces (Balkansky 2002:54–61; Feinman & Nicholas 1990:234; Kowalewski et al. 1989:240–5; Markman 1981:67), perhaps for defense or the need to keep prime agricultural land open on the valley floor.

In the Valley of Oaxaca, Monte Albán continued as a major political, religious, and demographic center with settlement increasing to 475 ha by the Pitao phase and a mean estimated population of 16,500 (Blanton 1978). By the Early Classic, Monte Albán was no longer the dominant demographic center in the valley, however. The communities of Jalieza as well as a cluster of sites around Dainzú, Macuilxóchitl, Tlacochahuaya, and Guadalupe (termed the DMTG cluster by Kowalewski et al. 1989:229–40) approached Monte Albán in size with estimated populations of 12,835 and 12,300 respectively. Other demographic nuclei included San Joaquín in the Ejutla Valley with an estimated population of 6,710 and El Palmillo, a terraced mountaintop site in the far eastern end of the Oaxaca Valley with an estimated population of 4,517 (Balkansky 2002, table 4.2; Kowalewski et al. 1989, table 8.3). These sites as well as some smaller demographic centers in the Central Valleys included mounded architecture, probably both public buildings and high-status residences. Both Jalieza and the DMTG complex have multiple clusters of mounded architecture and public plazas, suggesting barrio organization like at Monte Albán. Most of the Early Classic centers were small communities during the Terminal Formative, while many of the largest Terminal Formative sites declined by the Pitao phase. The data suggest that the social upheaval at the end of the Formative may have been accompanied by major settlement changes in the Central Valleys.

Settlement patterns suggest significant continuities in major demographic centers in the valley from the Pitao phase to the Xoo phase (Lind 1994). By the Xoo phase, Monte Albán covered 650 ha with an estimated 22,500 people. Jalieza continued as the second largest community in the valley with an estimated population of 16,000. The area of the Pitao-phase DMTG cluster included two large Xoo-phase sites: Macuilxóchitl with an estimated population of 6,222 and Tlacochahuaya with 5,352 people. Other major Xoo-phase demographic centers with their estimated populations include Loma del Trapiche (4,500) and Cerro de la Campana (3,900) in the Etla arm; El Choco (4,000) in the Valle Grande; and Santa Ana del Valle (3,600) and Lambityeco (2,700) in Tlacolula. As in the Pitao phase, most of the demographic centers included evidence for the presence of noble families and public buildings. Survey and excavation data suggest a continuation of the barrio organization first seen in the Nisa phase (Blanton 1978:75–93; Feinman et al. 2002:272, 2008).

Beyond the Central Valleys, researchers agree that, by the Early Classic, the rulers of Monte Albán had given up control of areas that may have been conquered during the Terminal Formative such as the Cuicatlán Cañada. The contraction of Monte Albán's influence in surrounding areas may have been a result of political relations with the powerful city of Teotihuacan in the Basin of Mexico. The relationship between these two great cities has been a focus of recent debate.

Monte Albán and Teotihuacan

Teotihuacan was the largest and most powerful city of Classic-period Mesoamerica. The city reached its greatest size during the Early Classic period when it grew to cover 20 km^2 with an estimated population of 100,000–150,000 people (Cowgill 1997, 2008). Most people lived in large apartment compounds and the city included a number of barrios occupied by foreigners, including people from Oaxaca, the Maya region, and West Mexico (Cowgill 2008:968). The civic-ceremonial center of the city was located along the Street of the Dead with massive public architecture such as the Pyramid of the Sun and the Pyramid of the Moon. Teotihuacan had wide-ranging contacts in Mesoamerica involving trade and the spread of political and religious ideas. Researchers have also debated the extent to which Teotihuacan may have conquered distant regions and perhaps came to control a large empire (Smith & Montiel 2001). Oaxaca is one of the areas where the impact of Teotihuacan has been debated.

Winter (1998) argues that the beginning of the Classic period in the Oaxacan highlands was marked by conquest and political domination

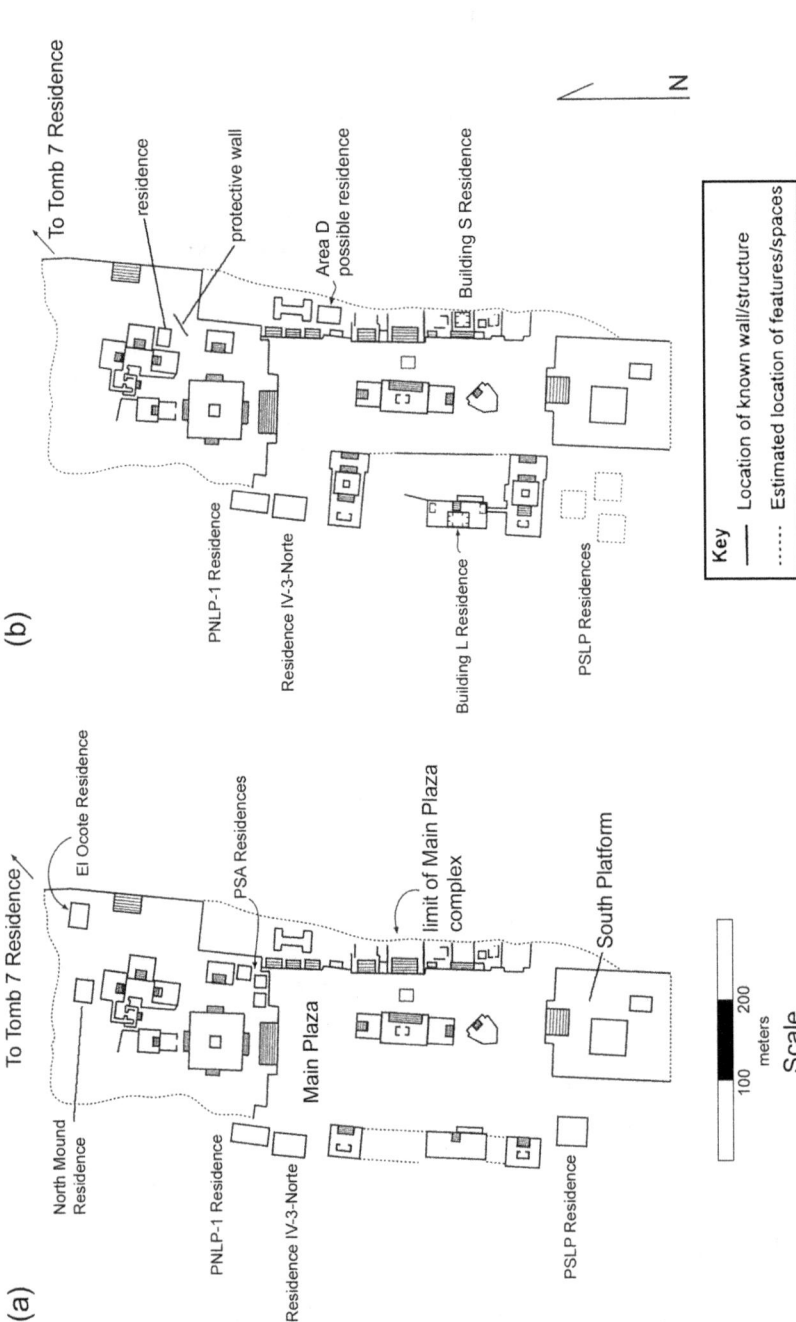

Figure 7.2 The Main Plaza of Monte Albán: (a) Pitao phase (AD 350–500); (b) Xoo phase (AD 500–800) (after Barber & Joyce 2006, figures 8.4 and 8.6; reproduced with permission of the University of Texas Press)

by Teotihuacan. He views this conquest as part of a broader pattern of imperial domination by Teotihuacan that included regions as distant as Kaminaljuyú in the Guatemalan highlands and Tikal in the Petén lowlands. In this section I discuss Winter's arguments and present an alternative model of Classic-period interaction.

Evidence for direct interaction between Monte Albán and Teotihuacan begins in the Tani phase (AD 200–350) with the establishment of the Zapotec barrio in the Tlailotlacan residential complex at Teotihuacan (Cowgill 1997:139). People living in Tlailotlacan maintained a Zapotec identity through the Classic period. They lived in typical Teotihuacan-style apartment compounds, but made Oaxaca Valley-style ceramics and urns, practiced Zapotec mortuary customs, and used the Zapotec script. Isotopic studies of human bone indicate that through the Classic period there was continual interaction with the Valley of Oaxaca and probably other diaspora communities (White et al. 2004).

Most of the evidence that Winter (1998) uses to support Teotihuacan conquest comes from a series of important discoveries made in the North Platform of Monte Albán during the Proyecto Especial Monte Albán (PEMA). In the eastern side of the platform, archaeologists excavated a large midden containing Basin of Mexico-style pottery, both imports and local imitations, along with typical Oaxaca Valley wares (Martínez López 1994). A Teotihuacan-style black limestone figurine was also recovered, along with hundreds of kilograms of cut mica and tools used to work the mica. The mica probably comes from sources near Monte Albán and was almost certainly traded to Teotihuacan. No evidence has been found for the use of mica at Monte Albán, but it was used to decorate braziers at Teotihuacan. Special deposits of mica made from slabs similar to those discovered at Monte Albán have been found in ceremonial rooms of the Viking Group in the Street of the Dead complex at Teotihuacan. Caso (1935:6) also discovered an offering within the altar of the Patio Hundido in the North Platform that included Teotihuacan-style figurines made of greenstone along with the remains of animals, probably an eagle and a jaguar.

Winter (1998:166) suggests that high-status residences on the North Platform without tombs might indicate the presence of foreigners since the majority of Zapotec houses included tombs, while those from Teotihuacan usually did not (figure 7.2a). A burial south of Building A on the North Platform was in a seated position that resembles central-Mexican mortuary practices. The burial included a possible Thin Orange bowl imported from central Mexico, greenstone figurines described by Caso and his colleagues (1967:102–3) as Teotihuacan style, local Oaxaca Valley pottery, and stone and bone ornaments. Winter (1998:167) suggests that this burial was a person from Teotihuacan. He also suggests that changes in burial customs during the Pitao phase, as well as a decline in the construction of monumental architecture at Monte Albán, might reflect influence by Teotihuacan. Winter's (1998) model is one of territorial imperialism with Teotihuacan conquering Monte Albán and installing administrators who ruled the polity during the Early Classic. He further argues that Teotihuacan conquered political centers in the Mixtec highlands.

Under conditions of territorial conquest evidence for large numbers of Teotihuacanos at Monte Albán and probably elsewhere in the Oaxaca Valley would be expected (see Schreiber 1987; Smith & Montiel 2001; Stark 1990). Military garrisons and administrative facilities with central-Mexican residences and public buildings would have been required to directly administer the Zapotec city. High-status residences on the North Platform and elsewhere at Monte Albán, however, are consistent with Zapotec architectural canons and differ greatly from the apartment compounds found at Teotihuacan (Barber & Joyce 2006:229–33; Winter 1986:353–61). Some of the elite residences on the North Platform were occupied both before and after the proposed conquest, showing occupational continuity. The lack of tombs in some residences, while unusual, could be an artifact of sampling bias. Several Late Classic Zapotec high-status residences also lacked tombs. Public buildings, while exhibiting some architectural elements linked to central Mexico, such as *talud-tablero* walls, exhibit continuities with earlier architecture as well. Urcid (2001) has identified several iconographic programs representing genealogies, military victories, and ritual practices of Early Classic rulers all executed using Zapotec, rather than central-Mexican, canons. Marcus (1983e) argues that several carved stones at Monte Albán record ambassadorial visits of Teotihuacan emissaries, although Urcid (2005:14–15) disagrees with Marcus based on epigraphic grounds (also see Von Winning 1983). Several elaborate late Pitao-phase tombs with Zapotec-style painted murals (e.g., Tombs 103 and 112) show the presence of prominent local nobility (A. Miller 1995:68–73; Urcid 2005:63–64).

Central-Mexican-style pottery in the Valley of Oaxaca is largely limited to Monte Albán and primarily associated with the midden on the North Platform. Interestingly, the ceramics from the midden include relatively little Thin Orange pottery (Martínez López 1994), a ceramic type that was traded outside of Teotihuacan's empire in extremely low quantities as a prestige item, but which occurred in much higher frequencies in conquered regions (Smith & Montiel 2001:258). Cylindrical tripod vessels like those found in the North Platform midden, are much more common in independent regions that interacted with Teotihuacan. Likewise, figurines could have been imported to Monte Albán as prestige goods, and diffusion of aspects of central-Mexican ritual practices would not be surprising given the political prominence of Teotihuacan.

If Teotihuacan did not incorporate Monte Albán into a territorial empire, then what was the relationship between these two powerful cities? At present, the possibility of hegemonic domination cannot be entirely excluded, which would include the establishment of tributary relations with local rulers left in place. Hegemonic relations could have resulted from the establishment of an asymmetrical alliance under the threat of warfare. If warfare was largely the purview of the nobility, it is possible that Teotihuacan could have defeated the lords of Monte Albán in battle, perhaps resulting in the destruction of iconographic programs at the end of the Formative. Recent epigraphic and iconographic research in the Petén lowlands suggests that a group of nobles affiliated with Teotihuacan formed an alliance with a local Maya faction to overthrow the ruling dynasty at Tikal (Martin & Grube 2000:29–31; Stuart 2000). While the precise relationship between Teotihuacan and Tikal remains controversial, direct involvement in the politics of the Maya lowlands probably lasted no more than a few generations. It is possible that a similar process occurred at Monte Albán.

Although some form of hegemonic relationship is a possibility, I think the evidence is more consistent with reciprocal economic and political relations between the rulers of Monte Albán and Teotihuacan. This model argues that nobles living on the North Platform during the Pitao phase imported elaborate ceramics and obsidian as well as ritual objects like the figurines. In return, nobles or attached specialists manufactured mica for export to Teotihuacan. The midden could have been the result of both the manufacture of mica for export and ritual feasting where exotic ceramics, including braziers for food preparation, were used and displayed. Feasting on the eastern side of the North Platform would have been an important ceremonial setting for interaction with visiting nobles and/or merchants from Teotihuacan, involving food preparation and consumption, ritual performances, and gift exchange. Feasting may have been a component of broader relations between Zapotecs and Teotihuacanos, perhaps involving the intermarriage of nobles, alliance, and trade. These relations would have been facilitated by the Zapotec barrio at Teotihuacan where people historically tied to the Valley of Oaxaca resided. Diplomatic and trade relations with Teotihuacan do not necessarily imply a lack of competition or even potential military threats between these two powerful cities. The Mixtec codices show that political relations among Postclassic communities were dynamic and often ambiguous (Byland & Pohl 1994; Jansen & Pérez 2007). More research is needed to clarify the nature of social relations between Monte Albán and Teotihuacan.

Elsewhere in Mesoamerica evidence for interaction with Teotihuacan at sites like Kaminaljuyú and Tikal in Guatemala, as well as Matacapán along the Gulf coast and Chingú in the northern Basin of Mexico, varies considerably and has led to major debates over the nature of interregional relations (Smith & Montiel 2001). There is little doubt that Teotihuacan's nobility were major players in Early Classic political economy, trade, and elite culture in many parts of Mesoamerica. Debates surround the degree to which Teotihuacan dominated an empire designed to control trade in materials like obsidian, cotton, ornamental shell, cacao, and greenstone. Smith and Montiel (2001) systematically review evidence for Teotihuacan imperialism and conclude that Teotihuacan was the capital of a hegemonic empire that dominated areas in and near the Basin of Mexico, but that evidence from more distant regions like the Maya lowlands, the Gulf coast, and Oaxaca does not support imperial domination. Future research will undoubtedly clarify the role of Teotihuacan in Classic-period developments throughout Mesoamerica.

Structures of authority: iconography, epigraphy, and mortuary ceremonialism

If the Oaxaca Valley was not ruled by Teotihuacan as current evidence indicates, then the political unrest at the end of the Formative must have been the result of internal political changes. As discussed in chapter 5, the dismantling and destruction of the Building L-sub and Building J programs suggests that social tensions between communal forms of authority and increasingly powerful nobility may have erupted in violence. I argue that the Classic-period archaeological record of the Central Valleys indicates that the outcome of this political upheaval was the further ascendancy of the nobility and the decreased importance of communal forms of authority such as the non-noble council of elders, warriors, and religious specialists perhaps represented on Building L-sub (Urcid 2008).

During the Classic period the political and religious significance of rulers was no longer muted in public art and architecture, which instead celebrated the religious and military power of nobles and their ancestors. Important nobles were depicted as intermediaries between common people and the divine, especially through the ability of the former to contact their deified ancestors. These data do not imply a straightforward cycling between more individualistic versus corporate forms of authority (cf. Blanton et al. 1996), since the authority of rulers continued to be derived to a great extent through the political and economic power of the corporate groups to which they belonged. Viewed from the perspective of an internal political transformation, the Classic period was a time when rulers exercised authority without the constraints of the powerful communal institutions of the Formative – institutions that had included commoners as well as nobles.

Major advances in understanding Classic-period social relations come from recent research on mortuary ceremonialism, epigraphy, and iconography by Javier Urcid (2001, 2005). Urcid's impressive research has focused on the decipherment of Zapotec hieroglyphic writing and the analysis of imagery in tombs and public monuments. As discussed in chapter 5, the earliest evidence for the Zapotec script dates to the Rosario phase, making it some of the earliest writing in Mesoamerica. By the Late/Terminal Formative short inscriptions were associated with the Building L-sub and Building J programs at Monte Albán. A larger corpus of writing is available for the Classic period, while themes represented in the imagery on carved stones and tomb murals shift from an emphasis on communal rituals and warfare to a focus on the aggrandizement of rulers and the nobility. Urcid (2001, 2005:5–15) shows how Zapotec writing, like other Mesoamerican scripts, is a mixed system with two components that are inextricably linked: narrative images and glyphs. Although the images are largely iconic, there are also indexical and symbolic components of Zapotec writing, including phonetic elements. Urcid (2001:409) refers to this as a logosyllabic system, although he notes that, toward the end of the Classic period, the script becomes more open with an increasing use of syllabic signs. Urcid (2001, 2005) shows that Zapotec and other Mesoamerican writing systems, including Mixtec, are most effectively analyzed from a contextual perspective, which considers the imagery and the broader archaeological context of the inscriptions. Such a contextual approach has yielded important new understandings of Classic-period Zapotec social and political relations.

Mortuary evidence from the Central Valleys shows a concern with constructing and maintaining memories of the genealogical relations of household heads (Urcid 2005). Most people were interred beneath the rooms or patio of their houses, although occasionally burials were located outside, but in the general vicinity of residences (figure 7.3). Urcid (2005:28–44) shows how conjugal pairs who were the heads of households in each generation were successively interred in tombs or, in the case of some lower-status residences, in stone-lined cists. Archaeologists often find that Zapotec tombs, when opened and explored, contain a jumble of skeletal remains of many individuals along with offerings such as pottery and jade with few articulated interments. Urcid argues that these remains

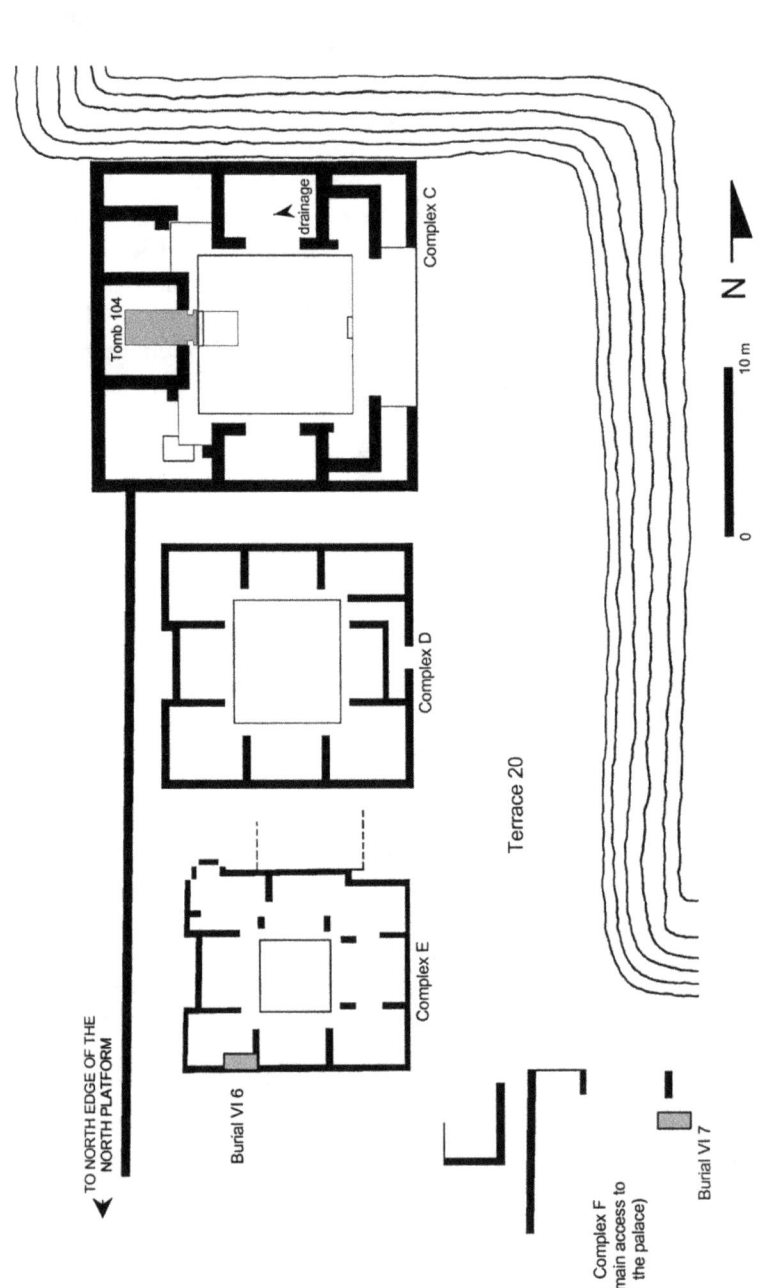

Figure 7.3 High-status residential complex showing the location of the tomb (Tomb 104) (after Urcid 2005, figure 4.1; redrawn with permission from Javier Urcid)

represent a sequence of household heads with the bones of earlier interments disarticulated and mixed due to later openings of the tomb for rituals and burial of descendants (also see Middleton et al. 1998).

Other members of the domestic group from infants to elders were interred in stone-lined cists, graves, and occasionally in reused pit features. High-status residences often included burials of adult females with elaborate offerings that Urcid (2005:40–1) interprets as the secondary wives of male household heads, which is consistent with evidence for polygyny among nobles at the time of the Spanish Conquest. Neonates and fetuses were often placed within ceramic vessels and usually did not include offerings, suggesting that they had not achieved full adult personhood. These patterns mean that individual residences usually had several different kinds of interments, including at least one tomb. In houses occupied over long periods, the tomb might be expanded, or additional tombs constructed.

The architectural elaboration of the tomb as well as the quantity and quality of offerings found in tomb and non-tomb interments correlates with other indicators of status such as the size and quality of domestic architecture (Urcid 2005; Winter 1986:353–61). Mourners often decorated the bodies with shell, bone, and greenstone ornaments, suggesting beautification and the marking of status or other social roles of the interred. Tombs and burials were accompanied by offerings of ceramic vessels, sometimes including urns that symbolized deities or ancestors. Dozens of vessels recovered from some tombs suggest the wide social networks of the deceased. In tombs, Zapotecs used red pigment to decorate the bones of earlier interments and at times bones of ancestors were removed for use as heirlooms in validating status (Urcid 2005:36–7). People often performed sacrificial rituals as part of the mortuary ceremony with dog sacrifices associated with both commoners and nobles, whereas bird sacrifice was restricted to nobles. Interments of rulers may have at times included human sacrifice.

Stone-masonry tombs and mausoleums of high-ranking nobles at Monte Albán and other important sites sometimes included extensive genealogical and ritual information recorded in narrative programs displayed on painted murals, urns, and figurines as well as on carved-stone facades, jambs, and lintels (A. Miller 1995; Urcid 2005). Genealogical narratives suggest kinship patterns similar to those recorded in codices and *lienzos* at the time of the Spanish Conquest where people belonged to corporate groups (lineages or ramages) with descent reckoned back through either the paternal or the maternal line to an apical ancestor, often considered to be the group founder. Genealogical relations were important for the social construction of status since proximity to the apical ancestor, as well as the prestige of that ancestor, produced the basis for inequality among corporate groups.

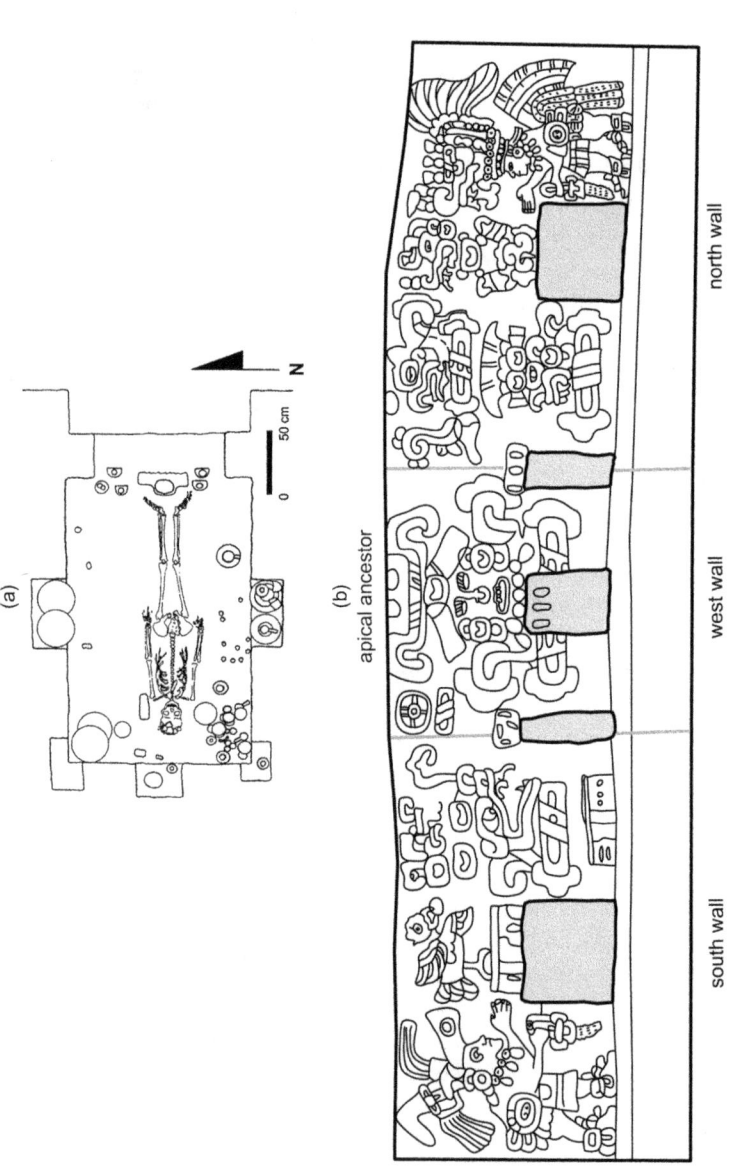

Figure 7.4 Tomb 104: (a) plan of tomb; (b) painted murals showing ancestors (after Urcid 2005, figure 4.2 and 4.4; redrawn with permission from Javier Urcid; drawing by Eric Berkemeyer)

Genealogical information was crucial to the trans-generational transfer of the material and symbolic resources of corporate groups (Urcid 2005:44).

The tombs with these narrative programs were some of the most elaborate ever discovered by archaeologists in Oaxaca. Zapotecs built tombs beneath residences with steps descending into the tomb from the patio above. Tombs typically included a main chamber attached to smaller rooms and sometimes vestibules, corridors, and internal stairs (figure 7.4).

Imagery was recorded in carved-stone monuments placed inside the tombs as well as stone lintels and door jambs. Even more spectacular are the examples of scenes, richly painted on plaster murals, that covered portions of the tomb walls (A. Miller 1995; Urcid 2005). The inside of the tombs would have been dark, humid, and cramped for participants in mortuary ceremonies, but the evocative imagery referencing genealogy and history along with the presence of deified ancestors would have created a powerful and emotionally moving setting.

Urcid (2005) examined the iconography and epigraphy of Tombs 104 and 105 from Monte Albán and Tomb 5 from the site of Cerro de la Campana in northern Etla. Though the imagery in the tombs is too complex to summarize in detail here, some generalizations are relevant (A. Miller 1995; Urcid 2005). Urcid (2005) argues that the imagery legitimated the social position of the nobles that commissioned the tomb's construction by establishing genealogical relations to important ancestors, especially the apical or founding ancestor of the corporate group to which the household was affiliated. There were as many as four sequential narratives represented in particular tombs, each commissioned by a different ruling couple. Different narratives were sometimes tied to the same apical ancestor, although the anchoring ancestor could change, perhaps reflecting the segmentation of the corporate group. Apical ancestors or ancestral couples are prominently displayed either as the largest glyphs placed at the back of crypts, or as busts depicting calendrical names protruding from entryways.

Imagery and hieroglyphic inscriptions on carved-stone monuments and murals record the genealogies of paramount couples, which usually include calendrical and sometimes personal names (Urcid 2005). Genealogies could cover centuries. For example, Cerro de la Campana Tomb 5 references at least 16 generations. Nobles depicted in the tombs are often shown beneath Glyph U, interpreted as the creator god, Pitáo Cozáana (Sellen 2002). Personages depicted in the tombs were richly attired, often wearing elaborate zoomorphic headdresses or helmets with images of Cocijo, crocodiles, or birds along with fine ornaments including beads, necklaces, crocodiles, feathers, bracelets, and headbands (A. Miller 1995; Urcid 2005). Personages sometimes exhibited dental modification and held feathered fans, incense pouches, or ornamental staffs. Gender was represented in elements of clothing with males often shown wearing short kilts or loincloths and women attired in blouses and long skirts. Ruling nobles were usually men dressed as jaguars with feline heads covering their faces and with clawed extremities over their hands and feet. These Zapotec kings were often shown paired with queens. Other figures depicted in the tombs were probably collateral kin related to the dynastic line who may have led communities subject to the ruling couple. The imagery suggests that descent was reckoned through the male line, although there were instances where powerful women figured prominently in the succession of rulers.

Important religious functionaries and warriors were depicted, further showing the diversity of social identities of Zapotec nobles (Urcid 2005). Male lords, including rulers, could be depicted as Xicani priests, distinguished by tied hairdos and zoomorphic buccal masks with upturned snouts. At the time of the Spanish Conquest, similar zoomorphic beings were depicted as flying figures with turtle carapaces termed Xicani in Zapotec or Yahui in Mixtec. These beings signaled both an alter ego into which priests could transform and the office of sacrificer, rainmaker, and keeper of sacred bundles who could communicate with ancestors. Some tombs depict processions of warriors and nobles shown wearing flayed facial skins that marked them as priests impersonating the deity Xipe Totec, who was associated with sacrifice and fertility. The evidence shows that members of ruling houses had the right to engage in warfare, take captives, play the ballgame, and offer human sacrifices as part of their role as rainmakers. Allusions to nobles as embodiments of earth, maize, lightning, rain, and the sacred calendar suggest a link between ancestors, land tenure, and the continuity of noble houses (Urcid 2005:154).

The imagery provides clues as to ceremonies performed to commemorate ancestors (Urcid 2005). Processions of priests, warriors, ballplayers, and lower-ranking people carrying offerings are shown paying homage to the funerary bundles of prominent couples. Offerings of incense, rubber balls, and small anthropomorphic stone artifacts as well as the sacrifice of birds to the ancestors were also rituals carried out in tombs. Ceremonies may have been calendrically timed based on the death dates of ancestors. The imagery also references the quadripartite division of the cosmos, especially the celestial, terrestrial, and underworld realms and the story of the cosmic creation and the origins of humans. I believe these allusions indicate that ritual communication with ancestors invoked the sacred covenant and was important in world-centering and the well-being of the cosmos.

The ritual importance of prominent ancestors suggests to me that they were revered not just by the nobility, but by commoners as well. A possible means through which noble ancestors were referenced and perhaps propitiated by commoners was through rituals involving ceramic figurines and whistles. Classic-period anthropomorphic figurines depict elaborately attired and ornamented personages often wearing zoomorphic headdresses that represent nobles (Martínez López & Winter 1994). Many elements of clothing and ornamentation on the figurines and whistles closely resemble that on elite personages shown in tomb art and in public monuments. Some figurines may depict Xicani priests (Martínez López & Winter 1994:68). Contextual data for the figurines are not well reported, although my impression is that, like their Formative predecessors, Classic figurines were used by both nobles and commoners in domestic settings. It is possible that the figurines represent important ancestors, perhaps the apical ancestors of high-ranking corporate groups. Regardless of their specific uses, the fact that they are attired as nobles suggests that these figurines represented and communicated something about the social distance between nobles and commoners. Interestingly, zoomorphic figurines were also common and the most frequent representations were of dogs and birds, both animals that were sacrificed to ancestors.

Genealogies of rulers as well as their ritual and political practices were also represented on carved-stone monuments. Carved stones at Monte Albán had complex histories of manufacture, use, repositioning, alteration, and reuse. Using analyses of chronology, style, form, and the themes depicted on imagery and writing, Urcid (2001, 2005) presents compelling reconstructions of the life history of these monuments, including those that were at one time components of longer narrative programs, such as those previously discussed from Building L-sub.

At least 11 different rulers of Monte Albán are depicted on carved stones from the Main Plaza (Urcid 2001, 2005:21–2). One of the earliest was an Early Classic ruler named Lord 5 Jaguar. Urcid (2005:22) argues that Lord 5 Jaguar commissioned a small commemorative building with lintels carved with scenes of 14 secondary nobles honoring him and his father. Lord 13 Night, a subsequent ruler probably from the end of the Early Classic, dismantled the earlier building and used the stones, including the carved lintels, to construct a larger building celebrating his enthronement and military victories. Carved stones set into the walls of the building include a depiction of Lord 13 Night elaborately attired and seated on a mat looking down on a procession of bound captives, one of which was attired in Jaguar skins indicating that he was an important ruler from a competing polity (figure 7.5).

The building commissioned by Lord 13 Night was eventually dismantled by one of his successors, probably in the Late Classic, and used as

Figure 7.5 The iconographic program of Lord 13 Night (drawing courtesy of Javier Urcid)

cornerstones in the South Platform. Caches of ceramic vessels, shell, and jade left in offering boxes were found at the base of the monuments. The vessels in the offering boxes date to the Tani phase (AD 200–350). Urcid (2001:358–62) suggests that these offerings were probably originally located elsewhere and reused when the South Platform was expanded and the carved monuments set as cornerstones. I suspect that the dismantling of these important buildings with their iconographic programs representing the sacred power of rulers was probably due to the usurpation of dynasties and attempts to erase earlier rulers from memory, or to termination rituals that transferred sacred power from the dead ruler to his or her successor. Common themes on other Classic-period monuments involve genealogy, funerary ceremonies, human sacrifice, the linkage of corporate groups through the marriage of prominent nobles, and the trans-generational transfer of corporate property and privileges (Urcid 2001, 2005).

By the Xoo phase genealogical narratives were increasingly represented on smaller stone slabs, friezes and lintels (figure 7.6). For the first time, stone monuments are found not only at Monte Albán, but also at political centers throughout the Central Valleys and surrounding mountainous regions. These monuments, often referred to as genealogical registers, relate information about descent in the context of several kinds of ceremonies (Urcid 1999, 2005). In some cases, several generations of noble couples are shown in scenes involving marital rituals. In other cases, a noble couple is shown conjuring the apical founding ancestor of their corporate group through the offering of bird sacrifices, burning rubber, and leaf bundles. Another theme involves ceremonies designed to validate the transfer of political and ritual authority from one generation to the next as invested in corporate land, property, and special offices. For example, a monument discussed by Urcid (2005:141) shows a personage dressed as the rain deity handing a symbolic lightning bolt to a successor, perhaps his son. Other monuments show a genealogy descending from an apical ancestor often depicted as a Rain god impersonator. The few monuments found *in situ* were discovered in tombs, although Urcid (2005:143–7) suggests that many were originally set in friezes or lintels of mausolea. A mausoleum with stone facades depicting a genealogical sequence was discovered above Tomb 6 in a high-status residence at Lambityeco.

To summarize, imagery on tomb art and carved-stone monuments shows how Classic-period political authority was more exclusionary and less communal than during the Formative (A. Joyce 2004:207–11; Urcid 2005:154–5). Genealogy became a key element of ideologies that legitimated the social position of corporate groups as well as rulers. Using Giddens' (1979:193–5) framework for understanding how ideology creates, maintains, and justifies

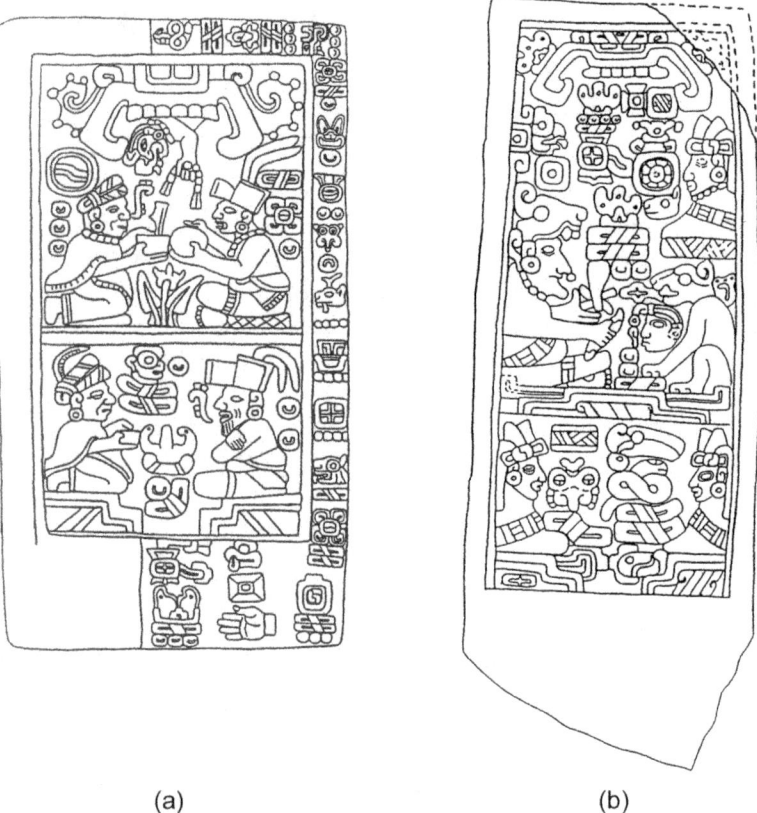

Figure 7.6 Xoo-phase genealogical registers from the Valley of Oaxaca: (a) Slab 6-6059, unknown provenance; Museo Nacional de Antropología e Historia (after Urcid 2005, figure 6.2; redrawn with permission from Javier Urcid); (b) Monte Albán Stela MA-VGE-2 (after Urcid et al. 1994, figure 3A; reproduced with permission from the Instituto Nacional de Antropología e Historia)

sectional interests, genealogy can be seen as having reified status distinctions among corporate groups since the prominence of apical ancestors was fixed. The imagery presented apical ancestors of noble groups as instrumental in the cosmic creation and their continued propitiation was crucial to world-centering rituals. This belief universalized the social position of the nobility by making nobles intermediaries between commoners and the divine, since nobles were both descended from and had privileged access to important ancestors. Wealth and status was further reified since rights to property, privileges, and special offices were held via membership in the corporate group. Members of ruling houses, for example, had the right to engage in warfare, take captives, play the ballgame, and offer human sacrifices. Status within the group was further reified as a function of a person's proximity to the apical ancestor. Indications that important offices could be inherited, such as that of rainmaker and paramount sacrificer, suggest the means through which other nobles as well as commoners could be excluded from positions of power. Evidence from Monte Albán's Main Plaza suggests that another way in which the exclusionary political authority of rulers was manifest was through access to and control over the ceremonial center.

Structures of authority: architecture and ceremonial space

Today when entering the Main Plaza of Monte Albán one is struck by the ruins of temples, ballcourt, and palaces that reference a distant time of ancient civilizations. The organized layout of the plaza leaves the impression of a chronological flatness demarcating a distant and mysterious past when the site was occupied that is utterly disconnected from the present. When looking down on the plaza from the North Platform, for example, it is difficult to visualize the site's 2,500-year life history during which it was built, remodeled, abandoned, reused, reconstructed, and eventually transformed into a World Heritage Site and tourist attraction (A. Joyce 2004, 2009a). This apparent temporal flatness belies the findings of archaeologists which show that the practices carried out in the Main Plaza as well as associated meanings and their political significance changed dramatically through time. The Classic period marks a time of major transformations in the use and political significance of the Main Plaza related to the rise of exclusionary political authority from the more communal forms of the Formative period.

A contextual analysis of monumental art and architecture on the Main Plaza indicates a shift away from large-scale public ceremonies during the Terminal Formative and toward practices restricted largely to the nobility during the Classic period (A. Joyce 2004). As discussed in chapter 5, Formative-period public art was visible to people on the plaza and stressed communal involvement in and benefits from warfare, sacrifice, and ritual, while muting the significance of nobles. Following the political upheaval at c.AD 200, most monuments were taken from their original locations, reset in building foundations, and often plastered over. Some monuments appear to have been intentionally broken (Urcid 2008). Classic-period iconography and architecture significantly altered the original sacred geography and ideological meanings of the plaza. With few exceptions, Classic-period Zapotec nobles placed monumental art in highly restricted settings such as in tombs (A. Joyce 2004:209–11; Urcid 2005). Rather than communal themes, Classic-period art foregrounded the ritual, political, and military power of the ruling nobility, their ancestors, and the corporate groups they led. Blanton's (1978:63–6) spatial analysis shows that during the Classic period access to the Main Plaza was increasingly restricted and controlled with only narrow access points at the corners of the plaza.

The construction of high-status residences on the plaza transformed it from a public space for large-scale ceremonies to a place of domestic activities (figure 7.2b). On the North Platform the El Ocote residence continued during the Pitao phase as did two possible high-status residences to the west and the PSA residence on the southeast corner of the platform (Barber & Joyce 2006:229–33). On the Main Plaza, the Area IV-Norte residence on the northwest corner continued as a high-status residence, while Zapotecs converted the Conjunto PNLP from a specialized shell-ornament production locus into a residence (PNLP-1). A high-status house was also constructed adjacent to the plaza just west of the South Platform. Continuity in the occupation of high-status residences during the Formative-to-Classic transition supports the argument for a continuation in the ruling dynasty and exclusionary forms of political authority as corporate institutions like the sodalities described by Urcid (2008) declined in power.

Additional high-status residences were built on the Main Plaza during the Xoo phase. At this time, the area west of the South Platform included 10 residences, although no more than five were occupied at any one time. Zapotecs built the largest of the Late Classic noble residences, Building S, on the southeastern end of the plaza; this residence included three contiguous patio groups. People also built a Xoo-phase residence on the top of the tall platform of Building L. The most elaborate Classic-period residences such as Building S, the PSA residence, and the residence of Tomb 104 were more elaborate and formalized than their Formative-period predecessors, consisting of three residential units separated by narrow passageways (Barber & Joyce 2006:233–9; Urcid 2005:49–50; Winter 1974:985–6). The size of these probable royal residences suggests that ruling houses at Monte Albán had expanded to include extended families and perhaps retainers. Additional research is needed to investigate the configuration of Classic-period ruling houses, however.

The construction of high-status residences around the Main Plaza would have dramatically altered its character relative to the Formative period. Instead of a public ceremonial space emphasizing community and the divine, Zapotecs transformed much of the Main Plaza into a residential area where the high nobility and their retainers carried out everyday domestic activities.

Figure 7.7 Photo of System M, a temple-patio-altar complex on the Main Plaza of Monte Albán (photograph by Arthur A. Joyce)

Commoners were increasingly excluded from the plaza. I suspect that large-scale public ceremonies in the Main Plaza were less frequent, and when carried out the presence of elite residences acted as constant reminders of the control of the plaza by the nobility.

Zapotec nobility conducted rituals in restricted ceremonial spaces around the Main Plaza that were set off from daily activities, as indicated by the construction of several temple-patio-altar (TPA) complexes (figure 7.7). The TPA consisted of a temple elevated on a platform that faced a patio with an altar in the center (Winter 1989a:45–6). In most cases, access to the TPA was restricted either by building a wall around the patio or by constructing a sunken patio. TPAs like the Patio Hundido on the North Platform date back to the Terminal Formative, although they are rare until the Late Classic when at least 10 were constructed at Monte Albán; others occur at administrative centers in the valley such as at Lambityeco and Macuilxóchitl. At Monte Albán, people built two TPAs on the west side of the Main Plaza, which effectively segregated portions of the plaza creating restricted ceremonial spaces. Activities within the patio would have been hidden from the view of people outside, further indicating a shift away from large-scale public ceremonies. TPAs created a boundary that ritual participants crossed between the mundane world of everyday activities and the divine world contacted through sacred rituals carried out in a restricted and hidden setting.

An increase in the construction of small temples during the Xoo phase created additional restricted ceremonial spaces (Martínez López 2002). Another indication of the appropriation of ceremonial space by nobles at Monte Albán comes from the incorporation of temples into two high-status houses: the Tomb 7 and PNLP-1 residences (Martínez López & Markens 2004:83). In both cases, Zapotecs constructed temples over earlier tombs, thereby associating the temple with the ancestors of the family that occupied the residence.

The trend toward restricted ceremonial spaces is found in administrative centers throughout the valley (Kowalewski et al. 1989:262–3). Winter (2001:296) identifies a common architectural complex in Xoo-phase political centers including Monte Albán, Cerro de la Campana, Loma del Trapiche, and Lambityeco, which consists of a high-status residence, ballcourt, TPA, and plaza in close association with one another. These complexes indicate a restricted arrangement of ceremonial space like at Monte Albán. Some of the larger sites, including Monte Albán, have more than one example of this architectural complex, suggesting that it is associated with the rulers of prominent corporate groups. At Lambityeco and Macuilxóchitl, people built a patio and altar adjoining a high platform (Mound 195) on which the probable residence of the ruling family was located, thereby creating what Lind (1994) has termed a palace-patio-altar complex (also see Faulseit 2008:32–4; Markens et al. 2008:202).

Identity and polity in the Central Valleys

By the Xoo phase there is evidence for uniformity in art and architecture in public and elite domestic contexts throughout the Central Valleys and religious practices were broadly shared (Urcid 2005; Winter 2001:295–7). These data could be used to argue for the existence of unifying political and religious institutions. Urcid's (2005) analysis of ruling genealogies, however, has found no evidence that communities like Cerro de la Campana or Lambityeco were ruled by the dynasty at Monte Albán. Archaeological and ethnohistoric evidence from the time of the Spanish Conquest also shows how similarities in art and architecture occurred over large areas of Mexico without political unification or integration.

Archaeological evidence from the Xoo phase does not suggest the kinds of practices and institutions that would have unified and integrated the Valley of Oaxaca. Political unification and integration can be achieved through elite control over large-scale economic systems. There is no evidence, however, for the kinds of large-scale agricultural systems, particularly involving irrigation, that could have been controlled by governments (Flannery 1983a). Monte Albán would have required provisioning by other communities (Nicholas 1989), which could have contributed to greater integration, but could have also created social tensions and provided political leverage to areas that generated surpluses.

The control and regulation of markets and specialized craft production by rulers is another means through which the Central Valleys could have been unified and integrated. Economies in the Central Valleys were complex with considerable evidence for productive specialization in goods like lithics, pottery, textiles, and shell and bone ornaments (Feinman & Nicholas 2004; Middleton et al. 2002). It is certain that markets also existed, although they are difficult to identify archaeologically. While most people in the Central Valleys were farmers, there is also evidence for specialized production for export at the household level. For example, at the Ejutla site, Feinman and Nicholas (2004) excavated a Classic-period residence finding evidence for a variety of productive activities including the manufacture of marine shell, onyx, and greenstone ornaments as well as ceramic vessels and figurines. The volume of these materials far exceeded what was necessary to supply the household, indicating that these products were exported. Evidence for the specialized production of ceramics has been found in low-status houses at Monte Albán (Fargher 2007; Markens 2004:415–21) and survey and excavation data suggest production of ceramics and lithics at numerous sites in the Central Valleys (Finsten 1995; Kowalewski et al. 1989:213–26, 272, 283, 298–9; Markens 2004; Sherman 2005:200–3).

Feinman and Nicholas (2004) have examined Classic-period economics through a multi-year field project at the site of El Palmillo. El Palmillo is one of the largest terraced hilltop sites in the Oaxaca Valley with over 1,400 terraces. The site overlooks the far-eastern end of the Tlacolula arm, one of the driest parts of the valley, where the productivity of maize would have been lower than in other areas, but which had a highly productive local resource in the form of the maguey plant. Excavation of six residential terraces at El Palmillo found that people engaged in a different set of crafting practices than those in Ejutla. Crafting included limited production of ceramics for local consumption as well as the specialized production of chert tools for export (Feinman & Nicholas 2004; Haines et al. 2004). The presence of stone tools used to process maguey, along with bone battens, needles, perforators, and ceramic and bone spindle whorls of the type used to spin maguey fiber, indicates specialized textile production. Each residence at El Palmillo manufactured a slightly different range of products, which were exchanged with other households both within the community and beyond. Exchange of specialized goods gave residents access to non-local goods including obsidian and stone ornaments.

The nature of household specialization was in part the result of raw material accessibility. The Ejutla Valley and the southern Valle Grande had preferential access to trade routes leading to Pacific coastal sources of shell. Likewise, eastern Tlacolula, where El Palmillo is located, has numerous chert sources and other sites in the area exhibit evidence for stone working.

Feinman and Nicholas (2004) argue that products such as ceramics and shell ornaments produced by household specialists most likely circulated through market exchange more than via tribute or redistribution. Craft specialization was primarily at the household level and was not directly managed by a bureaucratic elite (Feinman & Nicholas 2004; Markens 2004:421). It is also unlikely that nobles administered markets. Evidence for economic integration by rulers or by bureaucratic institutions is therefore weak at present.

Defense against common enemies can unify a populace under the leadership of administrators that organize military forces, build defensive works, and promulgate militaristic ideologies (Joyce & Winter 1996). During the Pitao phase, hilltop terraced sites, some with defensive walls, were common in the Central Valleys (Balkansky 2002:54; Elam 1989; Feinman & Nicholas 1990:234–6). Curiously, people in the Etla arm moved to lower elevations with few defensive sites, suggesting perhaps that this area was more directly affiliated with Monte Albán and therefore under its direct protection. It is possible that Monte Albán's leadership was successful in maintaining cordial relations with Teotihuacan, while communities in the southern and eastern parts of the Central Valleys felt more threatened (see Elam 1989:405). Acting as the chief arbiters of political relations with Teotihuacan would have given the rulers of Monte Albán leverage over other communities. Of course, communities in the Central Valleys may have faced threats from neighboring regions such as the Mixteca Alta. By the Xoo phase, evidence for interaction with Teotihuacan decreased as the Central Mexican metropolis began to fade in political power and influence, but many sites continued to be located in defensible hilltops (Elam 1989). Defensive and military concerns therefore may have resulted at least periodically in some degree of unity under the rulers and ruling institutions of Monte Albán, particularly as a result of relations with Teotihuacan.

Authority and Polity in the Classic Period 223

Overall, the evidence causes me to question the degree to which the Central Valleys were unified, integrated, and administered by a polity centered at Monte Albán (also see Balkansky 2002:65–6; Elson 2007; Winter 2004b:53–4). Instead, the data suggest a more dynamic and fragmented political landscape. Monte Albán was undoubtedly seen as a sacred place and a powerful political center whose rulers probably exerted direct control over the central part of the valley and perhaps into the Etla arm as well. Beyond this core region, I argue that the rulers of Monte Albán continuously negotiated relations with ruling dynasties of other political centers like Jalieza and the DMTG cluster who probably exerted some degree of political domination over surrounding communities, including the mobilization of tribute. The discovery of stone monuments with genealogies of prominent families, including those dressed as jaguars and rain-deity impersonators, indicates the presence of ruling dynasties in many Xoo-phase communities, including Cerro de la Campana and Lambityeco (Urcid 2005). Other sites with evidence for powerful nobles, public architecture, and perhaps ruling houses include Macuilxóchitl, El Choco, Reyes Etla, and Loma del Trapiche (Kowalewski et al. 1989, tables 9.2 and 9.6). Given the size of Monte Albán, it is likely that its rulers were able to set up tributary relations with many communities, but the nature of these relations was undoubtedly also dynamic. References to warfare and human sacrifice in Classic-period iconography show that political relations at times deteriorated to the extent that warfare broke out. Monte Albán may not have been able to dominate the valley militarily, given the size of sites like Jalieza and the DMTG cluster.

Both nobles and commoners embodied a variety of subject positions through which they negotiated their place in society including gender, age, status, corporate group, community, and occupational distinctions. People's identities included affiliations with a nested set of social groups from their immediate family and household to their corporate group and community. At a still larger scale, people undoubtedly belonged to more loosely defined supra-community affiliations that included a corporate group led by a ruling dynasty whose authority was materialized in their residences and tombs as well as the public places and monuments of a principal town or city. It is possible that, as a ritual center that referenced common origins, Monte Albán was the focal point of a still broader identity encompassing the Central Valleys and perhaps beyond. The degree to which this broader identity was a political reality would have varied, depending on Monte Albán's relations with and dominance over other communities.

Despite the exclusionary structure of Classic-period political discourse, I think that nobles and especially rulers had considerable flexibility to negotiate, reproduce, and transform their social position and relationships as well as that of their corporate group (also see A. Joyce 2004; Urcid 2005). Nobles advanced their interests by establishing alliances, especially through marital ties to other prestigious corporate groups. They could strategically emphasize descent from apical ancestors of either their maternal or their paternal lines and thereby foreground affiliations with different groups. The concern with genealogy and ancestors, especially in the context of tomb rituals, suggests that establishing genealogical linkages to powerful ancestors was crucial in negotiating and legitimating political power, including claims to land and other resources. The death of a ruler would have been a time of crisis and struggle over succession, requiring the invocation of genealogical relations and the renegotiation of alliances. Nobles also materialized their personal and corporate wealth and power through the production, consumption, and display of social valuables. The construction of elaborate residences, tombs, monuments, and public buildings created socially meaningful places that emphasized and could transform the political prominence of rulers and their corporate groups through citations to powerful ancestors and deities. Rulers and religious functionaries acted as intermediaries between people and the divine. At times rulers went to war to defeat competitors and ruling dynasties could mediate conflict through ballgame rituals. Other roles through which nobles engaged their social worlds included those of scribe, architect, muralist, and probably specialist in the production of elaborate sumptuary goods.

The exclusionary structure of political authority probably means that most commoners had little access to the upper echelons of Zapotec society, but this does not mean that non-elites were powerless or lacked agency. I argue that there was a diversity of subject positions through which non-elites negotiated social relationships. In addition to distinctions defined by age and gender, commoners also had access to a variety of occupations including farming, food preparation, raising children, and craft specializations such as the production of pottery, textiles, and shell ornaments. Local tradition, as well as the availability of key resources, provided constraints and opportunities for people to pursue particular occupations. Yet at El Palmillo the evidence suggests that households had considerable flexibility in adopting a mix of occupations – agricultural and crafting – through which they made a living and established networks of social relations with other households in the community and beyond. Feinman and his colleagues (2006; Haller et al. 2006) have found a weak correlation between the consumption of social valuables such as obsidian and greenstone with status. These data suggest that inequality may not have been tightly constrained by social status and that there was some mobility for people in terms of wealth and influence within their communities. Paleodietary and paleopathological studies at Monte Albán suggest that household heads buried in tombs may have had somewhat better diets and enjoyed better health than lower-ranking family members (Márquez & González 2001). Isotopic studies of diet also showed variation among barrios at Monte Albán, with higher-status barrios having somewhat greater access to meat (Blitz 1993).

Zapotecs for the most part established and negotiated their social and economic relations with the wider world, rather than having these relationships imposed on them by political authorities. Nobles and especially rulers, however, had a greater degree of control over people's access to the divine, since there is little evidence for non-elite domestic rituals other than mortuary ceremonies (Winter 2002:81–2; Winter et al. 2007:192). Prominent nobles and rulers had access to ritual buildings and spaces and filled certain religious offices, like that of Xicani priest, that gave them special access to the divine. The evidence suggests that, by the Classic period, Zapotec nobles were less concerned with large-scale ceremonies that engaged commoners and more focused on rituals involving restricted audiences of other elites.

Commoners and perhaps lower-ranking nobles must have been largely excluded from participation in important ceremonies carried out in restricted spaces such as TPAs, temples, and the tombs of powerful ruling dynasties. For Monte Albán's leading families, the Main Plaza was now both a ceremonial and a residential area. Unlike the Formative when there were no residences on the Main Plaza, Classic-period noble families and servants carried out their everyday domestic activities in and around the plaza. The bulk of the plaza may no longer have been a liminal space for contacting the divine with most rituals carried out in restricted areas like TPAs and temples that were removed from everyday life and the domestic sphere.

The ways in which commoners and perhaps nobles from hinterland communities experienced the plaza would have been colored by memories of its earlier uses and symbolism (A. Joyce 2004, 2009a). The evidence suggests to me that commoners were less actively engaged in the kinds of ritual performances and shared experiences that created a sense of belonging and identity with the symbols, rulers, and institutions of the polity. If local nobles actively competed and attempted to undermine the authority of Monte Albán, then central unifying symbols, especially surrounding the rulers of Monte Albán, would have been further weakened. The Main Plaza may have embodied an increasing separation, and perhaps tension, between the identity of commoners and rulers as well as between people in the center and periphery. Residences were increasingly enclosed and inwardly focused during the Late Classic, which might reflect these rising social tensions and divisions, especially among competing nobles and/or between nobles and commoners (Hutson 2002:68–9; Winter 1974). An unintended outcome of competition among the nobility and the disengagement of commoners from public ceremonies could have been to weaken the allegiance of commoners and lesser nobles to rulers and ruling institutions, especially to the distant rulers of Monte Albán. It is possible that for many people the Main Plaza and other restricted ceremonial spaces came to symbolize the evasion of the moral responsibilities of rulers to their people.

The exclusionary practices of Zapotec nobles therefore could have provided openings in hegemonic discourse and increased the degree to which commoners and lesser nobles penetrated ruling ideologies. Much of the social production of ideology during the Classic period seems to have been aimed at other nobles. Rulers, especially at Monte Albán were more concerned with shoring up support with other prominent families in the valley, probably as a result of increasing competition and conflict. By the Late Classic the nobility had grown in size and the social setting had become factionalized with numerous political centers. The collapse of Teotihuacan around AD 600 lessened the role of Monte Albán's rulers in negotiating relations with this powerful polity. Without the potential threat of Teotihuacan, rulers of other communities may have asserted greater independence and distanced themselves from Monte Albán. I argue that these factors led to increasing competition among ruling dynasties throughout the valley, which was negotiated ritually in highly restricted settings where genealogical relations and alliances could be worked out without undermining the authority of rulers in relation to commoners and lesser nobles (A. Joyce 2004). Nobles maneuvered for power through alliances and by strategic marriages, allowing individuals to claim descent from several powerful ancestors through multiple lines of descent. Evidence from the Mixtec highlands also suggests the possibility of increasing factionalism.

Classic-Period Polities of the Mixtec Highlands

In the Mixtec highlands, chronological divisions are not as well defined as in other parts of Oaxaca and so it is difficult to trace cultural changes through the Classic period (Spores 1972). Settlement data indicate that population growth and centralized polities emerged from the political chaos at the end of the Formative (Balkansky et al. 2000:376–9; Byland 1980:144–50; Kowalewski et al. 2009; Rivera 1999:229–34; Spores 1972:182–7). The Classic period saw the emergence of dozens of small polities that in many ways resembled those present at the time of the Spanish Conquest. Polities were centered on head towns, some urban in scale, where ruling families resided. Rulers exercised authority over small territories, probably no more than about 1,000 km^2. Most political centers and many other communities were located on defensible hilltops, and iconography as well as the presence of possible defensive walls indicates interpolity warfare. The fortunes of ruling dynasties probably varied depending on success in warfare and the establishment of strategic alliances and trade relations. Smaller political centers fluctuated from independence to being subject to more powerful polities (Balkansky et al. 2000:377). Like in the Central Valleys, evidence from the Mixteca Alta and Mixteca Baja suggests exclusionary forms of political authority and more formalized status distinctions. Iconographic, epigraphic, and architectural data show the emergence of a distinctive elite identity in the Mixtec highlands, although with important ties to the Valley of Oaxaca, the Basin of Mexico, and the lower Río Verde Valley. In the Mixteca, comparatively less information is available for understanding the practices and identities of common people because, with the exception of Cerro de las Minas, there have been few excavations in non-elite contexts.

More than a dozen political capitals have been identified in the Mixtec highlands. The largest centers covered over 200 ha and included Yucuñudahui in the Nochixtlán Valley and Cerro Jazmín near Yanhuitlán (Balkansky 1998b:481; Balkansky et al. 2000:377). Smaller centers such as Etlatongo and Jaltepec in the Mixtec Alta and Diquiyú in the Mixteca Baja measured around 100 ha (Balkansky 1998b:481; Jeffrey Blomster personal communication 2008). Communities in the 40- to 60-ha range included Huamelulpan and Cerro de las Minas as well as Ñuundaa in the Tamazulapan Valley, Cerro Encantado and Cerro de la Virgen in the Tlaxiaco Valley, Yucuninde in the Teposcolula Valley, and Cerro de la Caja in the Mixteca Baja (Balkansky 1998a:57; Byland 1980:321; Kowalewski et al. 2009:91, 257–60; Rivera 1999:27, 126; Winter 2007). Most polity capitals were located on defensible hills with commanding views of surrounding territory, continuing the pattern begun in the Late Formative. These sites were densely occupied with populations reaching several thousand people. Civic-ceremonial precincts with monumental architecture and high-status residences were located on hilltops, while people lived on the slopes with residential terraces built in steeper sections. Surveys suggest an expansion of agricultural terrace and *lama-bordo* systems, which appear to have stabilized hillslopes and lessened erosion to some extent (Joyce & Mueller 1997:85). The best-understood political centers are Yucuñudahui, Huamelulpan, and Cerro de las Minas.

Yucuñudahui

Yucuñudahui is located on a narrow L-shaped ridge that towers 400 m above the floor of the northern Nochixtlán Valley. Yucuñudahui means "hill of the rain god" in Mixtec and at the time of the Spanish Conquest it was known as a sacred mountain and place of creation (Hamann 2002: 358–63). The site was an important Ramos-phase demographic center that may have been affiliated with nearby Yucuita. As Yucuita declined at the end of the Ramos phase, people moved to Yucuñudahui, increasing the size of the community to 209 ha by the end of the Classic-period Las Flores phase (Plunket 1983).

The ceremonial center of Yucuñudahui extends along the narrow crest of the ridge. Areas were leveled and filled to create two monumental platforms that supported several large structures, perhaps temples, facing onto plazas, the largest of which reached about 200 m^2 (Spores 1984:30–48). Platforms are partially surrounded by low walls. High-status residences were located on terraces adjacent to and slightly below the plazas. A possible residential area, perhaps the house of the ruler, was also located on the eastern platform between two major substructures (Mounds C and E). In the depression between the platforms is a ballcourt. On the northern arm of Yucuñudahui's ridge, Caso (1938) excavated a high-status residence and an impressive Early Las Flores-phase stone-masonry tomb (Tomb 1). The tomb included painted murals and carved-stone slabs with calendrical glyphs as well as offerings of ceramic vessels. Midway along the ridge is an enormous limestone and chert quarry used to acquire lithics for stone tools and building materials.

Huamelulpan

Huamelulpan decreased from 212 ha during the Late Ramos phase to 45 ha by Las Flores, although it continued as a political and religious center (Gaxiola 1984; Winter et al. 1991). Most of the excavations have been in ceremonial or elite sectors, but survey suggests that commoners continued to reside on terraces around the site core (Balkansky 1998a).

Mixtecs continued to use and modify the Grupo de la Iglesia ceremonial complex during the Las Flores phase (figure 6.4). Two of the structures on Plaza 1 contained stone-masonry tombs, although only Tomb 7 was intact (Herrera 1991). The tomb was built and first used in the Early Las Flores phase, but the contents were later removed. In Late Las Flores, Tomb 7 was reused with an interment accompanied by 32 ceramic vessels, 14 carbonized corncobs, animal bones, and at least 99 unfired clay cones, possibly small incense burners. People left an offering above the tomb entrance that consisted of a possible hearth and 14 ceramic vessels. Since elaborate tombs were usually associated with high-status houses, it is possible that Plaza 1 was the residence of a noble family.

Gaxiola's (1984:55) excavations showed a reduction in the construction and use of the ceremonial platforms in the Grupo al Poniente de la Iglesia with only one of the large platforms continuing in use. Hieroglyphic inscriptions carved in the southeastern corner of the platform probably date to Las Flores (Gaxiola 1984:55; Javier Urcid personal communication 2008). Two Early Las Flores-phase residences were excavated in the northern part of the Grupo al Poniente de la Iglesia (Gaxiola 1984:64–71). One residence included a rectangular stone feature beneath a room containing the skulls of two people, perhaps sacrificial victims or revered ancestors. The second residence was more extensively excavated and had at least seven rooms with plaster floors surrounding a probable patio. The occupants probably used four of the rooms for storage or domestic activities, based on their small sizes and the presence of animal bones, chipped-stone tools and debitage, grinding stones, and a large storage jar. The other rooms were larger and were probably habitations. Beneath the floor of Room 5 was the burial of a male accompanied by 5 ceramic vessels. Just north of the house, a looted and badly damaged tomb was discovered with the remains of three adult women. The size and complexity of this residence indicate it was occupied by a high-status family.

A Late Las Flores-phase residence included two rooms with plaster floors and two probable hearths. Beneath the floor of the southern room (Room 1) were two stone-masonry tombs and three burials. Tomb 74-2 included one adult male and two adult females with 68 ceramic vessels. Interred near the top of the tomb were two burials: an adult male accompanied by a broken ceramic vessel (Burial 74-8) and the partial remains of two secondary interments, both adult females (Burial 74-9). About 30 cm to the north of Burial 74-9 was the interment of a child in a stone-slab *fosa* with three ceramic vessels, including an elaborate zoomorphic pot. The second tomb (Tomb 74-5) had a primary burial and three secondary ones, suggesting multiple uses, along with an offering of 54 ceramic vessels.

Cerro de las Minas

By AD 350, Cerro de las Minas had recovered from its collapse at the end of the Formative and once again became the dominant political center in the Huajuapan Valley (Winter 1991, 1994e, 2007). The Classic-period

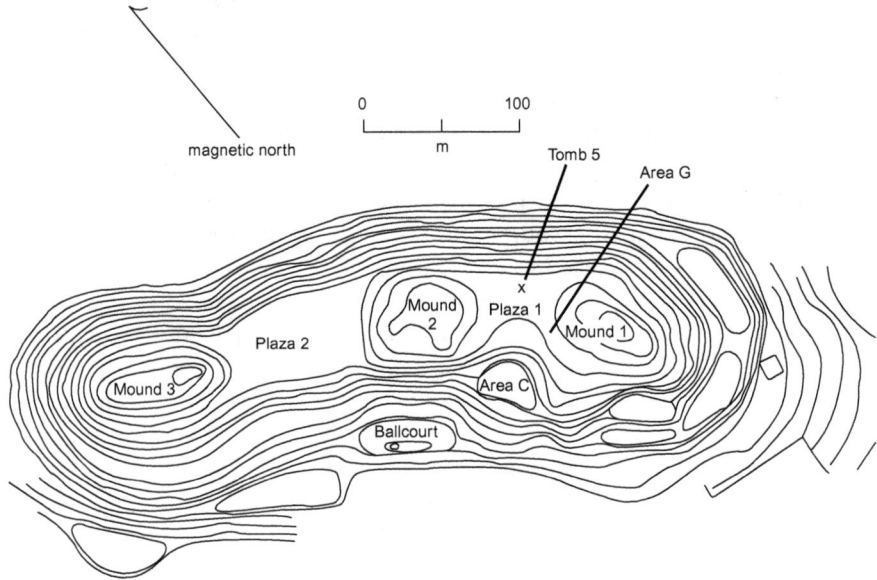

Figure 7.8 Plan of the site center at Cerro de las Minas (redrawn from Winter 1991, figure I.3; reproduced with permission from the Instituto Nacional de Antropología e Historia)

Ñuiñe-phase civic-ceremonial center is located on the site's summit, which supported three monumental platforms separated by two plazas (figure 7.8).

Structures on the platforms were poorly preserved, although buildings on Mound 1 and Mound 3 were probably temples. Evidence suggests that Mound 2 supported an Early Ñuiñe-phase high-status residence, probably the ruler's palace, which may have been converted into a temple in Late Ñuiñe times. Beneath the northeastern side of Plaza 1, Winter (1991, 2007) discovered the most elaborate tomb (Tomb 5) ever found in the Mixteca Baja, probably that of a ruling family. The ballcourt located below Mound 2 may have continued in use during Early Ñuiñe, but was partially dismantled and residences were built in the courtyard during Late Ñuiñe.

Excavations at Cerro de las Minas provide a large sample of Classic-period residences from various status levels (Winter 1991). Archaeologists exposed at least three contiguous high-status residences built on low platforms in Area G on the southeastern side of Plaza 1. It is possible that the three houses were components of a single large domestic compound similar to Building S at Monte Albán, probably the residence of the ruling family. The residences averaged 90 m² with each house consisting of multiple rooms surrounding a patio with plaster floors and well-made stone foundations (Acosta & Tercero 1991, figure 5). Residence G1 included a cist burial with a single individual accompanied by 15 ceramic vessels, a worked stone, and 42 shell beads as well as a burial of a child without offerings. Tomb 4 was a rectangular stone-masonry tomb located in residence G5. The tomb was reused with the remains of two individuals and an offering of nine ceramic vessels, an incense burner, two bone rings, three greenstone beads, two bone beads, and an obsidian bead.

Overlaying Structure G5 were two Late Ñuiñe-phase rooms with stone foundations (Winter & Acosta 1991). Mixtecs interred two stone-cyst burials beneath the floor of one room. Burial 1988/2 included the remains of three people accompanied by nine ceramic vessels, a worked stone, and a worked bone. Burial 1988/4 included remains of two people accompanied by eight ceramic vessels. The two rooms have been interpreted as separate residences, probably of servants or retainers of the noble families residing nearby (Winter 2007:95). Since high-status residences usually include a range of burial types, it is possible that the rooms were part of the high-status residential complex rather than servants' quarters. It is also possible that these residences postdate the occupation of the high-status houses.

Beneath the northeastern end of Plaza 1, Winter (1991, 2007) excavated the spectacular Tomb 5, one of the most elaborate tombs ever found in the Mixteca and the probable burial place of the household heads of a ruling family. Tomb 5 has an antechamber and a roughly square-shaped main chamber separated by a threshold with two jambs. The walls and floors of the tomb are coated with plaster. The tomb was remodeled at least once and was used during both the Early and the Late Ñuiñe phases. At least three individuals were interred in the tomb with the principal burial being an adult female. Offerings included 74 ceramic vessels; an urn and an urn fragment; 7 chert projectile points; a mano and metate; worked bone and stone along with over 1,100 beads, mostly shell, but also greenstone and obsidian; and a circular stone disc, possibly a mirror. The urn is one of the most beautiful examples of Ñuiñe-style urns ever discovered (figure 7.9). It was made from the orange-brown micaceous paste common to the region and was painted with red, orange, yellow, and green pigments. The urn had a square base, above which was a representation of the old fire god, wearing a buccal mask, and holding an object that might represent a gourd for tobacco used in rituals. Behind the figure was a cylindrical vessel and above the figure was a decorated cylindrical element.

In addition to the offerings, people placed two carved-stone slabs in the walls of the tomb. Each slab was carved with a year-glyph, probably the name of an ancestor, which is framed by Glyph U. The inclusion of

Figure 7.9 Ñuiñe urn from Cerro de las Minas Tomb 5 (redrawn from Winter 1991, figure VII.24; reproduced with permission from the Instituto Nacional de Antropología e Historia)

carved-stone slabs with the names of ancestors is a pattern found in other high-status tombs in the Mixtec highlands, including Yucuñudahui Tomb 1 and two tombs (Tombs 1 and 3) excavated on the slopes below the summit at Cerro de las Minas.

As argued by Winter (2007:96), the discovery of several tombs in residential precincts below the ceremonial center suggests a barrio organization with noble families or prominent commoners as barrio leaders. Probable commoner residences were excavated on terraces south of the site's summit (figure 7.10) and consisted of rooms with plaster floors around a patio (Montague & Winter 1991; Winter 2007). In the patio of a residence west of Plaza 1 were fragments of stone sculpture in the process of being worked, indicating that the occupants were making monuments probably for the ruling family on Plaza 1.

Burials from low-status houses included simple graves and stone-lined cists with between one and four bodies. Most interments included a few

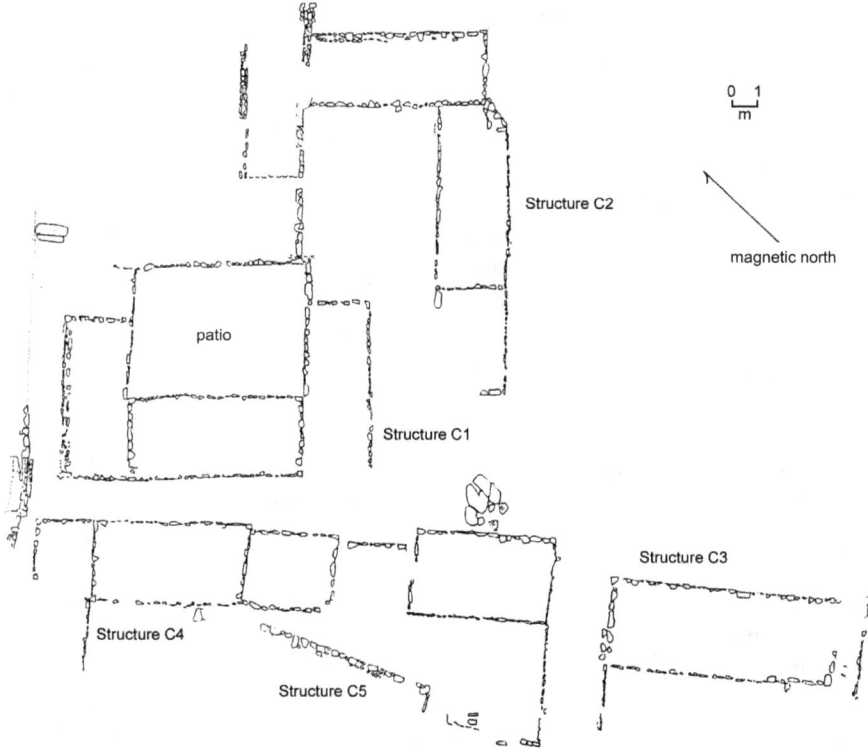

Figure 7.10 Plan of commoner residences at Cerro de las Minas (redrawn from Winter 1991, figure V.2; reproduced with permission from the Instituto Nacional de Antropología e Historia)

vessels and at times other objects such as bone needles, worked stone, and ornaments of bone or shell. The most elaborate burial included remains of four individuals and an offering of 22 ceramic vessels and a mano. Another burial included two bodies along with 2 ceramic vessels, 47 beads of shell and bone, 15 shell pectorals, a chert projectile point, and an intentionally modified human tooth.

Mixtec social structure, identity, and interaction

Classic-period status distinctions in the Mixtec highlands were much more clearly defined than during the Formative. The available evidence suggests that political authority was exclusionary with ruling families living in elaborate residences in restricted locations in the ceremonial core of political centers such as in Plaza 1 at Cerro de las Minas and perhaps the Grupo de la Iglesia at Huamelulpan. There are some indications that commoners were less actively engaged in communal projects that would have strengthened affiliations with rulers and ruling institutions. For example, at Huamelulpan and Cerro de las Minas, the volume of monumental architecture decreased relative to the Formative (Gaxiola 1984; Winter 2007; Winter et al. 1991). Public spaces at Classic-period centers are relatively small and often had elite residences built adjacent to them, suggesting a more private and restricted character. The evidence suggests that Classic-period political authority in the Mixteca more closely resembled conditions at the time of the Spanish Conquest than the more communal patterns seen during the Formative. Additional research, particularly in non-elite settings, is needed to more fully understand Classic-period social distinctions and political authority in the Mixtec highlands.

Regionally distinctive carved-stone monuments, writing, elaborate urns, large and architecturally impressive residences often associated with ceremonial spaces, and interment in impressive tombs with rich offerings can all be considered materializations of a distinct noble identity in the Mixtec highlands. Mortuary patterns resemble those from the Valley of Oaxaca with multiple generations of household heads interred in tombs or elaborate burials and other house members interred in more modest graves. Powerful nobles were celebrated in mortuary rites involving interment in elaborate tombs with impressive offerings such as with Cerro de las Minas Tomb 5, Yucuñudahui Tomb 1, and Huamelulpan Tomb 74–2. The large numbers of ceramic vessels in elaborate tombs indicate participation of many people in the mortuary ceremonies associated with the heads of noble families, suggesting extensive networks of relatives and allies. Since the principal individual in Tomb 5 at Cerro de las Minas was female, it is likely that women as well as men could hold considerable political power and may have been rulers as they were at the time of the Spanish Conquest. Ceramic urns, found primarily in tombs and elaborate burials, suggest associations with deities such as the old fire god. Noble identity and authority was based in part on ritual knowledge as indicated by the close association of high-status houses and ceremonial precincts. Rulers' houses may have included servants and retainers and the nobility sponsored the carving of stone sculptures by non-noble craftspeople (Winter 2007:95).

Noble identity and ideology was inscribed in the iconography and epigraphy of carved stones, slabs, and lintels (Moser 1977; Rivera 1999, 2000). Classic-period writing in the Mixteca, including the calendrical system, is derived from the Zapotec script but with a regionally distinctive style known as Ñuiñe (L. Rodríguez 1999). There are elements of Ñuiñe

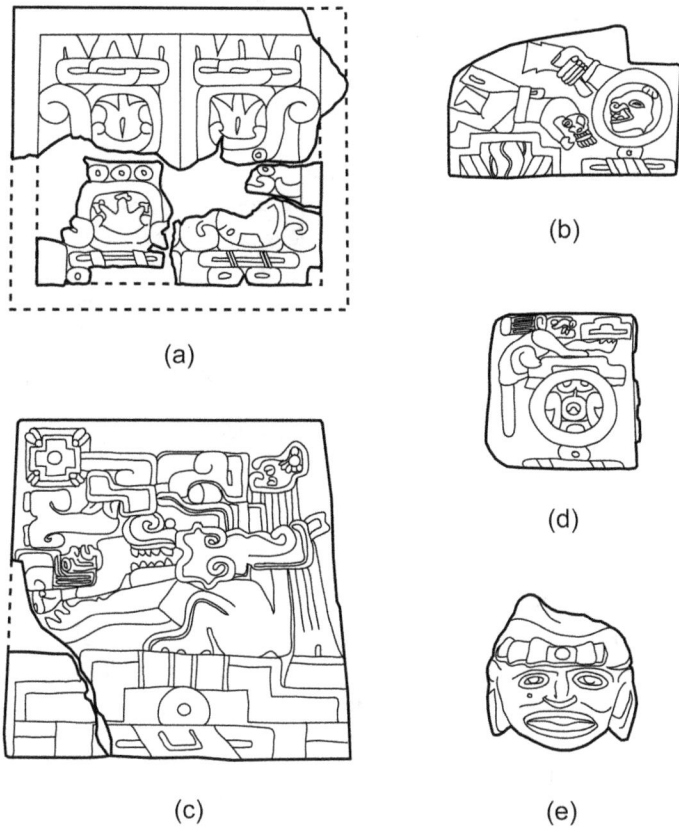

Figure 7.11 Classic-period carved stones from the Mixtec highlands: (a) carved slab from Yucuñudahui Tomb 1 (after Winter 2007, figure 1.9D); (b) Cerro de la Caja Monument 7 (after Rivera 2000, figure 3); (c) Cerro de la Caja Monument 2 (after Rivera 2000, figure 5); (d) Tequixtepec Monument 17 (after Moser 1977, figure 34); (e) stone sculpture of a human head (after Moser 1977, plate LXX)

script and iconography that also show influence from central Mexico, especially Teotihuacan.

Common themes include (figure 7.11):

1 calendrical dates that represent the names of rulers or important nobles. When dates are combined with Glyph U, they likely refer to deceased noble ancestors and are often found in tombs like Cerro de las Minas Tomb 5 and Yucuñudahui Tomb 1;

2   scenes depicting conquest and human sacrifice. These scenes often show a human figure inclined over a hill glyph with a sign representing a particular place such as the "Hill of the Lizard." Adjacent to the figure is a calendrical name of a ruler with a human hand holding a weapon, which extends over the inclined figure, representing the conquest of the identified place and probably the sacrifice of a ruler and/or war captive. Other scenes of sacrifice and conquest emphasize the calendrical name of the victorious ruler shown devouring a sacrificial victim;
3   depictions of rulers often shown in the guise of a jaguar or shown making ritual proclamations. Throughout Oaxaca, Classic-period rulers are often associated with jaguar imagery (e.g., Río Viejo Monuments 8 and 11) and rulers may have adopted the jaguar as their animal-spirit companion or *nagual*;
4   stone sculptures of human heads that probably represent decapitation sacrifices.

The iconography of carved stones therefore suggests that nobles directed military actions and performed important rituals such as human sacrifice. The iconography of Ñuiñe monuments communicated ideological principles. For example, the social position of rulers was reified through references to important ancestors and universalized via the foregrounding of the special ritual abilities of nobles, especially involving sacrifice.

Similarities in the culture of Mixtec nobles and those of other regions, particularly the Valley of Oaxaca, indicate participation in a network of interaction throughout western Mesoamerica. Mixtecs imported obsidian from central Mexico and the Gulf coast, shell from the Pacific and Atlantic coasts, jade from the Maya region, and small amounts of Thin Orange pottery manufactured in Tepeji and Ixcaquixtla, Puebla, but probably traded by people from Teotihuacan (Winter 1994e:210, 2007:102–3). The means of exchange (e.g., via merchants, direct relations among nobles, or down-the-line trade by commoners) are not well understood. It is likely that the spread of ideas and practices resulted from nobles of nearby polities intermarrying, forming alliances, and exchanging prestigious objects and ideas. Based on later ethnohistoric evidence it is likely that Mixtec nobles had periodic contacts with elites from powerful polities in distant regions such as Teotihuacan and Monte Albán. These contacts probably included diplomatic and trade relations as well as the formation of alliances that included intermarriage. Caso excavated a "Teotihuacan style" flexed burial at Yucuñudahui, although its date was uncertain (Plunket 1983:263). Studies of bone chemistry, DNA, or physical attributes would be needed to confirm that this burial was indeed a person from central Mexico.

Winter (2005b:95) suggests that Mixtecs may have been caught between the warring superpowers of Teotihuacan and Monte Albán with the former perhaps dominating the Mixteca. His arguments for Teotihuacan domination are based on general similarities in mortuary practices and ceramic styles, especially Thin Orange pottery. Comparative studies show, however, that similarities in ceramic styles are poor indicators of conquest (Stark 1990). Since the southern Puebla production centers of Thin Orange were only about 50 km north of the Mixtec Baja, it is likely that Mixtecs had direct contact with the producers. In fact, ceramics throughout Oaxaca and in much of western Mesoamerica exhibit stylistic crossties with pottery from the Basin of Mexico, including fine orange-paste semi-spherical bowls often with annular bases and cylindrical tripods with slab feet. Teotihuacan was the most powerful Classic-period polity in Mesoamerica and was probably broadly recognized as an important religious and political center, which may have encouraged Mixtec elites to emulate aspects of central Mexican culture. Based on the current evidence, it is unlikely that Teotihuacan or Monte Albán conquered and directly administered polities in the Mixtec highlands. Lower-intensity forms of conflict, including warfare for the purposes of taking captives or to establish tributary relations, are often difficult to identify in the archaeological record (A. Joyce 2003). Additional research is needed to more clearly define patterns of long-distance interaction.

Evidence for interaction among nobles within the Mixtec highlands is less controversial and includes warfare, exchange, alliance, and intermarriage among ruling dynasties. Although Mixtec nobles shared many aspects of elite culture, there is variation across regions and even between adjacent polities (Rivera 1999, 2000; Winter 1994e:208–17, 2005b:96–109, 2007:35–46). For example, Rivera (1999:247) identifies differences in monumental architecture between the competing polities of Cerro de la Caja and Chazumba in the Mixteca Baja. Carved stones and elaborate urns are more common in the Mixteca Baja. Representations of conquest and sacrifice appear to be more common in the northern Mixteca Baja than in regions to the south. Since the northern Baja was multilingual at the time of the Spanish conquest with speakers of different Mixtec dialects and Chocho-Popoloca, it is possible that conflict was more frequent and/or intensive across ethnolinguistic boundaries. A single writing system, however, was used throughout the Mixtec highlands. Variation in high-status mortuary practices suggests differences in identity probably linked to social roles. For example, some tomb interments were accompanied by large numbers of ceramic vessels (e.g., Huamelulpan Tombs 7, 74-2 and 74-5), while other tombs had tremendous quantities of ornaments as well as pottery (e.g., Cerro de las Minas Tomb 5). This type of variability is also seen in elaborate burials (Cerro de las Minas Burials 1988/5 and 1990/7). These data suggest that, while nobles were connected to a pan-Mesoamerican noble identity, they also exhibited distinctions related to regional, polity, occupational, and perhaps ethnic affiliations.

Commoners had diverse lives growing crops, making crafts, preparing food, raising children, socializing with neighbors, playing, exchanging goods at markets, performing rituals, marrying, and dying (Spores 1969, 1984:28–48; Winter 1994e, 2005b, 2007). Most people were farmers, growing maize, beans, and squash often through the use of agricultural terraces and *lama-bordo* systems to limit erosion in this mountainous landscape. Terrace systems were a form of landscape capital (Erickson 1999), which required considerable inputs of labor to construct, but which if maintained could persist and be used by people for centuries. Some people produced crafts like textiles, ceramics, and shell ornaments, although little is known concerning patterns of production, consumption, and exchange. An oven associated with a residence excavated at Yucuita was used for the manufacture of lime for plaster (Deraga 1981). Evidence for the specialized production of stone sculptures associated with a commoner house at Cerro de las Minas suggests specialists commissioned by or attached to the nobility. Evidence for domestic rituals includes incense burners, dedicatory offerings interred beneath floors or outside houses, burials, and elaborate serving vessels probably used in feasting.

Variation in mortuary patterns indicates that commoners were distinguished by social roles and could achieve some degree of status and wealth. People were interred in graves, *fosas*, cists, and simple tombs with more elaborate burials probably representing household heads. Some interments included over a dozen ceramic vessels, suggesting the deceased was the center of an extensive social network. Burials with large quantities of adornments (e.g., Burial 1990/7), indicate that some commoners sought to elevate their status or represent special social roles through bodily ornamentation.

Gender identities are not clear from the available evidence. Several male interments were accompanied by projectile points, suggesting that hunting, warfare, or stone-tool-making may have been male gendered activities. Bone needles recovered from houses and burials suggest that women produced textiles. Classic-period figurines are found in domestic contexts, but have not been well described, although there is a shift from the modeled figurines of the Formative to the use of molds. Common figurine types include representations of clothed women as well as jaguars, bats, and dogs (Winter 2007:80).

Commoner identities were defined by affiliations with family and with the local community, which probably included religious and political leaders.

At Huamelulpan and Cerro de las Minas, noble residences are found not only in the ceremonial center, but also among low-status houses in residential sectors, suggesting the type of barrio organization present at the time of the Spanish Conquest. As discussed above, common people, particularly in rural settlements, may not have been strongly affiliated with regional rulers and ruling institutions.

Mixtec commoners came in contact with people from other communities through the exchange of basic goods at markets, intermarriage, migration, and possibly participation in warfare. These social relationships contributed to the formation of broader affiliations. For example, ceramics in the eastern part of the Mixteca Alta exhibit distinctive crossties with the pottery of the Valley of Oaxaca (Byland & Pohl 1994:56–7), probably reflecting greater levels of interaction by the people of these regions. On a smaller spatial scale, styles of ceramics, stone tools, and architecture vary across the Mixtec highlands (e.g., Gaxiola 1984; Rivera 1999; Winter 1989a:67–8), reflecting social distinctions related to regional and/or polity affiliation. Research on the practices and identities of non-elites and people outside political centers is crucial for a fuller understanding of Classic-period Mixtec society and culture.

Political Fragmentation and Centralization on the Oaxaca Coast

In the lower Río Verde Valley, the collapse of the Río Viejo polity was followed by a period of political fragmentation and perhaps competition among multiple polities. By the Late Classic Yuta Tiyoo phase (AD 500–800) Río Viejo reemerged as a regional center. Though centralized political authority returned to the lower Verde, I argue that rulership was now exclusionary and hierarchical, focused on the power of ruling dynasties.

Early Classic political fragmentation and the roots of exclusionary authority

A dramatic disruption in regional sociopolitical organization occurred in the lower Río Verde Valley following the abandonment of Río Viejo's acropolis at c.AD 250. Río Viejo decreased from 200 ha in the Chacahua phase (AD 100–250) to 75 ha in the Coyuche phase (AD 250–500) and several other large sites in the floodplain declined significantly in size or were abandoned. The total occupational area in the regional survey, however, increased from 699 ha to 807 ha over the same period. People moved into higher elevations, perhaps due to conflict, as the percentage of the occupational area in the piedmont increased from 38 percent in the Chacahua phase to 63 percent in the Coyuche phase. During the Early Classic, the region contained as many as eight prominent communities of roughly equivalent size that may have been the centers of competing polities.

Evidence of practices that reproduced community and supra-community identities like large-scale feasting and caching, communal mortuary rituals, and the construction and use of monumental buildings decreased during the Coyuche phase. There were modest renovations to mixed-use and residential platforms at Río Viejo and minor additions to the acropolis at San Francisco de Arriba (A. Joyce 2005:25; Workinger 2002:96–231), but there do not appear to have been large-scale building projects. Places that were the focus of public ritual during the Terminal Formative, such as the acropoli at Río Viejo and Yugüe, were either abandoned or little utilized. Evidence for large-scale feasting and ritual caches has not been found in the Early Classic. Workinger (2002:204–8) excavated six modest offerings in the acropolis at San Francisco de Arriba, consisting of one to four ceramic vessels or broken pottery fragments.

Burials occur most often as individual interments and there is no evidence of the dense cemeteries of the Formative. Most burials were unaccompanied by offerings or occasionally had a single ceramic vessel or other objects like animal bone or worked stone. Two remarkable high-status burials have been recovered at Río Viejo, however. Burial RV-B7 was an adult male interred with 22 ceramic vessels, 11 greenstone beads, 2 shell ear flares, and a conch shell. Burial RV-B15 was an adult female with 29 ceramic vessels and 2 green obsidian blades. Two burials had dental filing and one of these also exhibited cranial modification. Bodily alterations may have referenced an aspect of status or occupation unrelated to one's commensal networks, since one of these interments lacked offerings and the other had only a single vessel (also see Geller 2004:388–90, 400–1).

During the Coyuche phase the focus of long-distance contacts among coastal Chatinos became Teotihuacan in the Basin of Mexico. Of the 356 obsidian artifacts excavated from Early Classic contexts, 80 percent were from Pachuca, which is the highest known percentage for a region outside the central Mexican highlands (A. Joyce 2003:66). All of the Early Classic Pachuca obsidian thus far excavated in the region has been from the demographic centers of Río Viejo and San Francisco de Arriba. Test excavations at two smaller Early Classic sites recovered eight obsidian artifacts, but none were green. These data suggest that leaders of prominent communities competed for access to Pachuca obsidian, excluding others in the process. A small proportion of Early Classic ceramics in the lower Verde exhibit formal and decorative attributes often linked to Teotihuacan including Thin Orange pottery, cylindrical tripod vessels with slab feet, coffee-bean appliqués, and *candeleros*. Some of these sherds were probably from imported vessels, although sourcing studies have not yet been carried out. Pottery with central Mexican attributes is more common in high-status contexts such as with Burials RV-B7 and RV-B15 from Río Viejo. In return for obsidian and fancy pottery, lower-Verde people probably exchanged coastal products like cotton, cacao, and ornamental shell, which were highly sought after by the nobility of Teotihuacan (Kolb 1987; Santley 1983). Iván Rivera's (2007) discovery of a remarkable carved-stone monument depicting a figure attired in central-Mexican-influenced dress at the site of Cerro de la Tortuga, 40 km northeast of Río Viejo, suggests the possibility of a Teotihuacan presence in the broader coastal region. Conquest of parts of the coast by Teotihuacan cannot be entirely excluded (A. Joyce 2003; however see Workinger 2002:398–401).

I argue that the collapse of Río Viejo resulted in major changes in social relations and identity in the lower Río Verde Valley. During the Early Classic political authority and social affiliation did not extend much beyond the local community, or at most a small group of interacting settlements. Ceremonial offerings and mortuary rituals were smaller in scale and emphasized individual or familial identities rather than community or supra-community affiliations. Rather than the corporate body emphasized in communal cemeteries, the focal point of Early Classic mortuary ceremony became the individual body whose treatment referenced social networks that converged on that body. Influential people built status and authority within the local community, and did not face the contradictions between local identity and a political authority dependent on supra-community affiliations. Though additional research is needed, political fragmentation and more atomized social affiliations may have created conditions where exclusionary forms of political authority could develop.

Late Classic centralization and the reemergence of Río Viejo

The political fragmentation of the Coyuche phase was followed in the Yuta Tiyoo phase by population nucleation and political centralization with the regional capital once again situated at Río Viejo (A. Joyce 2005:24–5). Late Classic settlement in the full-coverage survey zone covers 605 ha. Chatinos moved back into the floodplain as the occupational area recorded there increased from 22 percent of the total settlement area in the Early Classic to 56 percent by the Late Classic.

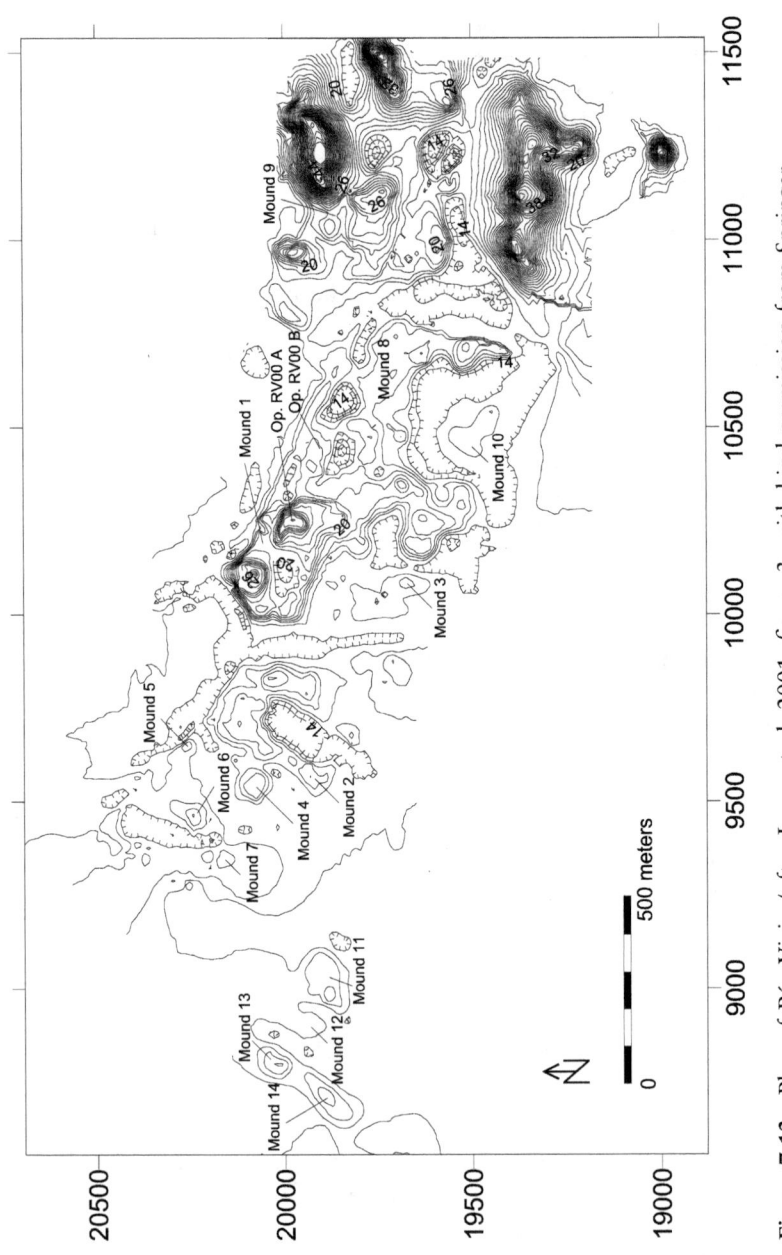

Figure 7.12 Plan of Río Viejo (after Joyce et al. 2001, figure 3; with kind permission from Springer Science+Business Media)

Río Viejo grew to its maximum area of 250 ha with most people living on large residential and mixed-use platforms (figure 7.12). Chatinos reoccupied the acropolis, which once again became the site's civic-ceremonial center. Evidence that Mound 1 was a locus of important public ceremonies, and probably the ruler's residence, includes the presence of three Late Classic carved-stone monuments depicting rulers (Urcid & Joyce 2001), a public plaza, and a sunken patio probably for elite-restricted activities. An excavation 50 m south of Mound 1 recovered thick deposits of Late Classic sherds from fancy serving vessels, suggesting elite domestic activities or perhaps feasting (A. Joyce 1991a:480). Our excavations on the acropolis exposed Late Classic building foundations, although they were poorly preserved, due to the later reuse of foundation stones. Other prominent Late Classic sites such as San Francisco de Arriba, Charco Redondo, and Cerro del Chivo range in size from 26 ha to 58 ha and have monumental buildings and carved-stone monuments.

Although the Late Classic saw the return of centralized rulership, evidence indicates that the Río Viejo polity no longer was characterized by the corporate political structures of the Terminal Formative (A. Joyce 2005: 24–5, 2008a:230–4). Yuta Tiyoo-phase social relations are continuous in many respects with Coyuche-phase patterns, including little evidence for communal building projects, large-scale feasting and caching, and communal mortuary ceremonialism. Excavations at Río Viejo and San Francisco de Arriba indicate that, rather than large-scale projects, construction of monumental buildings involved relatively minor renovations of structures largely built in the Formative (A. Joyce 1999, 2005; Workinger 2002). Commoners presumably participated in public rituals in the civic-ceremonial centers of these sites.

Iconography from Late Classic carved stones suggests a more exclusionary form of political power legitimated through the aggrandizement of rulers, their ancestors, and their place in the line of dynastic succession (figure 7.13). A total of 13 carved-stone monuments have been dated stylistically to the Yuta Tiyoo phase at Río Viejo (Urcid & Joyce 2001). They are carved in low relief and are made of the local granite, which along with erosion of the monuments often makes it difficult to see the details of the imagery in strong sunlight. To draw, photograph, and record these monuments, we have used artificial lights powered with a car battery to illuminate them at night, which allows us to manipulate the shadowing on the stones and more clearly see the imagery. In the semi-tropical lowland environment of the lower Río Verde, the lights attract thousands of insects, which buzz around our heads as we try to record the monuments.

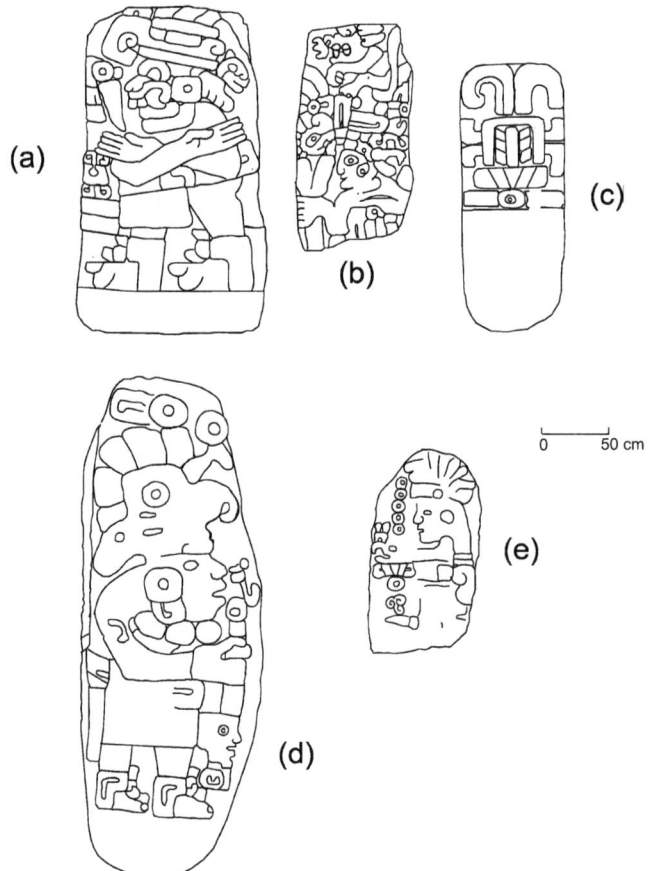

Figure 7.13 Yuta Tiyoo-phase carved-stone monuments from Río Viejo: (a) Monument 8; (b) Monument 11; (c) Monument 14; (d) Monument 6; (e) Monument 15 (after Joyce et al. 2001, figure 4; with kind permission from Springer Science+Business Media; drawings by Javier Urcid)

Most of the carved stones depict nobles, probably rulers of Río Viejo, dressed in elaborate costumes and sometimes accompanied by their name in the 260-day ritual calendar. For example, Monument 8, located on the acropolis, depicts a noble identified by his hieroglyphic name "10-Eye." The figure wears an elaborate headdress, ear spools, sandals, a loincloth tied with a waistband, and a jaguar buccal mask with prominent fangs. The headdress includes the profile head and paw of a jaguar as well as the imagery of Glyph U, which refers to a mythological bird and the ancestors.

Monument 11 depicts a noble holding a zoomorphic staff. The person wears a composite pendant and an elaborate headdress that has a jaguar protruding from its back. Above the figure are the glyph "2 Jaguar" and the "blood" glyph, probably a reference to autosacrificial bloodletting. In addition to actual depictions of rulers, two carved stones (Monuments 1 and 14) each include only a single glyph, probably the calendrical name of a ruler. Monument 1 depicts the glyph "2 Jaguar" and presumably refers to the same ruler as shown on Monument 11. Carved stones at other sites are similar in style to those from Río Viejo and include either depictions of nobles or calendrical names. The nobles referred to on these monuments may be local rulers or members of Río Viejo's ruling dynasty.

As argued by Urcid (2005:20–7), people depicted on monuments dressed in jaguar skins were almost certainly rulers. The jaguar was a powerful symbol of rulership throughout Mesoamerica linked to warfare, sacrifice, divination, governance, and ritual authority. The jaguar probably represented a powerful *nagual* into which rulers transformed as a means of communicating with ancestors and deities. In addition to the monuments from Río Viejo, Monument 1 from Tututepec also shows a noble dressed as a jaguar, suggesting that separate dynasties may have ruled different communities in the region. It is possible that rulers of less powerful communities paid tribute to the rulers of Río Viejo.

The coastal script shows clear similarities to Zapotec epigraphy, supporting the idea that the distribution of speakers of Chatino, a branch of the Zapotecan language, was wider in antiquity than today (Urcid 1993:161). Certain iconographic conventions also show connections to the Mixteca Baja and central Mexico, including imagery from Teotihuacan and Xochicalco (Urcid & Joyce 2001:212). Evidence for trade with Teotihuacan declined during the Yuta Tiyoo phase, although obsidian data support possible contacts with Xochicalco, an important Epiclassic city in Morelos. For example, the percentage of Pachuca obsidian fell from 80 percent in the Early Classic to 6 by the Late Classic, indicating decreasing trade with Teotihuacan. The most common source of Late Classic obsidian (44 percent) was Ucareo in Michoacan (Joyce et al. 1995:11–12), which was the dominant source of obsidian recovered from workshops at Xochicalco (Sorensen et al. 1989). Monuments of similar style to those of the lower Verde have been found along the coast from south central Oaxaca to eastern Guerrero at urban centers like Piedra Labrada, El Ciruelo (also known as Cola de Palma), and Río Grande (Gutiérrez 2008; Urcid 1993). Common representational themes include rulers attired as jaguars as well as allusions to the ballgame and human sacrifice, suggesting that warfare may have been a feature of interpolity relations along the coast and that dominant ideologies stressed special ritual abilities of nobles involving sacrifice and nagualism.

The aggrandizement of nobles as well as their physical and symbolic separation from commoners is also indicated by data from the ceremonial site of Cerro de los Tepalcates. Cerro de los Tepalcates is located on a rocky hill that rises 120 m above the salt flats just north of the coastal lagoons. From the top of the hill, one is afforded a spectacular view of the estuaries, surf, and the expanse of the Pacific Ocean. During the rainy season, the site becomes a virtual island as the salt flats north of the hill flood. At Cerro de los Tepalcates, hieroglyphic inscriptions that appear to be calendrical names of rulers are carved into boulders and we discovered the remains of a probable looted tomb. Since no tombs have been discovered elsewhere in the region, these data suggest that rulers may not have been interred in their communities, but rather in sacred non-residential sites as they often were at the time of the Spanish Conquest. The evidence from Cerro de los Tepalcates is suggestive of modern Chatino conceptions of the underworld (Greenberg 1981:83). For Chatinos, the underworld is divided into two layers. The nearest is Kanil xa, a realm half ocean and half land where various deities and the devil reside. Beneath this first layer and across the ocean is the land of the dead.

Based on the available data, commoners were primarily farmers who lived in modest wattle-and-daub houses (A. Joyce 2005:24–5; Joyce et al. 2001:354). Evidence for specialized production of gray-ware pottery comes from a test excavation and surface collections on Mound 4 at Río Viejo. Commoners continued to be buried as individuals or in small family groups in residential settings usually without offerings or accompanied by a few ceramic vessels and occasionally objects like ground-stone axes, shell beads, worked bone, and greenstone beads. An adult burial recovered from Mound 7 at Río Viejo, however, was interred with three ceramic vessels, two ground-stone axes, a shell necklace consisting of 69 beads, two bone pendants, two pieces of worked bone, one greenstone bead, and a piece of worked granite. This burial suggests that commoners had some social mobility and could enhance their status through beautification. Future research needs to explore more fully the dimensions of social difference beyond noble and commoner distinctions and how these differences were implicated in social change.

The data indicate a return to centralized political authority during the Late Classic with the reemergence of Río Viejo. In contrast to the Terminal Formative, commoners were less engaged in large-scale public projects and rituals that reproduced supra-community identities, while rulers set themselves apart from their subjects in monumental art and mortuary practices.

I interpret these data as suggesting that, like in the Oaxaca Valley and in the Mixteca, Classic-period political organization was characterized by a less communal, more exclusionary ideology with commoners less actively engaged in the kinds of ritual performances and shared experiences that created a sense of belonging and identity with polity symbols, rulers, and institutions.

In the Mixtec highlands as well as in the lower Río Verde Valley and the Valley of Oaxaca, evidence indicates an increasing separation between commoner and noble identities toward the end of the Classic period and perhaps rising tensions within the nobility. As I argue in the next chapter, these trends may have contributed to the collapse of ruling institutions and the dramatic social transformations that culminated at c.AD 800.

eight
Collapse and Reemergence

By approximately AD 800 virtually all of the Mixtec, Zapotec, and Chatino cities and political centers were in decline with people relocating to other communities. The collapse of Oaxaca's Classic-period polities was part of a political transformation that affected all of Mesoamerica. Between AD 600 and 900 many complex polities collapsed, including Teotihuacan, Tikal, Copán, and Palenque. The specific timing, causes, histories, and consequences of the collapse varied across Mesoamerica. Most regions, however, experienced dramatic changes in political institutions and ruling ideologies, including political fragmentation, depopulation of many major cities, and the loss of power by ruling dynasties (Diehl & Berlo 1989; Webster 2002). Some regions such as the Copán Valley, Honduras, and parts of the Petén lowlands were depopulated. Explanations for the collapse vary, but usually focus on some combination of warfare, landscape degradation, climate change, and internal political unrest.

In Oaxaca, the causes of the collapse are debated, although many archaeologists agree that factional competition among prominent corporate groups and their constituencies was an important factor (Elson 2003:155–6; A. Joyce 2004; Kowalewski et al. 1989:251; Lind 1994, 2008; Sherman 2005:306–10; Winter 2003:116). The disengagement of people from rulers and ruling institutions was probably another significant factor. When the social and political relations that linked ruling dynasties began to crumble in factional competition, many people may have declined to support rulers, especially those of powerful political centers like Monte Albán and Río Viejo. Although the initial success of these polities was a result of the engagement of commoners in rituals, labor projects, and military actions that came to be important political symbols, the collapse may have been an unintended outcome of people's exclusion from many of these same symbolically, emotionally, and politically charged practices.

In the Oaxacan highlands, research on the collapse and the period immediately following it has been hampered by the inability to distinguish Early

Postclassic ceramic phases, although research by Markens and colleagues (Markens 2004, 2008; Martínez López et al. 2000) is beginning to resolve this problem in the Valley of Oaxaca. In the lower Río Verde Valley, an Early Postclassic ceramic phase is well defined and supported by radiocarbon dates (Joyce et al. 2001:375–8). The data suggest that the Early Postclassic saw a significant reduction in inequality and it may have taken two or three centuries for strong social hierarchies to reemerge. The period of relative equality ends between AD 1000 and 1200 with the founding of new ruling dynasties.

During the Late Postclassic (AD 1100–1521), Oaxaca was broken up into dozens of small polities each ruled by a great house centered on a hereditary ruler who resided in a principal town (Blomster 2008a). These polities are often referred to as *cacicazgos* – a term taken by the Spanish from the indigenous peoples of the Greater Antilles – as well as city-states, principalities, or petty kingdoms. The exceptions to this general pattern were Tututepec in the lower Río Verde region and Tehuantepec in the southern Isthmus of Tehuantepec, which grew into major cities and the capitals of small empires. Mixtec and Zapotec nobles participated in an extensive network of interaction with elites throughout western Mesoamerica. The formation of alliances, exchange, warfare, and intermarriage led to the spread of a distinctive style of noble culture involving art, architecture, writing, dress, and cuisine known as the Mixteca–Puebla style that materialized a distinctive noble identity. By the fifteenth century many areas of Oaxaca were conquered or under threat by the Mexica Empire, although Tututepec remained independent. With the arrival of the Spanish in AD 1521, the prehispanic history of the Mixtec and Zapotecs ended and the period of colonial oppression and transformation began.

This chapter examines the Oaxacan Postclassic, bringing us full circle to the contact period discussed in chapter 2 (figure 8.1). In addition to the archaeological record, understandings of the Postclassic are enriched by the Mixtec codices as well as by Spanish and indigenous documents from the early colonial period.

The Collapse in the Oaxacan Highlands

Evidence in the Oaxacan highlands indicates a major historical transformation during the Early Postclassic, especially in relation to symbols and institutions of rulership (Blomster 2008a; Markens 2004, 2008; Markens et al. 2008:207–10; Winter 1989b, 2003). Causes of the collapse are not well understood although, in the Valley of Oaxaca, archaeological data from the end of the Xoo phase suggest that Monte Albán's nobility were

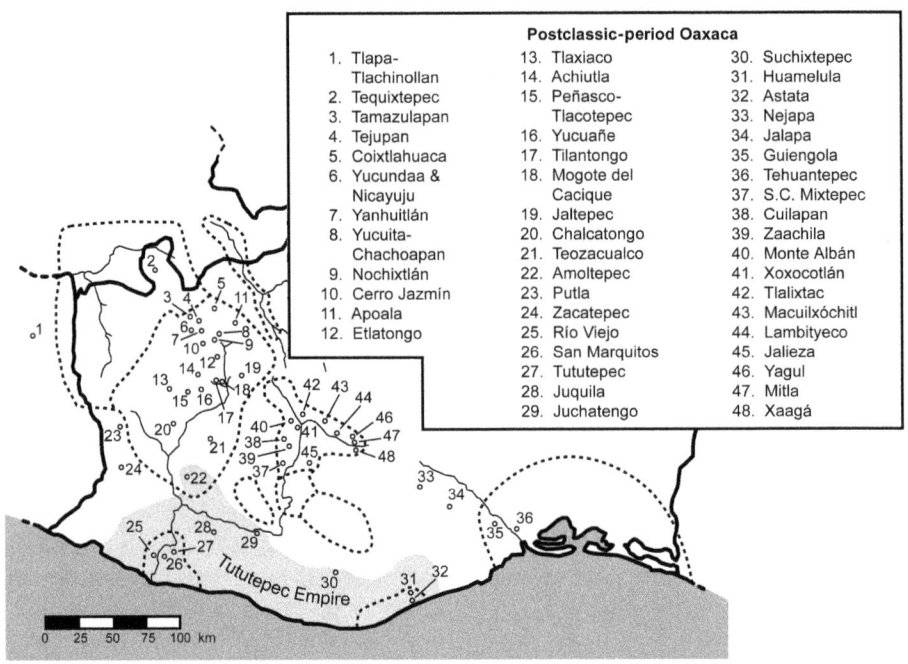

Figure 8.1 Postclassic-period archaeological sites in Oaxaca (drawing by Eric Berkemeyer)

increasingly isolating themselves from the general population as people began to leave the city and as ruling institutions failed (Blanton 1978:100; A. Joyce 2009a; Winter 2003). At this time, many of Monte Albán's elite residences were abandoned or were rebuilt on a smaller, more modest scale. Zapotecs built several new high-status residences in the Main Plaza complex in restricted locations often protected by walls. For example, a high-status house constructed on the North Platform included a diagonal adobe wall that blocked the view of people below (Winter 2003:106–12). Elsewhere in the valley, at political centers including Lambityeco and San Lorenzo Albarradas, there is evidence that monumental-building programs or tombs were left unfinished, suggesting that the collapse of ruling institutions may have occurred relatively quickly (Kowalewski et al. 1989:297; Lind 2001: 126). Conflict among Zapotec ruling houses is suggested by Lind's (2008) research at Lambityeco. He argues that the increasing wealth and power of the ruling dynasty at Lambityeco resulted in its replacement or overthrow by the rulers of Monte Albán (Lind 2008:183–9). A new ruler from Monte Albán replaced the local dynasty, but this was short lived as Lambityeco collapsed and was abandoned within a century.

Chronological problems make it difficult to generate inferences concerning the Early Postclassic, especially in the Mixteca (Kowalewski et al. 2009:328–9). Kowalewski and colleagues (2009:313–14) argue that much of the Mixteca Alta outside of the Nochixtlán Valley may have been abandoned by the Late Classic, indicating an early onset for the collapse that included emigration or a fall in population as early as c.AD 600. The recent delineation of the Liobaa phase has yielded provisional understandings of Early Postclassic social change in the Valley of Oaxaca, although until the revised chronology is applied to survey data and more extensive excavations are carried out in Liobaa-phase sites, it will be difficult to make definitive arguments. There has been considerable debate concerning Liobaa-phase demography and social organization (e.g., Marcus & Flannery 1990; Winter 1989b), although recent research suggests a period of fragmentation with the collapse of political centers like Monte Albán and Jalieza, dispersal of people into smaller communities, and perhaps a decrease in regional population (Markens 2004:429–33; Markens et al. 2008; Winter 2003; Winter et al. 2007). People carried out rituals at sites like Monte Albán and Macuilxóchitl that had been major Xoo-phase centers, but which were largely or entirely abandoned by the Early Postclassic. In other cases, Liobaa-phase practices were more mundane, such as at Lambityeco where Zapotecs built fires to render salt in the ruins of important Xoo-phase buildings. Markens and his colleagues (2008:207) excavated a Liobaa-phase house at Macuilxóchitl, which included a simple tomb containing chipped-stone debitage and a projectile point.

The most dramatic changes involved the collapse of ruling institutions and dynasties. The evidence demonstrates that ruling institutions failed and nobles lost the bulk of their wealth and political authority. Temples, elaborate residences, and ceremonial spaces previously controlled by the nobility were abandoned. Monumental art and writing ceased. The evidence at present suggests a profound collapse in ruling institutions as well as in settlement and perhaps demography, to the extent that it might be viewed as a rupture in the dominant discourse. Additional research is crucial to better understand this critical period in Oaxaca's prehispanic history, however. Additional chronological refinements are needed along the lines of Markens' recent work (Markens 2004, 2008; Martínez López et al. 2000), as well as reanalyses of survey data and excavations in smaller communities that may not have undergone major demographic disruptions.

At Monte Albán, Liobaa-phase evidence shows that as the architecture of the Main Plaza fell to ruins people returned to conduct rituals in the empty ceremonial center (Herrera 2002; A. Joyce 2009a). Ritual practices involved the placement of offerings in Classic-period tombs and TPAs. The most common objects in ritual deposits were miniature ceramic vessels, incense burners, *penates* (small stone figurines), and obsidian blades, all of which were associated with death, sacrifice, and ancestors. The data indicate that rituals in TPAs and tombs were being carried out to contact deities and ancestors to petition them for health and prosperity and perhaps to bring harm to enemies.

Zapotecs removed the contents of several tombs from Classic-period high-status residences and replaced them with offerings of miniature vessels and *penates*. The people who reused tombs must have known their location and may have been the descendants of the nobles who had lived in the residences and were buried in the tombs. The removal of bones from ancestral tombs referenced memories of a glorious past, but also the changed circumstances of Early Postclassic nobles now removed from their spatial and symbolic association with the sacred mountain and apparently living in much humbler circumstances in communities on the valley floor.

Liobaa-phase offerings recovered in TPAs, especially those in the North and South Platforms, consisted of thousands of objects resulting from repeated rituals over the course of several centuries, which suggests the continuous "feeding" of sacrificial offerings to the divine (Herrera 2002; A. Joyce 2009a). The use of common objects such as miniature utilitarian ceramics and obsidian artifacts suggests that a much broader range of people participated in these rituals relative to the highly restricted practices of the Classic period. Offerings in TPAs commemorated earlier ceremonies and the deeper history of the Main Plaza as a sacred mountain of creation. Yet the rituals also created new memories of a sacred past and a cosmic creation that was no longer dominated by powerful nobles, but instead was the product of the sacred work of a much wider range of people, thereby constituting the more egalitarian social relations of the Early Postclassic. Early Postclassic offerings at Monte Albán are related to an expansion of similar rituals in other ruined sites and caves, involving communication with and sacrifice to gods and ancestors in places viewed as interfaces with the divine (Winter et al. 2007:195–6).

The Classic-Period Collapse and the Early Postclassic on the Oaxaca Coast

The Late Classic Yuta Tiyoo-phase polity centered at Río Viejo collapsed during the Early Postclassic Yugüe phase (Joyce et al. 2001). Regional settlement as measured by the occupational area in the full-coverage survey zone decreased from 605 ha in the Yuta Tiyoo phase to 452 ha in the Yugüe phase. Río Viejo continued as a demographic nucleus, although settlement declined from 250 to 140 ha. Another large community emerged at San Marquitos, which grew from 7 ha in the Yuta Tiyoo phase to 191 ha in the Yugüe phase. Regional settlement shifted back toward the piedmont with 62 percent of the occupational area in the full-coverage survey located there, versus only 34 percent during the Late Classic. The data also indicate a cessation in the construction and use of monumental buildings to house rulers and ruling institutions.

The lack of monumental building activities is mirrored in a reduction in monumental art with only three stone monuments tentatively dated stylistically to the Yugüe phase (Urcid & Joyce 2001). The iconography and location of the monuments indicate a shift away from exclusionary forms of authority (figure 8.2). Yugüe-phase sculptures were highly visible and accessible since they were located on a hill on the southeastern end of the site, as opposed to locations on public buildings where many Yuta Tiyoo-phase stones were placed. Late Classic monuments depicted rulers with elaborate elements of royal dress such as jaguar headdresses, masks, staffs of office and often with their calendrical names and allusions to important rites like sacrifice. Yugüe-phase sculptures depict personages that lack the glyphs and elaborate attire of the Late Classic. For example, Monument 3 depicts a topless female wearing a skirt or *posahuanco* in the traditional style of the Oaxaca coast. Urcid and Joyce (2001:211) suggest that the Early Postclassic stone monuments depict deities, although they cannot rule out living nobles or ancestors.

Figure 8.2 Early Postclassic carved-stone monuments from Río Viejo (after Joyce et al. 2001, figure 4; with kind permission from Springer Science + Business Media): (a) Monument 3; (b) Jamiltepec Monument 1 (originally located at Río Viejo)

Explanations for the collapse of Río Viejo's ruling institutions are more difficult to demonstrate (A. Joyce 2008a; Joyce et al. 2001). Population decline due to landscape degradation or drought are not indicated, although ongoing paleoenvironmental studies are investigating the possibility. The movement of people into defensible piedmont locations and the unusually high frequency of projectile points from Yugüe-phase sites suggest the possibility that conflict was a factor. It is unclear whether conflict was intraregional, involving members of the fragmented Río Viejo polity, or if it involved foreign incursions. Another possible factor was the disruption of social networks that contributed to the legitimation of political authority. As polities like Teotihuacan began to collapse around AD 600, these networks of trade, alliance, and intermarriage were increasingly disrupted, which may have begun to undermine Río Viejo's rulers. Regardless of the specific set of factors, by c.AD 800, Río Viejo's rulers were no longer able to mobilize the support of their followers as people left the political center.

Evidence for the social transformations of the Early Postclassic comes from horizontal excavation of two residential areas at Río Viejo (Operations A and B; Joyce et al. 2001; King 2003). In both of these areas, excavations were originally designed to investigate Classic-period residences, but we were surprised to find that an extensive Early Postclassic occupation overlay the Classic-period remains. The excavations provided some of the most surprising and important evidence for Early Postclassic social change in all of Oaxaca. Operation A exposed 242 m^2 on Mound 1-Structure 2, the eastern portion of the acropolis (figure 8.3). Two houses were completely excavated as well as portions of three others along with a patio. Operation B exposed portions of seven structures on Mound 8, approximately 180 m southeast of the acropolis. The structures in both operations were low platforms, measuring approximately 11 m by 5 m by 0.5 m high, that supported wattle-and-daub superstructures. The size and form of the buildings in the two areas were virtually identical and the relatively modest architecture and burial offerings indicate commoner status.[9] Dozens of similar structures have been observed on the surface over a broad area of Mound 8 and in other parts of the site. The excavations at Río Viejo along with the regional survey data suggest little variation in wealth and status during the Yugüe phase, although additional sampling is needed to confirm this pattern.

King (2003:371–2) argues that differences in mortuary practices between the two areas reflect identities linked to separate barrios. Interments in Operation A included adults and children buried outside structures and without offerings. An unusual burial in the patio included a primary interment of an adult female accompanied by a secondary male burial as well as evidence for the use of fire in the mortuary ritual (Joyce et al. 2001:359).

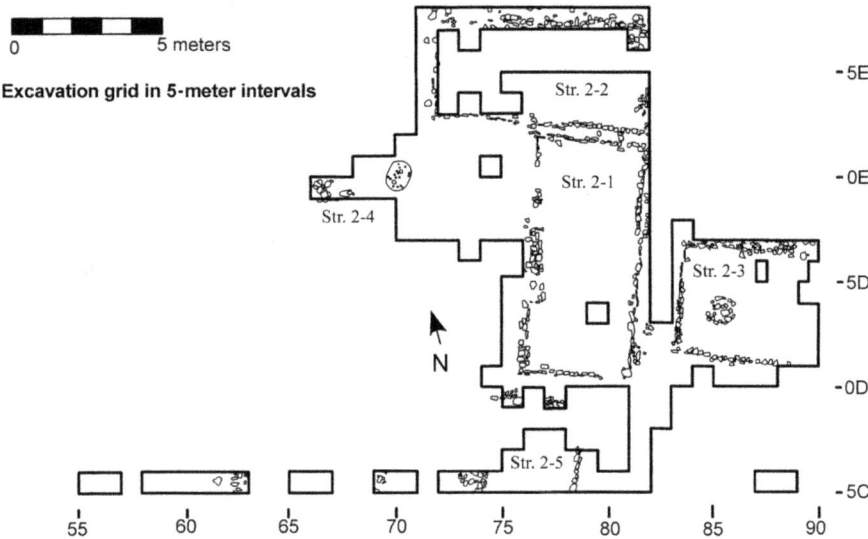

Figure 8.3 Plan of Operation RV00 A at Río Viejo (after Joyce et al. 2001, figure 7; with kind permission from Springer Science + Business Media)

The female was tightly flexed, probably indicative of a bundle burial, and placed directly over the male. In Operation B, adults and sub-adults were buried beneath the floors of two residences (King 2003:194–8). Unlike in Operation A, the burials in Operation B were placed side-by-side with uniformity in position, orientation, and offerings. Offerings typically included from one to three ceramic vessels located near the person's feet; some bodies had additional items including quartz axes, obsidian blades, and shell pendants. The mortuary evidence suggests that distinctions based on age were more clearly marked then those based on gender (King 2006).

Artifacts associated with the residences indicate domestic practices such as food processing and consumption, working of lithics, textile manufacture, ceramic production, and household rituals involving figurines (Joyce et al. 2001; King 2003). Costume ornaments include small pendants, buttons, and ear flares. People in both residences had ceramic imitations of copper bells, probably made locally and used as costume ornaments. Imported goods included a few greenstone beads, a small turquoise pendant, obsidian, and pumice. Fragments of at least two alabaster bowls were recovered in Operation A, although they were found in disturbed contexts and could not be definitively associated with the Yugüe phase. Social valuables recovered from the Operation A residence might also have been reused from earlier deposits dating to the time when the acropolis was a public building.

Our excavations exposed a worked monumental stone measuring 1.42 m by 1.09 m by 0.48 m laying on the surface of the patio in Operation A. The upper surface of the stone exhibited 15 ground or pecked depressions similar to those observed on other worked monumental stones and boulders at the site (Urcid & Joyce 2001:205–8). The use of these stones is unclear, although they could have been milling stones or perhaps had a ceremonial use.

Analyses of spindle whorls indicate that people made textiles from locally available cotton in excess of what was needed for household consumption (King 2003:298–317). People therefore probably traded textiles, perhaps for highland products like obsidian. Obsidian from seven different sources was recovered from Operation A (n = 54). The most common sources were Ucareo (n = 17) in West Mexico and Zaragoza (n = 12) overlooking the Gulf-coast lowlands (Levine & Joyce 2007). Yugüe-phase ceramics exhibit stylistic ties to Cholula and the Basin of Mexico, probably reflecting interaction with these regions (Joyce et al. 2001:375–8).

The excavations show that, by the Early Postclassic, the acropolis was no longer the civic-ceremonial center of the community, but instead was a locus of commoner residences (Joyce et al. 2001). The stones used by Chatinos to construct Early Postclassic residential platforms appear to have been obtained by dismantling the foundations of Late Classic public buildings on the acropolis. The transformation of the acropolis must have occurred shortly after the collapse since there is stratigraphic continuity between the Yuta Tiyoo- and the Yugüe-phase occupations. The presence of low-status houses on the acropolis shows that Early Postclassic people did not treat the earlier sacred spaces, objects, and buildings with the same reverence they had been afforded previously. The Late Classic acropolis with its public buildings, plaza, sunken patio, and carved-stone portraits of rulers was a monument expressing the sacred authority and political power of the nobility. By the Early Postclassic, the occupation of the acropolis by commoners and the dismantling of public buildings for reuse as foundation stones to construct residences suggest the denigration of earlier sacred spaces, symbols, objects, and buildings.

A more dramatic example of the disjuncture in political discourse is marked by the discovery of a fragment of a Late Classic carved stone (Monument 17) reutilized in an Early Postclassic structure wall excavated in a low-status residence in Operation B (King 2003:188–90). The carved stone depicts a noble with an elaborate feathered headdress. Before the residents placed the carved stone in the wall of the house, this monument had first been broken and then reused as a metate. The ground portion of the metate was on the side opposite the ruler's image, leaving us with an apt metaphor for the collapse, as people were grinding corn on the image of a ruler's face. Hamann (2008b:147) points out that since representations of nobles in Mesoamerica were often interpreted as the living selves of those persons, the use of a ruler's portrait as a grinding stone would have been an especially powerful symbolic act. At least four other Classic-period carved stones were also reset in walls during terminal, presumably Early Postclassic, construction phases. It is unlikely that, only a few generations after the collapse of the Río Viejo polity, the earlier meaning of these monuments would have been lost and they would simply have been considered as convenient building materials (for an extended discussion see A. Joyce 2008a:239–40).

The regional data indicate that the Classic-period collapse dramatically affected rulers, ruling institutions, and dominant ideologies, but had a less severe impact on the lives of commoners. The survey data do not indicate a major demographic decline and people living at Río Viejo in the Early Postclassic participated in a vibrant and diverse domestic economy involving the production of crafts including pottery, textiles, and stone tools. The lack of powerful rulers, who probably controlled long-distance trade in the Classic period, allowed common people access to trade routes and social valuables obtained through the increasingly commercialized economies of the Postclassic (Joyce et al. 2001; King 2008).

The way in which earlier symbols of rulership were treated in the Yugüe phase suggests to me that commoners increasingly penetrated and perhaps actively resisted the dominant ideology in the years prior to the political collapse (Joyce et al. 2001). Although the collapse in the lower Verde probably did not involve a commoner rebellion, allegiance to the nobility may have been weak given the exclusive and perhaps coercive character of Late Classic political authority. Chatinos may not have supported rulers in the face of external military incursions, internal factional competition, or economic hardship due to environmental change. By the Early Postclassic, people were free of the coercive power of the nobility and were able to publicly oppose and subvert the meanings of traditional symbols of power. The collapse of ruling institutions would have been manifest on a continuous basis as people, some living on the acropolis and dismantling its buildings, looked out onto the deteriorating remains of the once sacred space that had been the centerpiece of the Late Classic polity. The evidence from Río Viejo suggests that a hidden transcript of Late Classic resistance had become public.

Early Postclassic social change in the lower Río Verde Valley is therefore much better understood than in the Oaxacan highlands, in large part because of the clearly defined ceramic phase. Additional research throughout Oaxaca is needed, however, to better understand the causes and consequences of this major historical transformation. Fortunately, the Late Postclassic period is better understood because of multiple data sets – archaeological, epigraphic, and ethnohistoric – that can be brought to bear on the last few centuries before the arrival of the Spanish.

Postclassic Heroic History

The history of Mixtec and Zapotec peoples during the four centuries prior to the Spanish Conquest is much better understood than the Early Postclassic because of the wealth of prehispanic and early colonial-period documents, although few have surfaced for the Chatino. Until recently, archaeological research on the Late Postclassic was relatively sparse, although recent projects at Tututepec (Yucu Dzaa in Mixtec) and Yucundaa have reversed this trend (Joyce et al. 2004; Levine 2007; Pérez 2006; Spores 2005). In chapter 2, Mixtec, Zapotec, and Chatino culture and society of the Late Postclassic was discussed based largely on the ethnohistoric record. In this section, I will focus less on social, economic, political, and religious practices and identities and more on historical developments relying on the Mixtec codices, early colonial documents, and the archaeological record.[10] There is an unavoidable bias toward Mixtecs since they authored most of the preserved documents.

The Mixtec codices provide indigenous perspectives on the social transformations of the Late Postclassic. The codices are remarkable screenfold books made from bark paper or deer skin. They were covered with a thin layer of chalk on which were painted vivid scenes in the Late Postclassic Mixtec script. Only a handful of the codices survived the Spanish Conquest and they are invaluable both as the remnants of a vibrant literature and for the historical and religious information that they contain.

I view the codices and early colonial indigenous documents as examples of what Marshall Sahlins (1985:35, 1991) termed "heroic history" where the actions of structurally central individuals (e.g., divine kings) are interpreted as having massive implications for their society as a whole (Joyce et al. 2004). Such heroic agents are "socio-historical individuals," who reciprocally link a larger system with individual action. On the one hand, heroic agents are understood to embody larger social orders (Sahlins' *instantiation*). On the other, the actions of those agents are understood to have massive implications for their societies (Sahlins' *totalization*). My use of heroic history is focused on questions of instantiation: that is, how broad social transformations were understood through the actions of powerful figures. Since the codical histories often refer to events that occurred centuries before they were painted, it is difficult to make arguments about the totalizing effects of powerful rulers. The key is that sixteenth-century Mixtecs understood their histories as personified in elite heroes. Parallels between the codex-recorded exploits of Mixtec heroes and archaeological evidence strengthen and enrich the historical inferences drawn from both sources. Since the subject of the codices was invariably the nobility, the archaeological record also provides insights into possible elite biases in the codical narratives and broadens the historical picture to the lives of non-elites during the Late Postclassic.

Dynastic origins

The histories recounted in the Mixtec codices span the period from the late ninth century to the first few decades after the arrival of the Spanish (Byland & Pohl 1994; Jansen & Pérez 2005, 2007; Troike 1974). The tenth century as recorded primarily in the codices *Vienna* and *Nuttall* involves the divine creation and the founding of ruling dynasties. These accounts blend sacred time and symbolic dates with people and events that were probably related in some fashion with Mixtec history (Jansen & Pérez 2007:92–3). As discussed in chapter 2, the codices recount how the deity Lord 9 Wind ordered the Mixtec world by bringing a new religious cult to the region. Jansen and Pérez (2007) argue that this cult may have drawn legitimacy from associations with the sacred mountain of Monte Albán, which the archaeological record shows was a place where important Early Postclassic rituals were conducted. Ringle and colleagues (1998) argue that cults related to Quetzalcoatl spread throughout Mesoamerica during the Early Postclassic and the one linked to Lord 9 Wind may have been a local Mixtec expression. Cult followers include noble couples shown born from a sacred tree in the Valley of Apoala (Yuta Tnoho). These nobles founded the ruling houses of many important political centers of the Late Postclassic, including Tilantongo (Ñuu Tnoo), Achiutla (Ñuu Ndecu), Jaltepec (Añute), and Yanhuitlán (Yodzo Cahi). At this time, these four communities constituted an alliance linked to Apoala. At the time of the Spanish Conquest, rulers traced their ancestry to these lineage founders.

The tenth century record includes the War of Heaven where the cult followers of Lord 9 Wind defeat earth-associated Stone Men and sky-descending Cloud Men, which allows the cult to spread throughout the Mixteca (Jansen & Pérez 2007:135). Codical scholars have associated the War of Heaven with the violent collapse of Classic-period polities, followed by the founding of the ruling houses of the Late Postclassic (Byland & Pohl 1994:11–14; Hamann 2002:358–63; Jansen & Pérez 2007:133–41).

Alternatively, the War of Heaven could represent conflict between the more egalitarian communities of the Early Postclassic and followers of the new religious cult. Jansen and Pérez (2007:149) argue that the Stone Men were depicted as an "anonymous collective, without given names," which would be consistent with views of Early Postclassic social organization. More important than their historical relations to the collapse is the political significance of the codices during the Late Postclassic when they were painted. Hamann (2002:359–60) argues that the codical creation stories transformed memories of the collapse in ways that legitimated the authority of Late Postclassic nobles. The codices legitimated noble authority by showing that the royal houses of polities like Tilantongo and Achiutla had existed since the creation of the current world. Noble ancestors participated in the events of the creation and the formation of the sacred covenant that established the fundamental relations between people and the gods.

The epic of Lord 8 Deer "Jaguar Claw"

After the War of Heaven, events depicted in the codices are presented more frequently as dynastic history (Jansen & Pérez 2007). In the early eleventh century, two powerful rulers emerge from the Apoala alliance, Lord 9 Wind "Stone Skull" of Tilantongo and Lord 8 Wind "Twenty Eagles" of Cerro Jazmín/Suchixtlán (Chiyo Yuhu). They established an alliance in the year 1013, but as the eleventh century proceeded, relations eroded between the two polities. In the year AD 1081 the rivalry came to a climax as Tilantongo's ally, Lord 10 Eagle of Jaltepec, defeated Cerro Jazmín/Suchixtlán. A major player in this eleventh-century political rivalry was the powerful Death Priest, Lord 5 Alligator "Rain Sun," leader of a supreme council of four high priests at Tilantongo and keeper of the sacred bundle. In the year 12 Reed (AD 1063) the codices show the birth of the first son of Lord 5 Alligator and his second wife, Lady 11 Water "Blue Parrot." The son was named Lord 8 Deer "Jaguar Claw" and his birth was accompanied by omens foretelling a future of both triumph and tragedy. Lord 8 Deer "Jaguar Claw" would become the most celebrated figure in the Mixtec codices and indeed his life would be marked by great victories, but end in tragedy.

The main accounts of Lord 8 Deer's life come from the codices *Nuttall*, *Bodley*, and *Colombino-Becker*, which record his rise to power, first in the lowland coastal town of Tututepec, and later in his hometown of Tilantongo. Although Lord 8 Deer would eventually become the ruler of both Tilantongo and Tututepec, neither of his parents had genealogical ties to the ruling families of these polities (Joyce et al. 2004). Instead, Lord 8 Deer's rise to power was based *not* on the inheritance of an existing polity, but on the foundation of a new one. When he was 18 years old, Lord 8 Deer left Tilantongo and set out for the coast with the specific goal of founding a kingdom. The journey began with an important meeting with the powerful oracle Lady 9 Grass at her cave shrine in Chalcatongo (figure 8.4a).

At this meeting, Lord 8 Deer received a series of objects used in ceremonies accompanying the founding of politico-religious centers, including a sacred bundle, a flint staff, a golden fish, and a skull shield. Lord 8 Deer and his followers then travel to the coast bearing the ritual objects from Chalcatongo. The journey ends with Lord 8 Deer burning incense inside a ballcourt. This scene is followed by a procession of seven individuals, each carrying one of the sacred objects from Chalcatongo into the compound place sign of Tututepec-Juquila (figure 8.4b). The codices, therefore, present Lord 8 Deer as a person who performs rituals of foundation in the process of coming to the lower-Verde region. Following his arrival, the codices depict Lord 8 Deer conquering a series of places, apparently consolidating his power on the coast.

We argue that Lord 8 Deer was able to found a kingdom at Tututepec because of a combination of advantageous historical, political, economic, and ecological circumstances (Joyce et al. 2004:285–6). The archaeological record shows that at the beginning of the twelfth century the lower Río Verde region would have been vulnerable to outside conquest following the collapse of Río Viejo and ensuing political fragmentation and unrest. Lord 8 Deer may have pursued a strategy designed to take advantage of the ecological verticality of a highlands-to-coast corridor. The lower-Verde region was characterized by great agricultural productivity as well as a diversity of resources sought by highland peoples, such as cacao, salt, quetzal feathers, cotton, and fish. Access to coastal resources may have been a factor in Lord 8 Deer's ability to form an alliance with a powerful highland polity that contributed to his success in establishing Tututepec.

The codices depict a meeting between Lord 8 Deer and a group of foreign travelers led by Lord 4 Jaguar "Serpent" (Joyce et al. 2004:285–7). The foreigners carry fans and staves, the insignia of merchants, and wear a distinctive black facemask that marks them as culturally Tolteca-Chichimeca (Pohl 1994:83–108). The alliance is sealed by one of the most famous events depicted in the codices. In this scene, Lord 8 Deer is shown having his nasal septum pierced by a Tolteca-Chichimeca priest who then ornamented Lord 8 Deer's nose with a turquoise jewel. The nose-piercing rite occurred in AD 1097 and invested Lord 8 Deer with the title of *tecuhtli*, designating membership in the Tolteca-Chichimeca royal house (figure 8.4c). Gaining the title of *tecuhtli* was part of a strategy by which Lord 8 Deer claimed rulership of Tilantongo, his birthplace, and established

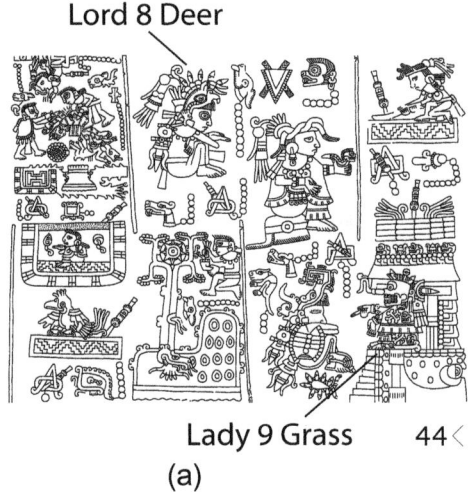

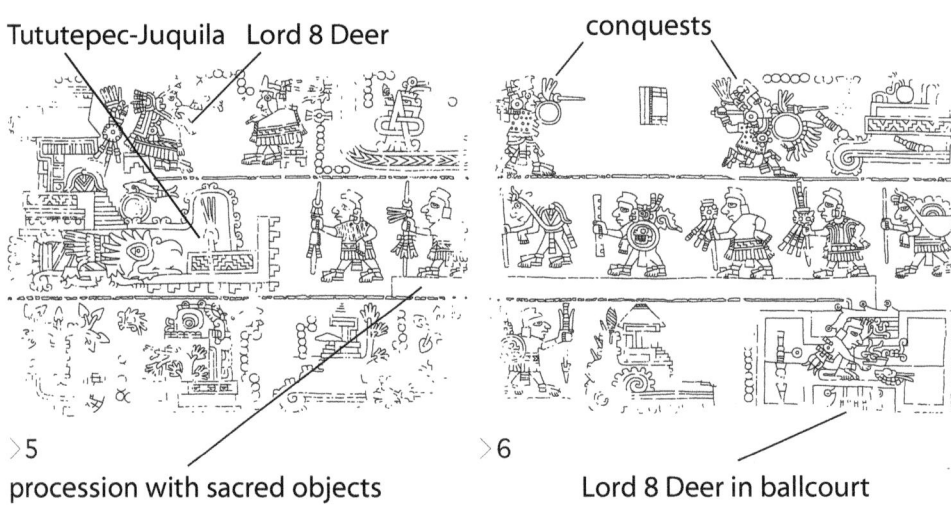

that polity's second dynasty following the death of the young, childless ruler Lord 2 Rain "Ocoñaña" in AD 1098. The alliance between Lord 8 Deer and the Tolteca-Chichimeca was mutually beneficial. Lord 8 Deer gained a powerful military ally as well as a means of legitimating his claim to the thrones of both Tututepec and Tilantongo. The broader Tolteca-Chichimeca alliance, in turn, gained access to highly valued coastal goods.

Following his ascendancy to the throne of Tilantongo, the codical story of Lord 8 Deer takes on a darker tone as he is increasingly corrupted by power. Lord 8 Deer initiates a series of conquests and strengthens alliances with communities in the highlands (Jansen & Pérez 2007:224–9). He then participates in a journey with Lord 4 Jaguar, although scholars disagree as to whether the trip was historical – perhaps to Cholula and eventually Chichén Itzá – or whether it was largely a symbolic journey to the sacred realm (cf. Byland & Pohl 1994:151–62; Jansen & Pérez 2007:229–39). The journey is followed in the *Codex Nuttall* by a scene showing Lord 8 Deer's half-brother, Lord 12 Movement, being murdered in a sweat bath (figure 8.4d). Codical scholars suspect that Lord 8 Deer arranged the murder to eliminate a potential rival. Lord 8 Deer then conquers the town of Xipe Bundle, sacrificing most of the ruling family, although a child, Lord 4 Wind "Yahui," survives. Ironically, 14 years later in AD 1115, Lord 4 Wind arranged for the assassination of Lord 8 Deer thereby completing the tragedy. Lord 8 Deer was buried in the sacred cave at Chalcatongo where he initially received the objects that began his rise to power more than 30 years before.

After Lord 8 Deer

Over the next several years Lord 4 Wind solidified control over the realm of his victim, Lord 8 Deer, establishing an alliance with Lord 4 Jaguar,

Figure 8.4 (*opposite*) Scenes from the Mixtec codices (drawings by Byron Hamann): (a) the meeting of Lord 8 Deer and Lady 9 Grass at Chalcatongo; *Codex Nuttall*, codex page 44 (the sequence begins at the lower right-hand corner and then proceeds right to left; after *Codex Zouche-Nuttall* 1987); (b) Lord 8 Deer and followers arrive at Tututepec showing the placement of sacred objects in the temple; *Codex Colombino-Becker*, codex pages 5 and 6 (the sequence begins at the lower left-hand corner and then proceeds back and forth across the two-page span; after *Codex Colombino* 1892); (c) the nose-piercing rite of Lord 8 Deer; *Codex Nuttall*, codex page 52 (after *Codex Zouche-Nuttall* 1987); (d) the murder of Lord 12 Movement; *Codex Nuttall*, codex page 81 (after *Codex Zouche-Nuttall* 1987) which was sealed through the same nose-piercing rite. Lord 4 Wind then shifted the ruling seat from Tilantongo to Mogote del Cacique (Ñuu Yuchi), thereby eclipsing the power of both Tilantongo and Jaltepec.

Following the death of Lord 4 Wind in AD 1164 at the age of 72, the large area that had been united by his predecessor, Lord 8 Deer, began to fragment (Byland & Pohl 1994:176–81, 246–55; J. Zeitlin 2005:11–21). The dynasty of Lord 4 Wind at Mogote del Cacique declined in influence and the late twelfth and thirteenth centuries were a time of political fragmentation and competition among numerous dynasties. The codices focus on the histories of four powerful ruling houses at Tilantongo, Teozacualco (Chiyo Cahno), Achiutla, and Tlaxiaco (Ndisi Nuu). The ruling lineages of Tilantongo and Teozacualco, allied through descent from Lord 8 Deer, extended their power in the late thirteenth century through the marriage of Lady 4 Rabbit of Teozacualco to Lord 5 Flower, a nobleman from the powerful Zapotec community of Zaachila. Subsequent marital alliances further strengthened the ties among the towns of Tilantongo, Teozacualco, and Zaachila as well as with Tlaxiaco and later Jaltepec. The alliance among these ruling houses allowed them to dominate fourteenth-century political relations, including military expansion into Nahuatl-speaking areas of southern Puebla.

Marriage with Zapotec royal houses brought Mixtecs into the Valley of Oaxaca. Some researchers suggest that Mixtecs may have gained control over large parts of the Oaxaca Valley (Bernal 1966; Paddock 1966b), although more recent studies show that the Mixtec presence was more limited (Flannery & Marcus 1983d). Mixtecs who married into Zapotec noble houses brought dependents that established residences, especially in the western valley at communities like Cuilapan and Xoxocotlán.

Prehispanic Zapotec histories are restricted to early colonial documents like the *Lienzo de Guevea*, the *Genealogy of Macuilxóchitl*, and the *Genealogy of Quialoo* as well as the *Relaciones Geográficas* and later Spanish histories (Burgoa [1674] 1989; Oudijk 2002; J. Zeitlin 2005). The histories recorded in these documents are more limited than those in the codices, although there are points of consistency between the Mixtec and Zapotec histories, especially surrounding the Zaachila dynasty. The earliest period mentioned in the Zapotec documents is recorded in the *Genealogy of Quialoo* from Santa Cruz Mixtepec in the Valley of Oaxaca, which shows that the community's ruling dynasty was established in the early twelfth century (Markens et al. 2008:196). Zaachila is depicted as having played an important role in founding Mixtepec's royal dynasty, showing that the former was already a powerful community. By the late fourteenth century Zaachila emerged as the dominant community in the Valley of Oaxaca. The rulers of Zaachila expanded into the southern Isthmus of Tehuantepec, probably to administer conquered lands on the Pacific coast (Oudijk 2002:76). The Zapotecs may have established a number of strategic communities and fortressed garrisons at this time, including Nejapa, Jalapa, and the hilltop fortress site of Guiengola (Oudijk 2002:76).

The rulers of Zaachila set up strategic alliances within the Valley of Oaxaca. For example, around AD 1370 the lord of Zaachila established an alliance with the ruler of Macuilxóchitl (Markens et al. 2008:195–6; Oudijk 2002:85–6). The alliance was sealed through a marriage arranged by the ruler of Zaachila whereby a noblewoman of Cuilapan, then subject to Zaachila, was married to the lord of Macuilxóchitl. That the alliance was not equal was indicated by the *Relación Geográfica* of Macuilxóchitl, which recorded that the community was obligated to send soldiers when ordered by the lord of Zaachila.

In the mid-fifteenth century, a succession struggle led to a decline in Zaachila's political prominence (Oudijk 2002:76; J. Zeitlin 2005:20–1). After losing the power struggle at Zaachila, Lord Cosijopii, a member of the ruling family, established his court at Tehuantepec, which further weakened Zaachila. Though Tehuantepec grew into a major city, Zaachila was eclipsed by Cuilapan as the major power in the Valley of Oaxaca. Political factionalism and conflict among the Oaxaca Valley's ruling houses encouraged migration to the southern Isthmus of Tehuantepec and into the Zapotec Sierra. The rulers of Tehuantepec began a series of conquests of towns inhabited by Zoque and Huave speakers in the Isthmus, consolidating control over the region and establishing a small empire (J. Zeitlin 2005:26–38, 52–7).

By the mid-fifteenth century Mixtecs and Zapotecs were increasingly threatened by the expanding Mexica Empire (Blomster 2008a:34–5; Byland & Pohl 1994:181–7; Oudijk 2002). In AD 1458 the important trading center of Coixtlahuaca was brutally defeated by the Aztec army of Emperor Motecuhzoma Ilhuicamina. Over the next several decades the Mexica expanded further into the Mixteca establishing tributary relations with communities including Yanhuitlán, Achiutla, Jaltepec, Tlaxiaco, and Nochixtlán (Atoco). The Aztecs eventually conquered towns in the Valley of Oaxaca, including Zaachila. In the late fifteenth century, an Aztec army under the emperor Ahuitzotl sought to conquer Tehuantepec. In response the Zapotec ruler Cosihuesa established an alliance with the Mixtec ruler of Achiutla. Aztecs attacked the combined Zapotec–Mixtec army at the mountaintop fortress of Guiengola, but the siege failed and a truce was established through the marriage of Ahuitzotl's daughter to Cosihuesa. That marriage resulted in the birth of a son, Lord Lachi, later known as Cosijopii II, who ruled

Tehuantepec when the Spanish arrived in AD 1522. The Aztec incursion into Oaxaca was halted to the south by the powerful empire of Tututepec.

As examples of heroic history, indigenous documents instantiate large-scale social changes in the lives of prominent nobles. To gain a broader view of Postclassic social transformations and to consider biases that might be contained within indigenous histories it is crucial to consider the archaeological record.

Lord 8 Deer "Jaguar Claw" and the Archaeology of Tututepec (Yucu Dzaa)

The region where relationships between the codical histories and the archaeological record have been most explicitly examined is the lower Río Verde Valley (Joyce et al. 2004; Levine 2007). Research has focused on the relationship between the codical narratives of Lord 8 Deer "Jaguar Claw" and the rise of the Late Postclassic imperial center of Tututepec as inferred from the archaeological evidence. The archaeological record shows that around the beginning of the twelfth century the region was vulnerable to outside conquest following the collapse of Río Viejo. Codical records suggest that Lord 8 Deer took advantage of these circumstances to found a new Mixtec polity at Tututepec in the lower Río Verde Valley.

Today Tututepec is a small Mixtec community of several thousand people in the rugged foothills overlooking the lower Río Verde floodplain. Yet when walking in the town, and for many kilometers around it, one comes across the remains of the once great city of Tututepec, or Yucu Dzaa in Mixtec. The hills surrounding the town are covered with hundreds of prehispanic terraces as well as artifacts like pottery and stone tools. Paths still traveled on by people and burros have been cut several meters into bedrock and undoubtedly date to the era of the Tututepec Empire, if not before.

Archaeological data are consistent with the founding of Tututepec and a major immigration into the region early in the Late Postclassic Yucudzaa phase. Although settlement at Tututepec dates back to the Late Formative, by the Early Postclassic Yugüe phase the site covered only 1 ha. The almost complete absence of Yugüe-phase settlement suggests that the Late Postclassic city did not develop out of an earlier community, but was founded instead as a new political center. Regional settlement data are consistent with massive immigration into the region as the occupational area in the survey zone increased from 452 ha during the Yugüe phase to 2,317 ha by the Yucudzaa phase; a 512 percent increase. Archaeological and linguistic evidence further concurs with the codices, indicating that the founding of Tututepec was the result of an intrusion of Mixtec-speaking peoples who replaced the local population, probably Chatino speakers, as the dominant group in the region (Joyce et al. 2004).

The full-coverage survey found that Late Postclassic Tututepec covers 2,185 ha, making it the largest site by area known in Late Postclassic Mesoamerica (Michael Smith 2005). In comparison, the Aztec capital of Tenochtitlán covers 1,250 ha. While Tututepec is larger than Tenochtitlán, its dispersed settlement pattern indicates a much lower population density with the site's population estimated at 16,388 (Joyce et al. 2004:288). Settlement in the region as a whole was highly nucleated with Tututepec accounting for 94 percent of the occupational area. Tututepec had a complex internal organization with multiple zones of public architecture, high-status residences, specialized craft production, and ritual activities (Joyce et al. 2004). The data suggest the specialized production of ceramics, textiles, and perhaps obsidian artifacts with these goods and others exchanged in a local markets (Joyce et al. 2004:288; Levine 2007). Architectural remains include hundreds of residential terraces as well as mounded architecture and structure foundations. Most of the terraces and foundations visible on the surface were relatively modest in architectural elaboration and presumably from commoner residences. There were five separate areas with mounded architecture, which might reflect elite residences and/or public buildings associated with particular barrios or *siqui*. A ballcourt discovered in the northeastern end of the site might be the location of Lord 8 Deer's ballcourt ritual depicted in the codices (Workinger 2002:150–8). A possible ballcourt was also identified near Tututepec's center, on the hill known as Cerro de los Pájaros.

The civic-ceremonial core of the site was the large platform on which the colonial church is located. Oral histories suggest that the church platform supported the Late Postclassic and early colonial ruler's palace and perhaps the site's Temple of Heaven depicted in the codices. This claim is supported by the presence of four stone discs originally from friezes that are now placed into the walls of the church. The disc frieze is an architectural decoration shown on palaces and temples in the codices.

Located until recently on the southeastern end of the church platform, and now moved to the community museum, is a group of eight carved stones that include monoliths, zoomorphic tenoned heads, and a feline sculpture. Monument 6 is the most significant because of its resemblance to Tolteca-Chichimeca iconography (figure 8.5). Many researchers have compared this monument to the Atlantid Warriors from Pyramid B at Tula (e.g., Jorrín 1974:68; Pohl 1999:184), the original Tolteca-Chichimeca

Figure 8.5 Tututepec Monument 6 (after Joyce et al. 2004, figure 11; © 2004 Society for American Archaeology; reproduced by permission of *Latin American Antiquity*, volume 15, number 3)

capital. Monument 6 is probably a repres-entation of the central-Mexican deity Itzpapalotl, the Obsidian Butterfly, based on the stiff pose, *tezcacuitlapilli* back mirror, and *quechquemitl* lined with what may be an obsidian knife border – all are characteristic of the goddess (Pohl 1999:184). The monument provides archaeological support for Lord 8 Deer's alliance with the Tolteca-Chichimeca. Early colonial documents as well as oral histories also record that people of Tututepec and its subject communities claimed to be Tolteca-Chichimeca and worshipped Itzpapalotl (Joyce et al. 2004:290). If the church platform was the original location of most of the stone monuments, the buildings on the platform would have been some of the most architecturally elaborate in Late Postclassic Oaxaca.

Excavations by Marc Levine (2007) exposed the remains of three residences built on separate terraces in the northern part of the site. Levine (2007) sought to investigate the domestic economy of Tututepec's Late Postclassic residents through household excavations. He chose an area of the site in the hot, dusty hills approximately 1.25 km north of the church platform. The excavation area overlooked the Yuta Ñaña stream and on clear days it was possible to see the ocean in the distance to the south.

Collapse and Reemergence 269

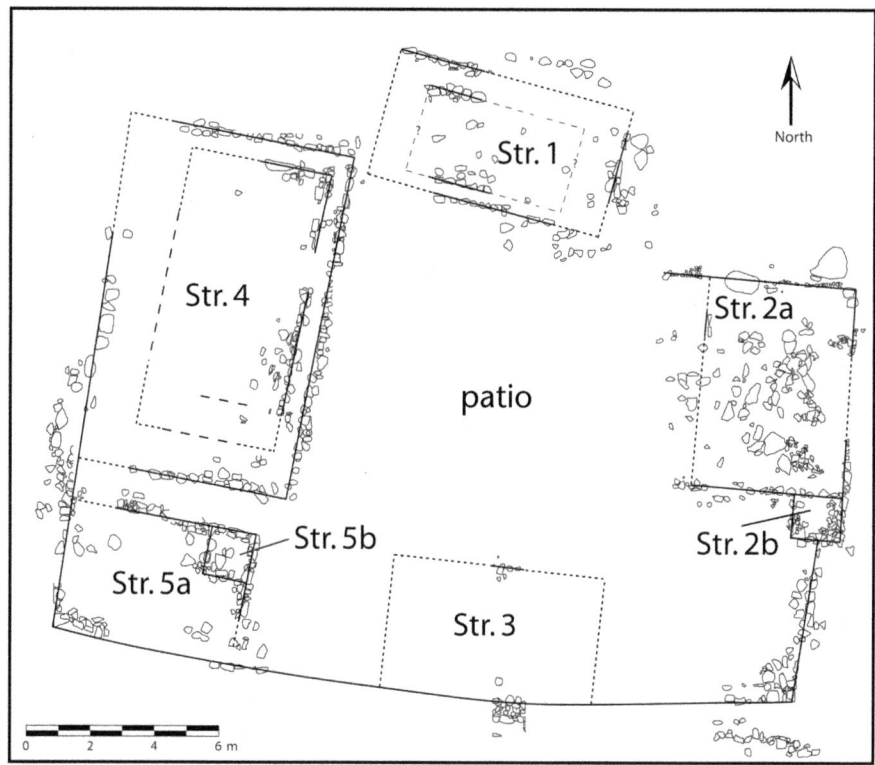

Figure 8.6 Residence A at Tututepec (drawing courtesy of Marc Levine)

In this area, which Levine calls Barrio la Poza, he recorded the remains of at least a dozen households built on terraces. He tested one domestic unit and carried out extensive horizontal excavations in two others designated Residences A and B respectively. Both residences excavated by Levine (2007) consisted of several rooms with stone foundations surrounding a patio (figure 8.6).

Artifact assemblages from the residences included social valuables like elaborately painted Mixteca-Puebla style polychrome pottery along with copper bells and "axes." Spindle whorls were common in both residences, indicating the production of cotton textiles for local use and exchange. Levine recovered over a thousand obsidian artifacts with the most common sources being Pachuca (43 percent) and Orizaba (54 percent). The high frequency of Pachuca obsidian indicates exchange with Aztec *pochteca* merchants who likely sought cotton cloth, cacao, and other coastal products in return (Levine & Joyce 2007). Frequencies of polychrome ceramics, obsidian, and copper artifacts far exceeded what has been found in excavated non-royal residences in the Oaxacan highlands, indicating that Tututepec's commoners had greater access to these social valuables and so probably benefited from the overall political and economic power of Tututepec. Comparative analyses of architectural features and artifact assemblages indicate that the inhabitants of Residence A enjoyed somewhat greater wealth than their Residence B counterparts, although commoners inhabited both residences.

Polychromes in the Mixteca–Puebla style were used principally in the context of feasting (Forde 2006). The polychromes were broadly available and communicated popular notions of ideology and corporate identity, especially involving themes of warfare, sacrifice, and the sacred covenant. In contrast, the codices focused on elite narratives and were probably consumed almost exclusively by audiences of nobles thereby materializing a highly exclusionary ideology. Forde (2006:160–1) argues that polychromes were a material medium through which commoners negotiated power in relation to the exclusionary ideologies of the nobility. Nobles had to frame dominant ideologies so that they had widespread appeal, whereas commoners were able to appropriate aspects of Tututepec's prestige in establishing popular identities.

The size, wealth, and complexity of Tututepec as shown by the survey and excavation data are consistent with early colonial accounts that describe the site as the center of an expansionistic empire that dominated much of southern Oaxaca (Spores 1993). Early colonial records indicate that at its maximum extent Tututepec controlled an empire extending from the modern Oaxaca–Guerrero border east to Huamelula, south to the Pacific Ocean, and north approximately 80 km to towns such as Zacatepec, Juchatengo, and Suchixtepec. Tututepec threatened towns as distant as Achiutla, 125 km to the north, and Tehuantepec, 250 km east. Tututepec had exchange relations with Aztec Tenochtitlán, but political relations between the two empires were tense.

Late Postclassic Archaeology of the Oaxacan Highlands

The Late Postclassic in highland Oaxaca was a time of population growth and the reemergence of powerful ruling dynasties. With the exception of the Tequixtepec–Chazumba area of the Mixteca Baja (Rivera 1999:239–40), evidence from regional surveys indicates that population reached its peak in the centuries before the arrival of the Spanish (Balkansky 2002:72; Balkansky et al. 2000:379–83; Drennan 1989:380; Feinman & Nicholas 1990:237–40; Finsten 1996; Kowalewski et al. 2009:315–17; Markman 1981:67; Nicholas 1989:501–3). Late Postclassic sites tend to be more dispersed and have less monumental architecture than sites from the Classic period. Only a handful of major political centers have monumental architecture on a scale approaching that of the Classic period, including Cuilapan (Sa'a Yucu), Mitla, and Macuilxóchitl in the Oaxaca Valley as well as Yucundaa and Achiutla in the Mixteca Alta. Clusters of sites separated by bands of sparsely occupied territory often correspond to Late Postclassic polities discussed in ethnohistorical documents (Balkansky et al. 2000:380–1; Kowalewski et al. 1989:348).

The largest sites in terms of size and the quantity of monumental architecture do not always correspond to their historical importance as presented in the codices. For example, architecture at Tilantongo and Zaachila is relatively modest (Balkansky et al. 2000:380–2; Kowalewski et al. 1989:329), although archaeological data from both sites provide links to codical histories. At Zaachila an elaborate tomb contains the image of a stucco figure with the hieroglyphic name Lord 5 Flower – perhaps referencing the Zaachila nobleman who married into the ruling house of Teozacualco. The Temple of Heaven at Tilantongo, mentioned prominently in the codices, has been identified archaeologically by Byland and Pohl (1994:135–6).

Evidence for the Mexica incursions into Oaxaca has been difficult to identify archaeologically. Hilltop fortresses associated with many sites suggest the presence of an external threat, but Aztec artifacts are rare. Places where Aztec ceramics are most concentrated correspond to areas where ethnohistoric documents indicate the presence of garrisons such as at Coixtlahuaca (Bernal 1948–9) and in the El Plumaje section of Monte Albán (Blanton 1978:103). Pachuca obsidian is found throughout the Oaxacan highlands and probably reflects exchange with *pochteca* merchants (Byland 1980:164; Winter 1989c).

Political centers of the Oaxaca Valley

In the Valley of Oaxaca, the regional survey project shows that population reaching its maximum during the Chila phase. The largest sites in the Valley of Oaxaca included Mitla, Cuilapan, and Macuilxóchitl with populations estimated at just over 10,000 people, while Yagul, Tlalixtac, and Jalieza had populations of over 6,000 (Kowalewski et al. 1989:317–30). The most extensively studied of these are Mitla and Yagul.

Yagul is located on a volcanic-tuff hill in the Tlacolula arm of the valley. Excavations by Bernal and Gamio (1974) exposed the site's ceremonial center with several large patios surrounded by monumental buildings as well as a ballcourt and a large residential complex, probably of the ruling nobility. Paths lead from the ceremonial center up to the summit of the hill, which was a walled fortress. Many of the walls are still standing and the hilltop commands a spectacular view of the surrounding valley so that invading forces could be tracked for many kilometers.

The residential complex is known as the Palace of the Six Patios (Barber & Joyce 2006:239–40; Bernal & Gamio 1974:13–62), which consists of six patios, intricately connected, each surrounded by four narrow rooms with triple entryways (figure 8.7). Room interiors were usually stuccoed and painted red. Patio F differs from the general pattern, suggesting a public as well as a residential use. Instead of opening onto the patio, the south room of Patio F opened outward toward the ballcourt and patio complexes below (figure 8.8a). The room included a low bench perhaps for receiving people. People within the room would have been visible from the public areas below. Patio F was more accessible with openings on both sides of its south room, which contrasts with the highly restricted access of the other patios.

Figure 8.7 Photo of the Palace of the Six Patios at Yagul (photograph by Arthur A. Joyce)

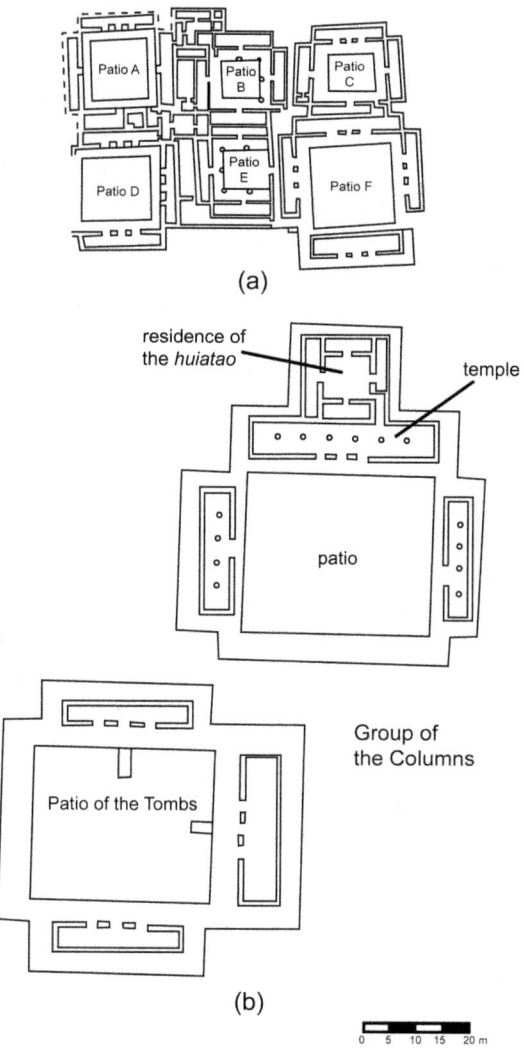

Figure 8.8 Plans of Late Postclassic high-status residences in the Valley of Oaxaca: (a) Palace of the Six Patios at Yagul (redrawn from Bernal 1966, figure 8; reproduced with permission from the Instituto Nacional de Antropología e Historia); (b) Group of the Columns at Mitla (after Pohl 1999, figure 8.1; reproduced with permission from Oxford University Press, Inc.)

Mitla was both a city and the most important religious center in the Valley of Oaxaca (Bernal 1966; Flannery & Marcus 1983e). The site is located in the far-eastern part of the Tlacolula arm at the base of a series of volcanic escarpments that rise to the north. During the Late Postclassic, Mitla was a burial place for the Zapotec nobility as well as the town where the great priest and powerful oracle resided. A thriving Zapotec community continues at Mitla and when it was visited in the late 1920s and early 1930s by the ethnographer Elsie Clews Parsons (1936:2) she was told that the souls of all Zapotec people come to Mitla, "their earth-strong pueblo," known as Liobaa or "place of tombs." A hilltop fortress provided defense in times of war as at Yagul. The site center includes several elaborate multi-patio residential complexes (Barber & Joyce 2006:241–2). The colonial-period church was built directly on the foundations of one of these residential complexes (the Church Group) and parts of the prehispanic structure were dismantled for building materials.

Like the Yagul palace, the Group of the Columns at Mitla was a combined residential and public space near the center of the city (figure 8.8b). The group consists of two large patios (measuring about 40 m on a side) surrounded by four rooms set on high platforms (Barber & Joyce 2006: 241–2). Both the interior and the exterior walls were elaborately decorated with stone mosaics (figure 8.9; less elaborate mosaics are present in tombs and monumental buildings at the nearby sites of Yagul and Xaagá). The southern patio contains two large cruciform tombs that were probably the repositories for the ancestral bundles cared for by the great priest. The northern patio group resembled Patio F at Yagul, but on an even larger scale. Facing the patio on its north side was a temple with six columns that provided access through a narrow passageway to a high-status house. A public patio and temple therefore fronted a highly restricted residence.

The Arroyo and Church Groups at Mitla both have rooms with murals painted on the lintels above the entrances. While the murals are incompletely preserved, Pohl (1999) argues that those on the Church Group record codex-like narratives, including creation sagas of the Mixtec and Tolteca-Chichimeca and the story of the founding of Mitla by Zapotec priests. The Arroyo Group murals depict a Zapotec creation story very similar to the first-sunrise narratives recorded in the Mixtec codices (Pohl 2005).

The scale of the palaces at Yagul and Mitla suggests an increase in the size of the ruling family perhaps resulting from polygamous marriages. The number of co-resident support personnel of ruling families, including retainers and slaves, may have increased as well. A probable commoner residence excavated at Macuilxóchitl with two interconnected patio groups

Collapse and Reemergence 275

Figure 8.9 Photo of stone mosaics at Mitla (photograph by Arthur A. Joyce)

(Winter et al. 2007:200–2) indicates that the size of some non-elite households also may have been greater than during earlier periods.

The Palace of the Six Patios and the Mitla residences continue the trend first seen in the Xoo phase of the most elaborate high-status residences consisting of multiple patio groups connected by narrow passageways (Barber & Joyce 2006:239). Like the Tomb 7 residence at Monte Albán, the Yagul and Mitla palace complexes also include temples. These data suggest that the power of the ruling dynasties of the Chila phase resembled the exclusionary patterns of the Classic period. The public roles of certain nobles were inscribed in the architectural linkage of their residences to public spaces. Public buildings and spaces associated with elite residences created a formal frame of reference for the activities of members of ruling houses. Access to the most important religious symbols, including sacred bundles and codices, were highly restricted. While important public rituals and religious symbols were under the control of the nobility, commoners participated in religious practices in domestic settings, especially involving life-cycle rituals of birth and death, as well as perhaps rituals associated with caves and shrines (Winter et al.

2007:205). Markens and his colleagues (2008:205) note a new form of mortuary practice in low-status houses at Macuilxóchitl and Xaagá, where people buried as many as 50 secondary interments in tombs or beneath house floors.

Pohl (2005) shows that the location of the creation event depicted on the Arroyo Group lintel at Mitla is almost certainly the Main Plaza at Monte Albán, which underscores the continuing significance of the hilltop as a sacred place. Like the creation stories in the Mixtec codices, the Arroyo Group lintel was a means by which the social position of ruling dynasties was reified – linking their origins to the cosmic creation so as to foreclose the possibility of dynastic collapse or replacement in the midst of a time of intense political competition. The identification of the Main Plaza as a place of creation represents another appropriation of the ceremonial precinct by the nobility, although in this case it is an appropriation of the plaza's past to legitimate political relations in the Late Postclassic present.

The appropriation of the symbolism of the Main Plaza by the nobility is also indicated by the continued use of the plaza for ritual purposes, especially the reuse of earlier tombs. The most elaborate example of tomb reuse was Tomb 7, which was built as early as the Terminal Formative (Martínez López 2002:227). During the Chila phase, Tomb 7 was reused to inter at least nine people with one of the most elaborate offerings ever discovered in the Americas, including hundreds of artifacts of gold, silver, copper, amber, jet, coral, shell, obsidian, turquoise, rock crystal, ceramic, and tecali along with more than a dozen bones carved with codex-style images (Caso 1969). The tomb was opened on multiple occasions for rituals and the placement of additional interments. Ceremonies in Tomb 7 were highly restricted with only important nobles and religious specialists participating. The codices indicate, for example, that powerful bundles associated with deified ancestors were cared for and propitiated by a specialized group of high priests (Pohl 1994:31–2). As a place of creation and the burial of powerful ancestors, the Main Plaza embodied a shared origin and ancestry of Zapotec peoples, although one that legitimated noble authority and internalized distinct elite and commoner identities. In addition to rituals, a defensive wall was also built over the South Platform creating a fortress for people living in surrounding communities. Late Postclassic commemorative practices, including the interment of nobles and ritual offerings, have been noted in other abandoned ceremonial centers including Cerro de las Minas, Huamelulpan, Yucuñudahui, San José Mogote, and Macuilxóchitl (Faulseit 2008:27; Flannery & Marcus 1983f:290; Hamann 2008b; Markens et al. 2008:208; Spores 1984:55; Winter 1991:34–6; 2007: 104).

Although powerful ruling dynasties competed for political dominance in the Late Postclassic, evidence suggests that Zapotec commoners had a significant degree of economic flexibility. Markets were available at political centers as well as in smaller communities and in boundary locations between polities (Kowalewski et al. 1989:339–40; Pohl et al. 1997). With the exception of the production of some prestige goods such as codices and goldwork, markets and craft production do not appear to have been controlled by the nobility. Survey data suggest the specialized production of a variety of craft goods, including pottery, obsidian, chert tools, textiles, salt, lime, and ground-stone tools (Kowalewski et al. 1989:348–64). Production centers often cluster near the location of raw materials such as salt near Tlacolula, chert near Mitla, and ceramic production associated with major clay sources such as those at Atzompa. Kowalewski and his colleagues (1989:354) suggest that craft specialists had considerable flexibility in exchanging products in multiple markets both within their own polity and in surrounding ones. It is possible that areas with access to fertile agricultural land may have generated agricultural surpluses for market exchange.

Tehuantepec

Research in the southern Isthmus of Tehuantepec provides evidence for the movement of Zapotecs into the region as documented in the ethnohistoric record (J. Zeitlin 2005:32–4). Evidence for the immigration of Zapotecs includes settlement reorganization along the Río los Perros, construction of the hilltop fortress of Guiengola, and establishment of new communities where people made pottery in the style of the Oaxaca Valley that differed from local traditions.

Settlement-pattern data along the Río los Perros show a dramatic disruption in settlement with the abandonment of the Early Postclassic regional center, a major reduction in the occupational area, and a shift in site location (J. Zeitlin 2005:26–33). These data suggest the destruction and dislocation of Zoque communities by the invading Zapotecs. In the early colonial period, the Río los Perros marked the boundary between largely Zapotec-speaking communities, in the western coastal plain, and Zoque villages to the east. Judith Zeitlin (2005:31–2) further identifies a series of distinct ceramic styles in lagoon-shore sites along the coast that may represent Huave-speaking villages. Huave speakers today occupy similar coastal areas in the southern Isthmus and ethnohistoric documents portray them as having had special relationships with Aztec merchants. The high frequency of obsidian from the lagoon-shore sites might reflect special access to central Mexican goods traded via *pochteca* merchants.

Guiengola is more substantial than typical hilltop fortresses like those at Yagul and Mitla, suggesting that people may have remained there for long periods or that there was a permanent resident population (Peterson & Mac Dougall 1974). In addition to impressive defensive walls, the site includes the remains of low-status houses and a ceremonial center with large platforms, a ballcourt, tombs, altars, and a high-status residential precinct, perhaps the ruler's palace. J. Zeitlin (2005:65) notes a number of architectural similarities between the high-status residence at Guiengola and a public building she excavated at Tehuantepec.

The Zapotecs established their ruling dynasty at Tehuantepec, which quickly grew into a major urban center. Although the population of the Late Postclassic city of Tehuantepec is estimated at 25,000, much of the site lies beneath the colonial and modern town (J. Zeitlin 2005). Undoubtedly, there was a civic-ceremonial core with public buildings and a palace complex as at other Late Postclassic head towns, but it has not been located. J. Zeitlin (2005:35-6) surveyed and excavated an outlying barrio in the community of Santa Cruz Tagolaba in the southern end of the Late Postclassic urban center. Surface survey shows that the prehispanic barrio can be defined by a concentration of ceramics covering about 50 ha with a clear fall-off in artifacts beyond. Based on the surface evidence, the barrio may have been comprised of around 200 houses, primarily occupied by commoners (J. Zeitlin 2005:45). The barrio was centered around a ceremonial precinct including the remains of a two-room temple built on a small platform similar to temples found in the Oaxaca Valley. Across a wide earthen plaza, J. Zeitlin (2005:43) discovered two plaster-floored buildings, although only one was well preserved: an elaborate public building with a porticoed entrance, four plaster-faced adobe columns, and a long porch or veranda along the exterior walls. Artifacts associated with the building suggest ritual practices such as the burning of incense and the use of obsidian lancets for bloodletting. The evidence from the Santa Cruz Tagolaba barrio shows the presence of traditional Zapotec religious, political, and domestic practices. A fifteenth-century Spanish census of Tehuantepec recorded 49 barrios, which probably resembled the one at Santa Cruz Tagolaba (J. Zeitlin 2005:41), indicating the internal complexity of the Late Postclassic city.

Early colonial indigenous and Spanish documents suggest that the rulers of Tehuantepec consolidated control over the coast through conquest and alliance formation (J. Zeitlin 2005:25-6, 254). Some documents record alliances between the ruling houses of Tehuantepec and other communities through marriage. For example, documents show at least one marriage that linked the Chontal-speaking *cacicazgo* of Astata with Tehuantepec's ruling dynasty (Kroefges 2004:148–9). The degree to which Tehuantepec dominated this alliance is not clear. Other communities, like Nanacatepec or Guevea, acknowledged the authority of Tehuantepec's rulers (J. Zeitlin 2005:53). The likelihood that Tehuantepec's subject provinces also sought at times to rebel is indicated by the revolt of Jalapa's rulers just after the arrival of the Spanish, perhaps as a result of disputes concerning the succession of the young Lord Lachi several years earlier (J. Zeitlin 2005:77–8, 91–2). The Tehuantepec royal house enlisted the Spanish to help in putting down the revolt.

Mixtec polities

In the Mixteca Alta, clusters of settlements are found around major political centers including Yucundaa, Cerro Jazmín–Yanhuitlán, Achiutla, Tilantongo, Amoltepec, Peñasco-Tlacotepec, Yucuañe, Tejupan, Etlatongo, Jaltepec, Yucuita-Chachoapan, and Nochixtlán (Balkansky et al. 2000:380–2; Blomster 2004:71; Byland 1980:159; Byland & Pohl 1994:61; Kowalewski et al. 2009:323; Spores 1972:189), as well as Tequixtepec in the Mixteca Baja (Rivera 1999:339). The powerful, multi-ethnolinguistic (Mixtec, Tlapanec, Nahua) polity of Tlapa-Tlachinollan arose in eastern Guerrero (Gutiérrez 2003). The largest site in the Mixtec highlands is Yucundaa, covering at least 290 ha with an estimated population of more than 10,000 people (Spores & Robles 2007:337). Other centers range from about 50 to 200 ha. Population growth was supported by an expansion in agricultural terraces, especially the *lama-bordo* system (Kowalewski et al. 2009:318–19; Spores 1969). Pérez (2006) shows how *lama-bordo* terraces could have been constructed by agrarian households without the direct intervention of rulers. Stabilization of hill slopes by terrace systems may explain the impressive stream incision that took place in the Nochixtlán Valley at c.AD 1200 (Mueller & Joyce 2007).

Patterns of monumental architecture varied among Mixtec political centers in terms of volume and whether the civic-ceremonial core was located within the residential sector or at some remove (Balkansky et al. 2000:381; Kowalewski et al. 2009:321–3). At Etlatongo, Blomster (2008b) recorded the remains of a possible palace. A carved-stone slab discovered at Etlatongo, like one found at Tilantongo, may have been part of narrative scenes on palace benches. Blomster (2008b) argues that these scenes referenced broadly shared ritual themes found throughout much of western Mesoamerica and that they were used by Mixtec nobles in negotiating their political positions in the highly competitive landscape of the Late Postclassic. That the Etlatongo stone was intentionally damaged is consistent with evidence from the codices that such negotiations were unstable and that at times ruling dynasties were overthrown.

Yucundaa has the greatest volume of monumental architecture in the Mixtec highlands with a ballcourt, a royal residence, and a pubic plaza measuring 180 m by 170 m (Spores 2005; Spores & Robles 2007). The royal residence includes numerous rooms and patios constructed with plaster floors and walls along with elaborate stonework with mosaic facades. Several non-royal elite residences built on large platforms or terraces were excavated and these resembled noble houses at Yucuita and Chachoapan. Surrounding the site center is a raised stone causeway or wall that demarcated the civic-ceremonial center and was used for ritual processions, but may also have had a defensive function (Spores 2005:73). Houses of commoners on terraces below the site center were also excavated and *lama-bordo* terraces were mapped. Commoner residences excavated at Yucundaa along with others excavated at Nicayuju (Pérez 2006) and Yucuita (Lind 1979: 64–5) ranged from a single room to multiple rooms surrounding a patio. Status distinctions were evident in the artifact assemblages associated with low-status houses, which had far lower frequencies of social valuables like polychrome pottery, greenstone, and obsidian than high-status houses.

The Spanish Conquest

The next major social transformation in Oaxaca and throughout the Americas came with the arrival of European conquerors and colonists. Spanish forays into Oaxaca began in AD 1520 with an expedition led by Gonzalo de Umbría. In 1521, a small contingent of soldiers and horsemen as well as a larger native force led by Francisco de Orozco entered the Valley of Oaxaca (Dahlgren 1990:69–71). Resistance varied throughout the highlands and in some regions, particularly the Zapotec Sierra, indigenous peoples took up arms against the Spanish (Chance 1989:16–21).

Early colonial records show the ways in which indigenous people actively negotiated relations with the Spanish. For example, Lord Lachi, the Zapotec ruler of Tehuantepec, petitioned Cortés for peace even before the arrival of Orozco and agreed to ally with the Spanish against Tehuantepec's enemy, the coastal empire of Tututepec. In January 1522, Cortés dispatched his lieutenant, Pedro de Alvarado, and 200 Spanish soldiers to the Pacific coast where they were joined by an army from Tehuantepec. By early March 1522, Alvarado had violently conquered Tututepec. The Spanish garrison near Tututepec lasted less than a year, undoubtedly due in part to Mixtec resistance. Shortly thereafter, Lord Lachi enlisted the aid of the Spanish in putting down a revolt by the subject community of Jalapa and in 1524 the Zapotecs assisted Alvarado in the conquest of the Maya kingdoms of Chiapas and Guatemala (J. Zeitlin 2005:89–90).

Superficially at least, this alliance between the Isthmus Zapotec and the Spanish is consistent with the sorts of expedient military alliances formed among ruling houses before the conquest. It also shows the degree to which Spanish hegemony was dependent on the cooperation of indigenous rulers in many parts of Mesoamerica during the early years of the conquest. Yet, as in many areas, alliances between indigenous rulers and the Spanish were tenuous and short lived as the Spanish solidified control and began to assert their dominance. By the late 1520s, the Isthmus Zapotecs were in revolt against the Spanish. Lord Lachi and many of his followers temporarily left the region, which significantly undermined a major Spanish shipbuilding effort (J. Zeitlin 2005:93–6). Relations between the Isthmus Zapotecs and the Spanish continued to be strained throughout the early colonial period.

In the decades following the arrival of the Spanish a series of epidemics including influenza and measles swept through Oaxaca, devastating indigenous communities. By relocating people and concentrating them in *congregaciones*, the Spanish colonial authorities created ideal conditions for the spread of disease. For example, demographic centers like Yucundaa and Nochixtlán were relocated from their prehispanic hilltop locations to valley floors (Spores 1984:106). The excavations at Yucundaa provide moving evidence of the impact of Spanish colonization (Spores 2005; Spores & Robles 2007). The site was a colonial center until the community was relocated around 1550. The Late Postclassic royal residence and non-royal noble residences were modified during the early colonial period with European architectural elements. A cache recovered from a commoner house may represent a successful attempt at concealing ritually important objects from the Dominican friars and indicates Mixtec resistance to Spanish colonial authorities. Excavations exposed the Dominican church and monastery built in the 1530s. A tragic example of the effects of the conquest is the recovery of hundreds of bodies of victims of the epidemics, many interred in multiple burials in the plaza (Spores & Robles 2007:347).

Although indigenous lords still exercised considerable power through the sixteenth century, the Spanish increasingly instituted political and economic control through the imposition of colonial institutions. Religious oppression and conversion to Catholicism began almost immediately with the construction of churches by the Dominicans. Indigenous nobles were baptized, took Spanish names, and adopted Spanish customs, dress, and language, although people also resisted colonial oppression and religious conversion as shown by numerous uprisings and by the famous idolatry trials at Yanhuitlán. Resistance is more powerfully represented by the daily reproduction of indigenous traditions, many of which survive up to the present day.

nine

Conclusions

This book presents a synthesis of the prehispanic history and cultural achievements of the Mixtecs, Zapotecs, and Chatinos of Oaxaca from a poststructural theoretical perspective. Oaxaca's indigenous peoples founded great cities like Monte Albán, Tututepec, and Huamelulpan. They created elaborate traditions of writing, mural painting, sculpture, ceramic arts, and textiles. Ancient Oaxacans built impressive buildings like the Mitla palaces, Río Viejo's acropolis, and Monte Alban's North Platform complex. They worshiped deities and ancestors via a sacred covenant using rituals such as the ballgame, human and autosacrifice, and the burning of incense. Prehispanic farmers developed productive agricultural systems, converting the natural environment into anthropogenic landscapes covered with terraces, fields, and settlements. Ancient Oaxacans lived rich and varied lives that can be seen in the different urban forms from Monte Albán's ceremonial core to the multiple-nuclei pattern of Mixtec cities like Huamelulpan and Monte Negro. Prehispanic history also varied as exemplified by the divergent outcomes of initial urbanization across Oaxaca. Yet the interconnectedness of prehispanic peoples in Mesoamerica is also apparent as in the appropriation of Olmec objects and ideas by Mixtecs and Zapotecs during the Early Formative, the migration of Mixtecs to Tututepec and Zapotecs to Tehuantepec during the Postclassic, or, less directly, through the detrimental impact of highland erosion that ironically had beneficial effects on the environments and people of the lower Río Verde Valley.

Throughout this book, I have explored the diversity of the lives and histories of prehispanic Mixtecs, Zapotecs, and Chatinos from a poststructural theoretical perspective that differs from previous approaches to Oaxaca's prehispanic past (e.g., Blanton et al. 1999; Marcus & Flannery 1996; Winter 1989a). In this chapter, I consider archaeological theory in Oaxaca and beyond, and discuss how poststructural theory builds upon and addresses shortcomings of previous approaches to Oaxaca's prehispanic past.

Poststructural theory argues that social and political formations (e.g., cities, polities, corporate groups) are instantiations of ongoing social relations simultaneously embedded in and both producing and reproducing social structure and tradition (e.g., Dobres & Robb 2000; Hodder & Hutson 2003; A. Joyce 2008a; Pauketat 2001; Shanks & Tilley 1992:116–34). Rather than assuming that social systems are integrated and coherent, a hallmark of functionalist theory, I view societies as fragmented and contested to varying degrees such that there is never complete closure to any system of social relations. Practices and the cultural and material conditions that constitute social formations are always negotiations among differently positioned actors – individuals and groups – distinguished by varying identities, interests, emotions, knowledge, outlooks, and dispositions. Large-scale social agglomerations like cities or regional polities therefore become inherently problematic in their production and reproduction. Such a poststructural view allows for a more diverse and dynamic view of society than is possible in functionalist theory and allows that all people in society have agency and power, not just social elites. I also advocate moving away from the societal typologies of cultural evolutionary theory because they tend to obscure the distinctive culture, history, and practices of past peoples. I argue that a focus on social practice moves us closer to the archaeological record of past human activity and its social and cultural significance, in contrast to abstract approaches that stress high-level forces such as the functioning of social and ecological systems or the unfolding of universal laws of history. In this chapter, I emphasize the ways in which a poststructural perspective advances understanding of prehispanic Mixtec, Zapotec, and Chatino history.

Beyond Functionalism and Neo-Evolutionism in Oaxaca

Oaxaca was one of the key regions where archaeologists first developed and applied functionalist theory, systems theory, and neo-evolutionary perspectives beginning in the 1960s and 1970s. This research included some of the most important and influential examples of the neo-evolutionary and systems perspectives applied to problems such as the origins of agriculture and the archaic state (Flannery 1968; 1976a; 1986; Spencer 1982). As discussed in chapter 1, for the past several decades, archaeologists have struggled to address problems with functionalism, systems theory, and neo-evolutionism. Oaxacan archaeologists were some of the first to move away from a focus on ecology and economy by considering religion and politics (e.g., Blanton 1978; Flannery 1976b), and they have begun to recognize a greater diversity of social types and evolutionary trajectories (Blanton et al. 1996).

Yet, as recently argued by a number of scholars, functionalism, neo-evolutionism, and a more general western materialism and utilitarian economics endure as the core of much archaeological theory in Oaxaca and beyond (e.g., Blanton 1998; Hodder & Hutson 2003; Janusek 2004:4; A. Joyce 2008a; Pauketat 2001, 2007; Yoffee 2005). People continue to be viewed as filling particular roles for the benefit of society that allow groups to function as integrated social systems. For example, some archaeologists still rely on definitions of chiefdom and state developed in the 1970s (e.g., Flannery 1972; Wright 1977) that were rooted in systems theory and neo-evolutionism, including assumptions of equilibrium and societal self-regulation (e.g., Flannery 1998; Spencer 2003; Spencer & Redmond 2001). Such a functionalist approach minimizes intrasocietal tensions and conflicts that are present in all groups and may be key sources of social change and innovation. These approaches also take a top–down perspective, viewing commoners as producers of basic staples and unskilled labor with little or no input into political process, while rulers are seen as the sole political decision-makers who drive social change (e.g., Flannery 1999).

An example of the persistence of functionalist, neo-evolutionist, and elitist perspectives is the "action theory" perspective of Marcus and Flannery (1996; Flannery 1999; also see Spencer 1990, 2003; Spencer & Redmond 2001). Action theory argues that leaders produce the innovations that drive cultural evolution at key points of transition during which societies evolve from one evolutionary stage to another. Rulers develop new political institutions, organize labor and military expeditions, delegate authority to specialized administrators, and regulate local political, religious, and economic activity. There is little or no consideration of the agency of commoners in political process, however (A. Joyce 2008a). Change is compressed into short periods emphasizing the differences between what are seen as long periods of stability (e.g., Flannery 1999; Marcus & Flannery 1996:244–5). History is therefore dominated by the periods of stability where evolutionary structures – political institutions, religious ideologies, and economic systems – remain relatively constant and tightly constrain people's agency and power and thus effectively integrate society (Flannery 1999).

Flannery and Marcus (Flannery 1983d; Flannery & Marcus 1983c; Marcus & Flannery 1994, 1996) have been innovative in using relational analogies from Oaxaca's ethnohistoric record to infer broad aspects of prehispanic culture, but they continue to view the Oaxacan past as evolving through traditionally defined neo-evolutionary stages like bands, tribes, chiefdoms, and states (Marcus & Feinman 1998; Marcus & Flannery 1996, 2004;

Spencer 2003; Spencer & Redmond 2001, 2004). Marcus and Flannery (1996:245) assert that, "there are stages in the rise of all archaic states that look provocatively similar." So for example, although Zapotec ethnohistory is used to identify prehispanic rulers' palaces in Oaxaca, the presence of a palace is in turn seen as a general hallmark of state organization throughout history (Flannery 1998; Marcus & Flannery 1996:160–1, 180–1; Spencer 2003:11,185; Spencer & Redmond 2004). Analogies that amplify the discussion of the evolution and functioning of Zapotec societies are therefore also drawn from societies far removed in space and time such as contact-period Hawaii, Greek city-states, and New Guinea "Big Men" societies (Flannery 1998; Marcus & Flannery 1996:87–8; 140–2; 155–8). Such analogies are justified by cultural evolutionist assumptions that these societies share fundamental structural and functional properties with Zapotec society at different points in its history, since they are seen as belonging to the same evolutionary stage. Analogies that assume broad similarities among societies remote in time and space have been questioned from a variety of theoretical perspectives (Johnson 1999:54–63; Schrire 1984; Stahl 1993:245–6) as have their cultural evolutionary foundations (A. Joyce 2008a; Pauketat 2007; Shanks & Tilley 1992:53–4; Yoffee 2005:228–32).

In archaeological theory there is an increasing tension between neo-evolutionary models that view the structures of particular evolutionary stages as similar regardless of historical circumstances, and recognition of the diversity of complex political formations and histories (e.g., Feinman & Marcus 1998; Trigger 2003). Researchers are increasingly challenging traditional evolutionist categories and general theories of social evolution (Barber 2005; Blanton et al. 1996, 1999:130–1; A. Joyce 2008a; Pauketat 2007; Yoffee 2005). While terms like chiefdom and state may still hold some utility if defined broadly and used for comparative purposes (cf. Yoffee 2005), in this book I have chosen to avoid the use of neo-evolutionist categories because I suspect they carry with them such theoretical baggage as to obscure the distinctive culture and history of the Mixtec, Zapotec, and Chatino peoples. Rather than imposing a western societal typology on the prehispanic past, I have explored the ways in which practices, ideas, and institutions produced a nested set of social identities that united, integrated, or divided people. In particular, I have been interested in the nature and scale of encompassing social affiliations that might be classified as polities and how they were reproduced, negotiated, and transformed. This perspective focuses attention on the culture and history of the Mixtec, Zapotec, and Chatino rather than on forcing the Oaxacan evidence into universalistic societal typologies and cultural evolutionary schemes.

I have also avoided the use of evolutionary terminology in part as an exercise to explore how the prehispanic past might be understood without these terms. I hope that, if we do not impose neo-evolutionist categories on the archaeological record, it will open up thought and discussion – that archaeologists will be better able to explore the genealogies of practice that constitute particular histories. What sorts of similarities and differences might be recognized among ancient and modern societies if we do not rely on neo-evolutionist categories as a basis for comparison? Some archaeologists might react to jettisoning discussion of the archaic state by viewing Oaxaca as less significant in terms of archaeological theory since it would be taken out of the running as a candidate for early statehood in Mesoamerica and beyond. Such a position reveals the progressive bias of neo-evolutionism, which tends to privilege societies based on where they fit on the neo-evolutionary scale of complexity. If we do not impose such progressive and universalistic models on the past, we might discover new insights through comparisons of economic relations, political institutions, agricultural systems, ideologies, and so on, regardless of where they fit in earlier evolutionary taxonomies. It is important to move away from evolutionist categories because neo-evolutionism and its contemporary descendants homogenize the past and make less significant the diverse lives and originality of hundreds of generations of prehispanic Mixtec, Zapotec, and Chatino peoples. This is especially true of the vast majority of ancient Oaxacans who were not rulers – the farmers, craft specialists, traders, workers, and inhabitants of rural communities – who have been discussed in this book, but who were often invisible in earlier archaeological treatments of political process.

Poststructural Theory and the Archaeology of the Mixtec, Zapotec, and Chatino

In this book I have examined the prehispanic Mixtec, Zapotec, and Chatino using a poststructural theoretical approach that embraces the distinctive history and diverse lives of ancient peoples. The key points of this approach are the following:

1 Poststructural theory emphasizes social differences and the varied subject positions of people in the past and how they changed through time (Butler 1990; Moore 1994; Ortner 1984, 1996; J. C. Scott 1990).
2 Social systems are viewed as instantiations of ongoing social practice simultaneously embedded in and both reproducing and transforming historical traditions (Bourdieu 1977; Giddens 1979; Sewell 1992).[11] Practice involves what people did in the past – both everyday activity and the unusual and/or unexpected such as important rituals, warfare,

and the arrival of exotic objects or strangers. The focus on social practice makes this perspective more empirically grounded than systems theory, neo-evolutionism, and other theoretical approaches that view human activity as caused by abstract high-level forces such as the functioning of ecological systems or the unfolding of universal laws of history.

3   Rather than integrated and coherent, as in systems theory and cultural evolutionism, the social systems that are continuously produced in practice are fragmented and contested to varying degrees (de Certeau 1984; Kertzer 1988; J. C. Scott 1990). Societies always contain polyvalent and potentially contestable symbols, meanings, practices, and institutions.

4   Society, culture, and history are viewed as the outcome of social negotiations among subjects differently positioned in relation to cultural meanings, resources, and therefore social power (Kertzer 1988; Pauketat 2001; J. C. Scott 1985, 1990). That is, the agency of non-elites – farmers, craftspeople, children, elders, merchants, and so on – as well as nobles must be considered in models of historical process. These points are discussed below in more detail for ancient Oaxaca and their broader implications are considered in relation to other theoretical positions.

Poststructural theory does not assume that societies exist as social wholes as in systems theory and other functionalist accounts (see Barber 2005; Hodder & Hutson 2003; Janusek 2004; A. Joyce 2008a; Meskell & Joyce 2003). Instead, an interest in subjectivity involves exploring people's affiliations with various complex, nested, overlapping, and partially contradictory collectivities and examining how the nature of these affiliations changed through time. Ancient Oaxaca was inhabited by men, women, children, elders, farmers, merchants, potters, weavers, priests, soldiers, rulers, scribes, architects, and many other social personae. Salient affiliations changed dramatically through the prehispanic period. For example, as discussed in chapter 3, people of the small, mobile groups that coalesced into early villages at the Archaic to Formative transition were distinguished by age, gender, and family, but the villages as a whole were still loosely affiliated with few practices that created a sense of shared history and identity. Early village life was therefore as much a social problem as it was an economic one. By the end of the Formative period (chapters 5 and 6), however, people had developed affiliations with a series of larger-scale collectivities including corporate groups, communities, and polities. Compared to farmers of the Early Formative, those of the Late Formative may have lived in similar houses and grown similar crops, but they had dramatically different relations with social elites, religious specialists, deities, important ancestors, and trade partners. As people lived and interacted they changed culture – the fields of knowledge into which people were born and lived – in ways that in turn altered subjectivity (cf. Foucault 1977, 1980). The nature of what it was to be a commoner, a man, a farmer, and a father, for example, changed through the prehispanic period as did the ways that these subject positions intersected and developed through individual lifetimes.

Rather than assuming general or universal laws of cultural evolution, poststructural theory views social change as a result of both everyday practice and creative accommodations to unanticipated and contingent circumstances (e.g., Giddens 1979; Sahlins 1981). For example, as discussed in chapter 4, in the late Early Formative a stronger community identity was forged through the continuous scaling up of rituals carried out in small public buildings and cemeteries at sites like San José Mogote, Tomaltepec, and Etlatongo. Households, barrios, and entire communities were increasingly distinguished by different economic practices involving routines of craft production along with foreign contacts through which exotic objects and ideas were acquired and adapted to local conditions. Some households were more successful than others in producing valued crafts and establishing external relations. These successes undoubtedly gave people greater influence within their communities and perhaps beyond, which began to amplify achieved status distinctions. Larger groups, mobilized by the construction and use of early ceremonial buildings such as Structures 1 and 2 at San José Mogote, also provided opportunities for leaders to expand their influence.

Later in the Formative, hereditary status distinctions emerged as a result of the conjuncture of many historical factors. As discussed in chapter 5, I argue that these factors included social tensions surrounding rising inequality, the decline of San José Mogote's regional power and prestige, destruction of San José Mogote's main temple in a raid, contact with and knowledge of regions where powerful hereditary rulers were already in place (especially the Gulf-coast Olmec), and at the same time the disruption of these external ties which threatened local alliances and economic relations. San José Mogote was in crisis and, while threats from raiding and disruptions of exchange were dealt with through military and economic means, Zapotecs saw these problems as inherently implicated in people's relations with the divine, which permeated all realms of social life. Whatever the exact set of circumstances, a prominent family, faction, or corporate group at San José Mogote initiated a series of innovations to deal with the political crisis involving new relations with the divine, including rituals like human sacrifice and an increased concern with important ancestors interred in tombs and celebrated as especially powerful in the world of the living. These new ideas and practices were developed out of earlier traditions of ancestor veneration and autosacrifice as well as from knowledge of powerful ruling institutions in regions like the Gulf coast, which contributed to the institutionalization of a distinctive noble status. Initially, incipient nobles probably had some difficulty in legitimating their position and ensuring that their special status was transferred to offspring. Practices through which noble status was inscribed in more enduring material media that contributed to the institutionalization of hereditary inequality included the construction of an elaborate residence in the ceremonial center on Mound 1 at San José Mogote and the production and exclusive use of effigy vessels depicting important deities.

Innovations in leadership as well as in ritual ideas and practices may have coalesced into a religious and political movement that culminated in the founding of Monte Albán. The social changes that accompanied the early years of Monte Albán further institutionalized hereditary inequality as nobles were increasingly associated spatially and symbolically with the new ceremonial center and with special access to divine forces and beings as well as success in warfare and control over social valuables. The founding of Monte Albán was an attempt to deal with social problems economically and politically, but also spiritually by establishing more potent means to contact divine ancestors and deities. People had to respond to the political crisis in this fashion because, for the Zapotec, the worlds of the living and of the divine were inseparable. Of course, much of the resulting history of Monte Albán could not have been anticipated – relocation of thousands to the hilltop center, provisioning problems, or changes in domestic economy. The founders of Monte Albán were dealing with immediate problems in ways that were appropriate to their culture and were not trying to found a city, establish a state, or achieve other hallmarks by which archaeologists have traditionally theorized the past. Many of the "major" developments in human history like the origins of cities and the collapse of centralized polities were the unintended consequences of people dealing with immediate contingencies in their lives.

Urbanization at Monte Albán and other early urban centers in Oaxaca created problems as well as new possibilities. People living on residential terraces in highland cities like Monte Albán and Huamelulpan, as well as those living in the dense residential sectors of Río Viejo in the coastal lowlands, had to deal with problems of reduced privacy, crowding, sanitation, and health as well as access and travel to agricultural lands (e.g., Storey 2006). The founding of early urban centers triggered dramatic changes in settlement and economy throughout their hinterlands as well. The provisioning of cities, particularly Monte Albán with its huge urban population, undoubtedly had complex implications – in terms of city–hinterland, status, and gender relations – that need to be more fully explored (see Kowalewski et al. 1989:123–6).

Major social changes like sedentism and urbanism must be treated as social problems that were the outcome of negotiations among differently positioned actors, and not simply societal or elite responses to economic, military, or ecological problems. People's divergent interests, views, dispositions, and social positions created tensions and conflicts that at certain points were actualized in competition and conflict, contributing to major social transformations. For example, as discussed in chapter 3, the new social formations of the Early Formative brought people together in permanent associations that created tensions surrounding courtship, mating, and sexuality, as reflected in the female figurines that may represent attempts by elders to control the identity and sexuality of young women (R. Joyce 2000). Since adulthood in prehispanic Mesoamerica was something that was constructed through the labors of elders, and since age was often materialized in bodily ornamentation and hair styles, it is not surprising that figurines, some worn as ornaments, became a locus for the negotiation of female gender identity and adulthood. Another example of intrasocietal conflict is the barrio organization seen in larger villages, such as San José Mogote and Yucuita, which probably reflects some tension surrounding early village life. This position contrasts with the view of early villages as tightly integrated by men's and women's rituals with a leader organizing and planning the construction and use of public buildings, organizing trade, attracting followers, and stimulating craft production (e.g., Marcus & Flannery 1996, chapter 7).

Through the Formative period, differences in wealth and status created social tensions within and between communities as prominent people, households, and perhaps corporate groups diverged from traditional egalitarian principles. These tensions and conflicting identities should not be seen as solely occurring between people or groups. Conflicting subject positions would have intersected within people's dispositions as well. The institutionalization of status distinctions may have been as much a conceptual problem for incipient elites torn between some desire to distinguish themselves, their families, and their corporate groups while at the same time viewing the world from within an egalitarian discourse that resisted such distinctions.

One of the most far-reaching transformations in the prehispanic history of Oaxaca was the coalescence of centralized polities and early urban centers at the end of the Formative. Previous models have argued that the founding and early development of Monte Albán was the result of warfare and conquest as well as of problems with provisioning the hilltop city that required the development of more effective administrative institutions (Marcus & Flannery 1996; Spencer 1982; Spencer & Redmond 2001) and a market (Winter 2006). In the Mixteca Alta, urbanization at sites like Huamelulpan and Monte Negro is seen as a response to the military threats posed by Monte Albán, although with new social institutions developing in response to local circumstances (Balkansky 1998a; Balkansky et al. 2004). These models of early urbanism imply that military and economic problems were responded to by social groups as a whole; with rulers directing settlement relocation and the formation of new administrative institutions for defense and economic integration. Resistance occurred, but only from outside the Monte Albán polity as communities like El Palenque fought against incorporation into the Zapotec polity.

A poststructural position assumes that polities are never fully holistic and integrated – that there are always internal differences that create tension and social conflict (Barber & Joyce 2007; Janusek 2004; A. Joyce 2008a). My interpretation of the archaeological record suggests that this was particularly true for the early years of political centralization and urbanism involving communities like Monte Albán, Río Viejo, Monte Negro, and Cerro de las Minas among others. While new large-scale public rituals, economic relations, and military actions contributed to the formation of broader social affiliations, it is difficult to believe that people left their homes to relocate to hilltop centers and gave allegiance and resources to an increasingly powerful nobility without creating some internal friction and alternative perspectives. At Monte Albán, the evidence discussed in chapter 5 indicates that early hereditary rulers shared power with more traditional communal institutions like the military sodalities discussed by Urcid (2008). The settings where tensions between alternative political institutions were played out probably included large-scale rituals, access to special ceremonial roles like that of rain-god impersonator, and decisions involving warfare and defense. As discussed in chapter 6, there is less evidence of powerful rulers in the Mixteca and on the coast. In the Mixteca, the nucleated centers of the Late/Terminal Formative may have been governed by corporate confederations that were probably loosely affiliated, unstable, and prone to fission.

Social divisions continued through the Classic period as local nobility increasingly pulled away from the rulers of powerful centers like Monte Albán, Río Viejo, and Yucuñudahui (chapter 7). The exclusionary ideologies of the Classic period that emphasized the power and special social roles of the nobility also meant that commoners were excluded from large public ceremonies and labor projects that had produced affiliations with political centers in the later Formative. These trends may have intensified after the collapse of Teotihuacan at c.AD 600, which removed a unifying external threat. Regardless of other factors like landscape degradation and climatic change, as discussed in chapter 8, these fault lines were instrumental in the collapse of centralized polities at the end of the Classic period.

Social distinctions were continuously negotiated and must be considered as fundamental to historical processes (Barber & Joyce 2007; Janusek 2004; A. Joyce 2008a; Pauketat 2001). For example, I argue in chapter 5 that political authority at Monte Albán during the Late/Terminal Formative involved an ongoing negotiation among members of hereditary and corporate institutions. The foregrounding of cosmic symbolism and communal images involving warfare, militarism, and ritual inscribed on the Building L-sub and Building J programs suggests a denial of contradictions between communal and hereditary forms of authority. The destruction of these iconographic programs at the end of the Formative, however, indicates that conflict eventually erupted between political factions. The ascendance of hereditary rulers celebrated in carved-stone monuments and tomb art shows that by the fifth century in the Valley of Oaxaca exclusionary forms of authority won out (chapter 7). The emphasis on genealogical connections to powerful apical ancestors in Classic-period imagery in turn reflects competition among ruling houses as they jockeyed for prominence. Classic-period iconography also indicates that competition among ruling houses at times led to warfare, sometimes culminating in the capture and sacrifice of enemy elites.

As considered in chapter 6, in the lower Río Verde Valley and the Mixtec highlands, friction surrounding the negotiation of early forms of centralized authority resulted in the collapse of political centers such as Río Viejo, Cerro de las Minas, and Monte Negro. It would take centuries for new urban centers to coalesce and for centralized political institutions to reemerge. By the Late Classic, exclusionary forms of authority are in evidence throughout the Mixteca and in the lower Río Verde Valley as in other areas of Mesoamerica with rulers celebrated in carved-stone monuments, ornate tombs, and elaborate residences.

Social negotiation did not just involve prestigious factions within society, but included common people as well (Barber 2005; Barber & Joyce 2007; Forde 2006; A. Joyce 2008a; Joyce et al. 2001; Joyce & Weller 2007; Levine 2007). The creation of large public ceremonial spaces at the end of the Formative can be seen as an accommodation by leaders to the interests of broad constituencies. This does *not* imply that rulers were consciously and strategically deceiving commoners to advance their personal and familial interests. As I have argued elsewhere (A. Joyce 2000, 2004), deities and ancestors were important agents in the worlds of Mixtecs, Zapotecs, Chatinos, and other Mesoamerica peoples so that dealing with political crises and other social problems required communication with the divine in concert with action in the world of the living. Likewise, leaders were expected to act for the benefit of their followers as "fathers" and "mothers" of the community.

Conversely, as the power of the nobility grew during the Classic period and as competition among ruling houses became more of a concern, access of commoners to the seats of divine power at ceremonial centers like Monte Albán and Cerro de las Minas *was* increasingly restricted. It is difficult to know the degree to which commoners may have sought distance from or actively resisted Classic-period rulers and ruling institutions. The evidence for the destruction and denigration of Late Classic monuments and public buildings by Early Postclassic people at Río Viejo suggests that there may have been a hidden transcript of resistance. At Monte Albán, the abandonment of some high-status residences and the building of new ones in restricted locations often protected by walls at the end of the Late Classic suggest that the nobility were experiencing some kind of threat. Regardless, commoners were not passive participants in political systems. The actions, interests, dispositions, and traditions of non-elites affected and altered elite decision-making, political economy, ideologies, and political institutions.

The non-elites of hinterland communities like El Palmillo and Ejutla also lived rich lives that on a daily basis were probably little affected by the powerful rulers of distant centers. People grew crops, raised children, produced a range of crafts, traveled to markets to exchange those products, buried their dead, carried out rituals in their communities, and paid service to the community and to local leaders. They negotiated their relations with their neighbors, leaders, deities, and ancestors through decisions involving land, craft production, market exchange, marriage and kinship, ritual, tribute, and communal projects. At political centers like Monte Albán and Río Viejo there was probably greater engagement between nobles and commoners. People in the hinterland and in smaller communities were probably largely disconnected from the nobility in their daily routines. More research is needed on the daily life of ancient Oaxaca's agrarian communities, however.

The archaeological and historical records show the great resilience and cultural achievements of the indigenous peoples of Oaxaca. Mixtecs, Zapotecs, and Chatinos experienced both gradual cultural transformations and periods of disjunctive social change. Periods of dramatic social transformation include those associated with early sedentism, the founding of urban centers, the Classic-period collapse, and the Spanish Conquest.

Despite these profound historical changes, continuities in belief and practice can be identified. Farming practices, many beliefs about the relationship between people and the divine, and certain forms of social organization (e.g., barrios and corporate groups) have deep histories in ancient Oaxaca that continue to the present. Indigenous culture and language survived through the oppression, forced acculturation, relocations, and genocide of colonialism. The ancient past can still be seen reflected in the beliefs and practices of living Mixtecs, Zapotecs, and Chatinos. Agency and power is manifest in the present as indigenous Oaxacans continue to assert their identities and negotiate their social circumstances as they did in the prehispanic past and will continue to do into the future.

Endnotes

1 Following the convention in Oaxaca archaeology, I use uncorrected radiocarbon dates when discussing ceramic phases and dates based on associated ceramics. When reporting specific radiocarbon samples, I will include both the uncorrected and the calibrated dates (one sigma ranges). Dates drawn from the codices are based on established concordances between Mixtec and Gregorian calendars (Byland and Pohl 1994:233).

2 A major paleoenvironmental field project during the summer of 2008 included investigations of geomorphology, soil carbonate isotopes, phytoliths, and tree rings as well as the extraction of sediment cores from lakes for pollen and isotope studies. The research promises to yield important paleoclimatological data as well as evidence for changes in vegetation through the Holocene.

3 Given the questions raised by Hardy (1993, 1996) concerning stratigraphy, lithic typology, and cultural sequences from Tehuacán and Oaxaca, I decided not to include the Archaic period phases in table 1.1 that were derived from studies of projectile points.

4 Marcus and Flannery (1996:125) disagree with the Valley of Oaxaca Settlement Pattern Project (Kowalewski et al. 1989:72–7) on the size of Rosario-phase settlement at San José Mogote. Marcus and Flannery (1996:125) give a figure of 60 to 65 ha, although they do not provide the rationale for their higher population estimate and the differences relative to the survey project. In contrast, Kowalewski and his colleagues (1989:72–3) provide a detailed justification for their settlement figures. Kowalewski and colleagues (1989:72) discuss the complexity of estimating settlement at San José Mogote and acknowledge that the site may have been larger than their conservative estimate. They choose to use the estimate of 34 ha to maintain consistency with size determinations of other sites in the valley. I agree with their rationale and have adopted their size estimate for San José Mogote.

5 Surveys in the Mixteca Alta were carried out before the definition of the Yucuita phase. The survey projects distinguished a Late Cruz phase, which encompasses the Cruz D and Yucuita phases.

6 The cemetery at Cerro de la Cruz has been misrepresented in several articles as the remains of a massacre (Balkansky 1998b:469–72, 2001; Redmond &

Spencer 2006:376). In his discussion of the burials in Structure 1, Balkansky (2001:560) states that "the still-articulated bodies, moreover, are piled together in rooms without apparent disturbance." In a later article, Redmond and Spencer (2006:376) claim that the burials from Cerro de la Cruz were found lying on the uppermost floor of Structure 1. Previously published descriptions and illustrations of the burials (Joyce 1991a, 1991b, 1994b, 2003; Joyce et al. 1998), however, demonstrate that "burial activities in both Structure 1 and Op. U [a nearby area with several interments] apparently occurred over a period of several generations, as shown by the frequent instances of later burials having disturbed earlier ones" (Joyce 1994b:158; also see Joyce 1994b, figure 9). The burials were interred *beneath* the uppermost two floors of Structure 1 (Joyce 1991a:213–14, 1994b:158; Joyce et al. 1998) and an analysis from the southern half of the structure, where stratigraphic relationships among burials could be clearly discerned, indicates that there were between 6 and 21 separate burial events (Joyce 1991a:732–9). Osteological analyses of the Cerro de la Cruz material have failed to yield evidence of traumatic wounds (Alexander Christensen, personal communication 2001; Joyce 1991a, appendix 1). Balkansky (2001:560) is incorrect when he argues that the age profile of the Structure 1 burials differs from formal cemeteries (see Joyce 1991a:255). The Chacahua-phase cemetery excavated by Barber (2005) at Yugüe further establishes the use of cemeteries during the Formative period in the lower Río Verde Valley. Workinger and Joyce (n.d.) provide a more detailed discussion of the misrepresentation of the evidence from Cerro de la Cruz.

7   Recent revisions of the ceramic sequence developed by Caso and his colleagues (1967) use locally significant names (e.g., Xoo is the Zapotec word for earthquake, an important prehispanic force and deity) to designate ceramic phases (Lind 1991–2; Markens 2004; Martínez López et al. 2000). This system replaces that of Caso and his colleagues (1967) who use a series of numbered phases for their Monte Albán chronology beginning with Period I. Flannery and Marcus (1994) defined a series of pre-Monte Albán phases using local place names to designate phases (e.g., Tierras Largas phase). The new system developed by Lind (1991–2) is now consistent in using local names for phases for the entire ceramic sequence (for a discussion of the history of research and debate on the Valley of Oaxaca ceramic sequence see Martínez López et al. 2000).

8   These population figures are based on the revised ceramic chronology, which combines the old Monte Albán periods IIIb and IV into a single Late Classic-period Xoo phase (see Lind 1994).

9   Since current evidence indicates that inequalities in wealth and power were minimal, King (2003:353) argues that there were no "elites" and therefore use of the term "commoner" is also inappropriate. I argue that the category "commoner" is justified, however, by the historical relations embodied in tradition and social memory, which would have reflected centuries of living under conditions of hierarchical political systems. It is also likely that the immediate descendants of Late Classic noble families continued to embrace an

identity as nobles during the Early Postclassic even if these families were no longer distinguished by unusual wealth or political power. In other words, commoner and noble identities were not just a product of the economic relations of the time, but were the result of historical relations embodied in people's dispositions. Early Postclassic people in the lower Río Verde Valley also participated in networks of long-distance trade and interaction, which would have brought them into contact with powerful nobles in other parts of Mesoamerica.

10 The following discussion represents a summary of key events represented in the Mixtec codices. For a more thorough discussion see Byland and Pohl (1994), Jansen and Pérez (2007), Pohl (1994), and Troike (1974) among others.

11 As used here, "social system" does not refer to the kinds of holistic, bounded, integrated, and self-regulating systems of anthropological functionalism, but instead simply refers to patterns of social relations that have some durability in time and space.

Bibliography

Abercrombie, Nicholas, Stephen Hill, and Bryan S. Turner. 1980. *The Dominant Ideology Thesis.* Allen and Unwin, London.
Acosta, Jorge R., and Javier Romero. 1992. *Exploraciones en Monte Negro, Oaxaca: 1937–1938, 1938–1939, y 1939–1940.* Instituto Nacional de Antropología e Historia, Mexico City.
Acosta, Ma. Del Rosario, and Geraldina Tercero. 1991. Cerámica y unidades habitacionales de Cerro de las Minas. *Notas Mesoamericanas* 13:129–46.
Aldenderfer, Mark. 2004. Preludes to Power in the Highland Late Preceramic Period. In *Foundations of Power in the Prehispanic Andes*, edited by Kevin J. Vaughn, Dennis Ogburn, and Christina A. Conlee, pp. 13–36. Archaeological Papers of the American Anthropological Association No. 14, Arlington, VA.
Alvarado, Fr. Francisco de. [1593] 1962. *Vocabulario en lengua mixteca.* Facsimile edited by Wigberto Jiménez Moreno. Instituto Nacional Indigenista and Instituto Nacional de Antropología e Historia, Mexico City.
Appadurai, Arjun. 1986. Introduction: Commodities and the Politics of Value. In *The Social Life of Things: Commodities in Cultural Perspective*, edited by Arjun Appadurai, pp. 64–91. Cambridge University Press, Cambridge.
Ashmore, Wendy. 1991. Site-Planning Principles and Concepts of Directionality among the Ancient Maya. *Latin American Antiquity* 2:199–226.
Ashmore, Wendy, and Jeremy Sabloff. 2002. Spatial Orders in Maya Civic Plans. *Latin American Antiquity* 13:201–16.
Balkansky, Andrew K. 1998a. Urbanism and Early State Formation in the Huamelulpan Valley of Southern Mexico. *Latin American Antiquity* 9:37–67.
Balkansky, Andrew K. 1998b. Origin and Collapse of Complex Societies in Oaxaca (Mexico): Evaluating the Era from 1965 to the Present. *Journal of World Prehistory* 12(4):451–93.
Balkansky, Andrew K. 2001. On Emerging Patterns in Oaxaca Archaeology. *Current Anthropology* 42(4):559–61.
Balkansky, Andrew K. 2002. *The Sola Valley and the Monte Albán State: A Study of Zapotec Imperial Expansion.* Memoirs of the University of Michigan Museum of Anthropology No. 36, Ann Arbor.

Balkansky, Andrew K., Stephen A. Kowalewski, Verónica Pérez Rodríguez et al. 2000. Archaeological Survey in the Mixteca Alta of Oaxaca, Mexico. *Journal of Field Archaeology* 27(4):365–89.

Balkansky, Andrew K., Felipe de Jesús Nava Rivera, and Teresa Palomares Rodríguez. 2008. Huamelulpan y Tayata, Oaxaca. *Arqueología Mexicana* 15(90):36–7.

Balkansky, Andrew K., Verónica Pérez Rodríguez, and Stephen A. Kowalewski. 2004. Monte Negro and the Urban Revolution in Oaxaca, Mexico. *Latin American Antiquity* 15(1):33–60.

Bamforth, Douglas B. 2007. *The Allen Site: A Paleoindian Camp in Southwestern Nebraska*. University of New Mexico Press, Albuquerque.

Barber, Sarah B. 2005. "Identity, Tradition, and Complexity: Negotiating Status and Authority in Pacific Coastal Mexico." Ph.D. dissertation, University of Colorado at Boulder.

Barber, Sarah B., and Arthur A. Joyce. 2006. When is a House a Palace? Elite Residences in the Valley of Oaxaca. In *Palaces and Power in the Americas*, edited by Jessica J. Christie and Patricia J. Sarro, pp. 211–55. University of Texas Press, Austin.

Barber, Sarah B., and Arthur A. Joyce. 2007. Polity Produced and Community Consumed: Negotiating Political Centralization in the Lower Río Verde Valley, Oaxaca. In *Mesoamerican Ritual Economy*, edited by E. Christian Wells and Karla L. Davis-Salazar. University Press of Colorado, Boulder, CO.

Bartolomé, Miguel, and Alicia Barabas. 1996. *Tierra de la palabra: Historia e etnografía de los Chatinos de Oaxaca*, 2nd edition. Instituto Oaxaqueño de las Culturas and Instituto Nacional de Antropología e Historia, Mexico City.

Beekman, Christopher S. 2008. Corporate Power Strategies in the Late Formative to Early Classic Tequila Valleys of Central Jalisco. *Latin American Antiquity* 19(4):414–34.

Bell, Catherine. 1992. *Ritual Theory, Ritual Practice*. Oxford University Press, New York.

Benz, Bruce. 2001. Archaeological Evidence of Teosinte Domestication at Guilá Naquitz, Oaxaca. *Proceedings of the National Academy of Sciences* 98(4): 2,104–6.

Bernal, Ignacio. 1948–9. Exploraciones en Coixtlahuaca, Oax. *Revista Mexicana de Estudios Antropológicos* 10:5–76.

Bernal, Ignacio. 1965. Archaeological Synthesis of Oaxaca. In *Handbook of Middle American Indians*, vol. 3: *Archaeology of Southern Mesoamerica*, part 2, edited by Robert Wauchope and Gordon R. Willey, pp. 788–813. University of Texas Press, Austin.

Bernal, Ignacio. 1966. The Mixtecs in the Archeology of the Valley of Oaxaca. In *Ancient Oaxaca*, edited by John Paddock, pp. 345–66. Stanford University Press, Stanford.

Bernal, Ignacio, and Lorenzo Gamio. 1974. *Yagul, el palacio de los seis patios*. Serie Antropológica No. 16. Instituto de Investigaciones Antropológicas, Universidad Nacional Autónoma de México, Mexico City.

Bernal, Ignacio, and Arturo Oliveros. 1988. *Exploraciones arqueológicas en Dainzú, Oaxaca*. Serie Antropológica No. 59. Instituto Nacional de Antropología e Historia, Mexico City.

Binford, Lewis R. 1962. Archaeology as Anthropology. *American Antiquity* 28:217–25.

Binford, Lewis R. 1968. Post-Pleistocene Adaptations. In *New Perspectives in Archaeology*, edited by Sally R. Binford and Lewis R. Binford, pp. 313–41. Aldine, Chicago.

Blanton, Richard E. 1978. *Monte Alban: Settlement Patterns at the Ancient Zapotec Capital*. Academic Press, New York.

Blanton, Richard E. 1998. Beyond Centralization: Steps Toward a Theory of Egalitarian Behavior in Archaic States. In *Archaic States*, edited by Gary M. Feinman and Joyce Marcus, pp. 135–72. School of American Research Press, Santa Fe.

Blanton, Richard E., Gary M. Feinman, Stephen A. Kowalewski, and Linda M. Nicholas. 1999. *Ancient Oaxaca*. Cambridge University Press, Cambridge.

Blanton, Richard E., Gary M. Feinman, Stephen A. Kowalewski, and Peter N. Peregrine. 1996. A Dual-Processual Theory for the Evolution of Mesoamerican Civilization. *Current Anthropology* 37(1):1–14.

Blanton, Richard E., Stephen A. Kowalewski, Gary M. Feinman, and Jill Appel. 1982. *Monte Albán's Hinterland*, part 1: *Prehispanic Settlement Patterns of the Central and Southern Parts of the Valley of Oaxaca, Mexico*. Prehistory and Human Ecology of the Valley of Oaxaca, vol. 7. Memoirs of the University of Michigan Museum of Anthropology No. 15, Ann Arbor.

Blanton, Richard E., Stephen A. Kowalewski, Gary M. Feinman, and Jill Appel. 1993. *Ancient Mesoamerica: A Comparison of Change in Three Regions*, 2nd edition. Cambridge University Press, Cambridge.

Blitz, Jennifer A. 1993. Shifting Dietary Patterns and Social Status at Monte Albán: From the Late Formative to the PostClassic. Paper presented at the 58th Annual Meeting of the Society for American Archaeology, St Louis, MO.

Blomster, Jeffrey P. 1998. Context, Cult, and Early Formative Period Public Ritual in the Mixteca Alta: Analysis of a Hollow-Baby Figurine from Etlatongo, Oaxaca. *Ancient Mesoamerica* 9:309–26.

Blomster, Jeffrey P. 2002. What and Where is Olmec Style? Regional Perspectives on Hollow Figurines in Early Formative Mesoamerica. *Ancient Mesoamerica* 13:171–96.

Blomster, Jeffrey P. 2004. *Etlatongo: Social Complexity, Interaction, and Village Life in the Mixteca Alta of Oaxaca, Mexico*. Wadsworth/Thomson Learning, Belmont, CA.

Blomster, Jeffrey P. 2008a. Changing Cloud Formations: The Sociopolitics of Oaxaca in Late Classic/Postclassic Mesoamerica. In *After Monte Albán: Transformation and Negotiation in Oaxaca, Mexico*, edited by Jeffrey Blomster, pp. 3–48. University Press of Colorado, Boulder, CO.

Blomster, Jeffrey P. 2008b. Legitimization, Negotiation, and Appropriation in Postclassic Oaxaca: Mixtec Stone Codices. In *After Monte Albán: Transformation and Negotiation in Oaxaca, Mexico*, edited by Jeffrey Blomster, pp. 295–330. University Press of Colorado, Boulder, CO.

Blomster, Jeffrey P., Hector Neff, and Michael D. Glascock. 2005. Olmec Pottery Production and Export in Ancient Mexico Determined through Elemental Analysis. *Science* 307:1068–72.

Boone, Elizabeth (ed.). 1984. *Ritual Human Sacrifice in Mesoamerica*. Dumbarton Oaks, Washington, DC.

Bourdieu, Pierre. 1977. *Outline of a Theory of Practice*. Cambridge University Press, Cambridge.

Brady, James E., and Wendy Ashmore. 1999. Mountains, Caves, Water: Ideational Landscapes of the Ancient Maya. In *Archaeologies of Landscape: Contemporary Perspectives*, edited by Wendy Ashmore and A. Bernard Knapp, pp. 124–48. Blackwell Publishers, Malden, MA.

Braudel, Fernand. 1973. *The Mediterranean and the Mediterranean World in the Age of Philip II*. Harper & Row, New York.

Braudel, Fernand. 1980. *On History*. Weidenfeld and Nicolson, London.

Brockington, Donald L. 1973. *Archaeological Investigations in Miahuatlán, Oaxaca*. Vanderbilt University Publications in Anthropology No. 7, Nashville, TN.

Brockington, Donald L., María Jorrín, and J. Robert Long. 1974. *The Oaxaca Coast Project Reports: Part 1*. Vanderbilt University Publications in Anthropology No. 8, Nashville, TN.

Brumfiel, Elizabeth M. 1991. Weaving and Cooking: Women's Production in Aztec Mexico. In *Engendering Archaeology: Women and Prehistory*, edited by Joan M. Gero and Margaret W. Conkey, pp. 224–51. Basil Blackwell, Oxford.

Buckler IV, Edward S., Deborah M. Pearsall, and Timothy P. Holtsford. 1998. Climate, Plant Ecology, and Central Mexican Archaic Subsistence. *Current Anthropology* 39(1):152–64.

Burgoa, Fr. Francisco de. [1674] 1989. *Geográfica descripción*. 2 vols. Editorial Porrúa, Mexico.

Butler, Judith. 1990. *Gender Trouble: Feminism and the Subversion of Identity*. Routledge, New York.

Butler, Judith. 1993. *Bodies that Matter: On the Discursive Limits of "Sex."* Routledge Press, New York.

Butterworth, Douglas. 1975. *Tilantongo: Comunidad mixteca en transición*. Instituto Nacional Indígenista, Mexico City.

Butzer, Karl W. 1982. *Archaeology as Human Ecology: Method and Theory for a Contextual Approach*. Cambridge University Press, New York.

Byland, Bruce. 1980. "Political and Economic Evolution in the Tamazulapan Valley, Mixteca Alta, Oaxaca, Mexico: A Regional Approach." Ph.D. dissertation, Pennsylvania State University, University Park.

Byland, Bruce E., and John M. D. Pohl. 1994. *In the Realm of 8 Deer*. University of Oklahoma Press, Norman.

Cahn, Robert, and Marcus Winter. 1993. The San José Mogote Danzante. *Indiana* 13:39–64.

Caso, Alfonso. 1935. *Las Exploraciones en Monte Albán, Temporada 1934–35*. Instituto Panamericano de Geografía e Historia, Publicación 18, Mexico City.

Caso, Alfonso. 1938. *Exploraciones en Oaxaca, quinta y sexta temporadas 1936–1937*. Instituto Panamericano de Geografía e Historia, Publicación 34, Mexico City.

Caso, Alfonso. 1942. Resumen del informe de las exploraciones en Oaxaca durante la 7a y la 8a temporadas, 1937–1938 y 1938–1939. *Actas del XXVII Congreso Internacional de Americanistas* 2(1939):159–87.

Caso, Alfonso. 1947. Calendario y escritura de las antiguas culturas de Monte Albán. *Obras completas de Miguel Othón de Mendizábal* 1:116–43.

Caso, Alfonso. 1949. El Mapa de Teozacoalco. *Cuadernos Americanos* 8(5):145–81.

Caso, Alfonso. 1956. El calendario mixteco. *Historia Mexicana* 5(20):481–97.

Caso, Alfonso. 1964. *Interpretación del Códice Selden 3135 (A.2)/Interpretation of the Codex Selden 3135 (A.2)*. Sociedad Mexicana de Antropología, Mexico City.

Caso, Alfonso. 1965. Zapotec Writing and Calendar. In *Handbook of Middle American Indians*, vol. 3: *Archaeology of Southern Mesoamerica*, part 2, edited by Robert Wauchope and Gordon R. Willey, pp. 931–47. University of Texas Press, Austin.

Caso, Alfonso. 1969. *El Tesoro de Monte Albán*. Memorias del Instituto Nacional de Antropología e Historia No. 3, Mexico City.

Caso, Alfonso. 1977. *Reyes y reinos de la Mixteca*, vol. 1. Fondo de Cultura Económica, Mexico.

Caso, Alfonso. 1979. *Reyes y reinos de la Mixteca*, vol. 2. Fondo de Cultura Económica, Mexico.

Caso, Alfonso, and Ignacio Bernal. 1952. *Urnas de Oaxaca*. Memorias del Instituto Nacional de Antropología e Historia No. 2, Mexico City.

Caso, Alfonso, Ignacio Bernal, and Jorge R. Acosta. 1967. *La cerámica de Monte Albán*. Memorias del Instituto Nacional de Antropología e Historia No. 13, Mexico City.

Caso, Alfonso, and Daniel F. Rubín de la Borbolla. 1936. Exploraciones en Mitla 1934–1935. *Instituto Panamericano de Geografía e Historia, Publicación 21*, Mexico City.

Castellanos, Abraham. 1989. *Monte Albán, Danni Dipaa: Cerro Fortificado*. Lásser Plus, Oaxaca.

Chadwick, Robert. 1966. The Tombs of Monte Alban I Style at Yagul. In *Ancient Oaxaca: Discoveries in Mexican Archeology and History*, edited by John Paddock, pp. 245–55. Stanford University Press, Stanford.

Chance, John K. 1978. *Race and Class in Colonial Oaxaca*. Stanford University Press, Stanford.

Chance, John K. 1989. *Conquest of the Sierra: Spaniards and Indians in Colonial Oaxaca*. University of Oklahoma Press, Norman.

Chance, John K. 2000. The Noble House in Colonial Puebla, Mexico: Descent, Inheritance, and the Nahua Tradition. *American Anthropologist* 102(3):485–502.

Chase, Arlen F., and Diane Z. Chase. 2007. Ancient Maya Urban Development: Insights from the Archaeology of Caracol, Belize. *Belizean Studies* 29(2):60–72.
Chase, Diane Z., and Arlen F. Chase (eds.). 1992. *Mesoamerican Elites*. University of Oklahoma Press, Norman.
Chiñas, Beverly. 1973. *The Isthmus Zapotecs: Women's Roles in Cultural Context*. Holt, Rinehart and Winston, New York.
Clark, James Cooper. 1912. *The Story of "Eight Deer" in Codex Colombino*. Taylor and Francis, London.
Clark, John E. 1997. The Arts of Government in Early Mesoamerica. *Annual Review of Anthropology* 26:211–34.
Clark, John E. 2001. Ciudades tempranas olmecas. In *Reconstruyendo la ciudad Maya: El urbanismo en las sociedades antiguas*, edited by Andrés Ciudad Ruiz, María Josefa Iglesia Ponce de Léon and María del Carmen Martínez Martínez, pp. 183–210. Sociedad Española de Estudios Mayas, Madrid.
Clark, John E. 2004. Mesoamerica Goes Public: Early Ceremonial Centers, Leaders, and Communities. In *Mesoamerican Archaeology*, edited by Julia Hendon and Rosemary Joyce, pp. 43–72. Blackwell, Oxford.
Clark, John E., and Michael Blake. 1994. The Power of Prestige: Competitive Generosity and the Emergence of Rank Societies in Lowland Mesoamerica. In *Factional Competition and Political Development in the New World*, edited by Elizabeth M. Brumfiel and John W. Fox, pp. 17–30. Cambridge University Press, Cambridge.
Clark, John E., Richard D. Hansen, and Tomás Pérez Suárez. 2000. La zona Maya en el preclásico. In *Historia antigua de México*, vol. 1: *El México antiguo, los orígenes y el horizonte preclásico*, edited by Linda Manzanilla and Leonardo López Luján, pp. 437–510. Instituto Nacional de Antropología e Historia, Mexico City.
Codex Bodley. 1960. Sociedad Mexicana de Antropología, Mexico City.
Codex Colombino. 1892. In *Homenaje á Cristóbal Colón: Antiguedades mexicanas publicadas por la junta colobina de México en el cuarto centenario del descubrimiento de América*. Oficina tipográfica de la Secretaría de Fomento, Mexico City.
Codex Zouche Nuttall. 1987. Akademishe Druck- und Verlagsanstalt, Graz.
Coe, Michael D. 1962. *Mexico*. Praeger, New York.
Coe, Michael. 1972. Olmec Jaguars and Olmec Kings. In *The Cult of the Feline*, edited by Elizabeth P. Benson, pp. 1–18. Dumbarton Oaks, Washington, DC.
Collingwood, Robin G. 1946. *The Idea of History*. Oxford University Press, Oxford.
Comaroff, John, and Jean Comaroff. 1992. *Ethnography and the Historical Imagination*. Westview Press, Boulder.
Connerton, Paul. 1989. *How Societies Remember*. Cambridge University Press, Cambridge.
Cook, S. F., and Woodrow Borah. 1968. *The Population of the Mixteca Alta, 1520–1960*. Ibero-Americana No. 50. University of California Press, Berkeley and Los Angeles.

Cook, Scott, and Martin Diskin (eds.). 1974. *Markets in Oaxaca: Essays on a Regional Peasant Economy of Mexico*. University of Texas Press, Austin.
Córdova, Fr. Juan de. [1570] 1989. *Vocabulario en lengua zapoteca*. Ediciones Toledo, Mexico.
Covarrubias, Miguel. 1946. El arte "olmeca" o de la venta. *Cuadernos Americanos* 28:153–79.
Cowgill, George L. 1997. State and Society at Teotihuacan, Mexico. *Annual Review of Anthropology* 26:129–61.
Cowgill, George L. 2004. Origins and Development of Urbanism: Archaeological Perspectives. *Annual Review of Anthropology* 33:525–49.
Cowgill, George L. 2008. An Update on Teotihuacan. *Antiquity* 82:962–75.
Cyphers, Ann. 1993. Women, Rituals, and Social Dynamics at Ancient Chalcatzingo. *Latin American Antiquity* 4(3):209–24.
Cyphers Guillén, Ann. 1997. Olmec Architecture at San Lorenzo. In *Olmec to Aztec: Settlement Patterns in the Ancient Gulf Lowlands*, edited by Barbara L. Stark and Phillip J. Arnold III, pp. 98–114. University of Arizona Press, Tucson.
Dahlgren, Barbro. 1990. *La Mixteca: Su cultura e historia prehispánicas*. Universidad Nacional Autónoma de México, Mexico City.
De Certeau, Michel. 1984. *The Practice of Everyday Life*. University of California Press, Berkeley.
De Cicco, Gabriel. 1969. The Chatino. In *Handbook of Middle American Indians*, vol. 7, edited by Robert Wauchope and Evon Z. Vogt, pp. 360–6. University of Texas Press, Austin.
De la Cruz, Víctor. 2002. Las creencias y prácticas religiosas de los descendientes de los Binnigula'sa'. In *La Religión de los Binnigula'sa'*, edited by Víctor de la Cruz and Marcus Winter, pp. 273–342. IEEPO-IOC, Oaxaca.
De la Cruz, Víctor. 2007. *El Pensamiento de los Binnigula'sa': Cosmovisión, Religión y Calendario con Especial Referencia a los Binnizá*. Instituto Nacional de Antropología e Historia, Mexico City.
De la Fuente, Julio. 1949. *Yalalag: Una villa Zapoteca serrana*. Serie Científica 1. Instituto Nacional de Antropología e Historia, Mexico City.
Deraga, Daria. 1981. "Dos unidades domésticas clásicas exploradas en San Juan Yucuita, Nochixtlán, Oaxaca." Unpublished Licenciatura thesis, Universidad Autónoma de Guadalajara, Guadalajara.
Díaz del Castillo, Bernal. [1580] 1955. *Historia verdadera de la conquista de la Nueva España*, 4th edition. Porrúa, Mexico City.
Di Castro, Anna, and Ann Cyphers. 2006. Iconografía de la cerámica de San Lorenzo. *Annales del Instituto de Investigaciones Estéticas* 89:29–58.
Diehl, Richard A., and Janet C. Berlo (eds.). 1989. *Mesoamerica after the Decline of Teotihuacan*, AD 700–900. Dumbarton Oaks, Washington, DC.
Dillehay, Thomas D. 1997. *Monte Verde: A Late Pleistocene Settlement in Chile*, vol. 2: *The Archaeological Context and Interpretation*. Smithsonian Institution Press, Washington, DC.
Dixon, E. James. 1999. *Bones, Boats and Bison: Archaeology and the First Colonization of Western North America*. University of New Mexico Press, Albuquerque.

Dixon, E. James. 2001. Human Colonization of the Americas: Timing, Technology, and Process. *Quaternary Science Reviews* 20:301–14.

Dobres, Marcia-Anne, and John E. Robb (eds.). 2000. *Agency in Archaeology*. Routledge, London.

Drennan, Robert D. 1976. *Fábrica San José and Middle Formative Society in the Valley of Oaxaca*. Prehistory and Human Ecology of the Valley of Oaxaca, vol. 4. Memoirs of the University of Michigan Museum of Anthropology No. 8, Ann Arbor.

Drennan, Robert D. 1989. The Mountains North of the Valley. In *Monte Albán's Hinterland*, part 2: *Prehispanic Settlement Patterns in Tlacolula, Etla, and Ocotlán, the Valley of Oaxaca, Mexico*, edited by Stephen A. Kowalewski, Gary M. Feinman, Laura Finsten, Richard Blanton, and Linda M. Nicholas, pp. 367–84. Memoirs of the University of Michigan Museum of Anthropology No. 23, Ann Arbor.

Dunbar, James, and C. Andrew Hemmings. 2004. Florida Paleoindian Points and Knives. In *New Perspectives on the First Americans*, edited by Bradley T. Lepper and Robson Bonnichsen, pp. 65–72. Texas A & M Press, College Station, TX.

Duncan, William N., Andrew K. Balkansky, Kimberly Crawford, Heather A. Lapham, and Nathan J. Meissner. 2008. Human Cremation in Mexico 3,000 Years Ago. *Proceedings of the National Academy of Sciences* 105(14):5,315–20.

Dunning, Nicholas P., Sheryl Luzzadder-Beach, Timothy Beach, John G. Jones, Vernon L. Scarborough, and T. Patrick Culbert. 2002. Arising from the Bajos: The Evolution of a Neotropical Landscape and the Rise of Maya Civilization. *Annals of the Association of American Geographers* 92:267–83.

Earle, Timothy. 1997. *How Chiefs Come to Power*. Stanford University Press, Stanford.

Ehrenreich, Robert M., Carole L. Crumley, and Janet E. Levy (eds.). 1995. *Heterarchy and the Analysis of Complex Societies*. Archaeological Papers of the American Anthropological Association No. 6, Arlington, VA.

Elam, J. Michael. 1989. Defensible and Fortified Sites. In *Monte Albán's Hinterland*, part 2: *Prehispanic Settlement Patterns in Tlacolula, Etla, and Ocotlán, the Valley of Oaxaca, Mexico*, edited by Stephen A. Kowalewski, Gary M. Feinman, Laura Finsten, Richard Blanton, and Linda M. Nicholas, pp. 385–407. Memoirs of the University of Michigan Museum of Anthropology No. 23, Ann Arbor.

Elson, Christina M. 2003. "Elites at Cerro Tilcajete: A Secondary Center in the Valley of Oaxaca." Ph.D. dissertation, University of Michigan.

Elson, Christina M. 2006. Intermediate Elites and the Political Landscape of the Early Zapotec State. In *Intermediate Elites in Pre-Columbian States and Empires*, edited by Christina M. Elson and R. Alan Covey, pp. 44–67. University of Arizona Press, Tucson.

Elson, Christina M. 2007. Late Classic Occupation at Jalieza: A Subregional Center in the Valley of Oaxaca. Paper presented at the 72nd Annual Meeting of the Society for American Archaeology, Austin, TX.

Erickson, Clark L. 1999. Neo-Environmental Determinism and Agrarian "Collapse" in Andean Prehistory. *Antiquity* 73:634–42.

Erickson, David L., Bruce D. Smith, Andrew C. Clarke, Daniel H. Sandweiss, and Noreen Tuross. 2005. An Asian Origin for a 10,000-Year-Old Domesticated Plant in the Americas. *Proceedings of the National Academy of Sciences* 102(51):18,315–20.

Erlandson, Jon M. 2007. Sea Change: The Paleo-coastal Occupations of Daisy Cave. In *Seeking Our Past: An Introduction to North American Archaeology*, edited by Sarah W. Neusius and G. Timothy Gross, pp. 135–43. Oxford University Press, Oxford.

Erlandson, Jon M., Michael H. Graham, Bruce J. Bourque, Debra Corbett, James A. Estes, and Robert S. Steneck. 2007. The Kelp Highway Hypothesis: Marine Ecology, the Coastal Migration Theory, and the Peopling of the Americas. *Journal of Island and Coastal Archaeology* 2(2):161–72.

Fargher, Lane F. 2007. A Microscopic View of Ceramic Production: An Analysis of Thin-Sections from Monte Albán. *Latin American Antiquity* 18(3):313–32.

Faulseit, Ronald. 2008. *Cerro Danush: An Exploration of the Late Classic Transition in the Tlacolula Valley, Oaxaca*. Report submitted to the Foundation for the Advancement of Mesoamerican Studies, Inc., Crystal River, FL (www.famsi.org/reports/07056/index.html).

Feinman, Gary M., and Joyce Marcus (eds.). 1998. *Archaic States*. School of American Research Press, Santa Fe.

Feinman, Gary M., and Linda M. Nicholas. 1990. At the Margins of the Monte Albán State: Settlement Patterns in the Ejutla Valley, Oaxaca, Mexico. *Latin American Antiquity* 1(3):216–46.

Feinman, Gary M., and Linda M. Nicholas. 2004. Unraveling the Prehispanic Highland Mesoamerican Economy: Production, Exchange, and Consumption in the Classic Period Valley of Oaxaca. In *Archaeological Perspectives on Political Economies*, edited by Gary M. Feinman and Linda M. Nicholas, pp. 167–88. University of Utah Press, Salt Lake City.

Feinman, Gary M., Linda M. Nicholas, and Helen R. Haines. 2002. Houses on a Hill: Classic Period Life at El Palmillo, Oaxaca, Mexico. *Latin American Antiquity* 13(3):251–78.

Feinman, Gary M., Linda M. Nicholas, and Helen R. Haines. 2006. Socioeconomic Inequality and the Consumption of Chipped Stone at El Palmillo, Oaxaca, Mexico. *Latin American Antiquity* 17(2):151–76.

Feinman, Gary M., Linda M. Nicholas, and Edward F. Maher. 2008. Domestic Offerings at El Palmillo: Implications for Community Organization. *Ancient Mesoamerica* 19(2):175–94.

Fernández, Deepika. 2004. "Subsistence in the Lower Río Verde region, Oaxaca, Mexico: A Zoological Analysis." Unpublished MA thesis, University of Calgary, Calgary.

Fernández, Rudolfo. 1981. "La estructura A de Yucuita. Arquitectura residencial urbana del preclásico superior en Oaxaca." Unpublished Licenciatura thesis, Universidad Autónoma de Guadalajara, Guadalajara.

Fernández Dávila, Enrique. 1997. San José Mogote, Etla: Origen de la Civilización Zapoteca. *Arqueología Mexicana* 5(26):18–23.

Fernández Dávila, Enrique, and Susana Gómez Serafín. 1988. *Arqueología de Huatulco, Oaxaca*. Colección Científica 171. Instituto Nacional de Antropología e Historia, Mexico City.

Finsten, Laura. 1995. *Jalieza, Oaxaca: Activity Specialization at a Hilltop Center*. Vanderbilt University Publications in Anthropology No. 48, Nashville, TN.

Finsten, Laura. 1996. Periphery and Frontier in Southern Mexico: The Mixtec Sierra in Highland Oaxaca. In *Pre-Columbian World Systems*, edited by Peter N. Peregrine and Gary M. Feinman, pp. 77–96. Prehistory Press, Madison, WI.

Flannery, Kent V. 1967. Culture History v. Cultural Process: A Debate in American Archaeology. *Scientific American* 217:119–22.

Flannery, Kent V. 1968. Archaeological Systems Theory and Early Mesoamerica. In *Anthropological Archaeology in the Americas*, edited by Betty J. Meggars, pp. 67–87. Anthropological Society of Washington, Washington, DC.

Flannery, Kent V. 1972. The Cultural Evolution of Civilizations. *Annual Review of Ecology and Systematics* 2:399–426.

Flannery, Kent V. (ed.). 1976a. *The Early Mesoamerican Village*. Academic Press, New York.

Flannery, Kent V. 1976b. Contextual Analysis of Ritual Paraphernalia from Formative Oaxaca. In *The Early Mesoamerican Village*, edited by Kent V. Flannery, pp. 333–45. Academic Press, New York.

Flannery, Kent V. 1983a. Precolumbian Farming in the Valleys of Oaxaca, Nochixtlán, Tehuacán, and Cuicatlán: A Comparative Study. In *The Cloud People: Divergent Evolution of the Mixtec and Zapotec Civilizations*, edited by Kent V. Flannery and Joyce Marcus, pp. 323–38. Academic Press, New York.

Flannery, Kent V. 1983b. Pleistocene Fauna of Early Ajuereado Type from Cueva Blanca, Oaxaca. In *The Cloud People: Divergent Evolution of the Mixtec and Zapotec Civilizations*, edited by Kent V. Flannery and Joyce Marcus, pp. 18–20. Academic Press, New York.

Flannery, Kent V. 1983c. Monte Negro: A Reinterpretation. In *The Cloud People: Divergent Evolution of the Zapotec and Mixtec Civilizations*, edited by Kent V. Flannery and Joyce Marcus, pp. 99–102. Academic Press, New York.

Flannery, Kent V. 1983d. The Legacy of the Early Urban Period: An Ethnohistoric Approach to Monte Albán's Temples, Residences, and Royal Tombs. In *The Cloud People: Divergent Evolution of the Zapotec and Mixtec Civilizations*, edited by Kent V. Flannery and Joyce Marcus, pp. 132–6. Academic Press, New York.

Flannery, Kent V. (ed.). 1986. *Guila' Naquitz: Archaic Foraging and Early Agriculture in Oaxaca, Mexico*. Academic Press, New York.

Flannery, Kent V. 1998. The Ground Plans of Archaic States. In *Archaic States*, edited by Gary M. Feinman and Joyce Marcus, pp. 15–58. School of American Research Press, Santa Fe.

Flannery, Kent V. 1999. Process and Agency in Early State Formation. *Cambridge Archaeological Journal* 9:3–21.

Flannery, Kent V., and Joyce Marcus. 1983a. The Growth of Site Hierarchies in the Valley of Oaxaca: Part I. In *The Cloud People: Divergent Evolution of the Zapotec and Mixtec Civilizations*, edited by Kent V. Flannery and Joyce Marcus, pp. 53–64. Academic Press, New York.

Flannery, Kent V., and Joyce Marcus. 1983b. The Rosario Phase and the Origins of Monte Albán. In *The Cloud People: Divergent Evolution of the Zapotec and Mixtec Civilizations*, edited by Kent V. Flannery and Joyce Marcus, pp. 74–7. Academic Press, New York.

Flannery, Kent V., and Joyce Marcus. 1983c. The Earliest Public Buildings, Tombs, and Monuments of Monte Albán. In *The Cloud People: Divergent Evolution of the Zapotec and Mixtec Civilizations*, edited by Kent V. Flannery and Joyce Marcus, pp. 87–91. Academic Press, New York.

Flannery, Kent V., and Joyce Marcus. 1983d. An Editorial Opinion on the Mixtec Impact. In *The Cloud People: Divergent Evolution of the Mixtec and Zapotec Civilizations*, edited by Kent V. Flannery and Joyce Marcus, pp. 277–9. Academic Press, New York.

Flannery, Kent V., and Joyce Marcus. 1983e. Urban Mitla and its Rural Hinterland. In *The Cloud People: Divergent Evolution of the Mixtec and Zapotec Civilizations*, edited by Kent V. Flannery and Joyce Marcus, pp. 295–300. Academic Press, New York.

Flannery, Kent V., and Joyce Marcus. 1983f. San José Mogote and the Tay Situndayu. In *The Cloud People: Divergent Evolution of the Mixtec and Zapotec Civilizations*, edited by Kent V. Flannery and Joyce Marcus, pp. 289–90. Academic Press, New York.

Flannery, Kent V., and Joyce Marcus. 1994. *Early Formative Pottery of the Valley of Oaxaca, Mexico*. Memoirs of the University of Michigan Museum of Anthropology No. 27, Ann Arbor.

Flannery, Kent V., and Joyce Marcus. 2000. Formative Mexican Chiefdoms and the Myth of the "Mother Culture." *Journal of Anthropological Archaeology* 19:1–37.

Flannery, Kent V., and Joyce Marcus. 2003. The Origins of War: New 14C Dates from Ancient Mexico. *Proceedings of the National Academy of Sciences* 100(20):11,801–5.

Flannery, Kent V., and Ronald Spores. 1983. Excavated Sites of the Oaxacan Preceramic. In *The Cloud People: Divergent Evolution of the Zapotec and Mixtec Civilizations*, edited by Kent V. Flannery and Joyce Marcus, pp. 20–6. Academic Press, New York.

Flannery, Kent V., and Marcus C. Winter. 1976. Analyzing Household Activities. In *The Early Mesoamerican Village*, edited by Kent V. Flannery, pp. 34–45. Academic Press, New York.

Forde, Jaime E. 2006. "Ideology, Identity, and Icons: A Study of Mixtec Polychrome Pottery from Late Postclassic Yuca Dzaa (Tututepec), Oaxaca, Mexico." MA thesis, University of Colorado at Boulder.

Foucault, Michel. 1965. *Madness and Civilization: A History of Insanity in the Age of Reason*. Vintage Books, New York.

Foucault, Michel. 1970. *The Order of Things: An Archaeology of the Human Sciences*. Tavistock, London.
Foucault, Michel. 1972. *The Archaeology of Knowledge (and the Discourse on Language)*. Pantheon, New York.
Foucault, Michel. 1973. *The Birth of the Clinic*. Tavistock, London.
Foucault, Michel. 1977. *Discipline and Punish*. Vintage, New York.
Foucault, Michel. 1980. Two Lectures. In *Power/Knowledge*, edited by Colin Gordon, pp. 78–108. Pantheon Books, New York.
Foucault, Michel. 1985. *The History of Sexuality*, vol. 2: *The Use of Pleasure*. Pantheon, New York.
Foucault, Michel. 1986. *The History of Sexuality*, vol. 3: *The Care of the Self*. Pantheon, New York.
Freidel, David A., Linda Schele, and Joy Parker. 1993. *Maya Cosmos: Three Thousand Years on the Shaman's Path*. William Morrow, New York.
Furst, Jill Leslie. 1978. *Codex Vindobonensis Mexicanus I: A Commentary*. State University of New York Institute for Mesoamerican Studies Publication No. 4, Albany.
Gadamer, Hans-Georg. 1975. *Truth and Method*. Seabury Press, New York.
Gaxiola, Margarita. 1984. *Huamelulpan: Un centro urbano de la Mixteca Alta*. Colección Científica 114. Instituto Nacional de Antropología e Historia, Mexico City.
Gay, José Antonio. 1881. *Historia de Oaxaca*. 2 vols. Impr. del Comercio, Mexico.
Geller, Pamela L. 2004. "Transforming Bodies, Transforming Identities: A Consideration of Pre-Columbian Maya Corporeal Beliefs and Practices." Ph.D. dissertation, University of Pennsylvania.
Geller, Pamela L., and Miranda K. Stockett (eds.). 2006. *Feminist Anthropology: Past, Present, and Future*. University of Pennsylvania Press, Philadelphia.
Geurds, Alexander, and Maarten E. R. G. N. Jansen. 2008. The Ceremonial Center of Monte Negro: A Cognitive Approach to Urbanization in Ñuu Dzaui. In *Urbanism in Mesoamerica/El Urbanismo en Mesoamérica*, vol. 2, edited by Alba Guadalupe Mastache, Robert H. Cobean, Ángel García Cook, and Kenneth G. Hirth, pp. 377–421. Instituto Nacional de Antropología e Historia/Pennsylvania State University, Mexico City and University Park.
Giddens, Anthony. 1979. *Central Problems in Social Theory*. University of California Press, Berkeley.
Giddens, Anthony. 1984. *The Constitution of Society: Outline of the Theory of Structuration*. University of California Press, Berkeley.
Gillespie, Susan D. 1991. Ballgames and Boundaries. In *The Mesoamerican Ballgame*, edited by Vernon L. Scarborough and D. R. Wilcox, pp. 317–45. University of Arizona Press, Tucson.
Gillespie, Susan D. 2000. Rethinking Ancient Maya Social Organization: Replacing "Lineage" with "House." *American Anthropologist* 102(3):467–84.
Gillespie, Susan D. 2001. Personhood, Agency, and Mortuary Ritual: A Case Study from the Ancient Maya. *Journal of Anthropological Archaeology* 20:73–112.

Goldberg, Paul, and Trina L. Arpin. 1999. Micromorphological Analysis of Sediments from Meadowcroft Rockshelter, Pennsylvania: Implications for Radiocarbon Dating. *Journal of Field Archaeology* 26(3):325–42.
Goldstein, Donna. 2003. *Laughter out of Place: Race, Class, Violence, and Sexuality in a Brazilian Shantytown*. University of California Press, Berkeley.
Goman, Michelle, Arthur A. Joyce, and Raymond G. Mueller. 2005. Stratigraphic Evidence for Anthropogenically Induced Coastal Environmental Change from Oaxaca, Mexico. *Quaternary Research* 63:250–60.
González Licón, Ernesto. 2003. *Social Inequality at Monte Albán Oaxaca: Household Analysis from Terminal Formative to Early Classic*. PhD dissertation, University of Pittsburgh.
Gramsci, Antonio. 1971. *Selections from the Prison Notebooks*. International Publishers, New York.
Greenberg, James B. 1981. *Santiago's Sword: Chatino Peasant Religion and Economics*. University of California Press, Berkeley.
Grove, David C. 1987. Chalcatzingo in a Broader Perspective. In *Ancient Chalcatzingo*, edited by David C. Grove, pp. 434–42. University of Texas Press, Austin.
Grove, David C. 1989. Olmec: What's in a Name? In *Regional Perspectives on the Olmec*, edited by Robert J. Sharer and David C. Grove, pp. 8–14. Cambridge University Press, Cambridge.
Grove, David C. 1997. Olmec Archaeology: A Half Century of Research and its Accomplishments. *Journal of World Prehistory* 11:51–101.
Grove, David C. 1999. Public Monuments and Sacred Mountains: Observations on Three Formative Period Sacred Landscapes. In *Social Patterns in Pre-Classic Mesoamerica*, edited by David C. Grove and Rosemary A. Joyce, pp. 255–95. Dumbarton Oaks, Washington, DC.
Grove, David C. 2000. Faces of the Earth at Chalcatzingo, Mexico: Serpents, Caves, and Mountains in Middle Formative Period Iconography. In *Olmec Art and Archaeology in Mesoamerica*, edited by John E. Clark and Mary E. Pye, pp. 277–96. National Gallery of Art, Washington, DC.
Grove, David C., and Susan D. Gillespie. 1992a. Ideology and Evolution at the Pre-State Level: Formative Period Mesoamerica. In *Ideology and Precolumbian Civilizations*, edited by Arthur A. Demarest and Geoffrey W. Conrad, pp. 15–36. School of American Research Press, Sante Fe.
Grove, David C., and Susan D. Gillespie. 1992b. Archaeological Indicators of Formative Period Elites: A Perspective from Central Mexico. In *Mesoamerican Elites: An Archaeological Assessment*, edited by Diane Z. Chase and Arlen F. Chase, pp. 191–205. University of Oklahoma Press, Norman.
Gruzinski, Serge. 1989. *Man-Gods in the Mexican Highlands: Indian Power and Colonial Society, 1520–1800*. Stanford University Press, Stanford.
Guernsey-Kappelman, Julia. 2001. Sacred Geography at Izapa and the Performance of Rulership. In *Landscape and Power in Ancient Mesoamerica*, edited by Rex Koontz, Kathryn Reese-Taylor, and Annabeth Headrick, pp. 81–111. Westview Press, Boulder.

Gutiérrez Mendoza, Gerardo. 2003. Territorial Structure and Urbanism in Mesoamerica: The Huaxtec and Mixtec-Tlapanec-Nahua Cases. In *El Urbanismo en Mesoamérica/Urbanism in Mesoamerica*, vol. 1, edited by William T. Sanders, Alba Guadalupe Mastache, and Robert H. Cobean, pp. 86–118. Instituto Nacional de Antropología e Historia/Pennsylvania State University, Mexico City and University Park.

Gutiérrez Mendoza, Gerardo. 2008. Four Thousand Years of Graphic Communication in the Mixteca-Tlapaneca-Nahua Region. In *Mixtec Writing and Society/Escritura de Ñuu Dzaui*, edited by Maarten E. R. G. N. Jansen and Laura N. K. van Broekhoven, pp. 71–107. KNAW Press, Amsterdam.

Haines, Helen R., Gary M. Feinman, and Linda M. Nicholas. 2004. Household Economic Specialization and Social Differentiation: The Stone-Tool Assemblage at El Palmillo. *Ancient Mesoamerica* 15:251–66.

Haller, Mikeal J., Gary M. Feinman, and Linda M. Nicholas. 2006. Socioeconomic Inequality and Differential Access to Faunal Resources at El Palmillo, Oaxaca, Mexico. *Ancient Mesoamerica* 17(1):39–56.

Hamann, Byron. 2002. The Social Life of Pre-Sunrise Things. *Current Anthropology* 43(3):351–82.

Hamann, Byron. 2008a. Landscapes of Divinity and Landscapes of Idolatry. Paper presented at Dumbarton Oaks Research Library and Collection, Washington, DC.

Hamann, Byron. 2008b. Heirlooms and Ruins: High Culture, Mesoamerican Civilization, and the Postclassic Oaxacan Tradition. In *After Monte Albán: Transformation and Negotiation in Oaxaca, Mexico*, edited by Jeffrey Blomster, pp. 119–68. University Press of Colorado, Boulder, CO.

Hardy, Karen V. 1993. "Preceramic Lithics in Central Mexico: An Examination of the Tehuacán and Oaxaca Chronological Sequences." Unpublished Ph.D. dissertation, University College, London.

Hardy, Karen V. 1996. The Preceramic Sequence from the Tehuacán Valley: A reevaluation. *Current Anthropology* 37(4):700–15.

Hayden, Brian. 1995. Pathways to Power: Principles for Creating Socioeconomic Inequalities. In *Foundations of Social Inequality*, edited by T. Douglas Price and Gary M. Feinman, pp. 15–86. Plenum Press, New York.

Hegmon, Michelle. 2003. Setting Theoretical Egos Aside: Issues and Theory in North American Archaeology. *American Antiquity* 68(2):213–43.

Helms, Mary W. 1991. Esoteric Knowledge, Geographical Distance, and the Elaboration of Leadership Status. In *Profiles in Cultural Evolution: Papers from a Conference in Honor of Elman R. Service*, edited by A. Terry Rambo and Kathleen Gillogly, pp. 333–50. Anthropological Papers, Museum of Anthropology, University of Michigan No. 85, Ann Arbor.

Hendon, Julia A. 2000. Having and Holding: Storage, Memory, Knowledge, and Social Relations. *American Anthropologist* 102(1):42–53.

Hendry, Jean Clare. 1992. *Atzompa: A Pottery Producing Village of Southern Mexico in the Mid-1950's*. Vanderbilt University Publications in Anthropology No. 40, Nashville, TN.

Hepp, Guy D. 2007. "Formative Period Ceramic Figurines from the Lower Río Verde Valley, Coastal Oaxaca, Mexico." Unpublished MA thesis, Florida State University, Tallahassee.

Herrera Muzgo Torres, Alicia. 1991. Tumba 7. In *Exploraciones arqueológicas en Huamelulpan, Mixteca Alta, Oaxaca. Informe temporada 1990*, edited by Marcus Winter, Alicia Herrera Muzgo T., Ronald Spores, and Vilma Fialko, pp. 62–77. Report on file Centro INAH Oaxaca, Instituto Nacional de Antropología e Historia, Oaxaca.

Herrera Muzgo Torres, Alicia. 2002. Ritos postclásicos en Monte Albán. In *La Religión de los Binnigula'sa'*, edited by Victor de la Cruz and Marcus Winter, pp. 343–70. IEEPO-IOC, Oaxaca.

Hillier, Bill, and Julienne Hanson. 1984. *The Social Logic of Space*. Cambridge University Press, Cambridge.

Hirth, Kenneth G. (ed.). 1984. *Trade and Exchange in Early Mesoamerica*. University of New Mexico Press, Albuquerque.

Hodder, Ian (ed.). 1982. *Symbolic and Structural Archaeology*. Cambridge University Press, Cambridge.

Hodder, Ian (ed.). 1987. *Archaeology as Long-Term History*. Cambridge University Press, Cambridge.

Hodder, Ian. 1999. *The Archaeological Process*. Blackwell, Oxford.

Hodder, Ian (ed.). 2001. *Archaeological Theory Today*. Polity Press, Cambridge.

Hodder, Ian, and Scott Hutson. 2003. *Reading the Past*, 3rd edition. Cambridge University Press, Cambridge.

Hodell, David A., Mark Brenner, and Jason H. Curtis. 2007. Climate and Cultural History of the Northeastern Yucatan Peninsula, Quintana Roo, Mexico. *Climatic Change* 83(1–2):215–40.

Holland, Dorothy, William Lachicotte, Jr., Debra Skinner, and Carole Cain. 1998. *Identity and Agency in Cultural Worlds*. Harvard University Press, Cambridge.

Hutson, Scott R. 2002. Built Space and Bad Subjects: Domination and Resistance at Monte Albán, Oaxaca, Mexico. *Journal of Social Archaeology* 2:53–80.

Jansen, Maarten E. R. G. N., and Gabina Aurora Pérez Jiménez. 2005. *Codex Bodley*. Treasures from the Bodleian Library, 1. University of Oxford, Oxford.

Jansen, Maarten E. R. G. N., and Gabina Aurora Pérez Jiménez. 2007. *Encounter with the Plumed Serpent*. University Press of Colorado, Boulder, CO.

Janusek, John. 2004. *Identity and Power in the Ancient Andes*. Routledge Press, New York.

Johnson, Matthew H. 1989. Conceptions of Agency in Archaeological Interpretation. *Journal of Anthropological Archaeology* 8:189–211.

Johnson, Matthew H. 1999. *Archaeological Theory*. Blackwell, Malden, MA.

Jones, Andrew. 2002. *Archaeological Theory and Scientific Practice*. Cambridge University Press, Cambridge.

Jones, John G., and Barbara Voorhies. 2004. Human and Plant Interactions. In *Coastal Collectors in the Holocene: The Chantuto People of Southwest Mexico*, edited by Barbara Voorhies, pp. 300–43. University Press of Florida, Gainesville.

Joralemon, Peter David. 1971. *A Study of Olmec Iconography*. Studies in Pre-Columbian Art and Archaeology No. 7, Dumbarton Oaks, Washington, DC.

Jorrín, María. 1974. Stone Monuments. In *The Oaxaca Coast Project Reports: Part I*, edited by Donald L. Brockington, María Jorrín, and J. Robert Long, pp. 23–81. Vanderbilt University Publications in Anthropology No. 8, Nashville, TN.

Josserand, J. Kathryn, Maarten E. R. G. N. Jansen, and Angeles Romero. 1984. Mixtec Dialectology: Inferences from Linguistics and Ethnohistory. In *Essays in Otomanguean Culture History*, edited by J. Kathryn Josserand, Marcus Winter, and Nicholas Hopkins, pp. 141–63. Vanderbilt University Publications in Anthropology No. 31, Nashville, TN.

Joyce, Arthur A. 1991a. "Formative Period Occupation in the Lower Río Verde Valley, Oaxaca, Mexico: Interregional Interaction and Social Change." Ph.D. dissertation, Rutgers University.

Joyce, Arthur A. 1991b. Formative Period Social Change in the Lower Río Verde Valley, Oaxaca, Mexico. *Latin American Antiquity* 2:126–50.

Joyce, Arthur A. 1993a. Interregional Interaction and Social Development on the Oaxaca Coast. *Ancient Mesoamerica* 4(1):67–84.

Joyce, Arthur A. 1993b. *The Interregional Impact of State Formation in Oaxaca*. Report submitted on research activities performed as a 1992–3 Kalbfleisch Fellow, American Museum of Natural History, New York.

Joyce, Arthur A. 1994a. Monte Albán en el contexto pan-regional. In *Monte Albán: Estudios recientes*, edited by Marcus Winter, pp. 63–76. Contribución No. 2 del Proyecto Especial Monte Albán 1992–4, Oaxaca.

Joyce, Arthur A. 1994b. Late Formative Community Organization and Social Complexity on the Oaxaca Coast. *Journal of Field Archaeology* 21(2):147–68.

Joyce, Arthur A. (ed.). 1999. *El proyecto patrones de asentamiento del Río Verde*. Report submitted to the Consejo de Arqueología, Instituto Nacional de Antropología e Historia, Mexico City.

Joyce, Arthur A. 2000. The Founding of Monte Albán: Sacred Propositions and Social Practices. In *Agency in Archaeology*, edited by Macia-Anne Dobres and John Robb, pp. 71–91. Routledge Press, London.

Joyce, Arthur A. 2003. Imperialism in Pre-Aztec Mesoamerica: Monte Albán, Teotihuacan, and the Lower Río Verde Valley. In *Ancient Mesoamerica Warfare*, edited by M. Kathryn Brown and Travis M. Stanton, pp. 49–72. AltaMira Press, Walnut Creek, CA.

Joyce, Arthur A. 2004. Sacred Space and Social Relations in the Valley of Oaxaca. In *Mesoamerican Archaeology*, edited by Julia Hendon and Rosemary Joyce, pp. 192–216. Blackwell, Oxford.

Joyce, Arthur A. 2005. La arqueología del bajo Río Verde. *Acervos* 7(29):16–36.

Joyce, Arthur A. 2006. The Inhabitation of Río Viejo's Acropolis. In *Space and Spatial Analysis in Archaeology*, edited by Elizabeth C. Robertson, Jeffrey D.

Seibert, Deepika C. Fernández, and Marc U. Zeder, pp. 83–96. University of New Mexico Press and University of Calgary Press, Albuquerque and Calgary.

Joyce, Arthur A. 2008a. Domination, Negotiation, and Collapse: A History of Centralized Authority on the Oaxaca Coast. In *After Monte Albán: Transformation and Negotiation in Oaxaca, Mexico*, edited by Jeffrey Blomster, pp. 219–54. University Press of Colorado, Boulder, CO.

Joyce, Arthur A. 2008b. Los orígenes de sacrificio humano en el periodo Formativo en Mesoamérica. In *Ideología política y sociedad en el periodo Formativo: Ensayos en homenaje al doctor David C. Grove*, edited by Ann Cyphers and Kenneth G. Hirth, pp. 393–424. Universidad Nacional Autónoma de Mexico, Instituto Nacional de Antropología e Historia, Mexico City.

Joyce, Arthur A. 2009a. The Main Plaza of Monte Albán: A Life History of Place. In *The Archaeology of Meaningful Places*, edited by Brenda Bowser and María Nieves Zedeño, pp. 32–52. University of Utah Press, Salt Lake City.

Joyce, Arthur A. 2009b. Theorizing Urbanism in Ancient Mesoamerica. *Ancient Mesoamerica* 20(2), in press.

Joyce, Arthur A., Laura Arnaud Bustamante, and Marc N. Levine. 2001. Commoner Power: A Case Study from the Classic Period Collapse on the Oaxaca Coast. *Journal of Archaeological Method and Theory* 8(4):343–85.

Joyce, Arthur A., J. Michael Elam, Michael D. Glascock, Hector Neff, and Marcus Winter. 1995. Exchange Implications of Obsidian Source Analysis from the Lower Río Verde Valley, Oaxaca, Mexico. *Latin American Antiquity* 6(1):3–15.

Joyce, Arthur A., and Raymond G. Mueller. 1992. The Social Impact of Anthropogenic Landscape Modification in the Río Verde Drainage Basin, Oaxaca, Mexico. *Geoarchaeology* 7:503–26.

Joyce, Arthur A., and Raymond G. Mueller. 1997. Prehispanic Human Ecology of the Río Verde Drainage Basin. *World Archaeology* 29(1):75–94.

Joyce Arthur A., Hector Neff, Mary S. Thieme, Marcus Winter, J. Michael Elam, and Andrew Workinger. 2006. Ceramic Production and Exchange in Late/Terminal Formative Period Oaxaca. *Latin American Antiquity* 17(4):579–94.

Joyce, Arthur A., and Errin T. Weller. 2007. Commoner Rituals, Resistance, and the Classic-to-Postclassic Transition. In *Commoner Ritual and Ideology in Ancient Mesoamerica*, edited by Nancy Gonlin and Jon C. Lohse, pp. 141–82. University Press of Colorado, Boulder, CO.

Joyce, Arthur A., and Marcus Winter. 1996. Ideology, Power, and Urban Society in Prehispanic Oaxaca. *Current Anthropology* 37:33–86.

Joyce, Arthur A., Marcus Winter, and Raymond G. Mueller. 1998. *Arqueología de la costa de Oaxaca: Asentamientos del periodo formativo en el valle del Río Verde inferior*. Estudios de Antropología e Historia No. 40. Centro INAH Oaxaca. Oaxaca, Mexico.

Joyce, Arthur A., Andrew Workinger, Byron Hamann, Peter Kroefges, Maxine Oland, and Stacie King. 2004. Lord 8 Deer "Jaguar Claw" and the Land of the Sky: The Archaeology and History of Tututepec. *Latin American Antiquity* 15(3):273–97.

Joyce, Arthur A., Robert N. Zeitlin, Judith F. Zeitlin, and Javier Urcid. 2000. On Oaxaca Coast Archaeology: Setting the Record Straight. *Current Anthropology* 41(4):623–5.

Joyce, Rosemary A. 1999. Social Dimensions of Pre-Classic Burials. In *Social Patterns in Pre-Classic Mesoamerica*, edited by David C. Grove and Rosemary A. Joyce, pp. 15–47. Dumbarton Oaks, Washington, DC.

Joyce, Rosemary A. 2000. *Gender and Power in Prehispanic Mesoamerica*. University of Texas Press, Austin.

Joyce, Rosemary A. 2003. Making Something of Herself: Embodiment in Life and Death at Playa de los Muertos, Honduras. *Cambridge Archaeological Journal* 13(2):248–61.

Joyce, Rosemary A. 2004a. Embodied Subjectivity: Gender, Femininity, Masculinity, Sexuality. In *A Companion to Social Archaeology*, edited by Lynn M. Meskell and Robert W. Preucel, pp. 82–95. Blackwell, Oxford.

Joyce, Rosemary A. 2004b. Unintended Consequences? Monumentality as a Novel Experience in Formative Mesoamerica. *Journal of Archaeological Method and Theory* 11:5–29.

Junker, Laura Lee. 2008. The Impact of Captured Women on Cultural Transmission in Contact-Period Philippine Slave-Raiding Chiefdoms. In *Invisible Citizens: Captives and their Consequences*, edited by Catherine M. Cameron, pp. 110–37. University of Utah Press, Salt Lake City.

Kearney, Michael. 1972. *The Winds of Ixtepeji: World View and Society in a Zapotec Town*. Holt, Rinehart and Winston, New York.

Kertzer, David. 1988. *Ritual, Politics, and Power*. Yale University Press, New Haven.

King, Stacie M. 2003. "Social Practices and Social Organization in Ancient Coastal Oaxacan Households." Ph.D. dissertation, University of California, Berkeley.

King, Stacie M. 2006. The Making of Age in Ancient Coastal Oaxaca. In *The Social Experience of Childhood in Ancient Mesoamerica*, edited by Traci Ardren and Scott R. Hutson, pp. 103–32. University Press of Colorado, Boulder, CO.

King, Stacie M. 2008. Interregional Networks of the Oaxacan Early Postclassic: Connecting the Coast and Highlands. In *After Monte Albán: Transformation and Negotiation in Oaxaca, Mexico*, edited by Jeffrey Blomster, pp. 255–91. University Press of Colorado, Boulder, CO.

Kirkby, Michael. 1972. *The Physical Environment of the Nochixtlán Valley, Oaxaca*. Vanderbilt University Publications in Anthropology No. 2, Nashville, TN.

Knapp, A. Bernard (ed.). 1992. *Archaeology, Annales, and Ethnohistory*. Cambridge University Press, Cambridge.

Kohler, Timothy, and George Gumerman. 2000. *Dynamics in Human and Primate Societies: Agent-Based Modeling of Social and Spatial Processes*. Oxford University Press, New York.

Kolb, Charles C. 1987. *Marine Shell Trade and Classic Teotihuacan, Mexico*. BAR International Series 364. British Archaeological Reports, Oxford.

Kopytoff, Igor. 1986. The Cultural Biography of Things: Commoditization as Process. In *The Social Life of Things: Commodities in Cultural Perspective*, edited by Arjun Appadurai, pp. 64–91. Cambridge University Press, Cambridge.

Kowalewski, Stephen A., Andrew K. Balkansky, Laura R. Stiver Walsh et al. 2009. *Origins of the Ñuu: Archaeology in the Mixteca Alta, Mexico*. University Press of Colorado, Boulder, CO.
Kowalewski, Stephen A., Gary M. Feinman, Laura Finsten, and Richard E. Blanton. 1991. Pre-Hispanic Ballcourts from the Valley of Oaxaca, Mexico. In *The Mesoamerican Ballgame*, edited by Vernon. L. Scarborough and David R. Wilcox, pp. 25–44. University of Arizona Press, Tucson.
Kowalewski, Stephen A., Gary M. Feinman, Laura Finsten, Richard Blanton, and Linda M. Nicholas. 1989. *Monte Albán's Hinterland*, part 2: *Prehispanic Settlement Patterns in Tlacolula, Etla, and Ocotlán, the Valley of Oaxaca, Mexico*. Memoirs of the University of Michigan Museum of Anthropology No. 23, Ann Arbor.
Kroefges, Peter C. 2004. "Sociopolitical Organization in the Prehispanic Chontalpa de Oaxaca, Mexico. Ethnohistorical and Archaeological Perspectives." Ph.D. dissertation, University at Albany, State University of New York.
Latour, Bruno. 2005. *Reassembling the Social: An Introduction to Actor-Network-Theory*. Oxford University Press, Oxford.
Lawler, Andrew. 2005. The Oldest Ritual? *American Archaeology* (Summer 2005):39–43.
Lees, Susan H. 1973. *Sociopolitical Aspects of Canal Irrigation in the Valley of Oaxaca*. Prehistory and Human Ecology of the Valley of Oaxaca, vol. 1. Memoirs of the University of Michigan Museum of Anthropology No. 5, Ann Arbor.
Leonard, Robert D. 2001. Evolutionary Archaeology. In *Archaeological Theory Today*, edited by Ian Hodder, pp. 65–97. Polity Press, Cambridge.
Lesure, Richard G. 1997. Figurines and Social Identities in Early Sedentary Societies of Coastal Chiapas, Mexico. In *Women and Prehistory: North America and Mesoamerica*, edited by Cheryl Claassen and Rosemary Joyce, pp. 227–48. University of Pennsylvania Press, Philadelphia.
Lesure, Richard G. 2004. Shared Art Styles and Long-Distance Contact in Early Mesoamerica. In *Mesoamerican Archaeology*, edited by Julia Hendon and Rosemary Joyce, pp. 73–96. Blackwell, Oxford.
Levine, Marc N. 2002. "Ceramic Change and Continuity in the Lower Río Verde Region of Oaxaca Mexico: The Late Formative to Early Terminal Formative Transition." Unpublished MA thesis, University of Colorado at Boulder.
Levine, Marc N. 2007. "Linking Household and Polity at Late Postclassic Period Yucu Dzaa (Tututepec), a Mixtec Capital on the Coast of Oaxaca, Mexico." Ph.D. dissertation, University of Colorado at Boulder.
Levine, Marc N., and Arthur A. Joyce. 2007. Examining Postclassic Change in Obsidian. Paper presented at the 72nd Annual Meeting of the Society for American Archaeology, Austin, TX.
Levine, Marc N., Arthur A. Joyce, and Paul Goldberg. 2004. Earthen Mound Construction at Río Viejo on the Pacific Coast of Oaxaca, Mexico. Poster presented at the 69th Annual Meeting of the Society for American Archaeology, Montreal, Canada.

Lind, Michael D. 1979. *Postclassic and Early Colonial Mixtec Houses in the Nochixtlán Valley, Oaxaca*. Vanderbilt University Publications in Anthropology No. 23, Nashville, TN.

Lind, Michael D. 1991–2. Unos problemas con la cronología de Monte Albán y una nueva serie de nombres para las fases. *Notas Mesoamericanas* 13:177–92.

Lind, Michael D. 1994. Monte Albán y el Valle de Oaxaca durante la fase Xoo. In *Monte Albán: Estudios recientes*, edited by Marcus Winter, pp. 99–111. Contribución No. 2 del Proyecto Especial Monte Albán 1992–4, Oaxaca.

Lind, Michael D. 2000. Mixtec City-States and Mixtec City-State Culture. In *A Comparative Study of Thirty City-State Cultures: An Investigation Conducted by the Copenhagen Polis Centre*, edited by Mogens Herman Hansen, pp. 567–80. The Royal Danish Academy of Sciences and Letters, Copenhagen.

Lind, Michael D. 2001. Lambityeco and the Xoo Phase (ca. AD 600–800): The Elite Residences of Mound 195. In *Procesos de cambio y conceptualización del tiempo, memoria de la primera mesa redonda de Monte Albán*, edited by Nelly Robles García, pp. 111–28. Conaculta/Instituto Nacional de Antropología e Historia, Mexico City.

Lind, Michael D. 2008. The Classic to Postclassic at Lambityeco. In *After Monte Albán: Transformation and Negotiation in Oaxaca, Mexico*, edited by Jeffrey Blomster, pp. 171–92. University Press of Colorado, Boulder, CO.

Lind, Michael D., and Javier Urcid. 1983. Lords of Lambityeco and their Nearest Neighbors. *Notas Mesoamericanas* 9:78–111.

Long, Austin, Bruce F. Benz, J. Donahue, A. Jull, and L. Toolin. 1989. First Direct AMS Dates on Early Maize from Tehuacan, Mexico. *Radiocarbon* 31: 1,035–40.

Lorenzo, José Luis. 1958. Un Sitio precerámico en Yanhuitlán, Oaxaca. In *Instituto Nacional de Antropología e Historia, Dirección Prehistoria, Pub. 6*. INAH, Mexico City.

Love, Michael. 1993. Ceramic Chronology and Chronometric Dating: Stratigraphy and Seriation at La Blanca, Guatemala. *Ancient Mesoamerica* 4(1):17–29.

Love, Michael. 1999. Ideology, Material Culture, and Daily Practice in Pre-Classic Mesoamerica: A Pacific Coast Perspective. In *Social Patterns in Pre-Classic Mesoamerica*, edited by David C. Grove and Rosemary A. Joyce, pp. 127–54. Dumbarton Oaks Research Library and Collection, Washington, DC.

MacNeish, Richard S. 1971. Speculation About How and Why Food Production and Village Life Developed in the Tehuacán Valley, Mexico. *Archaeology* 24(4):307–15.

MacNeish, Richard S., Melvin L. Fowler, Angel García Cook, Frederick A. Peterson, Antoinette Nelken-Terner, and James A. Neely. 1972. *The Prehistory of the Tehuacan Valley*, vol. 5: *Excavations and Reconnaissance*. University of Texas Press, Austin.

Marcus, Joyce. 1976. The Iconography of Militarism at Monte Albán and Neighboring Sites in the Valley of Oaxaca. In *Origins of Religious Art and Iconography in Preclassic Mesoamerica*, edited by Henry Nicholson, pp. 125–39. UCLA Latin American Center Publications, Los Angeles.

Marcus, Joyce. 1983a. The Genetic Model and the Linguistic Divergence of the Otomangueans. In *The Cloud People: Divergent Evolution of the Zapotec and Mixtec Civilizations*, edited by Kent V. Flannery and Joyce Marcus, pp. 4–13. Academic Press, New York.

Marcus, Joyce. 1983b. Zapotec Religion. In *The Cloud People: Divergent Evolution of the Zapotec and Mixtec Civilizations*, edited by Kent V. Flannery and Joyce Marcus, pp. 345–51. Academic Press, New York.

Marcus, Joyce. 1983c. On the Nature of the Mesoamerican City. In *Prehispanic Settlement Patterns*, edited by Evon Vogt and Richard Leventhal, pp. 195–242. University of New Mexico Press, Albuquerque.

Marcus, Joyce. 1983d. The Conquest Slabs of Building J, Monte Albán. In *The Cloud People: Divergent Evolution of the Zapotec and Mixtec Civilizations*, edited by Kent V. Flannery and Joyce Marcus, pp. 106–8. Academic Press, New York.

Marcus, Joyce. 1983e. Teotihuacan Visitors on Monte Albán Monuments and Murals. In *The Cloud People: Divergent Evolution of the Zapotec and Mixtec Civilizations*, edited by Kent V. Flannery and Joyce Marcus, pp. 175–81. Academic Press, New York.

Marcus, Joyce. 1992. *Mesoamerican Writing Systems*. Princeton University Press, Princeton.

Marcus, Joyce. 1998. *Women's Ritual in Formative Oaxaca: Figurine-Making, Divination, Death and the Ancestors*. Memoirs of the University of Michigan Museum of Anthropology No. 33, Ann Arbor.

Marcus, Joyce, and Gary M. Feinman. 1998. Introduction. In *Archaic States*, edited by Gary M. Feinman and Joyce Marcus, pp. 3–13. School of American Research Press, Santa Fe.

Marcus, Joyce, and Kent Flannery. 1990. Science and Science Fiction in Postclassic Oaxaca: Or, 'yes Virginia, there is a Monte Albán IV.' In *Debating Oaxaca Archaeology*, edited by Joyce Marcus, pp. 191–205. Anthropological Papers, Museum of Anthropology, University of Michigan No. 84, Ann Arbor.

Marcus, Joyce, and Kent Flannery. 1994. Ancient Zapotec Ritual and Religion: An Application of the Direct Historical Approach. In *The Ancient Mind: Elements of Cognitive Archaeology*, edited by Colin Renfrew and Ezra B. W. Zubrow, pp. 55–74. Cambridge University Press, Cambridge.

Marcus, Joyce, and Kent Flannery. 1996. *Zapotec Civilization*. Thames and Hudson, London.

Marcus, Joyce, and Kent Flannery. 2004. The Coevolution of Ritual and Society: New 14C Dates from Ancient Mexico. *Proceedings of the National Academy of Sciences* 101(52):18,257–61.

Markens, Robert. 2004. "Ceramic Chronology in the Valley of Oaxaca, Mexico, During the Classic and Postclassic Periods and the Organization of Ceramic Production." Ph.D. dissertation, Brandeis University.

Markens, Robert. 2008. Advances in Defining the Classic-postclassic Portion of the Valley of Oaxaca Ceramic Chronology: Occurrence and Phyletic Seriation. In *After Monte Albán: Transformation and Negotiation in Oaxaca, Mexico*, edited by Jeffrey Blomster, pp. 49–94. University Press of Colorado, Boulder, CO.

Markens, Robert, Marcus Winter, and Cira Martínez López. 2008. Ethnohistory, Oral History, and Archaeology at Macuilxóchitl: Perspectives on the Postclassic Period (800–1521 CE) in the Valley of Oaxaca. In *After Monte Albán: Transformation and Negotiation in Oaxaca, Mexico*, edited by Jeffrey Blomster, pp. 193–215. University Press of Colorado, Boulder, CO.

Markgraf, Vera. 1993. Climatic History of Central and South America since 18,000 yr B.P.: Comparison of Pollen Records and Model Simulations. In *Glacial Climates Since the Last Glacial Maximum*, edited by H. E. J. Wright, J. E. Kutzbach, T. I. Webb, W. F. Ruddiman, F. A. Street-Perrott, and P. J. Bartlein, pp. 357–85. University of Minnesota Press, Minneapolis.

Markman, Charles W. 1981. *Prehispanic Settlement Dynamics from Central Oaxaca, Mexico: A View from the Miahuatlán Valley*. Vanderbilt University Publications in Anthropology No. 26, Nashville, TN.

Márquez Morfín, Lourdes, and Ernesto González Licón. 2001. Estratificación social, salud y nutrición en un grupo de pobladores. In *Procesos de cambio y conceptualización del tiempo, memoria de la primera mesa redonda de Monte Albán*, edited by Nelly Robles García, pp. 73–96. Conaculta/Instituto Nacional de Antropología e Historia, Mexico City.

Martin, Simon, and Nikolai Grube. 2000. *Chronicle of the Maya Kings and Queens*. Thames and Hudson, London.

Martínez Donjuán, Guadalupe. 1994. Los Olmecas en el Estado de Guerrero. In *Los Olmecas en Mesoamérica*, edited by John E. Clark, pp. 143–63. Citibank, Mexico City.

Martínez Gracida, Manuel. 1888. *El Rey Cosijoeza y su familia*. Reseña Histórica y Legendaria de los Ultimos Soberanos de Zaachila, Mexico.

Martínez López, Cira. 1994. La Cerámica de estilo Teotihuacano en Monte Albán. In *Monte Albán: Estudios recientes*, edited by Marcus Winter, pp. 25–54. Contribución No. 2 del Proyecto Especial Monte Albán 1992–4, Oaxaca.

Martínez López, Cira. 1998. "Contextos mortuorios en unidades habitacionales de Monte Albán, Oaxaca, de la época II temprana a la época V." Licenciatura thesis, Escuela Nacional de Antropología e Historia, Mexico City.

Martínez López, Cira. 2002. La residencia de la tumba 7 y su templo: Elementos arquitectónico-religiosos en Monte Albán. In *La Religión de los Binnigula'sa'*, edited by Victor de la Cruz and Marcus Winter, pp. 219–72. IEEPO-IOC, Oaxaca.

Martínez López, Cira, and Robert Markens. 2004. Análisis de la función político-económico del conjunto Plataforma Norte lado poniente de la Plaza Principal de Monte Albán. In *Estructuras políticas en el Oaxaca antiguo*, edited by Nelly M. Robles García, pp. 75–99. Instituto Nacional de Antropología e Historia, Mexico City.

Martínez López, Cira, Robert Markens, Marcus Winter, and Michael D. Lind. 2000. *Cerámica de la fase Xoo (Epoca Monte Albán IIIB-IV) del Valle de Oaxaca*. Contribución No. 8 del Proyecto Especial Monte Albán 1992–4, Oaxaca.

Martínez López, Cira, and Marcus Winter. 1994. *Figurillas y silbatos de cerámica de Monte Albán*. Contribución No. 5 del Proyecto Especial Monte Albán 1992–4, Oaxaca.

Martínez López, Cira, Marcus Winter, and Pedro Antonio Juárez. 1995. Entierros humanos del proyecto especial Monte Albán 1992–1994. In *Entierros Humanos de Monte Albán: Dos Estudios*, edited by Marcus Winter, pp. 79–247. Contribución No. 7 del Proyecto Especial Monte Albán 1992–4, Oaxaca.

McCafferty, Sharisse D., and Geoffrey G. McCafferty. 1998. Spinning and Weaving as Female Gender Identity in Post-Classic Mexico. In *Reader in Gender Archaeology*, edited by Kelley Hays-Gilpin and David S. Whitley, pp. 213–30. Routledge, London.

Meltzer, David J. 1983. The Antiquity of Man and the Development of American Archaeology. In *Advances in Archaeological Method and Theory*, vol. 6, edited by M. B. Schiffer, pp. 1–51. Academic Press, New York.

Meltzer, David J. 2004. Peopling of North America. In *The Quaternary Period in the United States: Developments in Quaternary Science*, edited by Alan R. Gillespie, Stephen C. Porter, and Brian F. Atwater, pp. 539–63. Elsevier, Amsterdam.

Meskell, Lynn. 2001. Archaeologies of Identity. In *Archaeological Theory Today*, edited by Ian Hodder, pp. 187–213. Polity Press, Cambridge.

Meskell, Lynn, and Rosemary Joyce. 2003. *Embodied Lives: Figuring Ancient Maya and Egyptian Experience*. Routledge, New York.

Middleton, William D., Gary M. Feinman, and G. Molina Villegas. 1998. Tomb Use and Reuse in Oaxaca, Mexico. *Ancient Mesoamerica* 9(2):297–308.

Middleton, William D., Gary M. Feinman, and Linda M. Nicholas. 2002. Domestic Faunal Assemblages from the Classic Period Valley of Oaxaca, Mexico: A Perspective on the Subsistence and Craft Economies. *Journal of Archaeological Science* 29:233–49.

Miller, Arthur G. 1995. *The Painted Tombs of Oaxaca, Mexico*. Cambridge University Press, Cambridge.

Miller, Daniel (ed.). 2005. *Materiality*. Duke University Press, Durham.

Miller, Daniel, and Christopher Tilley. 1984. Ideology, Power and Prehistory: An Introduction. In *Ideology, Power and Prehistory*, edited by Daniel Miller and Christopher Tilley, pp. 1–16. Cambridge University Press, Cambridge.

Monaghan, John. 1990. Sacrifice, Death, and the Origins of Agriculture in the Codex Vienna. *American Antiquity* 55:559–69.

Monaghan, John. 1994. Sacrifice and Power in Mixtec Kingdoms. Paper presented at the 59th Annual Meeting of the Society for American Archaeology, Anaheim, CA.

Monaghan, John. 1995. *The Covenants with Earth and Rain*. University of Oklahoma Press, Norman.

Montague, Antonia, and Marcus Winter. 1991. Unidades habitacionales en la Plaza 3. In *Exploraciones arqueológicas en Cerro de las Minas, Mixteca Baja, Oaxaca. Temporadas 1987–1990, informe preliminar*, edited by Marcus Winter, pp. 56–82. Report on file Centro INAH Oaxaca, Instituto Nacional de Antropología e Historia, Oaxaca.

Moore, Henrietta L. 1994. *A Passion for Difference: Essays in Anthropology and Gender*. Indiana University Press, Bloomington, IN.

Moser, Christopher L. 1977. *Nuiñe Writing and Iconography of the Mixteca Baja*. Vanderbilt University Publications in Anthropology No. 19, Nashville, TN.

Mueller, Raymond G., and Arthur A. Joyce. 2007. Environmental Degradation and Erosion Related to Demographic Changes: Nochixtlán Valley, Oaxaca, Mexico. Paper presented at the 72nd Annual Meeting of the Society for American Archaeology, Austin, TX.

Nader, Laura. 1969. The Zapotec of Oaxaca. In *Handbook of Middle American Indians*, vol. 7: *Ethnology*, part 1, edited by Robert Wauchope and Evon Z. Vogt, pp. 329–59. University of Texas Press, Austin.

Nicholas, Linda M. 1989. Land Use in Prehispanic Oaxaca. In *Monte Albán's Hinterland*, part 2: *Prehispanic Settlement Patterns in Tlacolula, Etla, and Ocotlán, the Valley of Oaxaca, Mexico*, edited by Stephen A. Kowalewski, Gary M. Feinman, Laura Finsten, Richard Blanton, and Linda M. Nicholas, pp. 449–505. Memoirs of the University of Michigan Museum of Anthropology No. 23, Ann Arbor.

O'Brien, Michael J., and Dennis E. Lewarch. 1992. Regional Analysis of the Zapotec Empire, Valley of Oaxaca, México. *World Archaeology* 23(3):264–82.

O'Brien, Michael J., Roger D. Mason, Dennis E. Lewarch, and James A. Neely. 1982. *A Late Formative Irrigation Settlement below Monte Albán: Survey and Excavation on the Xoxocotlán Piedmont, Oaxaca, Mexico*. Institute of Latin American Studies, University of Texas Press, Austin.

Orr, Heather S. 1997. "Power Games in the Late Formative Valley of Oaxaca: The Ballplayer Sculptures at Dainzú." Ph.D. dissertation, University of Texas.

Orr, Heather S. 2001. Procession Rituals and Shrine Sites: The Politics of Sacred Space in the Late Formative Valley of Oaxaca. In *Landscape and Power in Ancient Mesoamerica*, edited by Rex Koontz, Kathryn Reese-Taylor, and Annabeth Headrick, pp. 55–79. Westview Press, Boulder.

Ortner, Sherry B. 1984. Theory in Anthropology Since the Sixties. *Comparative Studies in Society and History* 26:126–66.

Ortner, Sherry B. 1996. Making Gender: Toward a Feminist, Minority, Postcolonial, Subaltern, etc., Theory of Practice. In *Making Gender: The Politics and Erotics of Culture*, edited by Sherry B. Ortner, pp. 1–20. Beacon Press, Boston.

Oudijk, Michel R. 2002. The Zapotec City-State. In *A Comparative Study of Six City-State Cultures*, edited by Mogens Herman Hansen, pp. 73–90. The Royal Academy of Sciences and Letters, Copenhagen.

Oudijk, Michel R. 2008. The Postclassic Period in the Valley of Oaxaca: The Archaeological and Ethnohistorical Records. In *After Monte Albán: Transformation and Negotiation in Oaxaca, Mexico*, edited by Jeffrey Blomster, pp. 95–118. University Press of Colorado, Boulder, CO.

Paddock, John (ed.). 1966a. *Ancient Oaxaca: Discoveries in Mexican Archeology and History*. Stanford University Press, Stanford.

Paddock, John. 1966b. Mixtec Ethnohistory and Monte Alban V. In *Ancient Oaxaca: Discoveries in Mexican Archeology and History*, edited by John Paddock, pp. 367–85. Stanford University Press, Stanford.

Paddock, John. 1968. Una tumba en Ñuyoo, Huajuapan de León, Oaxaca. *Boletín del Instituto Nacional de Antropología e Historia*, Epoca 1, 33:51–4.
Paddock, John. 1983. Lambityeco. In *The Cloud People: Divergent Evolution of the Zapotec and Mixtec Civilizations*, edited by Kent V. Flannery and Joyce Marcus, pp. 197–204. Academic Press, New York.
Pareyón, Eduardo. 1960. Exploraciones arqueológicas en la Ciudad Vieja de Quiotepec, Oaxaca. *Revista Mexicana de Estudios Antropológicos* 16:97–104.
Parry, William J. 1987. *Chipped Stone Tools in Formative Oaxaca, Mexico: Their Procurement, Production, and Use*. Memoirs of the University of Michigan Museum of Anthropology No. 20, Ann Arbor.
Parsons, Elsie Clews. 1936. *Mitla: Town of the Souls*. University of Chicago Press, Chicago.
Pauketat, Timothy R. 2001. Practice and History in Archaeology. *Anthropological Theory* 1(1):73–98.
Pauketat, Timothy R. 2007. *Chiefdoms and Other Archaeological Delusions*. AltaMira Press, Lanham.
Pauketat, Timothy R. 2009. *Cahokia: America's Great City on the Mississippi*. Penguin Press, New York.
Peeler, Damon E., and Marcus Winter. 1992. Mesoamerican Site Orientations and their Relationship to the 260-day Ritual Period. *Notas Mesoamericanas* 14:37–62.
Pérez Rodríguez, Verónica. 2006. States and Households: The Social Organization of Terrace Agriculture in Postclassic Mixteca Alta, Oaxaca, Mexico. *Latin American Antiquity* 17(1):3–22.
Peterson, David Andrew, and Thomas B. Mac Dougall. 1974. *Guiengola: A Fortified Site in the Isthmus of Tehuantepec*. Vanderbilt University Publications in Anthropology No. 10, Nashville, TN.
Pires-Ferreira, Jane Wheeler. 1975. *Formative Mesoamerican Exchange Networks with Special Reference to the Valley of Oaxaca*. Prehistory and Human Ecology of the Valley of Oaxaca, vol. 3. Memoirs of the University of Michigan Museum of Anthropology No. 7, Ann Arbor.
Pires-Ferreira, Jane Wheeler. 1976. Shell and Iron-Ore Mirror Exchange in Formative Mesoamerica, with Comments on other Commodities. In *The Early Mesoamerican Village*, edited by Kent V. Flannery, pp. 311–26. Academic Press, New York.
Plunket, Patricia S. 1983. "An Intensive Survey in the Yucuita Sector of the Nochixtlán Valley, Oaxaca, México." Ph.D. dissertation, Tulane University.
Pohl, John M. D. 1994. *The Politics of Symbolism in the Mixtec Codices*. Vanderbilt University Publications in Anthropology No. 46, Nashville, TN.
Pohl, John M. D. 1999. The Lintel Paintings of Mitla and the Function of the Mitla Palaces. In *Mesoamerican Architecture as a Cultural Symbol*, edited by Jeff Karl Kowalski, pp. 176–97. Oxford University Press, New York.
Pohl, John M. D. 2002. Los dinteles pintados de Mitla. *Arqueología Mexicana* 10(55):64–7.

Pohl, John M. D. 2003. Royal Marriage and Confederacy Building Among the Eastern Nahuas, Mixtecs, and Zapotecs. In *The Postclassic Mesoamerican World*, edited by Michael E. Smith and Frances F. Berdan, pp. 243–8. University of Utah Press, Salt Lake City.

Pohl, John M. D. 2005. The Arroyo Group Lintel Painting at Mitla, Oaxaca. In *Painted Books and Indigenous Knowledge in Mesoamerica: Manuscript Studies in Honor of Mary Elizabeth Smith*, edited by Elizabeth H. Boone, pp. 109–27. Middle American Research Institute Publication No. 69, Tulane University Press, New Orleans.

Pohl, John M. D., John Monaghan, and Laura Stiver. 1997. Religion, Economy, and Factionalism in Mixtec Boundary Zones. In *Códices y Documentos sobre México: Segundo Simposio*, vol. 1, edited by Salvador Rueda Smithers, Constanza Vega Sosa, and Rodrigo Martínez Baracas, pp. 205–32. Instituto Nacional de Antropología e Historia y Consejo Nacional para la Cultura y las Artes, Mexico.

Redfield, Robert. 1941. *The Folk Culture of Yucatan*. University of Chicago Press, Chicago.

Redmond, Elsa M. 1983. *A Fuego y Sangre: Early Zapotec Imperialism in the Cuicatlán Cañada, Oaxaca*. Memoirs of the University of Michigan Museum of Anthropology No. 16, Ann Arbor.

Redmond, Elsa M., and Charles S. Spencer. 2006. From Raiding to Conquest: Warfare Strategies and Early State Development in Oaxaca, Mexico. In *The Archaeology of Warfare: Prehistories of Raiding and Conquest*, edited by Elizabeth N. Arkush and Mark W. Allen, pp. 336–93. University Press of Florida, Gainesville.

Redmond, Elsa M., and Charles S. Spencer. 2008. Rituals of Sanctification and the Development of Standardized Temples in Oaxaca, Mexico. *Cambridge Archaeological Journal* 18(2):239–66.

Renfrew, Colin, and Ezra B. W. Zubrow (eds.). 1994. *The Ancient Mind: Elements of Cognitive Archaeology*. Cambridge University Press, Cambridge.

Reyes, Fr. Antonio de los. [1593] 1976. *Arte en lengua mixteca*. Vanderbilt University Publications in Anthropology No. 14, Nashville, TN.

Ringle, William M., Tomás Gallareta Negrón, and George J. Bey III. 1998. The Return of Quetzalcoatl: Evidence for the Spread of a World Religion during the Epiclassic Period. *Ancient Mesoamerica* 9(2):183–232.

Rivera Guzmán, Ángel Iván. 1999. "El patrón de asentamiento en la Mixteca Baja de Oaxaca: Análisis del área de Tequixtepec-Chazumba." Unpublished Licenciatura thesis, Escuela Nacional de Antropología e Historia, Mexico City.

Rivera Guzmán, Ángel Iván. 2000. La iconografía del poder durante el Clásico en la Mixteca Baja de Oaxaca: Evidencia iconográfica y arqueológica. *Cuadernos del Sur* 15:5–36.

Rivera Guzmán, Ángel Iván. 2007. Una estela con icongrafía Teotihuacana en la costa de Oaxaca. Paper presented at the 72nd Annual Meeting of the Society for American Archaeology, Austin, TX.

Robb, John E. 1999. *Material Symbols: Culture and Economy in Prehistory*. Occasional Paper 26, Center for Archaeological Investigations, Southern Illinois University, Carbondale.
Robin, Cynthia. 2002. Outside of Houses. *Journal of Social Archaeology* 2(2): 245–67.
Robles García, Nelly M. 1986. Arquitectura de las unidades domésticas en la Mixteca Alta. *Cuadernos de Arquitectura Mesoamericana* 7:27–36.
Robles García, Nelly M. 1988. *Las unidades domésticas del Preclásico Superior en la Mixteca Alta*. BAR International Series 407. British Archaeological Reports, Oxford.
Rodríguez, Adolfo C., Gabriel Narváez C., Antonio Hernández M. et al. 1989. *Caracterización de la producción agrícola de la región costa de Oaxaca*. Universidad Autónoma Chapingo, Pinotepa Nacional.
Rodrigo Alvarez, Luis. 1983. *Geografía general del estado de Oaxaca*. Convocado por la Dirección General de Cultura y Recreación del Gobierno del Estado y la Sociedad Mexicana de Geografía y Estadística, Oaxaca.
Rodríguez Cano, Laura. 1999. El calendario de 260 días en las inscripciones de estilo ñuiñe. *Cuadernos del Sur* 5(14):15–34.
Romero Frizzi, María de los Angeles. 1994. Indigenous Mentality and Spanish Power: The Conquest in Oaxaca. In *Caciques and their People: A Volume in Honor of Ronald Spores*, edited by Joyce Marcus and Judith Francis Zeitlin, pp. 227–44. Anthropological Papers, Museum of Anthropology, University of Michigan No. 89, Ann Arbor.
Sahlins, Marshall. 1981. *Historical Metaphors and Mythical Realities*. University of Michigan Press, Ann Arbor.
Sahlins, Marshall. 1985. *Islands of History*. University of Chicago Press, Chicago.
Sahlins, Marshall. 1991. The Return of the Event, Again; with Reflections on the Beginnings of the Great Fijian War of 1843 to 1855 between the Kingdoms of Bau and Rewa. In *Clio in Oceania*, edited by Aletta Biersack, pp. 37–100. Smithsonian Institution Press, Washington, DC.
Sahlins, Marshall. 1996. The Sadness of Sweetness: The Native Anthropology of Western Cosmology. *Current Anthropology* 37(3):395–428.
Santley, Robert S. 1983. Obsidian Trade and Teotihuacan Influence in Mesoamerica. In *Highland-Lowland Interaction in Mesoamerica: Interdisciplinary Approaches*, edited by Arthur G. Miller, pp. 69–124. Dumbarton Oaks Research Library and Collection, Washington, DC.
Saul, Frank P., and Julie Mather Saul. 2001. Cosmetic Alterations of the Face and Body. In *Archaeology of Ancient Mexico and Central America: An Encyclopedia*, edited by Susan Toby Evans and David L. Webster, pp. 180–2. Garland Publishing, New York.
Schele, Linda, and David A. Freidel. 1990. *A Forest of Kings: The Untold Story of the Ancient Maya*. William Morrow, New York.
Schele, Linda, and Julia Guernsey-Kappelman. 2001. What the Heck's Coatépec? The Formative Roots of an Enduring Mythology. In *Landscape and Power in*

Ancient Mesoamerica, edited by Rex Koontz, Kathryn Reese-Taylor, and Annabeth Headrick, pp. 29–53. Westview Press, Boulder.

Schele, Linda, and Mary Ellen Miller. 1986. *The Blood of Kings, Dynasty and Ritual in Maya Art*. Kimbell Art Museum, Fort Worth.

Schiffer, Michael B. (ed.). 2000. *Social Theory in Archaeology*. University of Utah Press, Salt Lake City.

Schreiber, Katharina J. 1987. Conquest and Consolidation: A Comparison of the Wari and Inka Occupations of a Highland Peruvian Valley. *American Antiquity* 52(2):266–84.

Schreiber, Katharina J. 1992. *Wari Imperialism in Middle Horizon Peru*. Anthropological Papers, Museum of Anthropology, University of Michigan No. 87, Ann Arbor.

Schrire, Carmel. 1984. Wild Surmises on Savage Thoughts. In *Past and Present in Hunter Gatherer Studies*, edited by Carmel Schrire, pp. 1–25. Academic Press, Orlando.

Scott, James C. 1976. *The Moral Economy of the Peasant: Subsistence and Rebellion in Southeast Asia*. Yale University Press, New Haven.

Scott, James C. 1985. *Weapons of the Weak: Everyday forms of Peasant Resistance*. Yale University Press, New Haven.

Scott, James C. 1990. *Domination and the Arts of Resistance*. Yale University Press, New Haven.

Scott, John F. 1978a. *The Danzantes of Monte Albán*, part 1: *Text*. Studies in Pre-Columbian Art and Archaeology No. 19, Dumbarton Oaks, Washington, DC.

Scott, John F. 1978b. *The Danzantes of Monte Albán*, part 2: *Catalogue*. Studies in Pre-Columbian Art and Archaeology No. 19, Dumbarton Oaks, Washington, DC.

Seler, Eduard. 1904. The Wall Paintings of Mitla, a Mexican Picture Writing in Fresco. In *Mexican and Central American Antiquities, Calendar Systems, and History*, 24 papers by Seler, Forstemann, Schellhas, Sapper, Dieseldorff, translated from the German under supervision of Charles P. Bowditch, *Bureau of American Ethnology Bulletin* 28:247–324. US Government Printing Office, Washington, DC.

Seler, Eduard. 1908. Das Dorfbuch von Santiago Guevea. *Gesammelte Abhandlungen* 3:157–93.

Sellen, Adam T. 2002. Storm-God Impersonators from Ancient Oaxaca. *Ancient Mesoamerica* 13(1):2–19.

Service, Elman R. 1962. *Primitive Social Organization: An Evolutionary Perspective*. Random House, New York.

Sewell, William H. 1992. A Theory of Structure: Duality, Agency, and Transformation. *American Journal of Sociology* 98:1–29.

Shackel, Paul. 2000. Craft to Wage Labor: Agency and Resistance in America. In *Agency in Archaeology*, edited by Marcia-Anne Dobres and John E. Robb, pp. 232–46. Routledge, London.

Shanks, Michael, and Christopher Tilley. 1982. Ideology, Symbolic Power and Ritual Communication: A Reinterpretation of Neolithic Mortuary Practices.

In *Symbolic and Structural Archaeology*, edited by Ian Hodder, pp. 129–54. Cambridge University Press, Cambridge.
Shanks, Michael, and Christopher Tilley. 1992. *Re-Constructing Archaeology: Theory and Practice*, 2nd edition. Routledge, London.
Sharer, Robert J., and David C. Grove (eds.). 1989. *Regional Perspectives on the Olmec*. Cambridge University Press, Cambridge.
Sherman, R. Jason. 2005. "Settlement Heterogeneity in the Zapotec State: A View from Yaasuchi, Oaxaca, Mexico." Ph.D. dissertation, University of Michigan.
Smith, Adam T. 2003. *The Political Landscape*. University of California Press, Berkeley.
Smith, Bruce D. 1998. *The Emergence of Agriculture*. Scientific American Library, New York.
Smith, C. Earle, Jr. 1978. *The Vegetational History of the Oaxaca Valley*. Prehistory and Human Ecology of the Valley of Oaxaca, vol. 5, part 1. Memoirs of the University of Michigan Museum of Anthropology No. 10, Ann Arbor.
Smith, Mary Elizabeth. 1973. *Picture Writing from Ancient Southern Mexico: Mixtec Place Signs and Maps*, University of Oklahoma Press, Norman.
Smith, Mary Elizabeth, and Ross Parmenter (eds.). 1991. *Codex Tulane*. Middle American Research Institute, Tulane University, New Orleans.
Smith, Michael E. 1987. Household Possessions and Wealth in Agrarian States: Implications for Archaeology. *Journal of Anthropological Archaeology* 6:297–335.
Smith, Michael E. 2000. Aztec City-States. In *A Comparative Study of Thirty City-State Cultures*, edited by Mogens Herman Hansen, pp. 581–95. Royal Danish Academy of Sciences and Letters, Copenhagen.
Smith, Michael E. 2005. City Size in Late Postclassic Mesoamerica. *Journal of Urban History* 31:403–34.
Smith, Michael E. 2008. *Aztec City-State Capitals*. University Press of Florida, Gainesville.
Smith, Michael E., and Lisa Montiel. 2001. The Archaeological Study of Empires and Imperialism in Prehispanic Central Mexico. *Journal of Anthropological Archaeology* 20(3):245–84.
Smith, Monica L. 2003. Introduction: The Social Construction of Ancient Cities. In *The Social Construction of Ancient Cities*, edited by Monica L. Smith, pp. 1–36. Smithsonian Books, Washington and London.
Sorensen, Jerrel H., Kenneth G. Hirth, and Stephen. M. Ferguson. 1989. The Contents of Seven Obsidian Workshops around Xochicalco, Morelos. In *La Obsidiana en Mesoamérica*, edited by Margarita Gaxiola and John E. Clark, pp. 269–76. Colección Científica 176. Serie Arqueología. Instituto Nacional de Antropología e Historia, Mexico City.
Spaulding, Albert C. 1985. Fifty Years of Theory. *American Antiquity* 50(2): 301–8.
Spencer, Charles S. 1982. *The Cuicatlán Cañada and Monte Albán*. Academic Press: New York.

Spencer, Charles S. 1990. On the Tempo and Mode of State Formation: Neoevolutionism Reconsidered. *Journal of Anthropological Archaeology* 9:1–30.
Spencer, Charles S. 2003. War and Early State Formation in Oaxaca, Mexico. *Proceedings of the National Academy of Sciences* 100(20):11,185–11,187.
Spencer, Charles S., and Elsa M. Redmond. 2001. Multilevel Selection and Political Evolution in the Valley of Oaxaca, 500–100 B.C. *Journal of Anthropological Archaeology* 20:195–229.
Spencer, Charles S., and Elsa M. Redmond. 2004. A Late Monte Albán I Phase (300–100 BC) Palace in the Valley of Oaxaca. *Latin American Antiquity* 15(4):441–55.
Spores, Ronald. 1969. Settlement, Farming Technology, and Environment in the Nochixtlán Valley. *Science* 166:557–69.
Spores, Ronald. 1972. *An Archaeological Settlement Survey of the Nochixtlán Valley, Oaxaca*. Vanderbilt University Publications in Anthropology No. 1, Nashville, TN.
Spores, Ronald. 1974. *Stratigraphic Excavations in the Nochixtlán Valley, Oaxaca*. Vanderbilt University Publications in Anthropology No. 11, Nashville, TN.
Spores, Ronald. 1983. Origins of the Village in the Mixteca (Early Cruz Phase). In *The Cloud People: Divergent Evolution of the Mixtec and Zapotec Civilizations*, edited by Kent V. Flannery and Joyce Marcus, p. 46. Academic Press, New York.
Spores, Ronald. 1984. *The Mixtecs in Ancient and Colonial Times*. University of Oklahoma Press, Norman.
Spores, Ronald. 1993. Tututepec: A Postclassic-Period Mixtec Conquest State. *Ancient Mesoamerica* 4(1):167–74.
Spores, Ronald. 2005. Informe sobre las excavaciones en Yucundaa, Pueblo Viejo de Teposcolula. *Acervos* 7(29):70–4.
Spores, Ronald, and Nelly Robles García. 2007. A Prehispanic (Postclassic) Capital Center in Colonial Transition: Excavations at Yucundaa Pueblo Viejo de Teposcolula, Oaxaca Mexico. *Latin American Antiquity* 18(3):333–53.
Stahl, Ann B. 1993. Concepts of Time and Approaches to Analogical Reasoning in Historical Perspective. *American Antiquity* 58(2):235–60.
Stark, Barbara L. 1981. The Rise of Sedentary Life. In *Supplement to the Handbook of Middle American Indians*, vol. 1: *Archaeology*, edited by Jeremy A. Sabloff, pp. 345–72. University of Texas Press, Austin.
Stark, Barbara L. 1990. The Gulf Coast and the Central Highlands of Mexico: Alternative Models for Interaction. *Research in Economic Anthropology* 12:243–85.
Starr, Frederick. 1908. *In Indian Mexico: A Narrative of Travel and Labor*. Forbes and Co., Chicago.
Stockett, Miranda K., and Pamela L. Geller. 2006. Introduction: Feminist Anthropology: Perspectives on Our Past, Present, and Future. In *Feminist Anthropology: Past, Present, and Future*, edited by Pamela L. Geller and Miranda K. Stockett, pp. 1–19. University of Pennsylvania Press, Philadelphia.

Stoler, Ann. 1995. *Race and the Education of Desire: Foucault's History of Sexuality and the Colonial Order of Things*. Duke University Press, Durham.
Storey, Glenn R. (ed.). 2006. *Urbanism in the Preindustrial World: Cross-Cultural Approaches*. University of Alabama Press, Tuscaloosa.
Stuart, David. 2000. The Arrival of Strangers: Teotihuacan and Tollan in Classic Maya History. In *Mesoamerica's Classic Heritage: From Teotihuacan to the Aztecs*, edited by David Carrasco, Lindsay Jones, and Scott Sessions, pp. 465–524. University Press of Colorado, Niwot.
Sugiyama, Saburo. 1993. Worldview Materialized in Teotihuacán, Mexico. *Latin American Antiquity* 4(2):103–29.
Tamayo, Jorge L. 1964. The Hydrography of Middle America. In *Handbook of Middle American Indians*, vol. 1: *Natural Environment and Early Cultures*, edited by Robert C. West, pp. 84–121. University of Texas Press, Austin.
Taube, Karl. 1992. The Iconography of Mirrors at Teotihuacan. In *Art, Ideology, and the City of Teotihuacan: A Symposium at Dumbarton Oaks, 8th and 9th October 1988*, edited by Janet Berlo, pp. 169–204. Dumbarton Oaks, Washington, DC.
Taube, Karl. 1996. The Rainmakers: The Olmec and Their Contribution to Mesoamerican Belief and Ritual. In *The Olmec World: Ritual and Rulership*, edited by Jill Guthrie, pp. 83–103. Art Museum, Princeton University, Princeton, NJ.
Taube, Karl. 2000. Lightning Celts and Corn Symbolism: The Formative Olmec and the Development of Maize Symbolism in Mesoamerica and the American Southwest. In *Olmec Art and Archaeology in Mesoamerica*, edited by John E. Clark and Mary E. Pye, pp. 297–337. National Gallery of Art, Yale University Press, New Haven.
Tax, Sol. 1937. The Municipios of the Midwestern Highlands of Guatemala. *American Anthropologist* 39:423–44.
Terraciano, Kevin. 2001. *The Mixtecs of Colonial Oaxaca: Ñudzahui History, Sixteenth through Eighteenth Centuries*. Stanford University Press, Stanford.
Thieme, Mary S. 2001. Continuity of Ceramic Production: Examination and Analysis of Clay Materials from Santa María Atzompa. In *Procesos de cambio y conceptualización del tiempo, memoria de la primera mesa redonda de Monte Albán*, edited by Nelly M. Robles García, pp. 339–49. Instituto Nacional de Antropología e Historia, Mexico City.
Tilley, Chris, Webb Keane, Susanne Kuchler, Mike Rowlands, and Patricia Spyer (eds.). 2006. *Handbook of Material Culture*. Sage, London.
Tolstoy, Paul, and Louise I. Paradis. 1970. Early and Middle Pre-Classic Culture in the Basin of Mexico. *Science* 167:344–51.
Trigger, Bruce. 2003. *Understanding Early Civilizations: A Comparative Study*. Cambridge University Press, Cambridge.
Troike, Nancy. 1974. "The Codex Colombino-Becker." Unpublished Ph.D. dissertation, University of London.
Urcid, Javier. 1993. The Pacific Coast of Oaxaca and Guerrero: The Westernmost Extent of Zapotec Script. *Ancient Mesoamerica* 4:141–65.

Urcid, Javier. 1994a. Un sistema de nomenclatura para los monolitos grabados y los materiales con inscripciones de Monte Albán. In *Escritura Zapoteca prehispánica*, edited by Marcus Winter, pp. 53–79. Contribución No. 4 del Proyecto Especial Monte Albán 1992–4, Oaxaca.

Urcid, Javier. 1994b. Mound J at Monte Albán and Zapotec Political Geography during Period II (200 BC–AD 200). Paper presented at the 59th Annual Meeting of the Society for American Archaeology, Anaheim, CA.

Urcid, Javier. 1999. La lápida grabada de Noriega: Tres rituales en la vida de un noble Zapoteca. *Indiana* 16:211–64.

Urcid, Javier. 2001. *Zapotec Hieroglyphic Writing*. Studies in Pre-Columbian Art and Archaeology No. 34, Dumbarton Oaks, Washington, DC.

Urcid, Javier. 2002. La faz oculta de una misteriosa máscara de piedra. Memoria de la Segunda Mesa Redonda de Monte Albán. In *Sociedad y Patrimonio Arqueológico en el Valle de Oaxaca*, edited by Nelly M. Robles García, 213–48. Conaculta/Instituto Nacional de Antropología e Historia, Oaxaca.

Urcid, Javier. 2005. *The Zapotec Scribal Tradition: Knowledge, Memory, and Society in Ancient Oaxaca*. Foundation for the Advancement of Mesoamerican Studies Inc., Coral Gables, FL (www.famsi.org/zapotecwriting/).

Urcid, Javier. 2008. The Written Surface as a Cultural Code: A Comparative Perspective of Scribal Traditions from Southwestern Mesoamerica. Paper presented at the Symposium *Scripts and Notational Systems in Pre-Columbian America*, Dumbarton Oaks, Washington D.C.

Urcid, Javier. n.d. Huamelulpan: Prácticas Escriturales y Escultóricas a Través de su Historia. Manuscript in possession of the author.

Urcid, Javier, and Arthur A. Joyce. 2001. Carved Monuments and Calendrical Names: The Rulers of Río Viejo, Oaxaca. *Ancient Mesoamerica* 12(2):199–216.

Urcid, Javier, and Marcus Winter. 2003. Nuevas variantes glíficas zapotecas. *Mexicon* 25(5):123–8.

Urcid, Javier, Marcus Winter, and Raul Matadamas. 1994. Nuevos monumentos grabados en Monte Albán, Oaxaca. In *Escritura Zapoteca prehispánica*, edited by Marcus Winter, pp. 2–52. Contribución No. 4 del Proyecto Especial Monte Albán 1992–4, Oaxaca.

VanPool, Christine S., and Todd L. VanPool. 1999. The scientific nature of Postprocessualism. *American Antiquity* 64(1):33–53.

Von Winning, Hasso. 1983. The Hidden Low Reliefs at Monte Albán. *Masterkey* 57(2):57–62.

Voorhies, Barbara (ed.). 2004. *Coastal Collectors in the Holocene: The Chantuto People of Southwest Mexico*. University Press of Florida, Gainesville.

Wallrath, Matthew. 1967. *Excavations in the Tehuantepec Region, México*. Transactions of the American Philosophical Society, vol. 57, part 2, Philadelphia.

Watson, Patty Jo, and Mary C. Kennedy. 1991. The Development of Horticulture in the Eastern Woodlands of North America: Women's Role. In *Engendering Archaeology: Women and Prehistory*, edited by Joan M. Gero and Margaret W. Conkey, pp. 255–75. Basil Blackwell, Oxford.

Watson, Patty Jo, Steven A. LeBlanc, and Charles L. Redman. 1971. *Explanation in Archaeology: An Explicitly Scientific Approach*. Columbia University Press, New York.

Watson, Patty Jo, Steven A. LeBlanc, and Charles L. Redman. 1984. *Archaeological Explanation: The Scientific Method in Archaeology*, 2nd edition. Columbia University Press, New York.

Webster, David L. 2002. *The Fall of the Maya: Solving the Mystery of the Maya Collapse*. Thames and Hudson, London.

Whalen, Michael E. 1981. *Excavations at Santo Domingo Tomaltepec: Evolution of a Formative Community in the Valley of Oaxaca, Mexico*. Prehistory and Human Ecology of the Valley of Oaxaca, vol. 6. Memoirs of the University of Michigan Museum of Anthropology No. 12, Ann Arbor.

Whalen, Michael E. 1988. Small Community Organization during the Late Formative Period in Oaxaca. *Journal of Field Archaeology* 15:291–306.

White, Christine D., Michael W. Spence, Fred J. Longstaffe, and Kimberly R. Law. 2004. Demography and Ethnic Continuity in the Tlailotlacan Enclave of Teotihuacan: The Evidence from Stable Oxygen Isotopes. *Journal of Anthropological Archaeology* 23(4):385–403.

Whitecotton, Joseph W. 1977. *The Zapotecs: Princes, Priests, and Peasants*. University of Oklahoma Press, Norman.

Whitecotton, Joseph W. 1990. *Elite Ethnohistory: Pictorial Genealogies from Eastern Oaxaca*. Vanderbilt University Publications in Anthropology No. 39, Nashville, TN.

Whittaker, Gordon. 1980. "The Hieroglyphics of Monte Albán." Ph.D. dissertation, Yale University.

Willey, Gordon R. and Jeremy A. Sabloff. 1993. *A History of American Archaeology*, 3rd edition. Freeman, New York.

Winter, Marcus. 1972. "Tierras Largas: A Formative Community in the Valley of Oaxaca, Mexico." Unpublished Ph.D. dissertation, University of Arizona, Tucson.

Winter, Marcus. 1974. Residential Patterns at Monte Albán, Oaxaca, Mexico. *Science* 186(4,168):981–7.

Winter, Marcus. 1976. The Archaeological Household Cluster in the Valley of Oaxaca. In *The Early Mesoamerican Village*, edited by Kent V. Flannery, pp. 25–32. Academic Press, New York.

Winter, Marcus. 1982. *Guía zona arqueológica de Yucuita*. Centro INAH Oaxaca, Oaxaca, Mexico.

Winter, Marcus. 1984. Exchange in Formative Highland Oaxaca. In *Trade and Exchange in Early Mesoamerica*, edited by Kenneth G. Hirth, pp. 179–214. University of New Mexico Press, Albuquerque.

Winter, Marcus. 1986. Unidades habitacionales prehispánicas en Oaxaca. In *Unidades habitacionales mesoaméricanas y sus areas de actividad*, edited by Linda Manzanilla, pp. 325–74. Serie Antropológica No. 76. Instituto Nacional de Antropología e Historia, Mexico City.

Winter, Marcus. 1988. Periodo prehispánico. In *Historia de la cuestión agraria mexicana: estado de Oaxaca*, vol. 1: *Prehispánico-1924*, edited by Leticia Reina, pp. 23–106. Gobierno del Estado de Oaxaca, Universidad Autónoma Benito Juárez de Oaxaca, Mexico.

Winter, Marcus. 1989a. *Oaxaca: The Archaeological Record*. Minutiae Mexicana, Mexico.

Winter, Marcus. 1989b. From Classic to Post-Classic in Pre-Hispanic Oaxaca, Mexico. In *Mesoamerica after the Decline of Teotihuacan, AD 700–900*, edited by Richard A. Diehl and Janet C. Berlo, pp. 123–30. Dumbarton Oaks, Washington, DC.

Winter, Marcus. 1989c. La obsidiana en Oaxaca prehispánica. In *La obsidiana en Mesoamérica*, edited by Margarita Gaxiola G. and John E. Clark, pp. 345–62. Colección Científica 176, Serie Arqueología. Instituto Nacional de Antropología e Historia, Mexico City.

Winter, Marcus. (ed.). 1991. *Exploraciones arqueológicas en Cerro de las Minas, Mixteca Baja, Oaxaca. Temporadas 1987–1990, informe preliminar*. Report on file Centro INAH Oaxaca, Instituto Nacional de Antropología e Historia, Oaxaca.

Winter, Marcus (ed.). 1994a. *Monte Albán: Estudios recientes*. Contribución No. 2 del Proyecto Especial Monte Albán 1992–4, Oaxaca.

Winter, Marcus. 1994b. Los altos de Oaxaca y los Olmecas. In *Los Olmecas en Mesoamérica*, edited by John E. Clark, pp. 129–41. El Equilibrista, Mexico City.

Winter, Marcus. 1994c. *Tesoros del Museo Regional de Oaxaca/Oaxaca Regional Museum Treasures*. Honorable Ayuntamiento de Oaxaca, Oaxaca.

Winter, Marcus. 1994d. El Proyecto Especial Monte Albán 1992–4: Antecedentes, intervenciones y perspectivas. In *Monte Albán: Estudios recientes*, edited by Marcus Winter, pp. 1–24. Contribución No. 2 del Proyecto Especial Monte Albán 1992–4, Oaxaca.

Winter, Marcus. 1994e. The Mixteca prior to the Late Postclassic. In *The Mixteca-Puebla Concept in Mesoamerican Archaeology*, edited by Henry B. Nicholson and Eloise Quiñones Keber, pp. 201–21. Labyrinthos, Culver City, CA.

Winter, Marcus (ed.). 1995. *Entierros humanos de Monte Albán*. Contribución No. 7 del Proyecto Especial Monte Albán 1992–4, Oaxaca.

Winter, Marcus. 1998. Monte Albán and Teotihuacan. In *Rutas de intercambio en mesoamérica*, edited by Evelyn C. Rattray, pp. 153–84. Universidad Nacional Autónoma de México, Mexico City.

Winter, Marcus. 2001. Palacios, templos y 1300 años de vida urbana en Monte Albán. In *Reconstruyendo la ciudad Maya: El urbanismo en las sociedades antiguas*, edited by Andres Ciudad Ruiz, María J. Iglesia Ponce de Léon, and María del Carmen Martínez Martínez, pp. 253–301. Sociedad Española de Estudios Mayas, Madrid.

Winter, Marcus. 2002. Religión de los Binnigula'sa': La Evidencia Arqueológica. In *La Religión de los Binnigula'sa'*, edited by Victor de la Cruz and Marcus Winter, pp. 45–88. IEEPO-IOC, Oaxaca.

Winter, Marcus. 2003. Monte Albán and Late Classic Site Abandonment in Highland Oaxaca. In *The Archaeology of Settlement Abandonment in Middle America*, edited by Takeshi Inomata and Ronald W. Webb, pp. 103–19. University of Utah Press, Salt Lake City.

Winter, Marcus. 2004a. Excavaciones arqueológicas en El Carrizal, Ixtepec, Oaxaca. In *Diidxa biaani", diidxa" guie": palabras de luz, palabras floridas*, edited by Vicente Marcial Cerque, pp. 17–48. Universidad del Istmo, Tehuantepec, Mexico.

Winter, Marcus. 2004b. Monte Albán: su organización e impacto político. In *Estructuras políticas en el Oaxaca antiguo*, edited by Nelly M. Robles García, pp. 27–59. Instituto Nacional de Antropología e Historia, Mexico City.

Winter, Marcus. 2005a. Producción y uso de figurillas tempranas en el valle de Oaxaca. *Acervos* 7(29):37–54.

Winter, Marcus. 2005b. La cultura Ñuiñe de la Mixteca Baja: nuevas aportaciones. In *Pasado y presente de la cultura mixteca*, edited by Reina Ortiz Escamilla and Ignacio Ortiz Castro, pp. 77–115. Universidad Tecnológica de la Mixteca, Mexico.

Winter, Marcus. 2006. La fundación de Monte Albán y los orígenes del urbanismo temprano en los altos de Oaxaca. In *Nuevas ciudades, nuevas patrias. Fundación y relocalización de ciudades en mesoamérica y el mediterráneo antiguo*, edited by María Josefa Ponce de León, Rogelio Valencia Rivera, and Andrés Ciudad Ruiz, pp. 209–39. Sociedad Española de Estudios Mayas, Madrid.

Winter, Marcus. 2007. *Cerro de las Minas: Arqueología de la Mixteca Baja*, 2nd edition. Centro INAH Oaxaca, Oaxaca, Mexico.

Winter, Marcus, and Ma. Del Rosario Acosta. 1991. Unidades habitacionales asociadas a la Plaza 1. In *Exploraciones arqueológicas en Cerro de las Minas, Mixteca Baja, Oaxaca. Temporadas 1987–1990, informe preliminar*, edited by Marcus Winter, pp. 83–108. Report on file Centro INAH Oaxaca, Instituto Nacional de Antropología e Historia, Oaxaca.

Winter, Marcus, William O. Autry, Jr., Richard G. Wilkinson, and Cira Martínez López. 1995. Entierros humanos en un área residencial de Monte Albán: Temporadas 1972–1973. In *Entierros Humanos de Monte Albán: Dos Estudios*, edited by Marcus Winter, pp. 11–78. Contribución No. 7 del Proyecto Especial Monte Albán 1992-4, Oaxaca.

Winter, Marcus, Margarita Gaxiola, and Gilberto Hernández. 1984. Archaeology of the Otomanguean Area. In *Essays in Otomanguean Culture History*, edited by J. Kathryn Josserand, Marcus Winter, and Nicholas Hopkins, pp. 65–108. Vanderbilt University Publications in Anthropology No. 31, Nashville, TN.

Winter, Marcus, Alicia Herrera Muzgo T., Ronald Spores, and Vilma Fialko. 1991. *Exploraciones arqueológicas en Huamelulpan, Mixteca Alta, Oaxaca. Informe temporada 1990*. Report on file Centro INAH Oaxaca, Instituto Nacional de Antropología e Historia, Oaxaca.

Winter, Marcus, Robert Markens, Cira Martínez López, and Alicia Herrera Muzgo T. 2007. Shrines, Offerings, and Postclassic Continuity in Zapotec Religion.

In *Commoner Ritual and Ideology in Ancient Mesoamerica*, edited by Nancy Gonlin and Jon C. Lohse, pp. 183–210. University Press of Colorado, Boulder, CO.

Winter, Marcus, Cira Martínez López, and Robert Markens. 2008. Early Hunters and Gatherers of Oaxaca: Recent Discoveries. Paper presented at the 73rd Annual Meeting of the Society for American Archaeology, Vancouver, Canada.

Winter, Marcus, and Antonia Montague. 1991. *Excavaciones menores en depósitos de la fase Ñudée, ladera sur (Areas E y J)*. In *Exploraciones arqueológicas en Cerro de las Minas, Mixteca Baja, Oaxaca. Temporadas 1987–1990, informe preliminar*, edited by Marcus Winter, pp. 134–9. Report on file Centro INAH Oaxaca, Instituto Nacional de Antropología e Historia, Oaxaca.

Winter, Marcus C., and Jane Wheeler Pires-Ferreira. 1976. Distribution of Obsidian Among Households in Two Oaxacan Villages. In *The Early Mesoamerican Village*, edited by Kent V. Flannery, pp. 306–11. Academic Press, New York.

Workinger, Andrew. 2002. "Coastal/Highland Interaction in Prehispanic Oaxaca, Mexico: The Perspective from San Francisco de Arriba." Ph.D. dissertation, Vanderbilt University.

Workinger, Andrew, and Arthur A. Joyce. n.d. The Scope of Conflict in Formative Oaxaca. In *Blood and Beauty: Organized Violence in the Art and Archaeology of Mesoamerica and Central America*, edited by Heather Orr and Rex Koontz. Cotsen Institute Press, Los Angeles, in press.

Wright, Henry T. 1977. Recent Research on the Origin of the State. *Annual Review of Anthropology* 6:379–97.

Wylie, Alison. 1985. The Reaction Against Analogy. In *Advances in Archaeological Method and Theory*, vol. 8, edited by Michael B. Schiffer, pp. 63–111. Academic Press, Orlando.

Wylie, Alison. 1992. On 'Heavily Decomposing Red Herrings': Scientific Method in Archaeology and the Ladening of Evidence with Theory. In *Metaarchaeology*, edited by Lester Embree, pp. 269–88. Boston Studies in the Philosophy of Science. Kluwer, Boston.

Wylie, Alison. 2000. Questions of Evidence, Legitimacy, and the (Dis)union of Science. *American Antiquity* 65(2):227–38.

Yaeger, Jason. 2003. Untangling the Ties that Bind: The City, the Countryside, and the Nature of Maya Urbanism at Xunantunich, Belize. In *The Social Construction of Ancient Cities*, edited by Monica L. Smith, pp. 121–55. Smithsonian Books, Washington and London.

Yoffee, Norman. 2005. *Myths of the Archaic State: Evolution of the Earliest Cities, States, and Civilizations*. Cambridge University Press, Cambridge.

Zeitlin, Judith Francis. 1978. Changing Patterns of Resource Exploitation, Settlement Distribution, and Demography on the Southern Isthmus of Tehuantepec, Mexico. In *Prehistoric Coastal Adaptations*, edited by Barbara L. Stark and Barbara Voorhies, pp. 151–78. Academic Press, New York.

Zeitlin, Judith Francis. 2005. *Cultural Politics in Colonial Tehuantepec*. Stanford University Press, Stanford.

Zeitlin, Robert N. 1978. Long-distance Exchange and the Growth of a Regional Center. In *Prehistoric Coastal Adaptations*, edited by Barbara L. Stark and Barbara Voorhies, pp. 183–210. Academic Press, New York.

Zeitlin, Robert N. 1990. The Isthmus and the Valley of Oaxaca: Questions about Monte Albán Imperialism in the Pacific Lowlands. *American Antiquity* 55:250–61.

Zeitlin, Robert N. 1993. Pacific Coastal Laguna Zope: A Regional Center in the Terminal Formative Hinterlands of Monte Albán. *Ancient Mesoamerica* 4:85–101.

Zeitlin, Robert N. 2007. Early Cultures of Middle America. In *Encyclopedia of Archaeology*, edited by Deborah Pearsall, pp. 162–82. Elsevier, Oxford.

Zeitlin, Robert N., and Arthur A. Joyce. 1999. The Zapotec Imperialism Argument: Insights from the Oaxaca Coast. *Current Anthropology* 40(3):383–92.

Index

Page numbers referring to figures are shown in italics; n following a number denotes an endnote.

Abasolo, *68*, 92, 103, *120*, 147, 148
Achiutla (Ñuu Ndecu), 61, *250*, 259, 260, 264, 265, 270, 271, 279
Acosta, Jorge R., 10, 166–7
"action theory," 26, 285
age *see* identity
agency, 20, 25–7, 56, 224, 284–5, 288, 295
agricultural practices, 2, 5, 11, 16, 37, 40, 41, 50, 53, 54, 60, 66–72, 73, 106, 130, 162, 165, 169, 179, 200, 224, 277, 284, 287, 290
  and anthropogenic landscapes, 38, 40, 163, 180, 283
  floodplain agriculture, 41, 51–2, 69, 163, 181, 261
  gender and agriculture, 49, 70; *see also* gender
  irrigation, 76, 154, 221
  Lama bordo/terracing, 52–3, *53*, 163, 165, 169, 227, 238, 279–80, 283
  slash-and-burn, 51; *see also* environmental change
agricultural staples
  avocado, 51, 53, 77
  beans, 51, 67, 69, 70, 77, 238
  bottle gourds, 51, 67, 71, 231
  cacao *see* exchange goods

chiles, 51, 66, 67, 70, 77
cotton, 2, 48, 51, 54, 206, 241, 256, 261, 269, 270
maguey, 49, 51, 53, 68, 221–2
maize, 22, 51, 56, 60, 64, 67, 69–70, 72, 77, 99, 106, 108, 149, 174, 183, 212, 221, 238
manioc, 51
squash, 51, 67, 69, 70, 77, 238
tomato, 67
Aldenderfer, Mark, 100
alliances, 2, 47, 61, 106, 130, 186, 205, 224, 226–7, 259–63, 265, 268, 278–9, 281, 289
  and polity formation, 45, 157, 205
  and royal marriage, 45, 47–8, 89, 116, 44, 157, 177, 224, 226, 236–7, 249, 254, 264, 265
Alvarado, Fray Fransisco de, 8
Alvarado, Pedro de, 1, 3, 42, 280–1
Amoltepec, *250*, 279
ancestors *see* religion
Annales School, 32
Apoala (*Yuta Tnoho*), 59–60, 61, *250*, 259–60; *see also* religion
Astata, *250*, 278
Authority, 17, 29–30, 31, 48, 63, 98, 119, 196, 245, 251, 254, 256, 285

administrative centers, 47, 119, 150, 157, 179, 225, 227, 279, 293
centralized political authority, 71, 116, 118, 180, 186–95, 239, 246, 293
emerging hierarchy, 85, 91, 93, 110–15, 121, 125, 141–6, 162
exclusionary authority, 48, 73–4, 163, 178, 197, 206–7, 215, 217–20, 223, 224, 226, 227, 233–4, 239–41, 253, 257, 260, 276, 293
ruling houses, 45, 47–8, 50, 60, 212, 217–8, 223, 250, 259, 264–5, 271, 275, 278, 281, 293, 294
succession/succession struggles, 45, 48, 50, 212, 224, 243, 265, 279
see also noble/high status identity; resistance; social organization/society; status
Aztec, 1, 24–5, 43, 49, 154, 179
Aztec empire, 46, 55, 152, 153, 196, 267, 270
Emperor Ahuitzotl, 265
Emperor Motecuhzoma Ilhuicamina, 265
incursions into Oaxaca, 45, 265–6, 271
Pochteca merchants, 54, 55, 269–70, 271, 277
Tenochtitlán, *1*, 267, 270

Bajos de Chila, *161*, 180
Balkansky, Andrew K., 13, 104, 163, 165, 166, 169–70, 173, 296–7n
Barber, Sarah B., 187–8, 191, 193, 297n
Barrio Tepalcate, 68, *198*
Basin of Mexico, 54, 65, 66, 81, 82, 88, 89, 91, 92, 93, 124, 144, 186, 198, 201, 203, 206, 227, 237, 240, 256
Beringia, 65
Bernal, Ignacio, 10, 11, 272

Blanton, Richard E., 11, 73, 92, 94, 111, 119, 218
Blomster, Jeffrey P., 13, 89–90, 92, 93, 162, 279
bodily adornment/ornamentation, 25, 45, 78, 82, 87, 88, 89, 91, 96, 104, 108, 109, 122, 113, 116, 118, 136, 143, 157, 170, 185, 238, 213, 291
beautification, 89, 96, 103, 112, 115, 175, 185, 209, 246
costumes/headgear, 89, 97, 244, 255
greenstone, 54, 86, 102–3, 106–8, 112–13, 116, 143, 144, 148, 152, 156, 164, 170, 175, 189, 192, 203, 206, 209, 221, 224, 231, 240, 246, 255, 280; bead belts, 106, 113; ear spools, 89, 96, 98, 106, 109, 113, 156, 244
jaguars/jaguar imagery, 62, 90, 92–3, 198, 203, 212, 213, 223, 236, 238, 244–5, 253
jewelry/ornaments/ornamentation, 22, 25, 45, 48, 49, 54, 59, 78–9, 81–2, 86–9, 96, 102–9, 113, 116, 118, 124, 143–4, 156–7, 164, 175, 185, 198, 204, 206, 209, 211–12, 213, 218, 221–2, 224, 233, 237–8, 241, 255, 261, 291
mirrors, 86–8, 96, 98, 105, 112–13, 116, 192, 231, 268
shell sashes, 185
see also exchange goods
bodily modification
cranial modification, 97, 103, 108, 112, 124, 164, 167, 240
dental modification, 156, 164, 167, 192, 211, 240
Borbolla, Rubin de, 11
boundary/border lands, 3, 7, 54–5, 61, 153, 220, 237, 277
buffer zones, 122–3, 154
see also conflict; imperialism; warfare
Bourdieu, Pierre, 20, 22–3

Braudel, Fernand, 32–3
Burgoa, Fray Fransisco de, 8, 45
Butler, Judith, 24, 25
Byland, Bruce E., 10, 271, 298n

Caballito Blanco, 120, 158
caching, 98, 187, 189, 192, 194, 215, 240, 243, 281; see also religion
Cacicazgos, 249, 278
Calendrics, 9, 58, 123, 178, 211, 228, 234–6, 245, 246, 253, 296n
captives/slaves, 23, 46, 49, 50, 55, 62, 63, 123, 127, 129, 136, 144, 151, 152, 158, 170, 177, 198, 212, 213, 217, 236, 237, 274
carved stone imagery, 4, 10, 13, 25, 100, 123, 129, 132–9, 154, 158, 159, 167, 170, 174, 178, 197, 198, 204, 207, 209, 211, 213, *214*, 215, *216*, 228, 229, 231–2, 234–6, *235*, 237, 241, 243–6, *244*, 253, 256–7, 267, *268*, 279, 293; see also religion
Caso, Alfonso, 9–11, 14, 15, 153, 203, 228, 236, 297n
celts (greenstone), 102, 113
Cerro de la Caja, *198*, 227, *235*, 237
Cerro de la Campana, *198*, 201, 211, 220, 223
Cerro de la Cruz, 14, *161*, 181, *182*, 183–6, 187, 188, 194, 296–7n
  public cemetery, 183, *184*, 185, 188, 296–7n
Cerro de la Tortuga, 241
Cerro de la Virgen, *161*, 186, 189, 191, 192, 193
Cerro de la Virgen, Tlaxiaco Valley, *198*, 227
Cerro de las Minas, 12, *161*, 162, 172–4, 177, 179, 195, *198*, 199, 227, 229–30, *230*, 232, *232*, *233*, 233–4, *235*, 237–9, 276, 292, 293, 294
Cerro de los Tepalcates, 246

Cerro del Chivo, *198*, 243
Cerro Jazmín/Suchixtlán (Chiyo Yuhu), 40, *161*, 162, 195, *198*, 199, 227, *250*, 260, 279
Cerro Tilcajete, *120*, 157–8
Chalcatongo, 61, *250*, 261, 263
Chalcatzingo, *1*, 123, 137, 139, 140, 141
Charco Redondo, *161*, 180, 185, 186, 189, *198*, 243
Chazumba, *198*, 237, 270
chert, 53, 62, 6–66, 67, 85, 86, 157, 221–2, 228, 231, 233, 277
Chiapa de Corzo, *1*, 124, 141, 144
Chiapas, 89, 92, 93, 106, 113, 124, 144, 281
Chichén Itzá, *1*, 263
chiefdom model, 19, 73, 91, 111, 113, 115, 285–6
children, 49, 76, 77, 79, 96, 102–3, 107, 108, 109, 112–13, 115, 119, 143, 146, 147, 149, 170–1, 183, 185, 197, 224, 229, 231, 238, 254, 263, 288, 294
Cholula, *1*, 256, 263
Chontal see language families
Christianity, 24, 30, 33
Clark, John E., 72, 81, 82, 93, 115
coastal script, 245
codices, 4, 7, 8, 9, 44, 45, 47, 48, 49, 54, 56, 58, 59, 60, 61, 62, 136, 205, 209, 249, 258, 259–64, 267, 270, 271, 274, 275, 276, 277, 280, 298n
  Codex Bodley, 60, 260
  Codex Colombino-Becker, 3, 8, 260, 262, 263
  Codex Mendoza, 153
  Codex Selden, 8
  Codex Vienna, 8, 59–60, 259
  Codex Zouche-Nuttall, 8, 60, 259, 260, 262, 263
Coe, Michael D., 136
Coixtlahuaca, 11, 41, *250*, 265, 271

collapse, 12, 13, 32, 33, 119, 179, 195–6, 199, 226, 229, 239, 241, 247, 248, 249–58, 259, 260, 261, 266, 276, 290, 293, 294
Colonial period *see* Spanish conquest
comales, 140, 146, 149, 162, 189
commoners/commoner identity, 29–32, 46, 48–50, 56, 62–3, 126, 127, 130, 139, 142, 143–8, 151, 165, 175, 176, 191, 193, 194, 197–8, 207, 209, 212–13, 216–17, 219, 223–6, 228, 232–4, 236, 238–9, 243, 246–7, 248, 254, 256–7, 267, 270, 274–8, 280, 281, 285, 289, 292, 293, 294, 297n, 298n; *see also* identity; subjectivity
communal labor/communal projects, 48–50, 100, 113–16, 125, 184–5, 189, 191, 196, 197, 234, 243, 294
communitas, 103
conflict, 18, 19, 20, 24, 47, 50, 120, 121–5, 127, 130, 146, 151, 152, 154, 159, 177, 179, 180, 187, 195, 196, 197, 198, 224, 226, 237, 240, 250, 254, 260, 265, 285, 291, 292, 293
  social contradictions, 29, 33, 117, 141, 146, 149, 178, 197, 241, 293
  social tensions, 18, 19, 20, 24, 30, 50, 74, 79, 83, 85, 96, 98, 103, 108, 109, 117, 119, 127, 130, 141, 146, 149, 150, 159, 178, 180, 186, 194, 196, 197, 206, 221, 225, 226, 247, 285, 286, 289, 291, 292
  see also resistance; warfare
Copán, *1*, 248
Cordova, Fray Juan de, 8
corporate/communal social organization, 15, 31, 46, 49–51, 74, 83, 85, 92, 94–5, 102, 103, 108, 111, 115–17, 119, 122, 125, 127, 141, 144–5, 146, 159, 163, 164, 166, 167, 173, 177–9, 183, 185, 191, 194, 197, 205, 206–7, 209, 211, 213, 215–18, 220, 223–4, 241, 243, 248, 270, 284, 288, 289, 291, 292, 293, *295*
Cortés, Hernán, 1, 2, 3, 280
cosmos *see* religion
Coxcatlán Cave, *1*, 68, *68*
craft specialization/crafting, 49, 54, 85–6, 89, 98, 104–6, 108, 110, 112–13, 116, 125, 146, 148–50, 157, 162, 169, 218, 221–2, 224, 238, 246, 267, 277
  ceramics: Atzompa clay source, 277; ceramic compositional studies, 176; cream ware pottery, 157, 176; G-12 conical bowls, *140*, 150, 176, 187; kilns, 149; polychromes *see* Mixteca-Puebla style
  stone tools, 53, 54, 69, 77, 86, 149, 169, 238–9, 257, 277
  textiles, 48, 49, 50, 51, 54, 143, 221–2, 224, 238, 255, 256, 257, 267, 269, 277, 283
  woodworking, 68, 76, 86, 105, 167
  see also exchange goods; exchange relations
Cueva Blanca, 66, *68*
Cuicatlán, 153
Cuicatlán Cañada, 6, 12, 153–4, 201
Cuilapan (Sa'a Yucu), 10, 45, 50, *120*, 158, *250*, 264–5, 271
cultural evolution/neo-evolution, 11–12, 18–20, 32, 73, 111, 113, 119, 192, 195, 284–9
Cyphers, Ann, 79, 93

De Certeau, Michel, 34
De la Fuente, Julio, 15
Di Castro, Anna, 93
Díaz del Castillo, Bernal, 3
Diquiyú, *161*, 162, 177, *198*, 227
direct historical approach, 7, 36

Diuxi, *68*, 84, 104
divination *see* religion
DMTG cluster, *198*, 200–1, 223
   Dainzú, 11, *120*, *138*, 139, 158, *198*, 200
   Guadalupe, *198*, 200
   Macuilxóchitl, *198*, 200, 201, 219, 220, 223, *250*, 251, 264, 265, 271, 274, 276
   Tlacochahuaya, *198*, 200, 201
domestic architecture, 73, 75, 83, 94–5, 186, 209, 220, 225, 229–30, 238, 255, 269
domesticated animals, 48, 53, 55, 62, 67, 77
domestication, 4, 64, 67–70, 76; *see also* agricultural staples; domesticated animals
Drennan, Robert D., 105, 106

economy, 54, 108
   domestic/subsistence economy, 38, 51–3, 64, 72–3, 76, 86–7, 108, 119, 129–30, 257, 268, 284, 288–90
   political economy, 3, 12, 15–16, 50, 54, 55, 85, 86, 98, 99, 105, 106, 119, 122, 128, 130, 143–4, 146–50, 157–9, 161, 163, 179, 186, 196, 199, 205–7, 215, 217, 221–2, 224, 225, 257, 258, 261, 270, 277, 281, 285, 287, 289, 290–2, 294, 298n
   see also exchange goods
Ejutla, *198*, 200, 221
Ejutla Valley, 6, 12, 39, 151, 157, 180, 200, 222, 294
El Chocho, *198*
El Ciruelo, *161*, *198*, 180, 245
El Mogote, *120*, 122–3, 147, 151, 152
El Palenque, *120*, 151–2, 157, 167, 292
El Palmillo, *198*, 200, 221–2, 224, 294

El Pocito, 66, *68*
embodiment, 15, 24–5, 27, 29, 31, 47–9, 57, 73, 79, 83, 84, 101, 103, 106, 109, 111, 118, 141, 163, 194, 197, 212, 223, 225, 258, 276, 297n, 298n; *see also* religion, nagualism
environmental change, 41–2, 66, 180–1, 257; *see also* agricultural practices
epidemics, 3, 281
Erickson, Clark L., 52
ethnic/ethnolinguistic affiliation *see* identity
Etlatongo, *1*, 13, *68*, 74, 84–5, 86, 87–90, *90*, 93, 104, *161*, 162, 163, *198*, 227, *250*, 279, 289
exchange goods
   alabaster, 48, 54, 255
   cacao, 2, 48, 51, 54, 206, 241, 261, 270
   ceramics *see* craft specialization/crafting
   copper, 2, 49, 54, 255, 269–70, 276
   cochineal dye, 53, 54
   cotton *see* agricultural staples
   gold, 2, 3, 48–9, 54, 59, 261, 276, 277
   greenstone/jade/turquoise *see* bodily adornment/ornamentation; celts
   magnetite, 86–7, 96, 98, 102, 113
   mica, 86, 96, 105, 106, 107, 109, 170, 173, 203, 205
   obsidian, *1*, 54, 62, 69, 72, 81–2, 86, 88–9, 96, 99, 102, 105, 122, 124, 126, 143, 144, 152, 156, 157, 166, 175, 186, 187, 205, 206, 222, 224, 231, 236, 240–1, 245
   obsidian sources: Altotonga, *1*, 105; Guadalupe Victoria, *1*, 82, 88, 105; Orizaba, *1*, 89, 269; Otumba, *1*, 81, 88–9, 105; Pachuca, *1*, 124, 186, 240, 245, 269, 271; Paredón, *1*, 186;

Ucareo, *1*, 245, 256; Zaragoza, *1*, 256; Zinepécuaro, *1*, 88
onyx, 143, 144, 221
pearls, 2, 48, 156
polychrome pottery *see* Mixteca-Puebla style
púrpura dye, 53
quetzal feathers, 49, 54, 261
salt, 2, 41, 53, 54, 55, 105, 149, 251, 261, 277
shell, 22, 41, 49, 54, 59, 69, 78, 81, 82, 86–7, 89, 96, 102, 104, 105, 106–7, 109, 143, 144, 152, 156–7, 164, 170, 173, 175, 183, 185, 187, 192, 206, 209, 215, 218, 221, 222, 224, 231, 233, 236, 238, 240–1, 246, 255, 276
silver, 48, 49, 54, 276
textiles *see* craft specialization/crafting
tobacco, 53, 59, 60, 81, 231
see also specific regions
exchange relations, 49, 54–5, 64, 81–2, 119, 124, 149–50, 151, 157, 175, 176–7, 186–7, 192, 194, 195, 222, 236–9, 241, 249, 267, 269–70, 271, 277, 289, 294
gift exchange, 127, 205
luxury goods, 106, 108, 115, 126–7, 192, 194
markets, 5, 16, 43, 54–5, 87, 146, 148, 149–50, 177, 179, 197, 221–2, 238, 239, 267, 277, 292, 294
see also craft specialization/crafting

Fábrica San José, *68*, 104–8, *120*, 128, 158
Fargher, Lane F., 149
feasting *see* religion
Feinman, Gary M., 221–2, 224
Feminist theory, 18, 19, 27; *see also* gender
Fernández, Deepika, 181
Fernández Dávila, Enrique, 121

figurines, 4, 25, 57, 78, 78–9, 83, 92, 93, 94–7, *97*, 98, 102, 105, 108, 109, 113, 142, 150, 183, 203, 205, 209, 212–13, 221, 238, 255, 291
hollow baby style, 90, *90*, 91, 93, 94, *95*, 102
imported figurines, 89, 90, 93, 105
jade figurines, 156
penates (small stone figurines), 252
see also identity; religion
Forde, Jamie E., 270
Foucault, Michel, 28–9, 33–4
Flannery, Kent V., 11, 66, 67, 69–70, 71, 72, 73, 74, 77, 79–81, 82, 92, 96, 99, 100, 107, 108, 110, 111, 112, 113, 116, 121, 122, 123, 124, 126, 129, 147, 153, 154, 155, 176, 285–6, 296n, 297n
functionalist theory, 18–19, 30, 284–6, 288, 298n

Gamio, Lorenzo, 272
García, Fray Gregorio, 59
Gaxiola, Margarita, 168, 170, 172, 229
gender *see* identity
genealogies, 7, 9, 44, 46–7, 48, 137, 178, 204, 207, 209, 211, 213, 215–16, *216*, 220, 223–4, 226, 260, 264, 293, 296n
Geurds, Alexander, 166
Gheo Shih, *68*, 68–9, 70
Giddens, Anthony, 20–1, 23, 28, 29, 215
gifting *see* exchange relations
glottochronology, 43, 64; *see also* language families
Grove, David C., 92
Guevea, 279
Guhdz Bedkol, *68*, 70
Guiengola, 45, *250*, 265, 277–8
Guilá Naquitz, *68*, 68–9
Gulf coast, 54, 70, 81–2, 84, 88–92,

93, 95, 105, 106, 113, 114–15, 123, 141, 206, 236, 256, 289–90; see also exchange goods; Olmec/"Olmec style"

habitus, 22–3
Hacienda Blanca, 68, 71, 74, 78, 104
Hamann, Byron, 257, 260
Hardy, Karen V., 69, 296n
Hayden, Brian, 115
Hepp, Guy D., 183
hermeneutics, 20
heroic history, 258–66; see also codices; Sahlins, Marshall
hidden transcript, 30–2, 257, 294
hieroglyphic writing, 4, 14, 118, 123, 135–7, 141, 144, 146, 170, 174, 207, 211, 229, 244, 246, 271
hilltop sites, 39, 45, 119, 128–32, 141, 147, 148, 157, 158, 162, 165, 170, 172–3, 177, 199, 200, 221, 222, 227, 265, 271–2, 274, 276, 277–8, 281, 290, 292
Hodder, Ian, 27
Holland, Dorothy, 27
Holocene epoch, 11, 38, 64, 66–7, 70
Honduras, 106, 248
households *see* identity
Huajuapan Valley, 41, 172–3, 229
Huamelula, 250, 270
Huamelulpan, 11, 12, 161, 161–3, 168–72, 169, 172, 174, 177–9, 195, 198, 199, 227, 228–9, 234, 237, 239, 276, 283, 290, 292
Huamelulpan Valley, 41, 84, 85, 86, 161, 168–9
Huatulco, 6, 15
Huave *see* language families
Huitzo, 68, 104, 109, 110, 120, 125

identity, 5, 24–5, 43–4, 46–51, 110, 120, 233–9
  age, 24–5, 49–50, 78–9, 82, 103, 110–12, 116, 102, 103, 118, 136, 167, 178, 183, 188, 223, 224, 255, 288, 291
  community/collective/corporate, 4, 15, 24–5, 31, 73, 82, 83, 84–8, 95, 100–1, 103, 104–10, 116, 119, 122, 141, 144, 146, 178, 181–5, 187–9, 191, 194, 238, 270, 288–9
  ethnic/ethnolinguistic affiliation, 22–3, 43–4, 50, 203, 220–2, 224–6, 238, 279
  gender, 15, 22–5, 28, 47, 49, 50, 70, 78, 79, 82, 86, 95, 96, 98, 102, 110–11, 118, 125, 149, 150, 178, 212, 223, 224, 238, 255, 288, 291
  household, 11, 12, 54, 55, 63, 74, 75–9, 81–3, 85–9, 95, 96, 98–9, 102, 103, 105, 106–7, 108–9, 110–11, 113, 115–17, 118, 126, 142, 143, 149, 162, 164, 169, 185, 207, 209, 211, 221–2, 223, 224–5, 231, 234, 238, 255–6, 268–9, 275, 279, 288, 289, 291
  kinship/family, 44, 46, 48, 49–50, 69, 75–7, 82, 88, 103, 108, 110–11, 112, 114, 117, 122, 125, 149, 165, 175, 177–8, 183, 209, 220, 223, 225, 229–32, 238, 246, 263, 265, 274, 294; see also genealogies
  occupation, 24, 25, 28, 50, 118, 120, 178, 197, 223–4, 238, 240
  personhood, 21, 25, 209
  sexuality, 24, 61, 79, 83, 96, 291
  status, 12, 22, 28, 46–8, 50, 56, 59, 63, 72, 73, 77–8, 79, 81, 82, 85, 87, 93–100, 103–16, 118–19, 121–5, 127, 130, 136, 141–5, 146, 147, 148, 149, 151–2, 156–8, 159, 162, 163, 164–7, 170–3, 175, 178, 181–6, 188, 192–4, 196, 204, 207–9, 215–18, 220, 221, 223–5, 227, 228–33, 234, 237–41, 246, 247,

250, 252, 254, 256, 267, 273, 274, 275–6, 278, 280, 289–91, 294
supra-community, 24, 147, 194, 197, 223, 240, 241, 246
see also commoners/commoner identity; noble/high status identity
ideology, 26, 29–32, 33, 55, 56, 63, 93, 128, 150, 173, 177, 194, 215, 217, 222, 226, 234, 236, 246–7, 248, 257, 270, 285, 292, 294; also see religion
imperialism, 152–4, 203–4, 206, 266
INAH (Instituto Nacional de Antropología e Historia), 12, 13, 15, 57
inquisitorial trials, 8, 56
inscription (social), 30, 33, 82
instantiation, 258, 266, 284, 287; see also Sahlins, Marshall
irrigation see agricultural practices
Isthmus of Tehuantepec, 6, 12, 15, 35, 38, 41, 43, 55, 68, 71, 82, 93, 186, 187, 249, 265, 277, 281

Jalapa, *250*, 265, 279, 281
Jalieza, *198*, 200–1, 223, *250*, 251, 271
Jaltepec (Añute), *198*, 227, *250*, 259, 260, 264, 265, 279
Jansen, Maarten E. R. G. N., 10, 166, 259, 260, 298n
Joyce, Arthur A., 14, 191, 253, 297n
Joyce, Rosemary A., 24, 25, 29, 49, 79, 89, 93, 95, 183
Juchatengo, *250*, 270
Juquila, *250*, 261, 262

Kennedy, Mary C., 70
King, Stacie M., 254, 297n
kinship see identity
Kowalewski, Stephen A., 11, 158, 163, 251, 277, 296n

La Blanca, *1*, 115, 123
La Consentida, *68*, 71

La Coyotera, *120*, 153
La Libertad, *1*, 124
La Providencia, *161*, 161–2
La Venta, *1*, 115, 123, 139, 141
Laguna Zope, 71
Lama bordo see agricultural practices
Lambityeco, 12, *198*, 201, 215, 219, 220, 223, *250*, 250–1, 275
Landesque capital, 52
language families
  Chontal, 43, 278
  Huave, 43, 265, 277
  Mixe-Zoquean languages: Mixe, 43; Zoque, 43, 265, 277
  Nahuatl, 43, 153, 264
  Otomanguean languages: Amuzgo, 43; Chatino (language), 35, 42, 43, 45, 245, 267; Chinantec, 43; Chocho, 43, 237; Cuicatec, 43, 154; Ixcatec, 43; Mazatec, 43; Mixtec (languages), 42, 43, 45, 55, 207, 237, 258, 267; Popoloco, 43, 237; Trique, 43, 55; Zapotec (languages), 35, 42, 43, 44, 45, 64–5, 141, 174, 203, 207, 234, 245, 277
Latour, Bruno, 26
Levine, Marc N., 187, 191, 268–9
Lienzos, 7, 9, 153, 209, 264
Lind, Michael D., 220, 250, 297n
Loma del Trapiche, *198*, 201, 220, 223
Lorenzo, José Luis, 68
Llano Perdido, *120*, 153

MacNeish, Richard S., 67–70, 82
mapas, 7, 9
Marcus, Joyce, 14, 58, 71–3, 77, 79–81, 92, 97–100, 107–9, 113, 116, 121–4, 126, 129, 136, 147, 153–5, 204, 285–6, 296n, 297n
Markens, Robert, 249, 251, 276
materiality, 19, 22, 24, 25
Mazatan region, 113–15

memory, 3–4, 24–5, 73, 83, 100, 185, 215, 297n; *also see* identity
men/male identity, 7, 24, 30, 47, 49, 55, 58, 60, 70, 76–7, 79, 81, 87, 92, 95–8, 101–3, 108, 112, 116, 136, 149, 156, 159, 170–1, 185, 188, 192, 209, 212, 229, 234, 238, 240, 245, 254–5, 259–60, 286, 288; *see also* gender
Mexica *see* Aztec
Miahuatlán Valley, 11, 12, 39–40, 151, 153, 157, 200
migration, 5, 45, 64, 127, 177, 200, 239, 251, 265, 266, 277, 283
mirrors *see* bodily adornment/ornamentation
Mitla (Liobaa), 10–11, 15, 56, *57*, 61, 65–6, 70, *250*, 271, *273*, 274–8, *275*, 283
Mixe-Zoquean languages *see* language families
Mixteca-Puebla style, 45, 249, 269–70
Mogote del Cacique (Ñuu Yuchi), *250*, 264
Monaghan, John, 10, 16, 56–7, 59, 60
Montague, Antonia, 173
Monte Albán, *1*, 4, 10–13, *13*, 34, 39, 118–59, *120*, *161*, 163, 165, 168, 173–8, 196, *198*, 199–207, 209, 211, 213, 215–23, 225–6, 230, 236–7, 248–52, *250*, 259, 271, 275–6, 283, 290–4, 297n
 Area IV-Norte, 156–7
 ballcourts, 131, 139, 155, 158, 217
 Building A, 203
 Building IV-sub, *133*, *133*
 Building J, *133*, 137–9, 144, 151, 153–4, 158, 159, 206–7, 293
 Building L-sub, *133*, 133–6, 139, 141, 144–6, 151, 159, 168, 174, 178, 206–7, 213, 293
 Building S, *202*, 218, 230
 Conjunto PNLP, 156–7, 159, *202*, 218, 220
 conquest slabs, 137, *138*, 153–4, 159
 Contact with Teotihuacan, 144, 196, 198–9, 201, 203–6, 222, 226, 235, 236, 237
 Danzantes, 134, *135*
 defensive constructions *see* warfare
 El Ocote residence, *133*, 156, *202*, 218
 founding, 11, 118–59, 174, 290–1, 294
 Main Plaza, 11, 13, 128, 131–4, *132*, *133*, 137, 139, 141, 142, 143, 144–5, 148, 150, 155, 156, 158, 159, 163, 178, *202*, 213, 217–19, 225–6, 250–2, 276; *see also* monumentality; religion
 Monument J-38, 137
 Monument J-41, *138*, 144
 North Platform, *132*, 133, *133*, 146, 174
 Patio Hundido, *133*, 155, 203, 219
 PSA residence, *202*, 218
 Residence A3, *133*, 147
 South Platform, 131, *132*, *133*, 155, *202*, 215, 218, 252
 Tomb 7, 10, 133, 220, 275–6
 Tomb 33, 143
 Tomb 43, 143
 Tomb 104, *208*, *210*, 218
 Tomb 105, 211
 Tomb 111, 143
 Tomb 174, 143
 Tomb 204, 142
 TPA (temple-patio-altar) complexes, *219*, 219–20, 225, 251–2
 Viborón, 137–8, *138*, 155
Monte Negro, 11, *120*, 154, *161*, 162–3, 165–7, *166*, *168*, 174, 177, 179, 192, 195, *198*, 199, 283, 292, 293
Monte Verde, Chile, 66
Montiel, Lisa, 206
monumental architecture, 33, 100, 115, 121, 128, 131, 147, 151,

163, 173–4, 176, 178, 186, 191, 204, 227, 234, 237, 271, 279–80
acropoli, 4, 163, 184, 186, 189–91, 194–6, 239–40, 243–4, 254, 255–6, 257, 283
adoratorios, 156, 170, 174
civic-ceremonial complexes, 10–11, 166, 173, 189, 201, 227, 230, 243, 256, 267, 278–80
residential platforms, 181, 240, 256
monumental art, 138, 179, 217–18, 246, 251, 253
monumentality, 118, 131, 160; *see also* public architecture; ritual architecture
Morelos/Morelos Valley, 89, 91, 106, 245
"Mother Culture" model *see* Olmec/"Olmec style"
murals, 4, 7, 59, 197–8, 204, 207, 209, *210*, 211, 224, 228, 274, 283; *also see* monumental art
music *see* ritual performance

nagualism *see* religion
Nahuatl *see* language families
Nanacatepec, 279
Nejapa, *250*, 265
Nicayuju, *250*, 280
Nicholas, Linda M., 221–2
noble/high status identity, 5, 46, 48, 59, 78, 87, 94, 96, 98, 107, 109, 113, 118–19, 123–5, 130, 141–2, 144, 192, 194, 198, 227, 234, 237–8, 240–1, 247, 249, 297–8n
noble/high status residences, 12, 99, 104–6, 109, 112, 114–15, 124–5, 142, 144, 147–9, 151–2, 156, 158, 165–7, 171, *172*, 173, 186, 193, 200, 203–4, 208–9, 215, 218, 220, 227–32, 234, 250, 267, 273–5, 278, 280–1, 294
nobles of Oaxaca (named): Cosihuesa, 265; Lady 4 Rabbit, 264; Lady 8 Grass "Cloud of Ñuu Dzaui," 44; Lady 9 Alligator, 59; Lady 9 Grass, 58, 61, *262*; Lady 11 Water "Blue Parrot," 260; Lord 2 Rain "Ocoñaña," 263; Lord 4 Jaguar "Serpent," 261, 263; Lord 4 Wind "Yahui," 263–4; Lord 5 Alligator "Rain Sun," 260; Lord 5 Flower, 264, 271; Lord 5 Jaguar, 213; Lord 5 Wind, 59; Lord 8 Deer "Jaguar Claw," 2, 49, 61, 260–4, *262*, 266; Lord 8 Wind "Twenty Eagles," 260; Lord 10 Dog "War," 44; Lord 10 Eagle, 260; Lord 12 Movement, *262*, 263; Lord 13 Night, 213, *214*; Lord Cosijopii, 265; Lord Lachi/Cosijopii II, 2, 265, 279–81
see also identity
Nochixtlán (Atoco), 54, *250*, 265, 279, 281
Nochixtlán Valley, 12, *40*, 40–1, 44, 52, *53*, 68, 70, 74–5, 78, 82, 84–6, 88–9, 93, 123, 161–3, 165, 176, 180, 195, 199, 227–8, 251, 279
Nopala, *161*, 180
Nuyoo, 16, 56–7, 60–1
Ñuiñe script, 234–5
Ñuundaa, *161*, *162*, *198*, 227

Oaxaca Human Ecology Project, 11, 67
obsidian *see* exchange goods
Ocelotepec, 153
Olmec/"Olmec style," 84, 87, 89–95, 97, 102–3, 105, 112, 114, 116, 141, 283, 289
"Mother Culture" model, 91
"Sister Culture" model, 91–2
Orozco, Francisco de, 280
Orr, Heather S., 14
Ortner, Sherry B., 26–7
Otomanguean languages *see* language families

Palenque, *1*, 248
paleoclimatic/paleoenvironmental data, 34, 37–8, 66
Parsons, Elsie Clews, 15, 274
Paso de la Amada, *1*, 113–15
Pauketat, Timothy R., 27
Peñasco-Tlacotepec, *161*, 161–2, *250*, 279
Peñoles region, 154
Pérez Rodríguez, Verónica, 53, 259–60, 279, 298n
personhood *see* identity
Piedra Labrada, *198*, 245
Piedra Parada Jamiltepec, *161*, 180
Pires-Ferreira, Jane Wheeler, 87, 105
Pleistocene epoch, 38, 64–6
Pohl, John M., 10, 271, 274, 276, 298n
political centralization, 160–96, 239, 241, 292
Popol Vuh, 59
poststructural theory, 15, 18–20, 22, 24, 27, 32, 34, 74, 283–4, 287–9, 292
practices of affiliation, 116, 147, 191
practice theory, 19–21, 26, 110
prestige goods *see* exchange goods
priests *see* religion
Proyecto Especial Monte Albán (PEMA), 13, 203
processual archaeology, 11, 18, 21–2, 30
public architecture, *80*, 111, 114–16, 122, 154, 155, 157, 158, 169, 179, 201, 223, 267; *see also* monumentality; ritual architecture
public transcript, 31
Pulque, 48, 51, 53–4, 60
Putla, 55, *250*

Quiotepec, *120*, 154

Redfield, Robert, 15
Redmond, Elsa M., 12, 151, 153, 154, 97

Relaciones Geográphicas, 7, 264
religion, 3, 5, 8, 15, 24, 56, 63, 95, 108, 118, 125–8, 130, 150, 177, 197, 284
ancestor worship/contact, 4, 21–3, 25–6, 28, 58, 61–3, 79, 89, 96, 108, 111–3, 126–7, 130, 136, 139, 140–2, 145, 150, 162, 185, 197, 198, 206, 209–13, 220, 229, 236, 245, 252–3, 260, 276, 283, 289–90, 293–4
apical ancestors, 46, 209, 211, 213, 215–17, 224, 293
ballgame, 97, 118, 139, 141, 158, 174, 212, 217, 224, 245, 283
Catholicism, 3, 8, 30, 281; *see also* Spanish conquest
cosmos/cosmology, 5, 29, 33, 58, 62–3, 88, 122, 134, 139, 145, 189, 197, 212
creation stories, 8, 25, 48, 56, 59–63, 134, 139, 146, 212, 216, 228, 250, 252, 259–60, 274, 276; *see also* Apoala
deities, 4, 21–6, 28, 36, 44, 56–61, 63, 93, 111, 118, 125–7, 130, 138–9, 141, 170, 174, 178, 209, 212, 215, 223–4, 234, 245–6, 252–3, 259, 268, 283, 289–90, 293–4, 297n: Creator God (Pitáo Cozáana), 211; Death God, 192; fertility/fertility deities, 36, 58, 60, 62–3, 89, 106, 127, 137, 139, 141, 174, 197, 212; Fire Serpent, 90, 92–3; Itzpapalotl/Obsidian Butterfly, 268; Jesus/The man of *yii*, 24, 56; Lady 1 Deer, 59; Lord 1 Deer, 59; Old Fire God, 231, 234; Quetzalcoatl/Lord 9 Wind "Stone Skull," 58–9, 259–60; Rain God/Rain God impersonation, 57, 59, 111, 135, 136, 139, 141, 143, 145–6, 158, 170, *171*, 174, 215, 228, 292; Were-jaguar, 90, 92–3; Wide-

billed Bird deity, 139, 170; Xipe Totec, 58, 212; *see also* ancestors
directional symbolism, 58, 134
divination, 58, 79, 96, 100, 139, 245
domestic ritual, 78–9, 95–6, 108–9, 142, 150, 225, 238, 255
life-crisis ceremonies, 79, 96
mortuary ritual, 4, 61, 77, 94, 102–4, 108, 116, 125, 163, 186–7, 194, 234, 238, 240–1, 255
nagualism, 79, 236, 245
religious/ritual specialists, 22, 24, 26, 61–3, 96, 137, 145, 155, 167, 178, 206, 276, 289
ritual architecture: ceremonial precincts, 73, 98, 100–1, 112, 118, 125, 131, 134, 142, 144, 150–2, 155, 158, 227, 234, 276, 278; building dedication ceremony, 61, 63, 122, 125, 134, 166, 189, 238; shrines, 57, 61, 63, 96, 261, 275; temples, 24, 47, 61, 98, 110, 122–8, 130–2, 134, 137, 155–9, 166–7, 174, 178, 217, 219–20, 225, 228, 230, 251, 263, 267, 271, 274–5, 278, 289; *see also* monumentality
ritual calendar, 49, 56, 58–9, 61, 123, 155, 212, 244, 259; *see also* calendrics
ritual dance and music performances, 60, 69–70, 81, 96–7, 100, 122
ritual feasting, 17, 48, 55, 60–1, 94–6, 99–100, 104, 108–9, 115, 122, 124, 126–7, 134, 139, 151, 156, 164, 170–1, 176, 183, 185, 187–8, 191, 205, 238, 240–3, 270
ritual paraphernalia, 26, 96–7, 112, 126, 166: conch shell trumpet 96, 185; stingray spines, 62, 89, 96, 106, 122

ritual performance, 21–2, 25, 31, 100, 104, 122, 125, 127, 131, 145, 156, 205, 225, 247; *see also* religion, ritual dance/music performances; religion, sacrifice
sacred bundles/mummy bundles, 47, 56, 61, 77, 156, 212, 215, 255, 260–1, 263, 274, 275, 276
sacred caves/cave sites, 21–3, 26, 56–7, 61, 68–70, 73, 137, 252, 261, 263, 275
sacred covenant, 60, 62–3, 107, 111, 126–7, 137, 139, 174, 212, 260, 270, 283
sacrifice, 17, 23, 28, 33, 36, 50, 56, 59–64, 69, 79, 89, 95, 105, 107–8, 111, 118, 122–3, 125–7, 134, 136–7, 139, 141, 144–6, 150–3, 155–6, 158, 174, 197–8, 209, 212–13, 215, 217, 223, 236–7, 245–6, 252–3, 270, 283, 289–90, 293: animal sacrifice, 62–3, 212; autosacrifice/bloodletting, 62–3, 64, 88–9, 95–6, 100, 108, 122, 124–6, 136, 139, 144, 146, 150, 174, 245, 278, 283, 290; copal burning, 62; human sacrifice, 23, 50, 56, 60, 62, 69, 111, 118, 123, 125–7, 136, 139, 141, 144, 151–2, 158, 198, 209, 212, 215, 217, 223, 236, 245, 289, 293; *see also* religion, nagualism; religion, shamanism
shamanism, 59, 64, 96; *see also* religion, nagualism; religion, sacrifice
underworld, 58, 61, 93, 95, 134, 136–7, 139, 212, 246
War of Heaven, 60, 259–60
Reyes Etla, *198*, 223
Reyes, Fray Antonio de los, 8, 43
resistance, 26, 29, 30–2, 50, 127, 151, 158, 257, 280–2, 292, 294; *see also* conflict

Ringle, William M., 259
Río Atoyac, 6, 39, 74, 110
Río Balsas, 41
Río Grande, *161*, 180, *198*, 245
Río los Perros, 277
Río Salado, 6, 39
Río Viejo, 4, 14, *161*, 183–7, 189–92, 194–6, *198*, 199, 236, 239–46, *242*, *244*, 248, *250*, 252–5, *253*, *255*, 257, 261, 266, 283, 290, 292–4
  Mound 1 acropolis, 189–90, *190*, 243, 254
Río Verde, 6, 39–41, 187
Río Verde Valley, lower, 6, 12, 14–15, 35, 38, 41–3, *42*, 51, 71, 84, 120, 155, 160–1, 163, 180–1, 185, 192, 195, 199, 227, 239, 241, 243, 247, 249, 257, 261, 266, 283, 293, 297–8n
Río Yanhuitlan, 89
ritual *see* religion
Rivera, Iván, 14, 237, 241
Robles García, Nelly M., 13, 164
Rodríguez Cano, Laura, 14
Romero Frizzi, María de los Angeles, 56, 166, 167

sacred covenant/reciprocal obligations *see* religion
Sahlins, Marshall, 23, 258
San Augustine de las Juntas, *120*, 149–50, 158
San Francisco de Arriba, *161*, 180, 184–6, 189, 191, *198*, 240, 243
San Joaquín, *198*, 200
San José Mogote, *1*, 68, 71, 74–5, 79–80, 82, 84–9, 92, *95*–6, 98–105, 107, 109–11, 113, 115–16, *120*, *121*, 120–5, 127–8, 130, 134, 141, 158, 276, 289, 291, 296n
  Area A barrio, 87–8, 98–100, 113
  Area C barrio, *80*, 81–2, 98, 102, 110
  Mound 1, 110, *121*, 121–2, 124–7, 130, 134, 290
San Lorenzo, *1*, 87, 91, 93, 113–15, 123
San Lorenzo Albarradas, *198*, 250
San Marquitos, *250*, 253
San Martín Tilcajete, 12, 122
Santa Ana del Valle, *198*, 201
Santa Cruz Mixtepec, *250*, 264
Santa Cruz Tagolaba, 278
Santa Teresa, *161*, 173
Saul, Frank P., 103
Saul, Julie Mather, 103
Scott, James, 30, 31
sedentism, 38, 64, 69–73, 77, 82, 291, 294
Sewell, William H., 33
shamanism *see* religion
Sherman, R. Jason, 158
Sierra Madre mountains, 2, 6, 35, 37, 41
"Sister Culture" model *see* Olmec/"Olmec style"
skull racks, 62, 153; *see also* conflict; warfare
Smith, Mary Elizabeth, 10
Smith, Michael E., 179, 206
social identity *see* identity
social memory *see* memory
social negotiation, 15, 27, 29–32, 48, 73–4, 79, 83, 84–7, 94–6, 98, 116–17, 119, 141, 146, 155, 160, 186, 191–2, 195, 223–6, 270, 279–80, 284, 286, 288, 291, 293–5
social organization/society, 6, 9, 17–21, 23, 26–8, 32, 34, 38, 46–7, 64–5, 67, 74, 79, 84, 115, 128, 150, 160, 162, 166, 178, 197, 199, 223–4, 239, 251, 258, 260, 268, 284–6, 288, 293, 295
  egalitarianism, 84–5, 98, 115–17, 119, 142, 160, 194, 196, 252, 260, 291

rural settlements/villages/hinterland, 4, 5, 11, 15, 30, 38, 64, 70–6, 81–4, 119, 129, 146–8, 149, 151, 162–3, 179, 188, 225, 239, 277, 287–8, 290–1, 294
social systems, 21–2, 30, 32, 104, 284–5, 287–8
sodalities, 136, 145, 168, 218, 292
transegalitarian society, 115
urbanism, 4–5, 12, 30, 64, 118–19, 128, 147–8, 150, 152, 162, 172, 179–80, 183, 186, 195, 197, 199, 227, 245, 278, 283, 290–4
social tension, 24, 30, 74, 83, 85, 108, 130, 159, 186, 194, 206, 221, 226, 289, 291; *see also* conflict; resistance; warfare
Soconusco, 54, 90, 93, 106
Sola Valley, 6, 12, 39, 151, 157, 200
space, 22, 30, 69, 73, 85, 88, 100–1, 104, 111, 114, 131, 139–40, 145, 155, 163, 165, 169, 174, 178–9, 183–4, 186, 189, 191, 194, 197, 217–20, 225–6, 234, 251, 256–7, 274–5, 293
place-making, 24, 61–2, 73, 95, 103–4, 118, 131, 141, 151, 179, 185, 191, 218, 223–4, 228, 240, 259, 276
sacred geography, 88, 217
see also memory; monumentality
Spanish conquest, 3–8, 10–11, 23, 34, 35–6, 42–4, 46, 49, 51, 55–6, 60, 73, 97, 126, 147, 163, 177–8, 209, 212, 220, 227–8, 234, 237, 239, 246, 258–9, 280–1, 292, 294
Catholicism *see* religion
colonialism/colonial oppression, 2–10, 16, 17, 23–4, 30–1, 35–6, 43–5, 48, 50, 58, 60, 145, 153, 249, 258, 264, 267–8, 270, 274, 277–8, 280–2, 295
congregaciones, 281

idolatry trials at Yanhuitlán, 23, 282
see also epidemics; resistance
Spencer, Charles S., 12, 151, 153–4, 297n
Spores, Ronald, 13, 164
state, 19, 153, 192, 199, 247, 249, 284–7, 290
status *see* identity
structuration, 20, 23
structure, 20–3, 26–7, 29, 33, 50, 196, 223–4, 233, 284
subaltern studies, 19, 27
subjectivity, 20–1, 24–7, 34, 96, 118, 178, 197–8, 288–9; *see also* identity
Suchixtepec, 250, 270
systems theory, 18–19, 21–2, 25–7, 32, 69, 284–5, 288, 298n

Tamazulapan Valley, 41, 162, 227
Tax, Sol, 15
Tayata, 13, 68, 84–6, 88, 104, *161*, 161–2
Tehuacán Valley, 6, 67–71, 89, 154, 296n
Tehuacán Valley Project, 67
Tehuantepec (site), 2–3, 15, 44–5, 55, 249, *250*, 265–6, 270, 277–80, 283
Tejupan, *250*, 279
Tenochtitlán *see* Aztec
Teopantecuanitlán, *1*, 123
Teotihuacan, *1*, 144, 196, 198–9, 201–6, 222, 226, 235–7, 240–1, 245, 248, 254, 293
contact with Monte Albán *see* Monte Albán
Zapotec barrio, 203, 205
Teozacualco (Chiyo Cahno), 9, *250*, 264, 271
Teposcolula, 13, 44, 55
Teposcolula Valley, 41, 44, 174, 195, 227
Tequixtepec, *235*, *250*, 279
Tequixtepec-Chazumba area, 270

terracing *see* agricultural practices
textiles *see* exchange goods
Tierras Largas, *68*, 71, 74, 78, 82, 85–6, 88, 92, 104, 108, *120*, 128
Tilantongo (Ñuu Tnoo), 84, 161–2, 165, *250*, 259–61, 263–4, 271, 279
Tlacolula, 55, 277; *see also* Valley of Oaxaca
Tlalixtac, *250*, 271
Tlapa-Tlachinollan, *250*, 279
Tlatilco, *1*, 123
Tlaxiaco (Ndisi Nuu), 55, *250*, 264–5
Tlaxiaco Valley, 41, 227
Tolteca-Chichimeca, 261, 263, 267–8, 274; *see also*; Tula
Tomaltepec, *68*, 74, 85, 87, 92, 98–9, *101*, 101–4, 110, *120*, 125, 146–50, 289
Totalization, 258; *see also* Sahlins, Marshall
trade *see* exchange goods; exchange relations
tribute, 45–6, 48–50, 62, 111, 113, 119, 130, 145, 147, 148, 153–4, 158, 179, 221–3, 245, 290, 294; *see also* exchange relations
Troike, Nancy, 10, 298n
Tula, *1*, 267
Tututepec (Yucu Dzaa), *1*, 1–3, *2*, 14, 44, 55, *120*, 153–4, *161*, 186, *198*, 245, 249, *250*, 258, 260–1, *262*, 263, 266–70, *268*, *269*, 280, 283

Umbría, Ganzalo de, 280
urbanism *see* social organization/society
Urcid, Javier, 13–14, 136, 145, 178, 204, 207, 209, 211, 213, 215, 218, 245, 253, 292

Valley of Oaxaca, 6, 11–12, 15, 35, 38–41, *39*, 45, 51, 55, 61, 65, 68, 71, 73–4, 78, 82, 84–93, 96–7, 104–7, 111, 114–16, 119–25, 127, 131, 138–41, 151–4, 157, 159–60, 162–3, 167, 175–7, 186–7, 199–200, 203–5, 216, 221, 227, 234, 236, 239, 247, 249, 251, 254–65, 271, 273–4, 280, 293, 296–7n
Etla Valley, 6, 39, 45, 71, 75, 84, 86–7, 99, 103, 109, 110, 116, 121–2, 128, 148, 151, 201, 211, 222–3
Tlacolula Valley, 6, 39, 55, 65, 67, 99, 101, 122, 147, 158, 201, 221–2, 272, 274, 277
Valle Grande, 6, 39, 122, 147, 151, 157–8, 201, 222
Valley of Oaxaca Settlement Pattern Project, 11, 65, 296n

warfare, 5, 17–18, 45–6, 48, 62–3, 118, 121, 123, 126–30, 134, 136–7, 139, 141, 144–6, 148, 151–5, 158, 170, 174, 176–7, 187, 197, 205, 207, 212, 217, 223–4, 227, 236–9, 245, 248–9, 270, 274, 287, 290, 292–3
defense/defensive construction, 48, 129, 131–2, 151, 154, 158–9, 177, 200, 222, 227, 274, 276, 278, 280, 292
raiding, 123, 130, 289
see also conflict
Watson, Patty Jo, 70
Whalen, Michael, 99, 101
Whittaker, Gordon, 14
wild resources, 66, 77
birds, waterfowl, 41, 53, 181
coastal resources, general, 2, 261
Coyol palm nut, 53
deer, 7, 48, 53, 66, 77, 96, 99, 105, 171, 192, 258
fish/shellfish, 2, 41, 53–5, 67, 72, 89, 104, 106, 108, 181, 261
iguana, 53
Nopal cactus, 53, 180

peccary, 53, 66, 77
rabbits, 53, 67, 77, 99, 171
Teosinte, 99
Zapote, 53
Winter, Marcus, 12–13, 67–8, 70, 75, 77, 81–2, 86, 122, 143, 150, 164, 168, 170, 172–3, 196, 199, 201, 203–4, 220, 230–2, 237
Wolf, Eric, 15
women/female identity, 24, 30, 49–50, 55, 58, 60, 70, 76, 79, 83, 86, 87, 96–8, 101–3, 107–9, 112, 116, 125, 149, 156, 159, 167, 170–1, 188, 192, 209, 212, 229, 231, 234, 238, 240, 253–5, 265, 288, 291; *see also* gender
Workinger, Andrew, 184, 240, 297n
Wylie, Alison, 17

Xaagá, *250*, 276
Xipe Bundle, 263
Xochicalco, *1*, 245
Xoxocotlán, 10, 45, *250*, 264

Yagul, 11, *120*, 147–8, *250*, 271–5, *272*, *273*, 278

Yalálag, 15
Yanhuitlán (Yodzo Cahi), 8, 23, *40*, 54, 56, 227, *250*, 259, 265, 279, 282
Yegüih, *120*, 122, 147
Yucuañe, *250*, 279
Yucuita, 12, *68*, 74–5, 82, 84–5, *161*, 162–4, 166, 174–5, *175*, 177–9, 195, *198*, 199, 228, 238, *250*, 280, 291
Yucuita-Chachoapan, 279
Yucundaa, 13, 44, *250*, 258, 271, 279–81
Yucuñudahui, 11, *198*, 199, 227–8, 232, 234–6, *235*, 276, 292
Yugüe, *161*, 183, 187–9, *188*, 191–5, *193*, *198*, 240, 252–257, 266, 297n
Yuzanú, 68, *68*

Zaachila, 11, 39, 45, 50, *250*, 264–5, 271
Zacatepec, *250*, 270
Zapotec Sierra, 265, 280
Zeitlin, Judith Francis, 15, 277–8
Zeitlin, Robert N., 15